BECOMING A TEACHER OF YOUNG CHILDREN

BECOMING A TEACHER OF YOUNG CHILDREN

FIFTH EDITION

Margaret Lay-Dopyera

Syracuse University

John Dopyera

Cumberland Hill Associates

McGRAW-HILL, INC.

New York   St. Louis   San Francisco   Auckland   Bogotá   Caracas
Lisbon   London   Madrid   Mexico   Milan   Montreal   New Delhi
Paris   San Juan   Singapore   Sydney   Tokyo   Toronto

This book was set in Optima by The Clarinda Company.
The editor was Lane Akers;
the production supervisor was Kathryn Porzio.
The cover was designed by Carol Couch.
Project supervision was done by The Total Book.
R. R. Donnelley & Sons Company was printer and binder.

This book was developed by Lane Akers, Inc.

BECOMING A TEACHER OF YOUNG CHILDREN

1 2 3 4 5 6 7 8 9 0   DOC   DOC   9 0 9 8 7 6 5 4 3 2

ISBN 0-07-036777-9

Library of Congress Cataloging-in-Publication Data

Lay-Dopyera, Margaret.
    Becoming a teacher of young children / Margaret Lay-Dopyera, John
Dopyera.
      p.   cm.
    Includes bibliographical references and index.
    ISBN 0-07-036777-9
    1. Early childhood education—United States.   2. Early childhood
educators—United States.   3. Teaching—Vocational guidance—United
States.   4. Child development—United States.   I. Dopyera, John.
II. Title.
LB1139.25.L39   1993
372.21'0973—dc20   92-14951

Chapter opening photo credits: *1* Cumberland Hill Associates; *2* Cumberland Hill Associates,
Inc.; *3* Cumberland Hill Associates; *4* Cumberland Hill Associates, Inc.; *5* Cumberland Hill
Associates; *6* Cumberland Hill Associates; *7* Cumberland Hill Associates, Inc.; *8* David M.
Grossman; *9* Cumberland Hill Associates, Inc.; *10* Cumberland Hill Associates, Inc.;
11 Cumberland Hill Associates, Inc.; *12* Cumberland Hill Associates, Inc.; *13* Cumberland Hill
Associates, Inc.; *14* Elizabeth Crews; *15* Cumberland Hill Associates, Inc.; *16* Cumberland Hill
Associates, Inc.; *17* Cumberland Hill Associates, Inc.; *18* Cumberland Hilll Associates, Inc.; *19*
Cumberland Hill Associates, Inc.; *20* Elizabeth Crews; *21* Elizabeth Crews;
22 Elizabeth Crews.

ABOUT
THE AUTHORS

MARGARET LAY-DOPYERA is emeritus professor of education at Syracuse University. She received her undergraduate training as an early childhood and elementary teacher at Edinboro State University. Her master's degree was in reading education from Pennsylvania State University and her doctorate in psychological foundations of education from the University of Florida. She taught in the public schools of Jamestown, New York and in the laboratory school at Antioch College in Yellow Springs, Ohio. At Syracuse University, she directed the early childhood teacher education program, developed a model day-care program, and served as associate dean for academic programs. She has authored many journal articles, chapters, and research reports and made significant contributions to professional organizations such as the National Association for the Education of Young Children and the National Association for Early Childhood Teacher Education. She and her husband and coauthor, John E. Dopyera, are relocating to a new home they have created in the woods of northwestern Pennsylvania, where they will continue to write and conduct research.

JOHN DOPYERA is president of Cumberland Hill Associates, a staff development firm with strong interests in the early childhood field. He received his undergraduate education at Reed College, in Portland, Oregon and his graduate degrees at Syracuse University. He has taught in the teacher education programs at Syracuse University, Pennsylvania State University, and Pacific Oaks College, where he also served as dean of faculty. He has more than 30 years of experience in conducting needs assessments and in designing, conducting, and evaluating training programs for education, human services, and business and industry. He has authored many journal articles, chapters, and research reports and has made significant contributions to professional organizations such as the American Society for Training and Development and the American Educational Research Association.

CONTENTS
IN BRIEF

CONTENTS

PREFACE

Teaching children from ages two through seven, the age span considered in this book, is challenging and difficult but invariably rewarding for those who carefully select and prepare for this career. Whether the teacher of young children works with a prekindergarten, kindergarten, or primary class in a public school or in a nursery school or child-care setting, the responsibilities are the same—to provide circumstances that support the development and learning of each child. The central objective of *Becoming a Teacher of Young Children* is to help you understand how you can fully prepare for this important professional role.

Part 1: Background, provides you with information about the profession and what you can expect if you become a teacher. It presents both advantages and disadvantages of a career in early childhood education. A chapter on the history of this field gives you a glimpse of how the field has developed and of its current status. This section should help you begin thinking through your commitment to a career as a teacher of young children. Your own commitment to teaching can only be derived from realistic knowledge of yourself and of what you will be encountering in the teaching role.

Sensitivity to children's development and behavior, the focus of Part 2, is a necessary quality in an effective teacher. Only if a teacher can accurately assess what children feel, need, can already do, and are learning to do, is there any assurance that what is provided in the program will be appropriate for them. In developmentally appropriate early childhood programs play is considered a most appropriate medium for facilitating children's growth, development, health, and learning, and it is within the context of play that you will learn most about each individual child. The function of Part 2 is (1) to help you understand the importance of play for young children; (2) to increase your awareness of how various theorists and researchers view child behavior and development; (3) to develop your ability to observe and describe children's feelings, interests and abilities; and (4) to increase your understanding of how such observations are used to guide your program decision making.

In Part 3, you will be helped to understand how and why differing approaches are used by professionals who work with young children. Three general perspectives on child development and early childhood education are presented and then extended through a discussion of five specific program models. There are, of course, many different ways of organizing time schedules, arranging and using classroom space, and establishing and maintaining ground rules for children's behavior. Consequently, the last four chapters of Part 3 help you develop the knowledge and skills to establish and maintain a productive classroom populated by children of diverse characteristics and backgrounds; to plan and manage lessons and activities; and to communicate effectively with children, parents, and co-workers.

Part 4 will help you develop your teaching resourcefulness. You will learn how to set up activity centers and conduct the kinds of activities that help children learn. The need for a broad and varied repertoire that allows you to provide for quite diverse individual needs is constantly demonstrated and emphasized throughout the section.

Part 5 is devoted to several issues confronting early childhood educators. In this section perspectives are offered on topics such as children in poverty; child-care arrangements; early learning; entry, grouping, and appropriate programs for kindergarten children; and testing throughout the prekindergarten, kindergarten, and primary grades.

The following procedures are recommended to maximize the benefits you derive from the text:

1. Make arrangements to have experiences with young children in which you observe and interact with them. If you are currently enrolled in a college teacher-preparation program, such field experiences may be arranged for you. If not, you should make your own arrangements for contact with children who are two through seven years of age. The following are possible ways to obtain this kind of experience:

   Volunteer your services to assist teachers in nursery school, day care, kindergarten, or primary grades. Make realistic commitments that you can dependably carry out.

   Arrange to baby-sit for children of varying ages.

   Volunteer to assist the persons responsible for church school classes.

   Volunteer to assist the librarians in the children's section of a public library.

   In Appendix 1, you will find Fieldwork Guidelines with specific directions and advice on how to gain the most from these experiences.

2. Develop a portfolio of materials related to your professional growth. Such a portfolio could contain papers and other writing for your early childhood education courses; collections of related news clippings, articles, and references; activity suggestions; directories of resources; and catalogs. Developing a usable system for collecting, storing, and retrieving reference materials defi-

nitely will help your professional growth. For suggestions in classifying these materials, refer to Appendix 2.

The process of becoming a competent teacher is continuous. This textbook and your current teacher-preparation program are merely the beginning. Nor will the process be completed when you have graduated and are employed as a teacher. As authors, our goal is to help you become a successful and effective teacher. The ultimate responsibility, however, is yours.

ACKNOWLEDGMENTS

We gratefully acknowledge our indebtedness to many friends and associates in the preparation of *Becoming a Teacher of Young Children.* Primary among those is our editor, Lane Akers. When the first edition of our text was published in 1977, it was Lane Akers who patiently and skillfully guided us through the preparation process. Our association with Lane in each of our revision efforts has increased our appreciation of his supportive style, gentle insistence, and sound judgment. In this edition we also have benefitted from the efficient and friendly guidance of production editor, Kate Scheinman.

We appreciate the opportunity to again use Martha Perske's sensitive drawings on our cover and in a pictorial essay. The drawings strongly enhance and extend the messages of the text. We also acknowledge the help of many of our friends and associates in acquiring the photographs used in this edition.

The list of those from whom we have gained insights and inspiration for our writing is so extensive at this point that proper acknowledgment is not possible. We especially want to acknowledge the continuing influence of Lyman Hunt, Jr.; the late Ira Gordon; the children, parents, and staff members of the Antioch College Experimental School in Yellow Springs, Ohio (with whom the senior author was associated in the early sixties); the Syracuse University Early Childhood Education Center; and the Syracuse University Bernice M. Wright Cooperative Nursery School. We have benefitted greatly from our visits to the Fayetteville Elementary School of the Fayetteville-Manlius School District, New York; the Daj Hammarskjold School No. 6 of Rochester, New York; the Coronation Public School in Cambridge, Ontario; the Elizabeth Zieglor Public School in Waterloo, Ontario; the Meadowvale Village School District of Mississauga, Ontario; the Love Elementary School of Jamestown, New York; the Meadville, Pennsylvania, Cooperative Preschool; and the Titusville, Pennsylvania, Public Schools' Early Childhood Learning Center. Sharing the problems and successes of dedicated and skilled teachers who are providing excellent programs for young children continues to be our major source of inspiration.

The experiences and reactions of the following teacher educators who have used and reviewed our text also have proved invaluable. Those who provided insights for us in this revision include Rosalind Charlesworth, Louisiana State University; Steven H. Fairchild, James Madison University; Blythe Hinitz,

Trenton State College; Suzanne Krogh, Western Washington University; Jane Baldwin Livingston, University of Minnesota at Duluth; Shirley Long, Transylvania University; Lillian Oxtoby, Manhattan Community College; Peggy Rega, Evangel College; Doris O. Smith, California State University at Fresno; Aline Stomfay-Stitz, Christopher Newport College; and Maurmi Summers, Ames Community College.

Finally, we gratefully acknowledge the influence of now-grown daughters, Barbara Dopyera Daley, Suzanne Dopyera Kuntz, and Caroline Dopyera in demonstrating to us the continuity between childhood and adulthood. We continue to find pleasure in their development and successes. With each new grandchild we feel renewed purpose and concern about the practices of early childhood educators. We hope that we are making a contribution to the preparation of teachers of young children that will significantly influence the quality of programs that our grandchildren and others of their generation experience. This edition of our textbook is dedicated to Megan Daley, Bryan Daley, and Elizabeth Kuntz.

Margaret Lay-Dopyera

John Dopyera

BECOMING A TEACHER OF YOUNG CHILDREN

PART ONE

BACKGROUND

To have a commitment to teaching young children means to be thoroughly and realistically convinced that it is something with which you wish to be personally identified. Most of us make only a limited number of firm commitments in our lives—perhaps to a person we care deeply about, to a religious conviction, to a way of life, to a political ideology, to an urgent cause. One's profession, especially if it is to be teaching, warrants a commitment of nearly this magnitude. Part 1 should help you decide whether you wish to be identified with and committed to an early childhood teaching career.

Chapter 1, A Career in Early Childhood Education, provides a range of information on the teaching profession. We first discuss the profound effects occupational choice can have on one's life. The crucial nature of this decision and the need to view it as one of the most significant you will ever make are emphasized. A discussion of various aspects of teaching young children follows, including certification requirements, teaching duties, types of positions, and the job market. We also attempt to convey in some detail the hassles and rewards that are encountered in this occupation. The total thrust of this chapter is to provide more realistic perspectives than you may currently hold on what is involved in becoming a teacher of young children.

Chapter 2, Historical Perspectives, provides a broad historical perspective on the evolution of early childhood education. You will learn that the lot of children has been very mixed throughout history and that even now, as we approach the twenty-first century, early education receives varying levels of support and encounters very diverse views about the most appropriate ways to rear and educate the young. The differing perspectives from earlier centuries are still debated by those active in the field today. As a prospective early childhood educator, you need to look at the roots of what is still a very young and growing profession. Thus, in Chapter 2, we offer you some glimpses into the past.

It is not the intent of Part 1 to convince you to become a teacher of young children. After learning what such a career entails and after examining your own attitudes more closely, you may feel that it is not right for you. However, if your motivation remains high after reading and deliberating on the contents of this part, we anticipate that you will have a deeper, firmer, and more realistic commitment than you currently have.

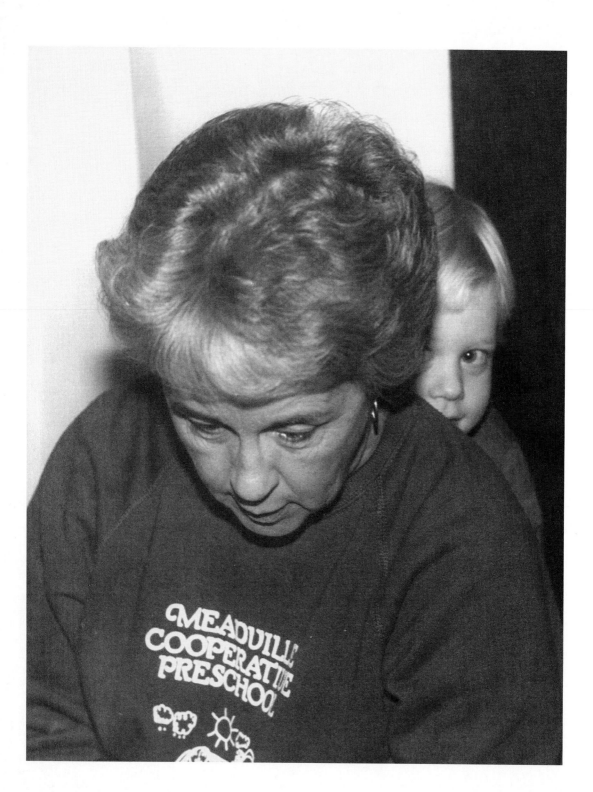

CHAPTER 1

A CAREER IN EARLY CHILDHOOD EDUCATION

OVERVIEW

This chapter has three objectives. The first is to emphasize the importance of decision making in your life, especially in the critical choice of profession. The second is to provide background on careers with young children, including certification for teaching, the current teaching milieu, the age-level divisions within early education, and other similar information. The third is to discuss the advantages and disadvantages of becoming a teacher of young children.*

DECISION MAKING

Each of our lives is an expression of what human beings are and can become. What you personally choose to be and do as you live your daily life is the means by which you make a contribution to the evolving conception of humankind. You are constantly engaged in making decisions about how you will spend your time, with whom, and about how you will describe what you have done. In so doing, you have already made a strong personal commentary about what human life is and can be.

Most of the choices you have made, however, probably have not seemed like choices. You probably have done what others around you were doing without much thought about its ultimate value. Even though we constantly face choices, we seldom ponder alternatives apart from what is expected of us. All of us typi-

*General guidelines for planning classroom observations and teacher interviews, establishing a fieldwork notebook, and participating in classroom activities are included in Part 1 of Appendix 1.

cally make our choices from such a narrow range of alternatives that there seems to be little reason to weigh one against another. Perhaps the human condition would improve dramatically if our daily decision making became considered rather than habitual and unthinking.

Certainly there is reason for strong deliberation before deciding on something as crucial as an occupational commitment. Some of the more important statements that you make with your life will be related to your chosen work. Many of the further choices available to you will be, to a large extent, dependent on restrictions and expectations imposed by the particular kind of work you do.

Teaching is not something in which one can be lightly engaged. Perhaps in some professions you can be, making only partial use of your abilities and interests while on the job and reserving major portions of yourself for nonwork pursuits. This is less possible in teaching. Teaching requires much more of a total personal commitment, of which you will become increasingly aware as you read through this chapter.

SOME BACKGROUND INFORMATION ON CAREERS WITH YOUNG CHILDREN

The care and education of our nation's children require a vast number of professionals. The number of people working with young children has increased

Shoe-tying at age three requires adult help. Providing help of this kind is one of the many tasks for teachers of young children. *(Permission of Bernice Wright Cooperative Nursery School)*

markedly during the last decades, and even more will be needed in the years ahead. In 1965, only 10.6 percent of children aged three and four were enrolled in any kind of program; by 1989 that figure had risen to 39 percent. The percentage of five- and six-year-olds enrolled in school programs also grew as public school kindergartens have become increasingly available. In 1965, 84.9 percent of children aged five and six were in programs; by 1989 that figure was 95.2 percent (National Center for Education Statistics, 1990). In addition to increased participation rates in early education programs, the sheer numbers of young children has been increasing. This population bulge, referred to as the baby-boom echo, has been increasing the need for child care and early childhood education staff. Figures 1-1 and 1-2 describe population fluctuations of the recent past and population projections to 1997. The rise in participation rates and recent increases in birthrates combine to make the field of early childhood education a promising employment choice.

In *Careers with Young Children: Making Your Decision,* Seaver, Cartwright, Ward, and Heasley (1979) identified five career patterns, which are displayed in Figure 1-3. Preschool teaching is just one of a number of career possibilities within the pattern of serving children directly. Clearly, you have diverse options to consider for careers with children. This book focuses on preparation for work with groups of children in the teacher role, but you will find that much of the material is relevant for related career choices as well.

FIGURE 1-1   Numbers of annual births, with projections: 1942 to 1997.
Source: From D. Gerald (1991), *Projections of Education Statistics,*
U.S. Department of Education, Office of Education Research and
Improvement.

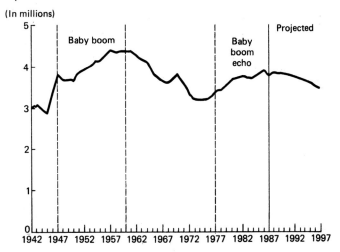

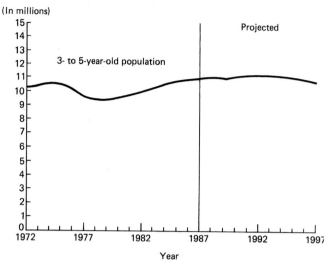

FIGURE 1-2   Preprimary population, with projections: 1972 to 1997.
Source: From D. Gerald (1991), *Projections of Education Statistics,*
U.S. Department of Education, Office of Education Research and
Improvement.

Age and Setting Differences

Although the various jobs of teaching have lots in common, some differences are marked. Preschool teachers usually work in conjunction with other adults in teaching the same group of children. Often the relationship between the adults is hierarchical. The National Association for the Education of Young Children (NAEYC) has designated four levels of early childhood teachers. These levels are illustrated in Figure 1-4. Those at levels 2, 3, and 4 often have responsibility for supervising the work of other teachers. Working as part of a teaching team is routine in nursery schools or prekindergarten programs (such as Head Start) and child-care centers.

Programs for preschool children vary greatly. The daily schedule may be that of a half-day nursery school (two and a half to three hours) or the extended day (eight hours or more) of child-care programs. Many preschool programs follow a public school calendar. Others, particularly child care, have few, if any, intervals when the program is not in operation.

Salaries for early childhood teaching also vary greatly, depending on the sponsorship and the type of program. In Head Start programs in Syracuse, New York, beginning teachers with a bachelor's degree received $15,738 ($9.15 per hour) during 1991–1992 and worked for 43 weeks during the year. In the same program, beginning teachers with an associate degree were paid $15,136 ($8.80 per hour) and with a Child Development Associate degree (CDA) and some experience were paid $14,878 ($8.65 per hour). Beginning salaries for prekindergarten, kindergarten, and primary teachers were $27,407 in the same

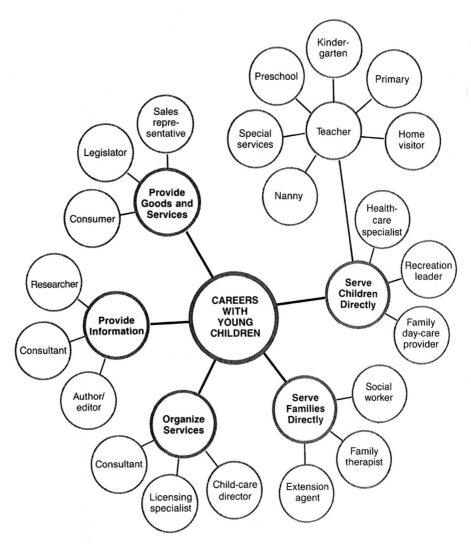

FIGURE 1-3   Careers with young children
Source: From J. W. Seaver, C. A. Cartwright, C. B. Ward, and C. A. Heasley (1979), *Careers with Young Children: Making Your Decision,* Washington, DC: National Association for the Education of Young Children.

community. The median pay for head teachers (level 3 of the NAEYC classifica-tion) in child-care centers in the same upstate New York area was $6.00 per hour or $12,480 annual pay for year-round 40-hour weeks. Associate teachers (level 2) received a median wage of just over $5.00 per hour or approximately $10,483 year-round pay.*

*These figures were obtained via telephone conversations between author and agencies involved, November 1991.

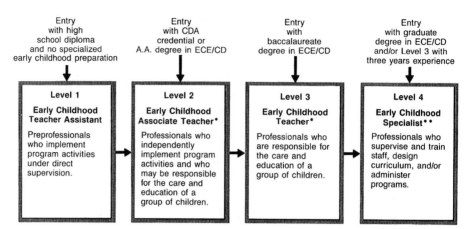

Entry with high school diploma and no specialized early childhood preparation	Entry with CDA credential or A.A. degree in ECE/CD	Entry with baccalaureate degree in ECE/CD	Entry with graduate degree in ECE/CD and/or Level 3 with three years experience
Level 1 **Early Childhood Teacher Assistant** Preprofessionals who implement program activities under direct supervision.	**Level 2** **Early Childhood Associate Teacher*** Professionals who independently implement program activities and who may be responsible for the care and education of a group of children.	**Level 3** **Early Childhood Teacher*** Professionals who are responsible for the care and education of a group of children.	**Level 4** **Early Childhood Specialist**** Professionals who supervise and train staff, design curriculum, and/or administer programs.

* Early childhood associate teachers and early childhood teachers may perform similar roles and functions. The different titles reflect the different patterns of formal education received and the extent of background knowledge of child development.

** The early childhood specialist can become qualified to perform a number of optional roles (such as program administrator in agencies with multiple programs, resource and referral specialist, parent educator, researcher, policy analyst) with successful completion of specialized education through college courses or formal credit for life experience.

FIGURE 1-4   Levels of early childhood teachers
Source: From NAEYC position statement on nomenclature, salaries, benefits, and the status of the early childhood profession (1984, November), *Young Children, 40,* 52–54.

It is an alarming state of affairs that day-care personnel, who have important responsibility for children in terms of type of care and long hours, are paid so poorly. An early educator looking for employment needs to be aware of the vast range in working conditions and in remuneration and benefits of otherwise comparable teaching positions. And, in addition, all concerned professionals need to work as advocates to improve the compensation and conditions of early education personnel.

Prekindergarten, kindergarten, and primary teachers' salaries in public schools are comparable to teachers at other grade levels. In many public schools the kindergarten teacher has sole responsibility for two groups of five- to six-year-old children. The groups typically range in size from fifteen to thirty-five children, one set attending in the morning and another in the afternoon. In other school districts, kindergarteners have full-day schedules, and in these situations the teacher has responsibility for one group all day long. The trend appears to be toward this latter arrangement.

The primary teacher, like the kindergarten teacher, typically has sole responsibility for children in a self-contained classroom. Although "special" teachers of art, music, and health may be available to teach or assist at certain time periods during the week, **aides** in the kindergarten or primary classroom are not commonly available. The class size in the primary grades typically ranges from fifteen to thirty-five or more children, with an average of twenty-five.

Comparisons with Other Professions

Teaching, like medicine and law, has been classified as a profession, since entry into the field requires professional training, state licensing, and even differential training for different roles and levels. As in other professional fields, professional organizations provide members with information, monitor the quality of programs, lobby for legislation, and attempt in various ways to advance the profession's goals and status. See Appendix 3 for a list of these early childhood education and child development organizations and associations.

However, in some significant respects, teaching is simply not comparable to other professions. There is, for example, a difference in clientele. In the typical situation, the clients of the early educator are small children who are seldom seen individually in the normal course of work. The task of the teacher is to work with groups, not individuals. All efforts to individualize instruction for any child must be done while maintaining attention to group concerns. This is quite a different matter than seeing one client at a time, as is typical in other professions.

Another interesting difference is the lack of long-term continuity with clients. A group of children with their parents are typically served intensively for a year or two and then are not contacted again as the group moves on to other teachers.

The parents, who might well be considered the real clients, do not usually initiate contact with a particular teacher to perform services for their children. They often have little opportunity to determine who will teach their children. Moreover, parents are usually unavailable for consultation while the teacher is performing professional functions, as opposed to most other professional relationships. The responsibilities of a teacher of children cover a much broader scope than that of other professionals. Even though there is often little opportunity for direct parental contact, the teacher is legally expected to serve **in loco parentis,** that is, to stand in the relation of parent and guardian to pupils, to regulate their conduct while under school supervision, and to take measures necessary for the pupils' safety, health, and welfare. The teacher has societal responsibilities that may sometimes influence his or her actions more heavily than the needs of the particular clients being served. What is done in a classroom is of significance to the broader community, and consequently, the demands on the teacher from community representatives (such as the board of education, administrators, and pressure groups) are sometimes far more influential than the needs and wishes of the children's parents, who are the direct recipients. This responsibility to the public appears to influence the performance of teachers, especially public school teachers, far more than it does the performance of social workers, nurses, doctors, psychologists, and other professionals.

Certification

There have been continuing efforts by state governments to set formal teacher **certification** requirements to ensure adequate educational experiences for the young. All states require that teachers in public schools be certified as qualified

TYPES OF PROGRAM SETTINGS

Nursery school

Program provided for children aged two, three, and/or four; typically a half-day program (two to three hours); the term nursery school traditionally refers to private or parent cooperative programs rather than to publicly supported programs.

Prekindergarten

Program generally restricted to children under age five for the year or years prior to entrance to kindergarten.

Kindergarten

Program generally restricted to children under age six for the year prior to entrance to first grade.

Preprimary

Program generally restricted to children under age six or seven for the years prior to entrance into first grade; may encompass what is typically identified as prekindergarten and kindergarten.

Primary

Program generally restricted to children aged six, seven, and eight in grades (or equivalents thereof) one, two, and three.

Child-care centers (or day-care centers)

Programs of four or more hours in duration; may accommodate varying ages, from infants through elementary school age (after-school care).

Family day care

Child care provided for a small group of children in the home of the caregiver who may or may not have had training for the role; may accommodate varying ages from infants through school age (after-school care).

Head Start

Program under federal support for economically disadvantaged children prior to entrance in regular public school programs; may be half-day or full-day; involves comprehensive services including nutritional and medical care; anticipates parental involvement.

Parent-child center

Programs providing health education and social services for impoverished parents and their infants and toddlers.

Backyard groups (mobile preschools)

Programs for small groups of neighborhood prekindergarten children conducted in the home of one of the children; may be coordinated by a professional and implemented by paraprofessionals and /or mothers.

Home programs (home visitor)

Programs for the instruction of a child in the home (to benefit both the child and the parent); professional (classroom teacher) or trained paraprofessional makes regular home visits; implemented at range of ages, either in connection with or separately from an in-class program.

In-home care (nanny program)

Program for a child or children within the parents' home.

Hospital schools

Program within hospital settings; may involve group attendance in a classroom or playroom and/or one-to-one teaching of children in their quarters.

Laboratory/demonstration schools

Programs within training and/or research settings such as universities, colleges, and institutes.

to teach by their departments of education. Many states require certification for teachers in private and parochial schools as well. Program administrators may also view certification as desirable for prekindergarten teaching.

Certification has typically been issued only to individuals having at least four years of approved college preparation. The four-year programs have consisted of professional study, as well as study in a range of scholarly disciplines. Some study of human behavior and learning is usually required. Several states require that teachers complete a fifth year of study or a master's degree, and some indi-

---

TYPES OF SPONSORSHIP FOR EARLY CHILDHOOD PROGRAMS

Private nonprofit	Church groups, Community Chest, etc.
Private profit	Owner-run franchises
Private (service to personnel)	Universities, business firms, hospitals, industries, etc.
Public (federal)	Head Start, parent-child centers, Title XX of Social Security Act
Public (state)	State-funded; may be administered through local school districts or social service agencies
Public (local)	Locally funded public school programs
Parent cooperatives and play centers	Neighborhood or community groups governed and maintained by the parents of children being served

Note: A given program can have multiple sources of funding and/or sponsorship.

---

vidual school systems have even more stringent certification requirements than those set by the state. In nearly all states, certification is issued by the state department of education on the basis of transcripts of credits and recommendations from approved colleges and universities. Certification is issued to applicants from other states only if prescribed programs have been completed at accredited colleges and if the coursework meets the specific requirements of that state.

In addition to the many four-year college programs that prepare students to meet state certification requirements, there are many two-year programs that prepare personnel for work in early education as associate teachers. Graduates of these two-year programs receive an **associate degree** from their institution, indicating specialized training. Persons with associate degrees take very responsible roles in many nonpublic nursery and child-care settings and work as **paraprofessionals** in public school settings and other situations where a team of teachers work together within a program.

Another category of credentialed professionals are child development associates, or CDAs. Currently the certification program for CDAs is administered by the Council for Early Childhood Professional Recognition, under the auspices of the National Association for the Education of Young Children. The certification is awarded to individuals who have been assessed and found competent to assume responsibilities for children from birth through age five. A CDA certificate can be earned by individuals who work in child-care centers, family daycare homes, or as home visitors. The majority of those receiving the CDA certification are employed in Head Start programs (Council for Early Childhood Professional Recognition, 1990). Some teaching experience and formal or informal education or training is required. Participation in workshops, seminars, and in-service programs may be considered sufficient training, and completion of a college program is not required. Many CDA training opportunities, however, are now incorporated into college programs.

The potential CDA must take primary responsibility for the day-to-day activities of a group of children. A person desiring to be a master teacher, a center director, or a curriculum specialist, however, needs competencies beyond those considered sufficient for a CDA.

PROS AND CONS OF BECOMING A TEACHER OF YOUNG CHILDREN

In this part of the chapter, we try to give you the "inside" view of what it is like to be a teacher of young children. You need to be aware of both the good side and the bad side, and we hope this discussion will help you to be more realistic.

The Need versus the Difficulty

A major reason for becoming a teacher is the opportunity to be engaged in work that is socially relevant and personally satisfying. There are few, if any, major social problems that cannot in some way be addressed in early education settings. Teachers have little reason to question whether the work they do is important or whether they can make significant contributions to the lives of others. Adults who serve as teachers of young children become second only to parents and siblings in their impact on the child. What a teacher does or does not do in the classroom can be influential years and even decades later, not just for the children in the classroom but also for those who they in turn will influence. We have never known of a teacher who doubted the crucial nature of his or her job. The needs children have for instruction, attention, and caring are obvious.

There are many persons, however, who eventually leave teaching because of a conflict between attaining their own personal teaching goals and adequately caring for children. There just is not enough time to do all that needs to be done. A teacher simply cannot meet all the needs of all the children in a typical classroom. One third-year teacher put it this way:

> When I started teaching—WOW! That first year was something else. Just the management of everything was so difficult that I thought I was really doing well if I just made it through the day with the kids and the equipment physically intact and if I kept myself from becoming psychologically undone in the process. A lot of it was a matter of getting my feet on the ground and my head together. But what continues to bug me, even after three years of experience, and I know it is true of the teachers who've taught twenty years also, is the hopeless feeling at the end of each day as I think about the individual children in my classroom who desperately needed and could really have benefited if I had given them more time and attention. If I concentrate on those kids the next day, it's just another set of kids I then neglect. I just can't do it. It's impossible to help them all as much as I feel they should be helped.

Would you have difficulty living with this feeling of never being able to do all that you think should be done for the children you teach? Of course, this is not a problem unique to teaching. Other professionals face the same dilemma. Physicians, for example, often end the day knowing that although they have helped many patients to a certain extent and some patients a great deal, many others needed more attention, more time, and more information than they were able to give. To continue to engage in medical practice, it is necessary for a physician to live with the constant knowledge of what is not being done that should be done. The social worker also encounters the seemingly endless needs of clients, and the same pressures face many other groups, both professional and nonprofessional.

Can you be satisfied with doing your best, knowing that your best is inadequate to the need? In teaching, the frustration of never doing "enough" can be balanced by the satisfaction of knowing that what has been done was well worth doing. Not all occupations offer this level of reward.

Creative Opportunity versus Criticism

Teaching continues to be more of an art than a science, despite an increasing accumulation of knowledge about classroom cause and effect. During the next decade, new knowledge will gradually be introduced into teaching practice. So much of teaching, however, is simply a matter of opinion, a personal judgment, that it is impossible to make many very definitive statements about what constitutes a good teacher or the most effective way to teach. This open-ended state of affairs has both its advantages and disadvantages.

The main advantage is the amount of latitude an individual teacher or a school system has in determining teacher methods. In the same city, at the same age level, it is often possible to find quite opposite arrangements in such basic matters as criteria for grouping children or standards for promotion. Even within a single school building it is not unusual to find teachers who disagree on issues of how reading should be taught, means of discipline, how to evaluate children's progress, and other important matters. Although there are convincing rationales for quite diverse views of how children should be educated and cared for, there is little solid evidence to justify any one particular view.

This creates a situation that prevents educators from saying, "This way has been demonstrated to be superior." The closest legitimate statement typically is, "Other ways have not been demonstrated to be superior to the way I favor." This, of course, leaves most issues within the realm of personal preference and thus allows you to experiment, to invent, and to fashion for yourself a style of teaching that is distinctly your own. The lack of consensus on crucial issues gives you plenty of opportunity to be creative as you become involved in seeking answers, solving problems, and inventing new procedures.

The problem with this open-ended state of affairs is that in the absence of a professionally accepted body of facts and operating procedures, anyone on the street can legitimately prescribe how schools should be run, how subjects should be taught, and how teachers and students should behave. Since there is no firm science of teaching, it is difficult to find grounds on which to persuade lay persons that they do not know as much about teaching as the certified teacher. After all, they went to school many years and were exposed to various teaching styles.

We have all seen teachers at work for approximately 10,000 hours by the time we are seniors in high school. Quite often laypersons have the opportunity to read as much up-to-date opinion on education in the popular press as the teacher has access to in professional journals. Given such exposure, it is inevitable that many will claim to know how schools should be run. Is this not true of you, for example? Do you not have a number of opinions on education based on your experiences as a student?

During the process of training, a teacher becomes aware that there are many legitimate ways to reach the same goals and that all the methods have drawbacks in certain situations and with certain children. In knowing this, a teacher is better prepared to exercise professional judgment regarding which method to use in any given situation. A layperson is less aware if the vast array of alternatives and consequently is more apt to think dogmatically. The result is that teachers, more than professionals such as electricians, druggists, physicians, and computer programmers, are confronted by people with partial but insufficient knowledge who tell them how their job should be done.

If you are to become a teacher, you must learn how to clearly and confidently state and defend your teaching goals and methods and to demonstrate progress in meeting these goals. Otherwise, you will be vulnerable to the self-proclaimed experts you will encounter, each of whom "knows" other superior ways of doing your job. You should be forewarned, however, that the teaching profession will give you many more opportunities to feel creative and innovative than opportunities to feel secure and protected by the knowledge that any particular teaching practice is the best way.

Classroom Freedom versus Situational Constraint

Teachers traditionally have had almost no control over some very significant aspects of their teaching, while maintaining almost total control over other aspects. The individual teacher often has little control over the number of children assigned to the classroom group, the composition of those groups, the equipment available, the scheduling of the program year, the length of the program day, and many other similar matters. They may be assigned a particular curriculum or be told to use a given set of commercial materials that largely prescribes their teaching activity. However, even during their first year, teachers are frequently left almost entirely to their own devices in matters of classroom instruction and management. There may be little help, counsel, or interest from others in the school about the teaching process.

The input of supervisors to individual teachers is often quite minimal. The administrators of public and private schools (and the directors of child-care centers) have quite a different set of responsibilities than the teacher. Whereas the teacher is primarily concerned with child management and instruction, administrators must focus on such noninstructional matters as public relations, ordering and distribution of supplies, scheduling of space, transportation, management of food operations, and other similar concerns. The opportunities for teacher-administrator discussion regarding issues of basic philosophy, objectives, or program structure are typically very limited.

Once they have been certified and employed, teachers are given an amazing amount of leeway to operate their classrooms as they wish, within the givens of number, mix, hours, general curriculum guides, physical space, and equipment. Unless their operation in some way violates the administrator's general perception of what should be happening, they normally operate without interference. One superintendent of a small school system flatly tells new teachers:

> I don't care what you do in your classroom. You use the methods you want. Of course, if I walk by your room and see something happening that I don't understand, I'll stop and ask you about it, and you had better have an objective in mind that I can understand. If you don't, I'll tell you to get things back in line. But until then you can do things the way you think best.

Teachers may find themselves reporting to superiors who have quite different views of how classrooms should be conducted and who, because of their

Teaching offers many opportunities to enjoy children's interests and contribute to their development. *(John James)*

administrative burden, lack the time and motivation to explore the significance of these differences. Conversely, many teachers have ample opportunity to discuss their views and concerns about education with interested administrators.

If you become a teacher, you should not assume that you will have close direction and assistance from the administrators to whom you report. You should prepare yourself to proceed quite independently. It may also be important that you not be "undone" by criticism—either by immediately giving in or by becoming defensive or antagonistic—but rather be able to justify your actions. To do this requires that you carefully cultivate your own competence and confidence.

Typically, teachers make their own decisions about when and where group learning activities will occur. *(Cumberland Hill Associates, Inc.)*

Sharing with Children versus Adult Isolation

Teachers of young children are likely to find some of their greatest rewards in sharing the freshness with which these children experience the world. "Innocence" or "simplicity of heart," although stereotyped terms, do reflect the honest wonder and delight with which children respond to phenomena such as snow falling, snails crawling, rhythmic speech patterns, or spring sunshine. Being a teacher of the young serves to keep one more in touch with the possibilities for sensory experiences than do most other occupations.

It is continuously intriguing to participate with children in their struggles to manipulate the physical environment, to use language, and to try to make sense out of what they are encountering. Every teacher has anecdotes about how pupils have figured and wondered and speculated about the objects and ideas they encounter. One of the authors, for example, especially remembers the wise conclusion of Ken, age seven, on hearing his classmates trying to top each with the magnitude of their own ages, the ages of their siblings, and the ages of their parents. Ken quipped, "Being older than other people is good, isn't it, until you start getting gray hair, and then it isn't so good."

Or the puzzlement of Gordon, age six, in struggling through a passage in an abridged version of *The Three Billy Goats Gruff* in which the text reads, "The first billy goat said, 'I want to go over the bridge. I want to eat the good green grass. I want to get fat.'" Gordon finished the passage saying, "You know, I knew that word *fat* 'cause it's just *at* with *f* on it first. But you know what I don't know? Why does the goat want to get fat? That gives you heart stroke. My uncle *died* of heart stroke because he was too fat." Why, indeed? What a boost for the adult, who long ago ceased to wonder about the why of the three billy goats trip-trapping over the bridge or the nature of the troll underneath, to experience it all over again with the fresh view of the child encountering the story for the first time.

Although there are many positive aspects of sharing one's workdays with children, the lack of opportunity for adult contact can be a problem for some teachers. Most prekindergarten programs have at least two adults per group of children, but this is more the exception than the rule for kindergarten and the primary grades. The problem with children as social companions is that although you can share and delight in their perspectives, there is no way they can share in most of yours. Yet your pupils are constantly there, in your charge, whether you feel like being with them or not. Once the school day is under way, there is little chance for a teacher to have a "time out." The complaint of many teachers of young children, especially beginners, is "I never even have a chance to go to the bathroom."

Thus, in contemplating teaching as a career, it is important that you first consider to what extent your morale requires adult interaction and, second, to what extent you are likely to provide yourself with necessary supportive relationships outside the work milieu.

Quite realistically, if you are the type of person who derives your greatest satisfactions from the exploration of new adult relationships, you should be aware that in teaching you may find fewer opportunities for this enjoyment than in many other professions.

Self-Development

Every act of self-improvement is an act toward improved teaching. A very exciting aspect of teaching is knowing that development of oneself as a person goes hand in hand with development of oneself as a teacher. Skills of organization, communication, breadth of knowledge, sensitivity, all of which are helpful in one's daily life, become especially important in teaching. Every teacher who helps children helps them according to his or her own strengths. Teaching is far more than the application of techniques. A teacher's personal qualities make teaching either boring and abrasive or rich and meaningful for children. It is difficult to think of any area of personal development that would not somehow improve teaching.

Arthur Combs (1974) describes the teaching process as using "self as instrument." He points out that in teaching, as in other "helping" professions such as nursing, counseling, and social work, "instantaneous responses" to unique situations are constantly required. The interchange between teacher and child is different at every moment, and a teacher must continuously react to each child in terms of the particular question, idea, or concern then being expressed. If teachers are to act instantaneously in a way that will benefit children's growth and learning, they must themselves be healthy, aware, and secure. They have an obligation and an opportunity to employ themselves fully in their work. In teaching, more than in most occupations, there is the possibility for uniting avocation and vocation.

CONSIDERING THE TASKS OF TEACHING

Let us next explore your perceptions of what it will be like to teach young children on a daily basis. When you imagine yourself teaching, what do you see yourself doing? This is a three-part task involving Table 1-1.

1 Before referring to Table 1-1, list all the things you can visualize yourself doing as a teacher of young children. Take no more than ten minutes to make your list.

2 Once you have made your list, look at Table 1-1, which lists many activities we have observed teachers of young children engaging in frequently. Compare your list with what is presented in the table. How would you characterize the differences?

3 With the items from your list and those from the table, do a self-survey to determine how you feel about the tasks associated with the teaching role. For each item, rate as follows:

++ really enjoy doing this
 + feel comfortable doing this
 0 uncertain
 − feel uncomfortable doing this (possibly due to inexperience)
−− would certainly not enjoy doing this

TABLE 1-1   TASKS OF TEACHERS OF YOUNG CHILDREN

Tasks	Rating
Plan for following days, weeks, etc. (objectives, activities, and materials, time allotments, procedures, setting arrangements, etc.)	
Maintain accurate attendance records for all children	
Maintain basic supplies in readiness for children's use	
Prepare materials for expressive activities (mix paints, prepare clay, etc.)	
Prepare equipment for use (take from storage, place in appropriate location)	
Prepare or select instructional materials (poster, flannel board, work sheets, etc.)	
Collect scrap materials from home and community to supplement those provided by commercial suppliers	
Interact with children individually and in groups (listen, ask questions, explain, give directions, discuss, relate personal experiences)	
Grant or deny children's requests	
Set and enforce standards for children's behavior	
Initiate and direct children's transitions from one location and type of activity to another	
Monitor (and sometimes intercede in) children's interactions or conflicts	
Observe and keep records on children's behavior and progress	
Conduct group-sharing sessions (oral or visual sharing of experiences, expressive products, work efforts, etc.)	
Conduct group lessons (plan, set objectives, select materials and activities, involve children, evaluate, etc.)	
Conduct music activities (singing, dancing, movement, use of instruments, listening, etc.)	
Involve children in mathematical activities (counting, comparing group sizes, ordering according to number or other dimensions, etc.)	

(continued)

TABLE 1-1   TASKS OF TEACHERS OF YOUNG CHILDREN (cont.)

Tasks	Rating
Involve children in activities or lessons that develop reading concepts or skills (function of written language, correspondence between written words and spoken words, between spoken sounds and letters, etc.)	
Print (manuscript printing) on paper, chalkboard, and posters (directions, announcements, reminders, notes, etc.)	
Show children how to correctly form and space letters and numerals	
Involve children in science activities (observing, inferring, experimenting with a variety of materials)	
Keep majority of children constructively occupied while working with an individual child or a small group	
Supervise or conduct playground activities	
Arrange and conduct field trips to other locations	
Supervise children's toileting	
Serve and supervise snacks and lunches	
Help children in dressing (zippers, ties, boots)	
Take care of ill or injured children until parents or medical personnel are available (vomiting, crying, drowsiness, bleeding, etc.)	
Maintain physical orderliness in classroom, replacing equipment and teaching materials after use	
Take care of or supervise care of classroom pets and plants	
Arrange displays on walls, tables, bulletin boards	
Create and maintain activity centers for particular purposes (planting and observing growth, printing, developing motor coordination, etc.)	
Communicate with parents via home visits, conferences, notes, etc.	
Work with other teachers to coordinate efforts and make joint program decisions	
Discuss or defend your teaching practices with supervisory personnel and fellow teachers	

As you consider your ratings for each item, that is your overall impression? If you were to be regularly engaged in these tasks, would you find them satisfying? Are there a sufficient number of tasks you believe would be satisfying to compensate for those toward which you feel negative?

SUMMARY

All of us make statements with the choices we make in our own lives about what humans are and can become. Some of the more potent statements are often made through one's work. The decision about occupation, especially if that occupation is to be teaching, is a critical one with far-reaching consequences.

Careers with young children form a number of different patterns: serving children and serving families, organizing services, providing information, providing goods and services. Within the category of service to children, teaching is only one of the many possibilities. Furthermore, teaching is done at different age levels, in different settings, and under varying sponsorship, each of which may be of significance to career choice.

In contrast with other professions, a teacher works with clients (children in groups) intensively for a period of a year or so and then terminates contact. The teacher serves *in loco parentis* yet may have minimal contact with parents during the course of providing services to the child. Policy is often influenced more by the general public than by the parents.

Certification requirements are set by states for work in public schools. These vary from state to state. Colleges and universities set up undergraduate programs for teacher preparation that meet state guidelines for coursework or performance criteria. Associate degrees for work with young children are awarded in two-year college programs and by the child development associate program.

The pros and cons of teaching could be summarized by the following:

"The need is so great but the task is so difficult."
"There's opportunity for inventiveness but everyone's an expert."
"In some areas there's no teacher authority and in others, total responsibility."
"There are joys in teaching but it's a lonely job."
"It matters who you are as a person."

There are various reasons for becoming a teacher of young children. Motives can range from the desire for economic security, to social approval and respect from the community, to interest in bringing about significant social change. Whatever the motivation, the commitment of teaching should be based on a realistic knowledge of oneself, the requirements for training, and the demands of the profession—if it is to lead to personal satisfaction and professional success.

SUGGESTED ACTIVITIES

1 Make a list of your reasons for considering teaching as a career. Consider whether the personal rewards that you anticipate from teaching young children reflect what you believe to be your values.

2 Try to visualize the way you would like your life to be ten years from now; twenty years from now. What is the likelihood that becoming a teacher will allow you to have the kind of life you want to have?

3 Select three states where you might wish to become employed. Write to their state certification divisions requesting their current certification requirements for teaching children in prekindergarten, kindergarten, and elementary grades. Address your inquiry to: State Certification Officer, State Department of Education, (State Capitol), (State).

4 Select three different locales (in the same state or in different states) where you might wish to teach. Contact the school district in these locations requesting the following types of information on prekindergarten, kindergarten, and primary grades: size of classroom groups, pupil-teacher ratios, per-child expenditure, hours per sessions, yearly calendar, salary schedule, provisions for sick leave, provisions for tenure, additional benefits.

5 Select three or more specific early childhood centers that are not under the supervision of the public school district. Request information from these centers similar to that suggested under item 4 above. To obtain a listing of such centers, look under Schools or Day Care and Nursery Centers in the yellow pages in a telephone directory.

ADDITIONAL READINGS

Ade, W. (1982). Professionalization and its implications for the field of early childhood education. *Young Children, 37*(3), 25–32.

Almy, M. (1975). *The early childhood educator at work.* New York: McGraw-Hill.

Anglin, L. W., Golmand, R., & Anglin, J. S. (1982). *Teaching: What it's all about.* New York: Harper & Row.

Ayers, W. (1989). *The good preschool teacher: Six teachers reflect on their lives.* New York: Teachers College Press, Columbia University.

Hendrick, J. (1987). *Why teach?* Washington, D.C.: National Association for the Education of Young Children.

Seaver, J. W., Cartwright, C. A., Ward, C. B., & Heasley, C. A. (1979). *Careers with young children: Making your decision.* Washington, D. C.: National Association for the Education of Young Children.

Stone, J. G. (1990). *Teaching preschoolers: It looks like this . . . in pictures.* Washington, D.C.: National Association for the Education of Young Children.

Watkins, K. P., & Durant, L., Jr. (1990). *Day care: A source book.* New York: Garland.

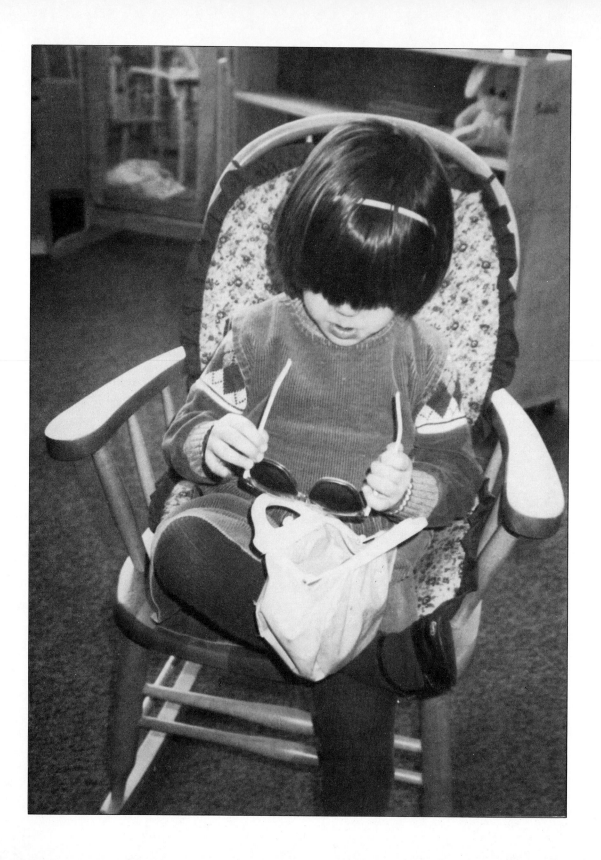

CHAPTER 2

HISTORICAL PERSPECTIVES

OVERVIEW

Children are angelic and pure. They must be protected from the corruption of evil influences.

Children are wild and savage. They must be tamed. Their spirits must be broken before they can become civilized.

Children are born evil, corrupt, selfish, and dangerous. They must be watched and punished to prevent them from following their natural inclinations.

Children are property. As property they may be used as servants, as toys, as sex objects, as ornaments to oneself. They may be given away or abandoned like any other possession.

Children are like miniature adults. They can do anything an adult can do although less well. They think and feel in adult ways although inferior in all their functions.

Children at birth are neither good nor bad. They are capable of rapid learning, however, and their natural temperament and physiological capabilities are gradually molded by the environments into which they are born.

All these views of children have been held by large numbers of people at some point in history. Variations on these beliefs can still be seen; sometimes an individual holds two or more of these views and justifies what others believe to be bizarre behavior by citing statements like those listed here. In this chapter, you will have brief encounters with various individuals and groups who differed markedly in their views about children. All are part of the Western heritage of concepts about childhood.

CHANGING VIEWS OF CHILDHOOD

We have very limited knowledge of how children were viewed during vast periods of human history. It would seem, however, that prior to the nineteenth century children were not thought of as persons with needs and rights. The early history of Western civilization is nearly devoid of reference to children. We do know that the ambivalence of Greek and Roman parents about caring for their dependent offspring sometimes led to infanticides. Children were, according to deMause (1974), "thrown into rivers, flung into dung heaps and cess trenches, potted in jars to starve to death, and exposed on every hill and roadside" (p. 25). Firstborns were more likely to be kept than those born later. Girl children were more often disposed of than males, and there were, therefore, tremendous imbalances in male and female populations. This state of affairs evidently persisted into the fourth century A.D.

Beyond the fourth century, children were probably less brutalized, but there is not much evidence that they were particularly valued. The offspring of well-to-do persons were routinely placed with others—nurses, masters, teachers—throughout their childhood. Those who were less well-off commonly apprenticed their children or hired them out as servants by age eight or ten.

By the eleventh, twelfth, and thirteenth centuries, childhood and children, in general, may have been viewed more favorably. The theme of the Nativity with mother and child often appeared in art and literature. In these scenes, the child, in the image of the infant Jesus, was in central focus. Despite the identification of childhood with the revered Christ child, the education and training of children was not considered very important by the early Christians or by the established church throughout the feudal period. Nurturing souls for a future world was the prime focus of the religious community. The advice of the early Christian leader Basil (c. 329–379) in his "Address to Young Men on the Right Use of Greek Literature" was, "We Christians, young men, hold that this human life is not a supremely precious thing. . . . We place our hopes on the things which are beyond, and in preparation for the life eternal do all the things that we do" (Braun & Edwards, 1972, p. 22). Preparation for life eternal did not include the need for a general education for children. Only children entering religious orders received schooling, and that was limited to topics such as church history, laws, and dogma. Otherwise, children did whatever adults around them did. Although offspring of nobility were cherished as the recipients of lineage rights, they were generally not treated differently in childhood than in adulthood. The concept of childhood as a separate life phase devoted to pursuits different from those of adults seems not to have existed in medieval society.

By the sixteenth century, the physical well-being of children was of more concern to adults. Still, there is little evidence of children's games, stories, or toys in the literature or art work from this period. The scenes depicted by the painter Brueghel, for example, included some children but showed children and adults engaging in the same activities.

THE ROOTS OF MODERN IDEAS OF CHILDHOOD

Throughout the last several centuries there has been increased interest in children as young persons with special needs and characteristics for which different settings and expectations are needed. From the great minds of the Reformation and Renaissance, there came surprisingly modern concepts about the nature, education, and rearing of children. The ideas of Martin Luther, Desiderius Erasmus, John Amos Comenius, John Locke, and Jean Jacques Rousseau infuse the heritage of early educators. Their writings show the emerging idea of childhood as a unique life stage needing special thought and care.

Sixteenth-, Seventeenth-, and Eighteenth-Century Theorists

The German radical Martin Luther (1483–1546), like the early Christians, was deeply concerned about preparing the citizenry for a personal knowledge of "God's word" and hence salvation. He believed that if each individual could become literate, he or she would have access to God's word as expressed in the Bible rather than depending on the interpretations of the established church. Luther proposed primary schools for all children, including girls, that were to foster a whole range of development—intellectual, religious, physical, emotional, and social. He wrote, "In my judgment there is no other outward offense that in the sight of God so heavily burdens the world, and deserves such heavy chastisement as the neglect to educate children" (Braun & Edwards, 1972, p. 26). Luther was as influential in establishing changes in thinking about children in his homeland as he was in bringing change in religious traditions.

A contemporary of Luther's, the Dutch humanist Desiderius Erasmus (1466–1536), also worked for reform of the church. Faced with the breakup of medieval feudalism into national and religious factions, he worked for unity and peace, trying to reconcile faith and reason. He, like Luther, had views on children's development and education. Unlike Luther, however, he was less inclined to view the world in terms of good versus evil. He pursued a career in writing and traveling to meet with many of the leading thinkers of the period. He was instrumental in increasing awareness of the value of human existence in the "here and now"—including the value of the lives of children.

John Amos Comenius (1592–1670), a bishop from Moravia (now Czechoslovakia), proposed principles of universal education that were clearly the forerunners of modern educational thought. Comenius saw the world as the expression of God and, therefore, he thought that all humans should be taught to know and appreciate it. His stance as a concerned citizen of the world stood out in bold contrast to the religious hatreds and persecutions of his day. He stressed the pliability of the young and the importance of early learning in shaping what a person becomes. One of the books he wrote in 1658, *The Visible World,* is considered the forerunner of all illustrated textbooks.

John Locke (1632–1704), an English philosopher exiled in Holland because of his opposition to the crown, was best known in his time as a defender of religious liberty and for political treatises against the absolute right of kings. His writings were avidly read by the English nobility opposed to the succession to the throne of the future King James II. He wrote on both political and philosophical topics. His writings about the nature of knowledge and how it is acquired by the young became very influential. He is most remembered for the idea of the child as a blank slate **(tabula rasa)** on which adults can write via their child-rearing practices. Despite this view, Locke advised study of children's individual natures so educational methods suitable for their differing inclinations could be chosen. He emphasized the application of reason to influence pliant young minds, and education, he advocated, was to be made pleasant rather than burdensome. Note the following advice:

> The great skill of a teacher is to get and keep the attention of his scholar: whilst he has that, he is sure to advance as fast as the learner's abilities will carry him; and without that, all his bustle and bother will be to little or no purpose. To attain this, he should make the child comprehend, (as much as may be,) the usefulness of what he teaches him; and let him see, by what he has learned, that he can do something he could not do before; something which gives him some power and real advantage above others, who are ignorant of it. To this he should add sweetness in all his instructions; and by a certain tenderness in his whole carriage, make the child sensible that he loves him, and designs nothing but his good; the only way to beget love in the child, which will make him hearken to his lessons, and relish what he teaches him (Braun & Edwards, 1972, p. 39).

The philosopher and social critic, Jean Jacques Rousseau (1712–1778), saw the world as full of injustice and corruptions and reacted to it by writing novels and treatises in which he advocated the overthrow of existent government systems and life-styles. Not surprisingly, he was banished from his native France, but his work continued to be very popular and influential there and elsewhere. He wrote prolifically. His novel *Emile* included wide-ranging advice on child rearing and education. Emile, the child in the novel, was brought up on an island untainted by evil influences. Emile's learning came from nature and his senses were developed under the guidance of his father and mother in the idyllic setting. Rousseau portrayed Emile as growing up whole and free and able.

In sharp contrast to what he advocated, Rousseau's own children, born to a "servant girl" with whom he became involved, were reported to have been abandoned to a foundling hospital. He was an emotional and temperamental person. Nevertheless, he convinced many of his contemporaries that his ideas were worth following. He wrote and spoke about how important it is to keep children from the corrupt and degenerate influences of society. He said a child "should be neither treated as an irrational animal, nor as a man; but simply as a child." He was one of the first of his time to advocate for the consideration of the early years as a life stage different from adulthood. Unlike Locke, Rousseau advocated the avoidance of verbal instruction, and he had little faith in reason or empirical data. Instead, he thought truth was to be gained only through one's own inner life.

Pioneer Educators of the Nineteenth and Twentieth Centuries

The men whose names and ideas are described in prior paragraphs had much to say about the education of the young. None of them, however, were directly involved with providing education or care for children other than, in some instances, their own. Some of the educators who followed, in addition to espousing theories about how children learn and develop, also created schools in which they put their ideas into practice. Johann Pestalozzi (1746–1827), for example, took in poor children and orphans from his rural area in Switzerland and cared for them and taught them. Although his school was a financial failure and closed after only five years, his teaching methods, as described in his writing, and his charismatic personality became very popular across Europe. He later founded a boarding school that was highly successful. His work influenced the German educator Friederich Wilhelm Froebel (1782–1852), who in 1841 developed a program for young children that he called a *kindergarten* (children's garden). Froebel wanted something more systematic than what he perceived as the promising but ill-defined approach of Pestalozzi. It is Froebel's kindergarten that set the initial pattern for the field of early childhood education.

Froebel was a deeply religious person who viewed human nature as innately good and the world as the living work and manifestation of God. He believed that humans were responsible for understanding the world and for living effective lives within it. He perceived of a unity of God, nature, and humans in which each person reflects the whole of the unity. His notion of the oneness of life led him to advocate the development of cooperation instead of competition in education. Froebel believed understanding would come from the study of opposites. He developed materials, called "gifts," that were representations of religious symbolism. One of the ten gifts consisted of a set of six colored worsted balls that to Froebel symbolized the unity of humans, God, and nature. Another gift included a ball, a cube, and a cylinder. The cube represented unity within diversity (many-sidedness), and the cylinder represented the joining of two opposite forms. He also developed a curriculum of "occupations" and of games, songs, nature study, and work in language and arithmetic that he believed would help young children develop an understanding of universal principles. Among the occupations were paper cutting, paper weaving, bead stringing, drawing, embroidering, and weaving.

Froebel felt that children should not be regarded as wax to be molded. Instead, he wanted to follow the nature of the children. The metaphor of the children's garden came from his belief that children, within a well-structured environment, should grow as plants and animals do, according to their own nature and potential. Froebel's writings suggested that teachers follow children's play activity interests rather than actively teaching. Froebel wrote descriptions of kindergarten practice that showed the application of his ideas. Even though he almost certainly intended these lessons as illustrative rather than prescriptive, his followers often slavishly imitated them.

Froebel's kindergarten practices were distinctly different from elementary schooling which had as its major focus the development of literacy for Biblical and classical studies. It is not surprising, therefore, that kindergartens were adopted as an appendage to the schooling provided for older children. Since kindergartens were seen as a separate part of schooling for younger children, the kindergarten practices had little impact on elementary teaching practices. In fact, in recent years kindergartens (programs for five-year-olds) have been modified to become more like elementary school.

The first Froebelian kindergarten in America was opened in 1855 by Margarethe Meyer Schurz (wife of German-American statesman, Carl Schurz) of Watertown, Wisconsin, in her own home. Susan Blow opened the first public school kindergarten in 1873 in St. Louis, Missouri. In the Boston area, Elizabeth Peabody, one of the Boston transcendentalists so prominent during this period, had started classes for young children by 1860. She was influenced by Schurtz to go to Germany to study the new kindergarten methods. After studying Froebel's methods, Peabody returned to the United States to lecture and to write and was involved in the initiation of many public and private kindergartens. By 1885, the Froebelian kindergarten was operating in many parts of the United States.

Maria Montessori (1870–1952), the first woman in Italy to earn a doctor of medicine degree, developed a *Casa dei Bambini* (children's house) in the slums of Rome in 1907. Fifty to sixty children between two and a half and seven years old attended the school for eight to ten hours per day. She developed a "prepared environment" that included teaching materials modeled after those developed by Edouard Sequin, noted for his work with the mentally defective. Her efforts, like Pestalozzi's, were directed toward the needs of the poor. Her school operated within tenements in the poorest sections of Rome; it demonstrated very positive effects.

The Montessori method soon spread around the world. Madame Montessori had an exhibition classroom at the World Fair in San Francisco in 1915 that impressed influential Americans. Her methods were countered in the United States, however, by some of the other educational leaders of that period. William Heard Kilpatrick, for example, compared her methods unfavorably with the popular ideas of John Dewey. Although pure Montessori programs did not persist in the United States despite initial enthusiasm, many of her special materials were adapted and used extensively in U.S. classrooms.

Some of the more influential ideas on early childhood programming in the United States and Canada came from the programs of Margaret McMillan (1860–1931), who with her sister, Rachel, became a champion of neglected British children. Because of their concerns over the poor health of school-age children, in 1911 they began sponsoring open-air nursery schools as a preventative measure. They enrolled children from ages one through six. They emphasized cleanliness and the prevention of health problems. Since many of the school activities occurred outside, the program became involved with gardening and in caring for animals. Natural play materials and objects garnered from junk heaps were used along with prepared materials.

McMillan, unlike Montessori, highly valued children's imaginative play, art, and movement. These activities, along with the perceptual-motor activities such as clay modeling and building with bricks, were central to the McMillan nursery schools. In addition, children were introduced to reading, writing, arithmetic, and nature study by age five.

In the United States, although kindergartens were adopted in some states and in most urban centers, schooling for the young was still fairly uncommon during the first two-thirds of the twentieth century. When, in 1925, Patty Smith Hill, a professor at Columbia Teachers College, invited those involved in early childhood education to a conference to discuss their mutual interests, there were only twenty-five people on her guest list. This group, however, became the nucleus of what became the National Committee on Nursery Schools in 1926 and was transformed into the National Association for Nursery Educators in 1929. This organization has evolved into what is now known as the National Association for the Education of Young Children with a membership of 77,000. Clearly, the field of early childhood education has been transformed since the 1920s.

Maria Montessori. *(Courtesy of the American Montessori Society)*

During the first half of this century, the development of preschool education in the United States came not through the established educational systems but, instead, through the sponsorship of philanthropic groups, university programs, and governmental agencies. The people connected with these efforts were pioneers, and in many instances, their efforts blossomed into distinguished training and research centers.

A nurse, Harriet Johnson, established a nursery school in New York City in 1919, which later became known as Bank Street. Patty Smith Hill also initiated a laboratory nursery school at Columbia Teachers College in 1921. In 1922, two other nursery schools were launched. Edna Noble White initiated a program in Detroit (the Merrill-Palmer Institute), and Abigail Eliot started the Ruggles Street Nursery School in Boston. All these schools had child-oriented philosophies in the McMillan tradition. Their programs provided long periods of unstructured play and little didactic instruction. Learning about self, others, and the world was seen as integral to the child's involvement in unstructured work and play activities. These programs were pacesetters for the nursery school movement, designed for three- and four-year-olds with a somewhat different orientation than the public school kindergartens.

During the 1920s and 1930s, a number of additional laboratory schools were developed around the country devoted to the systematic study of children's development and to the training of leaders for parenting and teaching. Examples were the Iowa Child Welfare Research Station, the Fels Research Institute, and the Gesell Child Guidance Clinic. Arnold Gesell at Yale University collected normative data on young children to demonstrate the orderliness of children's sequential maturational processes. The Yale studies, as well as comparable research studies at other universities (including studies by Louis Murphy and Eugene Lerner at Sarah Lawrence College and Joseph Stone and others at Vassar), were supported by grants from the Laura Spelman Rockefeller Fund. From 1923 to 1930, Laurence Frank administered that fund and championed the development of child study. Later he was instrumental in awarding funding to similar enterprises. The work begun at this time is reflected in every early childhood and child development text you will encounter in your professional preparation.

During the first half of the century, there were two brief periods when early childhood programs expanded rapidly in this country. Both periods stemmed from economic or wartime crises. During the 1930s depression years, nursery centers under the administration of the Public Works Administration were developed to employ out-of-work professionals and to enrich the lives of children from families beset by financial and social difficulties. Seventy-five thousand children aged two through five were enrolled. During World War II, day-care centers were established for mothers employed in defense industries. These depression and wartime centers served to educate the public about the nature and possibilities of early childhood education programs. Nevertheless, they were largely disbanded at the conclusion of each national emergency. Only in urban and wealthier areas were nursery schools available during the 1950s.

Freud, Piaget, and Sputnik

During the second quarter of this century, Sigmund Freud's (1856–1939) ideas became popular among educated Americans, some of whom linked his ideas of infant sexuality, the unconscious, and play therapy with nursery schools. These Freudians expected the expert guidance of professionals and the expressive opportunities of the nursery schools to optimally support their children's social, emotional, and physical growth.

Nursery school proponents of this period, whether Freudian or not, concurred on the value of play for children's development. Children in nursery schools were provided with a balanced "age-appropriate" program that included unstructured periods devoted to children's self-initiated play activities. The pri-

Jean Piaget. *(AP/Wide World Photos)*

mary concern of the nursery schools was the socialization of the young. The extent to which children were mastering concepts or developing academic skills was considered less important than whether they participated appropriately in daily routines and learned to get along with others. During this period, kindergarten also evolved in similar directions. It was unheard of in the 1950s for kindergartens to provide instruction in reading, writing, or mathematics. Lessons, when they occurred, were more likely to be concerned with developing social knowledge and awareness, language competence, and "readiness" skills than directly teaching academic content. Parents were routinely advised against encouraging or allowing early involvement with school learning.

Although his work was not influential in the United States until the 1960s, Jean Piaget (1896–1980) and his colleagues had been at work in Switzerland for decades developing ideas that had tremendous significance for those concerned with the development and education of young children. From 1925 to 1940, Piaget focused on the stages of human intellectual development, which he saw as universal. From 1940 to 1960, his work extended to perceptual development and the active role a child plays in creating and interpreting his or her perceptions. His continuing work and the work of his associates elaborated on how children come to understand scientific concepts. His scholarship was prolific, and when his work finally became publicized in the United States, it made a tremendous impact.

In 1957, the Soviets successfully launched the first missile, Sputnik, into space. In considering their stunning success, some Americans began to question why this impressive achievement had not been accomplished by the United States. Perhaps, they reasoned, if we did a better job of educating our young, we would have been first. The result was a renewed interest in mathematics and science education as well as in early education. The Montessori approaches, long defunct in the United States, were reinstituted and touted as a better preparation for later learning than the play-oriented nursery schools and kindergartens. Nancy Rambusch's Learning to Learn center in Stamford, Connecticut, based on Montessori's ideas, received wide publicity during this period. Other approaches that emphasized earlier academic learning were highlighted in the periodicals of the late 1950s and 1960s.

COMPENSATORY EDUCATION

The importance of the early years of life for learning were further emphasized in the writings of two influential men—J. McVicker Hunt and Benjamin Bloom. Bloom's (1964) book pointed out that 50 percent of the variation in intelligence test scores among seventeen-year-olds can already be predicted from test scores obtained at age four. This was widely quoted and interpreted to mean that if children were given better learning environments before school they would become smarter and would do better in subsequent schooling. J. McVicker Hunt's (1961) analysis in *Intelligence and Experience* (which helped to popularize Piaget's ideas in this country) also concluded that deficits in functioning follow early deprivation and, conversely, that benefits can be expected from early enrichment.

By the mid-1960s, a few experimental preschools such as the Perry Preschool Project developed by David Weikart and associates at Ypsilanti, Michigan, and the Early Education Project of Susan Gray in Nashville, Tennessee, were reporting that highly **disadvantaged** children from poor families made significant gains on intelligence scores when provided with a combination of educationally oriented preschool programs and home visits. This initial success spurred the development of many other programs with amazing variations in type of programming and target ages.

Head Start Programs

During the Kennedy and Johnson administrations of the 1960s, concern for the plight of the country's poor led to various kinds of remediating legislation. The overall "War on Poverty" included legislation creating **Head Start** programs to prevent the school failures common among poor children. In the summer of 1965, Head Start programs for four- and five-year-olds were launched across the land with the intent of improving the children's ability to function in mainstream society. Although the sponsoring legislation was framed in terms of a very broad set of goals that included health, social, and emotional development, as well as learning, many of the programs focused heavily on "school" goals. The **compensatory education** programs that resulted were often very unlike the nursery school models of prior decades.

An initial large-scale evaluation of Head Start results, the Westinghouse study (Cicirelli et al., 1969), failed to find the anticipated gains on achievement tests or intelligence tests. Consequently, policy makers' enthusiasm for the **intervention** began to wane. In addition, it was learned that comparable gains could be made by disadvantaged children whenever they first entered school. Nevertheless, the Head Start programs were tremendously popular, and they were continued despite lower expectations for their success in producing academic gains as measured by standardized tests. Health, nutrition, and remediation for disabling conditions were seen as particularly important outcomes of Head Start programs.

In the absence of confirming evidence of the educational value of preschool intervention programs, the governmental agencies responsible for these efforts mounted studies to try to determine whether certain types of program models were more effective than others. First, this was attempted through a national project called **Head Start Planned Variation,** which compared the implementation and outcomes of different preschool models. This study was followed by another project, **Follow Through,** which attempted to determine the effects of different models when their interventions were continued into the primary grades. The findings of these large studies were highly controversial due to disagreements among the experts over the appropriateness of the design, instruments, and interpretations of the findings. Nevertheless, the general conclusion was that programs that directly emphasize academic skills produce higher scores on achievement tests than programs that focus on more comprehensive goals. From these and other evaluation studies conducted during the 1960s and 1970s, two principles can be identified, as follows.

1 Program Outcomes Depend on the Program's Goals   Several studies found that different program emphases result in different outcomes. For instance, in the Head Start Planned Variation studies, it was found that the programs that specifically emphasized the recognition and labeling of letters, numerals, and shapes produced children better at these skills than did the other models. The Cognitively Oriented Curriculum, on the other hand, clearly produced greater increases in scores on the Stanford-Binet intelligence test (Smith, 1975).

Researcher Jane Stallings (1975) reported somewhat similar findings among the first- and third-graders in Follow Through. According to those findings, time spent in reading and math activities, accompanied by a high rate of drill, practice, and praise, contributed to higher reading and math scores. It was also learned, however, that children taught by those methods tended to accept personal responsibility for their failures but not for their successes, which they tended to attribute to their teachers and instructional materials. Children in the more open and flexible instructional approaches had higher scores on a nonverbal problem-solving test of reasoning. They took responsibility for their own successes but not for their failures. Further differences were found in absence rates. Children were absent less from classrooms in which there was a high degree of child independence, child questioning, adult response, individualized instruction, open-ended questions, and positive affect. Child absences appeared to be more frequent in classrooms where children often worked in large groups, adults used direct questions in academic work, and corrective feedback was used frequently (Needels & Stallings, 1975).

The findings of these and other studies confirm that the specific program encountered by children can make significant differences in what they learn and become.

2 Program Outcomes Depend on the Children   Different children benefit from different kinds of programs. Prescott (1972) observed children identified as thrivers or nonthrivers in both open and closed day-care programs and concluded that different kinds of children appear to thrive in each situation. She indicated that a closed structure appeared to offer a more useful experience for children who (a) trusted adults and were ready to meet task expectations; (b) did not trust adults and felt more secure with the clear expectations of the teacher-directed situation; and (c) tended to manipulate adults and children and needed exposure to limits that were firm and relatively impersonal. Open structures were seen as particularly useful for children who (a) needed experience in dealing with other children and adults in settings where they could learn coping skills other than compliance with adult expectations; (b) were shy and needed individual support for the development of initiative; and (c) could handle task demands but needed leeway for creativity and experimentation. Thus, different kinds of children, or the same children at different points in their development, might benefit from different kinds of program structures.

The Head Start Planned Variation studies also noted that for passive and less competent children greater gains on the Stanford-Binet intelligence measure occurred in the more directive models. The more competent and less passive children gained more, however, in the less directive models (Smith, 1975).

Robert Soar (1973) conducted a series of studies over a period of many years, first with middle-class children and then with low-income children in Follow Through programs, that produced contrasting findings for the different groups. He found that middle-class school-age children appeared to benefit most (in achievement) from moderate degrees of freedom and to benefit least from either very high or very low amounts of teacher-imposed structuring. The pattern was different for the low-income pupils in Follow Through whose achievement gains increased under greater control and structure.

These studies imply that a given program needs to be matched not only to target goals but also to the characteristics of the children enrolled. Consequently, educators cannot look to the findings of evaluation studies for simple answers on whether programs are effective or what effects come from particular kinds of programs.

The encouraging news from the early 1960s about the success of early intervention programs began diminishing as reports became available showing how differences between experimental and control groups disappeared as both groups continued on into elementary school. The initial positive impact on cognitive abilities and socioemotional development is not evident in test scores obtained beyond a two-year time span. A recent review of 210 research reports on Head Start's results (CSR, Inc., 1985) cited "virtually unanimous" findings of immediate positive gains but the enrollees "do not remain superior to those disadvantaged children who did not attend Head Start." These reports, on the other hand, included evidence of other positive outcomes in the areas of school success, children's health, and social and educational benefits to families and communities.

Evidence on the results of some selected high-quality programs present a more positive picture. Children who had participated in twelve of the 1960s model programs were located and assessed during the 1970s. The findings, as reported by Lazar, Darlington, Murray, Royce, and Snipper (1982), were hailed as substantiating belief in the effectiveness of early intervention. Experimental children had higher scholastic achievement during elementary school than control children, and fewer were placed in special education or retained in a grade. In one particularly well-researched program, The Perry Preschool Project (later versions were called the Cognitively Oriented Curriculum), information on 123 children of low socioeconomic status from ages three through nineteen was collected. Results indicated lasting benefits of preschool education in improved cognitive performance during early childhood; improved scholastic placement and achievement during the school years; decreased delinquency and crime, need of welfare assistance, and teenage pregnancy; and increased high school graduation rates, enrollment in postsecondary programs, and employment (Berrueta-Clement, Schweinhart, Barnett, Epstein & Weikart, 1984). These findings support the continuation and expansion of early education for the disadvantaged.

Over the years, congressional appropriations for Head Start have fluctuated in relation to changes in political climate. The growing evidence of the long-term life benefits to participants and to the society as a whole has lead to increased enthusiasm about early intervention. Despite this enthusiasm, expansions in funding have not paralleled the need. Only a portion of those qualified for Head Start participation are served. In 1990 Head Start programs enrolled 548,000 children, about 27 percent of those eligible. The Congress in 1990 authorized for the first time a series of funding increases which, if appropriations are also forthcoming, will, by 1994, allow all eligible three- and four-year-olds to participate and 30 percent of five-year-olds. The Head Start appropriation for fiscal year 1991 is $1.95 billion but could climb to $7.66 billion by fiscal year 1994 (Children's Defense Fund, 1991).

In addition to Head Start, a multitude of diverse intervention programs have been launched, including those that have a focus on parents prior to and at the birth of their children and during the first three years of life. Examples of such programs are the Minnesota Early Childhood Family Education Program, Missouri Parents as Teachers Program, Chicago Ounce of Prevention Fund, and Family Focus, Inc. Many states are gradually extending their financial commitments to preschool programs. Despite the expansion of existing programs and the development of new ones, the need for early intervention programs still far exceeds their availability.

PRESCHOOL FOR THE ADVANTAGED

Interest in preschool education for advantaged children has grown in recent decades as well. During the 1970s and the 1980s the program models, the equipment and materials, and the professional expertise developed for the early education of the poor were transferred to more affluent settings. Enrolling children from middle and upper classes in preschool programs has become increasingly popular. The willingness of parents to entrust the rearing and education of their preschool children to program personnel is a recent phenomenon and can be traced to a number of influences. One is the growing awareness of the benefits of early learning opportunities. Some young parents translate this into the need for formal group participation and seek out preschools and day-care centers to give their children special advantage. In the yellow pages of telephone directories of cities and small towns across the United States, advertisers under the category of "Day Care and Nursery Centers" now promise not only care but educational opportunities. Under names such as Little Learners, ABC Academy, Learn as You Grow Nursery School, Creative Environment Day Care, and Smart Day Care Inc., entrepreneurs attract an upper-middle-class clientele. A second reason that more parents are using preschools is that more and more women are choosing to remain employed for personal and financial benefits. Over half of the children in the United States under age three are reported to have mothers who have full-time jobs outside the home. The statistics for children under age six show even higher incidence of mother employment. In 1987, 56.8 percent of married or separated mothers and 70.5 percent of divorced mothers of children under age six were working outside the home (United States Department of Commerce, 1988). In summary, economic conditions and life-style expectations have converged to lead more parents to work and to place their children in day-care programs that they hope will be even more stimulating for their children than the home environment.

As the popularity of day care has grown, a rather curious juxtaposition of varying traditions has developed. Kindergartens, traditionally half-day programs (two and a half to three hours), do not provide sufficient child-care coverage to match the needs of working parents. Therefore, many children at age five attend not one, but *two* daily programs, a public school kindergarten and a day-care program. Increasingly, however, full-day kindergarten programs matching the full-day elementary school schedule are being instituted. In 1987, a survey of elementary school principals found that 34.9 percent had a full-day kindergarten schedule (National Association of Elementary School Principals, 1987). This change responds both to working parent demands for a longer program day and to a societal push for greater accomplishments from young children. Since the full school day is still not sufficient to accommodate the schedule of working parents, schools and other agencies are providing after-school programs as well.

According to some commentators on the current scene, the concept of childhood is once again undergoing radical shifts: The general public increasingly expects that children, advantaged and disadvantaged, will become enrolled in educational prekindergarten programs, sometimes under the sponsorship of the public school system and sometimes under private for-profit or nonprofit auspices. These expectations often encompass the belief that the "academics" will be stressed in such programs, and some parents begin work with toddlers on alphabet recognition, counting, learning shapes, and so forth to assist their children's success as new enrollees in these early education programs.

Urgent efforts to discourage these expectations have been mounted by leading psychologists and educators. Edward Zigler, a professor at Yale University and a former head of the federal Office of Child Development, for example, speaks out forcefully against the institutionalization of programs for all four-year-olds as part of the public school system. "We are driving children too hard," Zigler is quoted as saying. "We must allow children to enjoy their own childhood, their most precious commodity" (Fiske, 1985). Neil Postman (1982, 1985) warns of the "disappearance of childhood." He feels that there is significant evidence that once again children are being viewed and judged as part of an adult world. Children's dress, entertainment, literature, and style of life are, he says, becoming increasingly adultlike. Much in the current milieu seems to support this conclusion. In short, there is still little consensus about the nature of childhood. Although we have come to value the early years as a unique, crucial time of life, we still seem to hold very differing opinions on the nature of childhood. Some of the controversial issues presented briefly here will be more thoroughly examined in Chapter 22.

SUMMARY

The views held of children have fluctuated tremendously throughout human history. For much of that time span, children were not considered of any particular consequence. However, during the last few centuries, an increasing amount of thought and experimentation has been directed at how children may best be reared and taught. As we approach the year 2000, there still seems to be a grand mix of opinions about these matters. Should childhood be a time of intense preparation for adulthood? Should it be a magical and special time best left unspoiled by particular expectations for learning or performance? Is pleasurable learning the real essence of a magical childhood experience? Embedded within each of these contrasting views of children (each of which is further elaborated in Chapter 9) are the ideas of many great thinkers from the past. Words and images from Comenius, Rousseau, Froebel, Montessori, Dewey, and Piaget keep reappearing in today's writing on early childhood education. As an early childhood education professional, you will gain confidence from a firm knowledge of this heritage.

SUGGESTED ACTIVITIES

1 Construct a time line on which you place the persons and events mentioned in this chapter. From such a time line, develop a sense of the historical progression of early childhood education.
2 Select one person who has been described in this chapter as making significant contributions to the evolving concepts of childhood and early education and gather additional information from encyclopedias, reference books, and biographies to better understand the historical milieu and motivation of this person.
3 Select a given location and date (such as Rome in December 1837) and construct a scenario of what life might have been like for a child born into that milieu.
4 Compare the classrooms you recall from your own childhood with the classrooms in which you currently are observing or participating and analyze some of the major differences.
5 Interview persons older than yourself about how child rearing and educational practices have changed during their lifetimes.
6 Review the arguments in support of the compensatory education movement. To what extent are the arguments still valid? What are the obstacles to the implementation of broad-scale compensatory education programs?

ADDITIONAL READINGS

Baylor, R. M. (1965). *Elizabeth Palmer Peabody: Kindergarten pioneer.* Philadelphia, PA: University of Pennsylvania Press.

Borstelmann, L. J. (1983). Children before psychology: Ideas about children from antiquity to the late 1800s. In P. H. Mussen (Ed.), *Handbook of child psychology* (4th ed.) (pp. 1–40). New York: John Wiley.

Bradburn, E. (1989). *Margaret McMillan: Portrait of a pioneer* (2nd ed.). London: Routledge.

Braun, S. J., & Edwards, E. P. (1972). *History and theory of early childhood education.* Worthington, OH: Jones.

Greenleaf, B. K. (1978). *Children through the ages: A history of childhood.* New York: McGraw-Hill.

Hewes, D. (1980). *The Froebelian kindergarten as an international movement.* ERIC Reproduction Service Document No. ED 186 125.

Hymes, J. L., Jr. (1991). *Early childhood education: Twenty years in review. A look at 1971–1990.* Washington, DC: National Association for the Education of Young Children.

Kagan, S. L., & Zigler, E. F. (Eds.). (1988). *Early schooling: The national debate.* New Haven, CT: Yale University Press.

Kramer, R. (1988). *Maria Montessori: A biography.* Reading, MA: Addison-Wesley.

Lilley, I. M. (1967). *Frederich Froebel: A selection of his writings.* Cambridge, England: Cambridge University Press.

Montessori, M. (1974). *Dr. Montessori's own handbook.* New York: Schocken.

Postman, N. (1982). *The disappearance of childhood.* New York: Delacorte.

Schorsch, A. (1985). *Images of childhood: An illustrated social history.* Pittstown, NJ: The Main Street Press.

Weber, E. (1984). *Ideas influencing early childhood education: A theoretical analysis.* New York: Teachers College Press.

PART TWO

TWO

SENSITIVITY TO CHILDREN'S DEVELOPMENT

Teachers of young children need to understand many aspects of children's behavior and development including what children are capable of doing at any given time. Teachers need to infer from a child's behavior how that child is viewing the world and what his or her concerns and needs are. Accordingly, two major emphases of Part 2 are:

1 The development of your understanding of children's physical and motor development, affective and social development, and cognitive development
2 The development of your ability to study individual children as a basis both for your own teaching and for effective communication with others about the children

Prior to the chapters which develop the above two emphases, however, you will find a chapter focusing on children's play. It is extremely important that you begin your development of skills for observing and understanding children by recognizing the key role which play takes in their development and learning. In Chapter 3, *Play: The Key to Children's Learning and Development,* you will gain perspectives which will also serve you well in developing and managing programs for young children. The importance of deeply understanding and respecting children's play cannot be overemphasized.

Chapters 4 and 5 are concerned with physical characteristics and motor development, Chapters 6 and 7 with affective and social development, and Chapters 8 and 9 with cognitive development. Chapters 4, 6, and 8 concentrate on basic information about the progression of development and learning from birth through seven years. Chapters 5, 7, and 9 provide guidelines for studying the behavior of young children. The chapters also provide suggestions for compiling, organizing, and using information about a given child in order to plan appropriate learning experiences and to communicate with parents, colleagues, and other professionals.

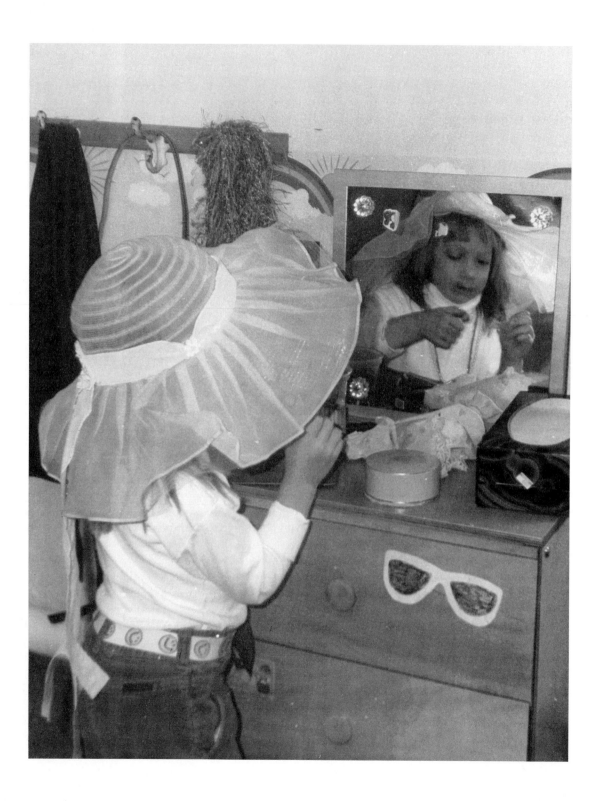

CHAPTER 3

PLAY: THE KEY TO CHILDREN'S LEARNING AND DEVELOPMENT

OVERVIEW

This chapter begins with a brief discussion of what play is, that discussion is followed by a more lengthy section on the benefits of play for children. The chapter then focuses on different types of play distinguished according to category systems developed by various researchers and theoreticians. The final section of the chapter points out that the observation of children's play provides a prime arena both for learning about development of young children and for developing a sensitivity to individual differences. Suggestions for appraising early childhood programs can help you choose a place to spend some time observing children at play.

DEFINITIONS OF PLAY

A simple definition of *play** is that play is what we do when we do whatever we want to do. Play is what we do when we don't have to follow a routine pattern or meet other's expectations or directions. Some may say that play is the opposite of work. In actuality, play and work are often closely aligned. Is the computer programmer who can hardly keep her hands off the keyboard whether at home or at her place of employment working or playing? Is the day-care worker who chooses to spend part of his Saturday in the children's section of a bookstore working or playing? Is the child who is hammering nails in a board one

---

*In contrast to this simple definition, our dictionary lists sixty-seven entries to capture the multiple meanings of the term *play*.

after another working or playing? Is the child who chooses to practice making letters on a chalkboard working or playing? Is the child who must constantly be reminded of her turn in the card game her mother insisted she "play" with her younger cousin working or playing? Obviously, what is often assumed to be work can also be play and vice versa.

Many different definitions and theories of play have been proposed by writers of varying persuasions. Garvey (1977) suggested that the following four conditions are descriptive of what most would consider play:

- Play provides pleasure to the player.
- Play focuses more on the player's enjoyment of the process than the acquisition of some particular end product.
- Play is voluntary and freely chosen by the player.
- Play involves active engagement by the player.

Some child development specialists have added further specifications to what they consider play, but they include at minimum the four above characteristics. These same specialists, although basically agreeing on what is and is not play as they watch children so engaged, may emphasize quite different benefits of that play, including (1) the enhancement of the child's quality of life, (2) therapy through the release of frustrations and negative emotions, (3) the intellectual growth synonymous with play, (4) the learning of the scripts of social life, (5) language development, (6) the enhancement of interpersonal communication, (6) the discharge of excess energy. Each of these benefits will be discussed in the upcoming pages.

BENEFITS OF PLAY

Quality of Life

Many teachers provide play opportunities for children simply because the teachers want to serve the emotional development of the children in their charge, creating pleasure and, thus, positively contributing to the quality of their childhood. Because of the enjoyment derived from play, the child is believed to develop a more positive outlook. According to this view, the happy child becomes a happy and productive adult. Much in the research literature supports this view. For example, a National Institute of Mental Health report summarizes as follows:

> It is common agreement in the field that growth, development, health, and high levels of cognitive and affective functioning in children are all associated with continuous, on-going participation in actions and interactions that are full of pleasure and playfulness (Lichtenberg & Norton, 1972, p. 17).

Many early educators have concerns that children who are deprived of the opportunity to amply engage in experiences of pleasurable play do not develop optimally. These educators warn against overvigorous programming by adults (who may feel under great stress) to too early move children into the rigors of routine, work, and formal schooling. David Elkind (1988), in his book

The Hurried Child, writes as follows about keeping play as a central part of children's early experience rather than "hurrying" them into the lessons and responsibilities similar to those of older peers and adults:

> No matter what philosophy of life we espouse, it is important to see childhood as a stage of life, not just as the anteroom to life. Hurrying children into adulthood violates the sanctity of life by giving one period priority over another. But if we really value human life, we will value each period equally and give unto each stage of life what is appropriate to that stage (p. 202).

Although there are many mysteries about why children play, how they learn to play, and the significance of that play, one clear fact remains generally undisputed. In Bruner's (1983) words, "Unless we bear in mind that play is a source of pleasure, we are really missing the point of what it is all about."

Play as Therapy

Sigmund Freud believed that children's interest in play resulted from their need to deal with conflicts which are universally experienced. As children play, especially in pretend activities, Freud believed that they used the mechanism of **projection** to deal with and cast off tensions and concerns and work out feelings about family relationships. He saw play as providing a personal **catharsis** and an opportunity to clarify and master emotions. Thus, a child confused by the mixed feelings regarding the addition of a new sibling to the family, may play at, successively, caring for, loving, punishing, mistreating a baby doll. Negative, frightened, and hostile feelings which are not directly acceptable and/or are not consciously perceived are believed to be successfully discharged through dramatic play. Many early childhood educators follow Freud's thinking in arranging for ample opportunities for "housekeeping" and "family" play in early childhood settings or, in the case of unusually intense emotional problems, in play therapy settings. These educators cite play as very desirable for children's psychological adjustment.

Play as Intellectual Development

Both the Swiss psychologist Jean Piaget and the Soviet psychologist Lev Vygotsky developed ideas about how play is related to intellectual development, although the ideas of these two influential theoreticians sometimes differ. Piaget emphasized the complementary processes of **accommodation** and **assimilation** as the means by which the internal mental organization (system of beliefs and knowledge) is altered. The human being, according to Piaget, adapts to new experience by creating, through mental imitation, interiorized images of what is encountered in the world. As new experiences do not fit the existent mental structure (internal schemes), humans modify internal images to fit the reality. This process of change was referred to by Piaget as accommodation. Assimilation, the complementary process, is the means by which those aspects of experience which do not require accommodation of existent mental structures are integrated. Assimilation is described by Piaget and Inhelder (1969) as the "filtering or modification of the input" and accommodation as "the modification of internal schemes to fit reality" (p. 6). Both processes are continuously operative, according to Piaget. Piaget considered play as a pure form of the assimilative aspect of intellectual development. It is in play that children try out what they perceive as the central aspects of what they have encountered, thus transforming the experience to a form which can be accommodated into existent mental structures. According to the Piagetian ideas, children engage in play to try out certain puzzling or interesting aspects of their world with complete control over what is pretended (that is, symbolically manipulated in imagery or action).

Piaget particularly emphasized the observation of play to obtain evidence of developmental change in children's symbolic abilities. Piaget (1962) explained, giving examples of his own children's behavior, that as early as the end of the first year of life infants begin to use one object to represent another and thus are able to assimilate their prior experiences, not in reality, but through the use of symbols. A piece of cloth, for example, is used by his daughter, Jacqueline, at fifteen months, to represent "make believe" going to bed:

> . . . [She] saw a cloth whose fringed edges vaguely recalled those of her pillow; she seized it, held a fold of it in her right hand, sucked the thumb of the same hand and lay down on her side, laughing hard. She kept her eyes open, but blinked from time to time as if she were alluding to closed eyes. Finally, laughing more and more, she cried "Ne'ne' (Nono)." The same cloth started the same game on the following days (p. 96).

In such **symbolic play,** Piaget saw the evidence of intellectual development in the use of a symbol. The ongoing consolidation (or assimilation) by children of their experiences through play provides confirmation of the developing internal representations of the world which later support abstract thought.

As children play, they become able to facilely establish and enter or depart from play **frames.** Our son-in-law was recently marveling over the ability of our granddaughter Megan, age two and a half, to engage in pretend activity. "Where does that come from?" he wonders. "She doesn't see me going around pretending that sand is food." Nevertheless, Megan "plays" that the doll is hungry and feeds both herself and the doll and all other interested bystanders as much sand as we care to pretend to eat. Megan knows the difference between when she is pretending and when she is not. She steps in and out of a **play frame.** Increasingly, she is incorporating the signals of play versus nonplay in her voice changes, posture, gestures, facial expressions. Although these behaviors are new and are relatively undifferentiated compared to what she will exhibit across the next years, she is already able to use words to ask others to join in her pretending. She can also take on and incorporate suggestions to elaborate her play. When I query "Does the dolly want a drink?" in the midst of a "sand" feeding, Megan shifts out of the play frame and says to me, "Where's a drink?" and then back in to say to the dolly, "Here's drink," as she shoves a block toward the dolly's face. Megan has a limited number of simple play scenes which she enacts at the present time—kitchen activities of cooking and eating, going shopping with purse and money, driving in a car or truck. As she has more experiences and develops more skill in pretending, she will increase the number of different scenes she can create and she will grow in her abilities to elaborate on a sequence of happenings within any one scene.

These activities, which are so common and so taken for granted that they may not be noticed by adults, are both the play and the work of the young child. To create play scenes requires symbolic representation in which some objects and actions are assigned a new and arbitrary meaning by a child. Decisions must be made on what will be done first and next and next. In play scenes, even simple ones, there is a beginning, a middle, and an end. Solitary play involves cognitive stretching; playing the same kind of scenes with others denotes immense achievement.

On the basis of some preliminary observational studies of doll play (Wolf, Rygh & Altshuler, 1984) some researchers hypothesize that children elaborate their concepts of other people in a regular and predictable manner. First, they only manipulate the dolls (e.g., put the doll to bed, comb the doll's hair). Later they show in their talk (spontaneous narration of play or the words they say on behalf of the dolls) that they are perceiving of the doll as performing the action as an independent action ("She is combing"). Soon thereafter they also refer to the doll's internal feelings—perceptions, sensations, and physical abilities ("He tired and sees bed. Goes to bed.") Later, there is talk of the doll's feelings and social relations ("She sad. Bear no let her play"). Finally, children's talk as they play with dolls includes reference to what the doll knows ("He remembers that it is in the house.") This progression is assumed to be a direct reflection of children's developing understanding of human abilities in themselves and others. The extent to which doll play contributes to or simply reflects these developmental changes is unclear. However, using Piaget's formulations, we would assume that children may be assimilating (practicing and consolidating) their recently acquired concepts of self and others through their actions in doll play.

The contribution of play to the development of cognitive abilities is stressed even more strongly in the writings of Lev Vygotsky than of Jean Piaget. Piaget emphasized that the progress made by the developing child could be assessed through observation of play. However, beyond being an index of children's growing maturity, Vygotsky identifies play as a key factor in causing the child's progress from one level of development to the next. Play is the child's way of expressing meaning. Children must pretend around an object, he said, in order to trigger and allow the expression of ideas. This, according to Vygotsky, is how the transformation from concrete to abstract thought occurs. When a child pretends, for example, that a stick is a horse, the stick "becomes a pivot for severing the meaning of horse from a real horse" (Vygotsky, 1976, p. 546). Thus for young children, who are otherwise incapable of abstract thought, play is the vehicle which removes situational restraints and allows going beyond the concrete to an abstract representation. Pretending assists in the development of representation by separating images from objects.

Unlike Piaget, Vygotsky explicitly addresses the role of adults in relation to children's play. Vygotsky helps us understand that through children's play, we can better understand what children currently understand and what the next steps may be. Vygotsky's term "zone of proximal development" refers to the area between a child's present actual level of functioning (what the child can do without help or support) and the performance level of the child with help and support from an adult or a more experienced peer. Vygotsky pointed out that it is this later level which can next be achieved. Interaction appropriately focused on the "zone of proximal development" facilitates that achievement. By understanding the developmental stages and thus more accurately predicting what a child at a given level might be able to successfully do with a bit of help, a teacher may become more effective in fostering the child's learning and development.

Play as Learning the Frames and Scripts of Social Life

Anthropologist Gregory Bateson described children's dramatic play or pretending as clarifying their understandings of societal norms and role prescriptions in various situations. He said that play "is the name of a frame for action" (Bateson, 1979, p. 139). Children within such a play frame clarify their **scripts** for living as they sort out and then practice the roles that are associated with varied contexts. As children play mother, father, baby, dog, police, doctor, and so forth, they demonstrate their increasingly differentiated knowledge of the organized cluster of behaviors that are identified with a particular status or position within their society. A role in most pretend situations assumes another complementary role in the same play scene. The role of mother is complementary to the role of baby. The role of doctor mandates the role of patient. Knowledge of the complementary role is illustrated by the players. Playing out a role in relation to someone other than oneself is believed to contribute to the child's development of self as a separate identity which is different from but related to others as well as to provide the means for understanding the perspective of others.

In play, children represent recurring experiences in what are sometimes referred to as *event schemata*. A schema is gradually elaborated and continues to serve as a regulator of behavior throughout the life of the individual. You, for example, have learned schemata for classrooms and the associated role scripts for student, instructor, projectionist, custodian. As a student in a frame of a college classroom, you do not typically address the class unless invited to do so by the instructor. Nor do you typically jump up in the middle of a session to erase the chalkboards or attempt to run the audiovisual equipment. You follow the schemata you have learned for the student role and sit passively waiting to see what the instructor has planned for your daily session. You also have schemata for restaurants, for churches, for bus rides. Having learned and well practiced

Let's pretend we're fixing fruit salad for lunch. *(Cumberland Hill Associates)*

the behaviors associated with role and setting, you as an adult give little attention to these matters. Children, however, have a great deal to learn as they playfully portray themes drawn from their lives. The observations by Forys and McCune Nicolich (1984) identified popular themes of three-year-olds as "adorning (i.e., dressing up, putting on jewelry, grooming), meal preparation, feeding and bedding the doll or baby, eating, cleaning, dressing-undressing the dolls." As children play and replay scenes of these types, they gradually incorporate more elaborations and more complex scripts, combining themes in new and innovative ways.

As children play, their activity is guided by thought processes which Bateson referred to as **metacommunication.** Metacommunication is the talk, internalized or spoken, about what will be done within the play frame. Listen to the solitary toddler putting a dolly to bed, waking it up, feeding it, changing its diapers, spanking it, and kissing it, and you often hear the talk which guides the actions you observe. It is believed to be within the context of this talk that the child consolidates prior experience and stretches to make sense of diverse encounters so that they may be enacted in play.

Play as Enhancing Language Development

The effects of play on language are strongly emphasized by linguists and early childhood educators as a justification for the use of play in early childhood programs. Throughout childhood there is evidence that interaction with peers is effective in enhancing language development. Infants and toddlers are encouraged by interaction with siblings and peers to persist in practicing and experimenting with sounds. Adults, however, often find such vocalizations boring or irritating. Once rudimentary language is acquired, a peer group is an extremely important stimulant to further language learning. Vocabulary (including common phrases), syntactic structures, and forms for negotiation and argument are gained as children engage in play. The following example of vocabulary development is cited by Ervin-Tripp (1991):

> A 4-year-old playing nurse said to another, "I'm going to give you a temperature." The nurse put something in the patient's mouth, so she appeared to give rather than to take; perhaps the child assumed the name for a thermometer was "temperature." The child's first use of the term is an approximation, which moves the child into a greater readiness to notice the word at the next visit to the doctor's office. We could say that play has prepared the child for future learning and lowered the future threshold for vocabulary heard in play (p. 92).

The use of **temporal conjunctions** such as *when, while, before, after* are important markers in language development as they indicate the development of complex sentences. Children use these terms and create more complex sentences more frequently in play interactions with peers than in other language situations. Joint planning for play evidently requires the use of terms which mark what and when things will happen. Other more advanced language usage which indicates causality *(because)*, verb auxiliaries *(gonna, hafta, can, will)* are observed first and most prominently in talk during peer play. Linguistic researcher Ervin-Tripp (1991) explains, "It is possible to see this skill only when children are involved in peer play, because when children talk to adults, the adults commonly dominate the organization, timing, content of talk, framing of what is to be done, and definition of the situation" (p. 95). In play, Ervin-Tripp continues, ". . . children imitate their models, receive corrections, copy predictable routines, figure out meanings from context, and then permute and recombine what they have learned" (pp. 95–96).

A great deal of evidence indicates that the language development of native speakers and the second-language learning of immigrant children is enhanced effectively during play interactions. In play encounters the necessary ingredients for language learning are naturally present. The learners are highly motivated to pay attention to the language that is heard. The language heard is simple enough to be understood (often because of context) but slightly in advance or different from the learner's expression. The learner has ample opportunity to practice the new language in one-to-one interchanges and receives feedback immediately as to the effectiveness of the language in the ongoing exchange. Language learning is indeed an important outcome of peer play interactions.

Play as Interpersonal Communication

Children as young as two and a half years old, motivated by the enjoyment of pretend play, attempt to engage in metacommunication about shared play frames with peers. Much more is involved than merely agreeing to create a play scene together. Negotiations are necessary about the characters to be played, the plot, the props. Discussion of the plot alternate with acting it out. Beyond the elaboration of language, as already discussed, children (1) learn the nuances of how to convey ideas and receive ideas, (2) build and clarify concepts, (3) coordinate their own views with other players. After carefully studying the processes of children in conducting make-believe events with peers, Garvey and Berndt (1976) declared "the point to be made about the communication of pretending is that a great deal of speech is devoted to creating, clarifying, maintaining or negotiating the social pretend experience" (p. 10).

In pretend play with peers, children must often "stretch" their abilities to think clearly about their inclinations and plans and to find the means for explaining those thoughts to others. When playing by themselves or even when playing with adults, there is less challenge than in peer play. As indicated above, adults can often guess at children's meanings and therefore are able to ease the communication burden for children. The result is that children rely on the adult to figure out what they mean from minimal communication. Pellegrini (1984) found, for example, that three- and four-year-old children engaged in more mature social cognitive play when other children were present than when only adults were present.

As children together build rules for their play activities (e.g., "Let's say that this is the house and this is the yard"), they increase their ability to see points of view other than their own. As children develop their abilities to coordinate their play ideas they are developing rather advanced cognitive strategies. Consider what we can observe in such play. The following kinds of metacommunicative messages used by preschoolers were reported by Schwartzman (1978):

1 Formation statements: "Let's play going shopping."
2 Connection statements, "Can I be the sister?"
3 Rejection statements, "No, he can't play with us."
4 Disconnection statements: "I'm not your father now."
5 Maintenance statements: "He broke it. Tell Mommy."
6 Definition statements: "This is the stove."
7 Acceptance statements: "Oh, yeah, the soup tastes good."
8 Counterdefinition statements: "This isn't our supper. This is just our cafeteria tray."

Statements such as the above are the signals children use to construct their roles and actions in the thematic play scene. They constantly maintain awareness of both the role of player and the role of writer-director of the play scene. They develop techniques for indicating to the other players when they are "in frame" and when they are "out of frame." For example, children sometimes "prompt" in their own natural voice but with a lower volume, giving a suggestion of how to improve on the action. This happens with almost no disruption of the flow of the other players. They sometimes "narrate" (tell the story which is being played), interrupting the narration to assume a role. For example, Robin who is playing aunt says to Royce who is playing father, "Pretend I came here . . . and I didn't see you. And you start to feed the baby and it cried. And I was scared cause I thinked you were a burglar." The narrator, back in frame, squeals dramatically, "Who is that? Help! Help! Police!" Royce behaves as Robin's script suggests he should, picking up the baby and simulating the baby's crying, "Waah! Waah! Mommy!" He then adds to the narration, "Let's say I was behind the door so you can't see me . . . " and so forth.

In the midst of the pretend scene, roles are sometimes switched, and possibly switched back, without loss of continuity. Children pause to discuss the merits of one kind of action versus another or even to have a squabble about roles and then may pick up or begin again with gusto. Sometimes scenes are repeated with new twists or with discussed improvements. The kind of thinking processes required to carry on these actions so often seen in shared dramatic play activities go considerably beyond what adults typically consider to be within the capabilities of young children.

Play as Discharge of Excess Energy

The desire of children to be engaged in physical activity is well recognized by anyone who has spent more than a few minutes with them. It is commonly believed that children need to be physically active before they can then settle down and pursue more sedentary activities. Thus, children in elementary school programs are sent out for recess breaks, and most children joyously run, chase, gallop, imitate active horses or rockets, ride bikes, and so on for as long as their teachers allow. Asked about their favorite time of day in school, children almost universally reply, "Recess!" Physical movement is even more important for preschoolers. Teachers are advised as follows by the National Association for the Education of Young Children: "Children at this age [prior to age five] need planned alternations of active and quiet activities. . . . Older children continue to need alternating periods of active and quiet activity throughout the day, beyond traditionally provided recess" (Bredekamp, 1987, p. 8).

The novice may tend to equate play with this need of children for active movement. Play, especially dramatic play, often includes active movement and may sometimes be rowdy and boisterous. Children's need to be physically active is typically naturally incorporated into children's play (unless there are adult restrictions which prevent this from happening). However, the benefits of play are not derived from structured exercise programs. Play and exercise are not the same!

Each of the above views of play serves to enrich our perceptions of the multiple ways in which this spontaneous activity on the part of children enlivens and contributes to their learning and development.

TYPES OF PLAY

If you reflect on the various types of play in which you engaged as a child, you may become aware that you think of very different types of activities as play. It will be useful to you to develop a more differentiated set of categories under the overall label of play.

In observing children, you will find it useful to differentiate between exploratory activity and subsequent play. According to a number of studies (e.g., Wohlwill, 1984), children first engage in actions which help them to know what the object does or what its perceptual properties are. Only after these become known does the child begin to find out what can be done with the object. It is at this latter stage that the object is used playfully to create planned variations or to represent some aspect of experience in a play frame. Note, therefore, the benefits to children of having access to familiar materials: Children who must constantly encounter new stimuli or respond to adult directions have little opportunity to go beyond exploration to engage in playful behavior. Sometimes well-meaning but unaware teachers continually introduce new materials, new tasks, new challenges, new experiences without giving children adequate opportunities to profit from thorough familiarity with what they have already encountered. Some planned redundancy in children's programs may foster play and creativity.

Other researchers have created different categories of play. The following are important for you to learn and begin to use as you observe children: **sensorimotor play, symbolic play, constructive play,** play of games with rules. These are the labels that Jean Piaget gave to the play he saw his own three children engage in as they advanced from one stage to another. Children, of course, are oblivious to these classifications. To the player, play is whatever gives involvement, excitement, challenge, and pleasure at the moment. As a teacher, though, familiarity with these labels and descriptions may help you to anticipate the appropriate kind of play for children at various stages of development.

Sensorimotor play is evidenced very early in the life of the young child. We observe sensorimotor play in the infant who has learned a particular schema, such as making a crib rattle by vigorously kicking and waving, and who does this with obvious pleasure. We also see sensorimotor play in the six-year-old who skips up and down the sidewalk "just for the fun of it." This kind of play is also sometimes called *practice* play as it is the performance of abilities which are already in the repertoire of the player but which nevertheless are reenacted again and again for pleasure. Adults too engage in sensorimotor play such as dancing, doodling, swimming. Do you?

Sensorimotor play often involves the actions of one's own body, as in skipping or dancing or swinging. Sensorimotor experimentation often also involves natural forces of gravity, momentum, time, electrical charges, etc. When this is the case, the playing child acquires the basis for understanding universal principles typically referred to as the principles of physical science. Thus, children who are playing with magnets or bubbles or swinging are gaining, along with their pleasure in the immediate activity, awareness which is drawn upon throughout their later lives in acquiring conceptual understanding of very complex phenomena.

Symbolic play is what we often call "pretending" or dramatic play. In effect, it is the playful representation of an actual object or experience. Symbolic play is seen very early in life. Children of twelve or thirteen months sometimes go through the motions of eating without food or simulate going to bed. Fein and Apfel (1979) report that in their study of twelve-month-old children most (80 percent) went through the motions of eating without food; some (32 percent) pretended to feed their mother; a few (19 percent) fed a doll. Toddlers have a number of pretend sequences which they use apart from the actual situations or persons being represented. They do so with gusto and evident gratification.

The next developmental step appears to be for the child to act as though toys were actively involved in pretend transactions. At that stage, the child may say to the doll he is putting to bed in the housekeeping corner, "Do you want to go to sleep now?" In the role of doll, he may say, "No!" Back to the other role, the question may come, "You don't want to go to sleep? Do you want me to read you a story?" What is required, of course, is that the player enact two roles, coordinating the joint actions. Miller and Garvey (1984) give examples of this kind of behavior at age three:

> " . . . Mary (38 months) spoke first in a whiny, lisping voice as Baby, 'I want my Kathy doll,' and then clearly and sternly as Mother to Baby doll, 'If you will just go to sleep'" (p. 124).

Beyond age three, the child becomes increasingly able to take on and sustain a particular role with toys or peers taking other roles. The child develops ability to coordinate his or her own self identity and actions with the role the other is taking and then extends this into the play sequence. Effectively implementing this kind of role coordination in mutually satisfying fashion is a very telling developmental indicator. The ability to create such a play scene requires a complexity and nimbleness of thought that is impressive, especially when negotiation with peers is involved. The players must reach agreement about the roles each will play and about the identity of objects to be mutually used. Players must project a set of events and engage in the ongoing coordination of actions, and each must be able to communicate through language about what he or she is doing and why. As Smilansky (1968) pointed out, the same abilities needed for successful participation in sociodramatic play (dramatic play in cooperation with other persons) are necessary to the understanding of literature and history.

The progression of children in using objects in their play is also of interest. Younger children typically use real objects or their replicas in their pretending and are stimulated in their play by having realistic replicas of dishes, fire hats, and so on. By age five, however, children's play is often well supported by raw materials (cartons, scarves, styrofoam pieces) that become, in imagination, a variety of objects to fit the projected scene. Some children continue to be quite dependent on the presence of objects which in some way resemble the actual object, whereas others are much less concerned with the appropriateness of the substitution and may use the same object for many different purposes. Some children also learn to use hand and/or body movements (miming) instead of handling actual objects to support the play they have in mind. Some researchers suggest that these differences are less a function of developmental progression than of cognitive style. Realistic objects continue to influence the play sequences for all children, however. The presence of a particular prop is often the invitation to children to pursue a particular play theme. Once the play is underway, however, it is the action in the play frame which suggests how an object will be used. Thus, for one group of three- to five-year-old children, a three-legged stool with a magnifying glass in its center became a telescope (to spot a fire), a toilet for the baby, a "workchair" for housework, a trailer to pack possessions to take a trip, and a milk carton (Bretherton, 1984).

Children's play with **manipulative materials** (abstract shapes or pliable forms) is sometimes referred to as **constructive play.** In constructive play, children create, for the fun of it, their own representations of selected aspects of the physical world with materials ranging from blocks to plasticene to Legos. A great deal of children's time is spent in this kind of play, either alone or with others. You may find it useful to distinguish between a child's **exploration,** during which there is an investigation of the properties of an object, and the subsequent use of that type of object to represent all or some part of a "pretend" activity or construction. Exploration may overlap with the sensorimotor play referred to earlier as children experiment with, practice, and master the properties of materials which are novel to them. This distinction may be particularly important for parents, teachers, caregivers who may need to provide time for exploration as a prelude to constructive play. Just handling, pounding, tasting, squeezing, throwing, bending, and so on of objects may not be the waste of time the unaware adult may think. As discussed previously, some teachers seem to think that they must always be introducing new stimulating toys to keep children interested. The net effect of this practice may be that children seldom get beyond exploration of one kind of material before that is whisked away and another presented. The younger the child, the more time is spent in exploration with novel materials prior to constructive and symbolic play (Switzky, Ludwig & Haywood, 1979; Voss, 1987). Teachers need to anticipate that toddlers and preschoolers will spend more time in exploratory actions and less time in actual play than children at ages five or six.

There is, of course, a great deal of overlap between various types of play. For example, it is not unusual within a single five-minute span to see a child playing with blocks, cheerily bang the blocks together (sensorimotor play), line the blocks up to create a rectangular enclosure (constructive play), and then, apparently influenced by hearing the record of "The Teddy Bear's Picnic" playing in the background, line up a row of teddy bears (spool-shaped blocks) who climb over the fence to have a picnic and a football game within the enclosure (symbolic play). Often children from age five onward spend as much or more time in creating a scene and "props" from the constructive play materials which are

Preschoolers learn many things when they represent their world through constructive play. *(Cumberland Hill Associates)*

accessible as they do in the actual playing out of the actions for which the scene is intended.

During the years from four to seven, children become interested in playing games with rules. Examples of such games are Duck Duck Goose, Musical Chairs, Hot Ball. Often these are sensorimotor activities which have conventions preestablished for players to use in guiding their actions. From age six and seven children increasingly elect participation in a variety of rule-governed games. They also continue to enjoy and embellish their abilities in symbolic play, both with their peers and on their own. Children create, practice, and present plays with increasingly elaborate plots and staging. They also create play scenes wherein parts are played by puppets, paper dolls, and all kinds of miniature toys. Children's interest in games with rules does not typically preclude their involvement in increasingly sophisticated fantasy enactments.

Another way of viewing play which is often used by researchers and by teachers categorizes the extent and type of interaction as **solitary play, parallel play, associative play, cooperative play.** Solitary play is, as the name implies, the play of a child without others' involvement. Although solitary play persists throughout childhood, it is the predominant mode for the early years. When another child is present, very young children also continue to play as though they were by themselves without interaction. This kind of play is called parallel play. When children play beside each other with the same materials and with some turn taking and verbal interchanges, clearly aware of the other's activity, the play is called associative play. When the players go beyond conversation and turn taking, to jointly plan and/or influence each other's actions, the play is referred to as cooperative play. Many researchers, Parten (1932) for example, have reported a direct progression with increasing age in the proportion of time that children spend in associative and cooperative play as compared to solitary and parallel play. These terms are more fully explained in Chapter 6, Affective and Social Development.

ASSESSMENT OF CHILDREN'S BEHAVIOR AND DEVELOPMENT IN PLAY SETTINGS

You have gained some perspectives on how play is viewed and valued as a central part of the developmental process. Throughout this textbook you will encounter strong emphases on facilitation of children's play. In most other publications on the care and education of young children, you will find similar thrusts. Note for example, the following statements from *Developmentally Appropriate Practice in Early Childhood Programs Serving Children from Birth through Age 8* (Bredekamp, 1987):

> Much of young children's learning takes place when they direct their own play activities. During play, children feel successful when they engage in a task they have defined for themselves, such as finding their way through an obstacle course with a friend or pouring water into and out of various containers. Such learning should not be inhibited by adult-established concepts of completion, achievement, and failure. Activities should be designed to concentrate on furthering emerging skills through creative activity and intense involvement.
>
> . . . the child's active participation in self-directed play with concrete, real-life experiences continues to be a key to motivated, meaningful learning in kindergarten and the primary grades (pp. 3–4).

It is, as indicated above, essential that the teacher of children through age eight be willing and capable of providing extensive and varied opportunities for age- and stage-appropriate play. In addition, professionals who are interested in assessing children's growth, development, and learning can learn much about the individual child, as well as about children's development in general, by observing play. Garvey (1979), for example, proposes that a child's competence level becomes apparent by listening to him or her play.

To develop your sensitivity to children's behavior and to assess a child's development through observations, you will need to locate situations in which children have ample opportunity to engage in exploratory behavior and to develop play activities of sufficient duration to allow full involvement. To fulfill the intent of this section of the textbook, you must locate such a setting. You may find this task difficult. Teachers vary greatly in their views of play and in their implementation of their beliefs, as you will learn if you talk with several.

The following questions which you or your instructor may address to personnel in prospective observation sites may be helpful in determining whether play is a central part of children's experience in the specific program:

1 What periods do you have in your daily schedule? How many different periods do you typically have? How long does each last?
2 During each of these periods (each in turn) is it okay for children to
   Talk with each other?
   Stop and rest?
   Go to the bathroom?
   Play with each other?
3 What activity centers (or areas) do you have in your classroom? Are they constant, or do you create new centers on a regular basis?
4 During what periods may children use these centers?
5 Do you have any ways in which you assign children to these centers? Are there any expectations for how long children may remain in these centers?
6 What are your ground rules or expectations for what children may or may not do in these centers?
7 What do you as a teacher do during different periods?

You might wish, for your own enlightenment, to observe children in programs of teachers who give contrasting answers to some of the above questions.

The best situations for observing children for the purpose of assessing their development have some of these attributes:

- There is a predictable time sequence with plenty of time for self-selected activities so that children can fully carry out a single project or have the chance to do several things of their own choosing.
- There is reliability across time in equipment and materials available. There may be one or two changeable theme-based activity centers, but a number of activity centers routinely are available that offer a variety of options for children's consideration. Children have open access to the centers, limited only by numbers wishing to use the materials at any given time. Once they become involved in a center, children are able to continue as long as they are productively involved. Ground rules for use of the centers are few but firm, with the expectation that only those who can follow the center's ground rules may have access to those centers.
- Children are allowed to freely converse as they play and work during these periods. Even excited clamorous talk is tolerated unless it disrupts others' activities.

- During these periods, teachers observe children's activities and move around the room showing through their demeanor and their comments that they are aware of and supportive of the children's constructive actions and interactions.

The above criteria are offered as a guide in selecting the kind of setting in which you can best develop your abilities to observe children's behavior. We also offer them as advance organizers for your thinking about the kind of program which many professionals in the field of early childhood education believe to be supportive of the optimal development and learning of preschool and primary age children. As you continue to study the materials in this text and in other guides to the field of early education, you will become increasingly aware of the benefits of play and of offering programming for children in which play takes a central role.

SUMMARY

Play is characterized as what one does when one does what one wants to do. Play is more formally characterized, as follows: The player finds play pleasurable, the player focuses on the process not the product, and the player is actively and voluntarily engaged. The benefits of play are myriad and are believed to include (1) enhancement of the child's quality of life, (2) therapeutic release, (3) intellectual growth, (4) learning of the frames and scripts of social life, (5) discharge of excess energy. Useful discriminations and categorizations regarding children's play behaviors include exploratory and subsequent play behaviors; Piaget's sensorimotor play, symbolic play, constructive play, play of "games with rules"; Parten's solitary play, parallel play, associative play, cooperative play.

There is general agreement in the field of early childhood education that play is very important and that much of young children's learning takes place when they direct their own play activities. Teachers therefore need to be able to "read" the nuances of children's play behavior. To develop sensitivity to children's behavior and to learn to assess an individual child's development through observation requires practice. This practice is best done in program situations which devote time and resources to support children's play. The observation guides incorporated in the upcoming chapters assume the availability of such program situations.

SUGGESTED ACTIVITIES

1 List as many different types of play as you can recall from your childhood. After you make an initial list, note whether you have included play across the entire span of the childhood years, including ages prior to school entrance. Try to remember your feelings about each type of play you have listed. How important was it to you? What do you remember about it? Do you think that type of play provided you with any lasting benefits?

2 Ask your friends to do the same kind of listing as in item 1 and interview them about their feelings and opinions of the value of that play. From this information, determine whether any common responses either confirm or question the information about play provided in this chapter.

3 Observe children in community settings available to you such as parks, laundromats, restaurants, bus stops. Note the extent to which play occurs in these informal settings. Look for any examples to confirm or question the information about play provided in this chapter.

ADDITIONAL READINGS

Almy, M., Monigham, P., Scales, B., & Van Hoorn, J. (1984). Recent research on play: The teacher's perspective. In L. G. Katz (Ed.), *Current topics in early childhood education* (Vol. 5). Norwood, NJ: Ablex.

Block, J. H., & King, N. R. (1987). *School play.* New York: Garland.

Bruner, J. (1983). Play, thought, and language. *Peabody Journal of Education, 60(3),* 60–69.

Forman, G. E., & Hill, F. (1984). *Constructive play: Applying Piaget in the preschool.* Menlo Park, CA: Addison-Wesley.

Garvey, C. (1977). *Play.* Cambridge, MA: Harvard University Press.

McCracken, J. B. (1987). *Play is FUNdamental.* Washington, DC: National Association for the Education of Young Children.

McKee, J. S. (Ed.). (1986). *Play: Working partner of growth.* Wheaton, MD: Association for Childhood International.

National Association for the Education of Young Children. (1985). *Toys: Tools for learning: Parents as partners series #571.* Washington, DC.: author.

Sawyer, J. K., & Rogers, C. S. (1988). *Helping young children develop through play: A practical guide for parents, caregivers, and teachers.* Washington, DC: National Association for the Education of Young Children.

Scales, B., Almy, M., Nicolopoulou, A., & Ervin-Tripp, S. (1991). *Play and the social context of development in early care and education.* New York: Teachers College.

CHAPTER 4

PHYSICAL AND MOTOR DEVELOPMENT

OVERVIEW

The following anecdotal account written by an early childhood teacher illustrates the primacy of physical activity in young children's behavior:

> Curtis runs into the playroom at full speed and slides to a stop with verbal screeching just short of a block tower Joey is building. "What 'cha doin'?" he says, but before Joey can answer, he runs in the other direction, kicks shoulder high with his left foot at some imaginary target, and says, "Got 'cha!" He wheels about and returns to the exact spot again kicking shoulder high, this time with his right foot. Again he says, "Got 'cha!" He then turns about, runs up the four-foot sliding board attached to the jungle gym, pivots halfway up, and sits down to slide to the bottom. At the bottom he stretches out, completely relaxed, watching the block tower teeter as Joey adds a cube. "Watch it!" he shouts and leaps up in time to catch one of the falling blocks.

Curtis is four years old. He is full of energy and enthusiasm. His gross motor abilities appear to provide him with great satisfaction. His body gives him pleasure in both its appearance and its performance. If Curtis's teachers are unaware of the central role that physical abilities play in his development at this age, they are missing a critical aspect of his being. And Curtis is not particularly unusual in this respect. Most young children, although perhaps not as able as Curtis, judge themselves more on the basis of their **motoric competence** than on any other criterion. Teachers of young children need to become as sensitive to these aspects of development as they are to cognitive or social behaviors.

In this chapter, we will first very briefly discuss the progress and significance of motor development and physical growth during the infant and toddler years. We will then describe in greater detail the motor and physical characteristics of children ages three through seven, including size and bodily proportions, bodily posture, physical attractiveness, **large-muscle development, fine-motor development, dominance,** physical defects, nervous traits, and health and disease indicators.

INFANTS AND TODDLERS

When did you last hold and wonder at a newborn baby? The human infant, although quite helpless, has amazing competencies from the day of birth. The differentiation process begins immediately and continues throughout the life span. Much of the early learning consists of establishing the source of experience: Is it coming from within or from outside oneself? Both are unknowns that must be learned.

Many recent studies have demonstrated the extent to which infants become actively involved in visually examining and, when possible, manipulating their environments to provide new experiences. They quickly develop expectancies based on their experiences and are disconcerted when events do not match what they anticipated would happen. For example, Lewis (1977) found that infants as young as one month showed surprise reactions when the voice of the person at whose face they were looking came, not from the face, but from a microphone placed in another location. In this and other situations, babies seem to seek the stimulation of novel experiences. Given a choice of a photograph of a familiar face versus a different face, infants gaze at the novel one. Also they prefer to look at the novel face rather than a photograph of the familiar face in a different orientation (Fagan, 1976).

The Swiss psychologist Jean Piaget studied in great detail the development of infants, especially his own children Lucienne and Laurent and proposed that there is no **intellect** at that age apart from **motor intelligence.** He said that it is, at least in part, through the child's own motor activity that mental structures are developed from which further thinking is derived.

The first year of life, according to Piaget, involves the development of successively more advanced **schemata,** or means for acting on the world and deriving information. At first, children use the schema of sucking (initially a **reflexive behavior**); later they use grasping (also initially a reflex). They taste and feel all that comes within range of their mouths and hands and visually examine the sights that surround them. Eventually they begin to coordinate the use of these separate ways of acting on the world and from this coordination come new schemata, or modes of learning. These include the awareness that something grasped is something to taste, something heard is something to look at, something seen is something to reach for and grasp. These new schemata are improved means (beyond separate actions such as sucking and grasping) for obtaining information. Knowing that the feel of something is dependably associated with its appearance is a tremendous advance in knowing about that object; knowing that one can navigate a felt object into one's mouth to taste and to explore orally is another significant realization about oneself as well.

A bit later, children begin to show some anticipation about which actions will cause particular outcomes. For instance, Piaget describes how his five-month-old daughter, Lucienne, upon looking at a doll hung from the hood of her bassinet, would consistently kick her feet to create movement and a swaying of the doll. In becoming aware that his or her own activity can affect what is seen or heard, the baby has acquired a very effective means for learning about the world. If you have ever watched babies at this age, you might have observed how enthralled and delighted they appear to be with their newfound ability to make things happen.

Infants increasingly learn how their own actions bring about effects on objects around them. By the end of the first year, an infant with a rattle or a bell will experiment with vigorous shaking, slow movements, and pauses followed by more movements. There is a very active manipulation of any object within reach to determine what it is like and its possible uses. By eighteen months, children have developed an awareness of **object permanency** (that is, they know that objects still exist when out of sight). These new concepts allow young children to manipulate objects more effectively in order to create effects and to solve simple problems.

Although these kinds of behaviors were noted by parents and other close observers of infants long before Piaget's ideas became known, they were typically considered to be the result of **biological maturation** and were not considered significant in terms of further development. Piaget's contribution has been to point out that it is, in part, the child's own functioning that transforms these initial schemata into more complex ones and that the higher forms of thinking and problem solving have their genesis in the infant's motor explorations.

A greater elaboration of the continuity from the **sensorimotor** period in infancy to the development of schemata for more complex thinking is presented in Chapter 8. In the present chapter, we will limit ourselves to briefly tracing how the child's increased motor efficiency leads to the ability to move from place to place and to manipulate objects and tools with increasing skill. The child who at age three or four can run, climb, and use pencils and scissors has certainly made dramatic progress since infancy.

A child's increasing competence in moving about generally includes the following progression: lifting chin, lifting chest, sitting with support, sitting alone, standing with help, standing when holding onto furniture, creeping, walking when led, walking, walking and pulling a toy on a string, jumping, running— and then the world! This difficult and involved progression ranges from helplessness to moving about very independently during the second year.

The ability to manipulate objects has its genesis in the baby's grasping. When the baby is able to sit alone, at around seven months, the handling of objects is greatly aided. By this age, infants can grasp and explore objects with both thumb and palm (instead of just the palm alone). Infants shake and bang objects to create sounds, transfer them from one hand to the other, and generally become quite engrossed in examining anything that comes within reach, such as stones, blocks, toys, silverware, cookies, or cotton balls. They learn about such sensations as prickly, soft, sticky, sour, pliable, hard, and rough. They gradually learn how to use their hands in coordination with their eyes to control the object being explored.

A crucial ability—and a difficult one to acquire—is that of consciously letting go of an object in hand. This often is not accomplished until late in the first year. To effectively pick up and put down objects, the baby must have considerable control of the fingers and especially of the opposing thumb. (Try to pick up and release an object without your thumb if you would like to gain a new appreciation of these carefully acquired skills.) After months of practicing hand manipulation of various objects, a two-year-old has normally learned such "advanced" feats as building a tower of six or seven blocks, making a train of three or more cubes, drawing misshapen circles and V's, turning individual pages of a book, or fitting square blocks into square forms in puzzles. Think of the learning this represents, the number of unsuccessful or partially successful efforts required before these tasks are mastered. Only a baby's parents or constant caretakers can appreciate how much effort this represents.

We hope the preceding discussion will lead you to appreciate what has already

Using a tool such as a shovel is a challenge for three-year-olds.
(Cumberland Hill Associates, Inc.)

been accomplished, both by the typical three-year-old and by those children who enter a preschool program without some of these motor skills. Some children will struggle much longer with these rudimentary skills of walking, balancing, and handling objects and will need far more tolerance than their more successful peers. Yet all too often they receive reprimands for their clumsiness simply because they do not equal the average attainment for their age.

AGES THREE THROUGH SEVEN

When you see young children at the library, the laundromat, or a concert, can you guess about how old they are? If you cannot, or if you feel unsure of your estimates, you might begin sensitizing yourself to the physical characteristics and motor abilities of children of various ages. You can do this by making it a practice to observe, predict, and verify (by asking the child or parent) the ages of children you encounter. You will find that your guesses will become more and more accurate. Besides, it is very interesting to compare the different responses of individual children and children of different ages to your question, "How old are you?"

Size and Weight

Tables of average heights and weights for varying ages may be interesting to study, but any conclusions drawn from them about the appropriate size for an individual child at any given time may be thoroughly misleading. Each child follows his or her own growth pattern, in both rate of growth and eventual size. Comparisons with agemates are virtually meaningless. For example, two 6-year-olds who weigh exactly the same may be faring very differently. As judged by previous growth rates and by expectations based on size of parents, one could be undersized, and the other could be overweight.

Adequacy of size cannot be judged at any one point in time. The pattern of growth across time and the parents' statures are essential in making such a judgment, but even with this information it is difficult to say whether a given height or weight is "normal" for an individual child. Teachers need to be very wary in making such appraisals. Although it is a well-known fact that inadequate nutrition, especially protein, restricts size, there are many nondietary causes of different growth patterns. It would be erroneous simply to assume that a small or thin child is not getting a proper diet.

Height and weight increases occur quite regularly during the early childhood years; however, changes in bodily configuration are more conspicuous. Three-year-olds find the task of reaching over their heads and touching the opposite ear an impossible one, but most six- and seven-year-olds can do this easily because they have longer arms. You might enjoy testing this out with the children whose ages you are trying to guess. Tell them that you can do a trick, then touch your opposite ear and find out if they can do it also.

You may note that many children who are large for their age are more "advanced" in other respects as well, such as motor coordination, academic skills, and social ability. Many explanations of this have been proposed. One is that such individuals have a genetic superiority that is evidenced in many ways. Another explanation is that optimal diet, physical care, and a stimulating learning environment result in advanced growth and social and intellectual development. A third is that being initially larger than one's agemates produces a natural superiority in social relationships and, consequently, a positive self-concept that facilitates development in all areas.

From a teacher's perspective, there is good reason to concentrate on helping all children view their current stage of growth as a launching point for further development. Teachers must also be aware of those instances in which larger size is not accompanied by advanced abilities and must develop their expectations accordingly.

Bodily Posture

Posture is the result of various adjustments used to balance the whole body. Despite frequent admonitions of parents and teachers to "sit up" and "stand straight," there is actually little a child can consciously do to improve posture. If opposing muscles are unequal, faulty balance between them results in poor posture. A better alignment of the body is not necessarily brought about by holding the head up or putting the shoulders back. It is achieved, instead, by good muscle tone, good skeletal development, and general physical and emotional good health.

Each child balances his or her body in the most functional way, given his or her individual mass and muscle tone. A stocky child balances the body in one way, a skinny child in another. Although a beautifully balanced body is an indication of health, one child's stance should not be modeled on another's, since significant bodily differences usually exist. Bodily posture is something a teacher might note and possibly use to evaluate a child's physical and emotional health, but it is not something that warrants direct action to bring about change.

A low center of gravity in a living organism leads to desirable stability. The young child has a high center of gravity that gradually shifts downward throughout the early years from just above the navel to just below it. This high center of gravity, along with incomplete muscle development, accounts for the frequent falls and comparative clumsiness of young children, in contrast to older ones. You may find it interesting to observe the number of times preschool children fall during active play, as compared with older children.

Physical Attractiveness

Despite all the admonitions to the contrary, such as "beauty is as beauty does" and "beauty is only skin deep," attractive features are a great asset. Although personal appearance is partly a matter of fashion, some people are never considered to be pretty or handsome. Worse yet, there are always some people whose features are so differently or unevenly arranged that they are universally seen as unattractive or ugly. Many children remain outside the current standards of attractiveness and, consequently, may identify more with villains and clowns than with attractive heroes and heroines.

As a teacher, you will be responsible for both children who match and children who deviate from your own and society's image of attractiveness. Can you care as much about a hollow-cheeked, sallow-skinned child with decaying teeth and large protruding ears as you can about a cute, freckle-faced redhead with an engaging smile and a stylish haircut? What effect will this have on the children you teach? You may wish to systematically examine your feelings about the appearance of others, especially children.

Large-Muscle Development

In working with children it will be helpful to become consciously attuned to movement. For a child, movement is almost everything. Keturah Whitehurst (1971), a physical educator, expresses this view as follows: "Movement means to young children, life, self-discovery, environmental discovery, freedom, safety, communication, enjoyment and sensuous pleasure" (p. 9). To be fully attuned to children, you must learn to see movement and to differentiate its many aspects, such as:

Agility   The ability to move flexibly, to stretch, bend, twist, spin, arch, leap, turn, throw, run, jump.

Strength   The effective alignment of body parts to push or release power.

Endurance   The extent to which movement(s) can be continued without need for rest.

Balance   The effective alignment of body parts to maintain the vertical center of gravity, which prevents falling.

Rhythm   The ability to pattern movements in a predictable, repetitive sequence.

Speed   The effective alignment of body parts to allow rapid and/or efficient movement through space.

The aspects of movement do not necessarily develop simultaneously. Strength and power are often associated with body size and build, whereas balance and agility show little relationship to physique or strength. There is relatively little relationship between strength and speed. Therefore, when observing children, you should look for and note specific movements rather than making broad evaluations such as "well coordinated" or "poor motor development."

It will be useful for you to learn the "typical" patterns of motor development by age levels, despite the many exceptions to these developmental progressions within any group of children. As you read through the following section, keep in mind that movements typical of four-year-olds are sometimes accomplished by three-year-olds and, conversely, are sometimes still unattained by children of

At four and five, tools become functional: "Make it smooth on top . . . and level too." *(Cumberland Hill Associates, Inc.)*

ages five and six. Knowledge of the general progression is more useful than the specific ages at which these accomplishments are attained.

Three-year-olds can run smoothly and easily, increase and decrease speed, turn corners sharply, and come to screechingly quick stops. Many three-year-olds alternate feet as they climb steps, rather than placing both feet on each step. They can also, just for fun, jump from a bottom step to the floor with both feet together. They can jump up and down using both feet without falling and can even (but ever so briefly) balance on one foot. They can walk along a sidewalk crack or a line for distances of 10 feet or so without falling off, and they can walk backward.

Most joyful of all, they can ride a three-wheeler! On wheels they can go faster and with less effort, can turn, stop, and back up and can extend the control they have gained over their own bodies to the vehicles. And they find it easy to do. Anyone who can do this, they seem to feel, could never be mistaken for a baby! In fact, one of the minor traumas for many three-year-olds in nursery school is the need to share their three-wheelers. On such occasions, they often pucker up and howl like the wee ones they really still are—or were not long ago.

Age four is the time for pushing out, for testing the limits of one's growing abilities and testing the tolerances of caregivers. Four-year-olds are likely to climb as high as they can on equipment or in trees, often bringing fear to the hearts of observing adults. Many are expert jumpers, able to make running and standing jumps, whereas most three-year-olds can only jump up and down in place. The three-wheeler has been well mastered by age four and is used for stunts and all kinds of special variations, such as backing rapidly, turning hairpin corners, rounding curves at top speed, or riding standing up. Many of the skills practiced at age three with total concentration are, at age four, nonchalantly incorporated into elaborate fantasy play. A bike speeding around the circle is likened to a racing car or a spaceship, and its rider may well be receiving and responding to vital messages from fellow pretenders as he or she navigates.

Five- and six-year-olds have efficient, coordinated skills for running, jumping, and climbing that, as at age four, are constantly employed in pretend play. They are also likely to become involved in jumping rope, jumping over objects, hopping and standing briefly on one foot, balancing on narrow planks or chalk lines, roller-skating, riding a two-wheeler, and keeping time to music by walking or skipping. Skipping, in particular, requires considerable coordination of muscles as well as a good sense of rhythm and is often not mastered by five-year-olds nor even some six-year-olds.

Seven-year-olds skip easily and can gallop to rhythmic music. They can skip and jump with accuracy into small spaces, as in hopscotch. In throwing a ball, the proper footwork and shifting of weight is often mastered, and accuracy (such as hitting a 4-foot target from a distance of 15 feet) greatly increases. At age seven, children run vigorously and can jump upward and forward with ease, using effective arm movements as they do so. Bike-riding skills are carefully rehearsed and perfected. Various motor skills are coordinated through games, races, gymnastics, and dramatic presentations.

When tackling a new motor skill, such as walking or jumping, children display remarkable concentration. Nothing else dilutes their attention. Only after much repetition can the new skill be combined with other behaviors in a more complex activity. For example, as children are learning to walk, they concentrate fully on maintaining balance and shifting weight effectively; only after much practice can they look around while walking or simultaneously walk and talk. Two- and three-year-olds, with full concentration, can barely manage to throw a ball in the general direction they wish it to go; as likely as not, they will drop it behind them or misdirect it entirely. Even at age four, only a small proportion of children have mastered throwing.

Between the ages of five and five and a half, approximately three out of four children learn to throw effectively. First attempts usually involve both hands and much body movement, but the movements gradually become more specialized. A patient adult who is willing to retrieve the ball is needed during the initial practice sessions. This practice often goes on and on, to the limits of adult tolerance for chasing off in all directions. Six-year-olds begin to catch balls with their hands rather than with outstretched arms or against their chests. Eventually, through patient and concentrated practice, the child acquires the balance and coordination needed to properly direct and catch the ball. The practice contin-

"Look how deep we made it. Let's get the water!" *(Cumberland Hill Associates, Inc.)*

ues with gradual improvement in strength, speed, and accuracy. The skill can then be employed in fantasy activities (such as, "Let's pretend that old box is a bear attacking us and that we throw rocks at it") or in organized games where throwing must be coordinated with running, jumping, and dodging in very complex and varied patterns.

These patterns of **differentiation** and **integration,** which are easily observed in regard to motor skills, are also descriptive of development in the social and cognitive areas and will be referred to repeatedly throughout this section. They illustrate a basic principle of child development. Development proceeds from the general to the specific. Differentiation refers to the processes by which broad patterns of behavior are refined into more functional and precise abilities; for example, scribbling is practiced and refined to the skills of drawing and writing. Integration, on the other hand, is the process of bringing various behavior patterns into coordinated interaction with one another, such as the coordination of hopping, leaning, and balancing in a game of hopscotch. These processes can be observed at all levels of development, and for a teacher making observations of children it is very important to determine not only whether a child can perform a particular skill (differentiation) but also whether that skill has been sufficiently mastered to allow integration with other actions.

Fine-Motor Development

There is a direct continuity in the development of fine-motor coordination, from gross movement through the processes of differentiation just described. Our use of the two separate headings *Large-Muscle Development* and *Fine-Motor Development* are merely for convenience of presentation and should not be inferred to signify two distinct streams of development.

Beginning with the ability to use the thumb in opposition to the fingers during the first year, hand and finger manipulation becomes increasingly skillful. Before age two, a child typically carries little toys or blocks about individually and drops them in unstructured piles, but two- and three-year-olds can perform a large variety of hand movements, such as stringing large beads, copying a circle or cross, folding paper, or making large letters (especially those with vertical or horizontal lines only, such as *E, H, L,* and *T*).

At ages three and four, many of the abilities needed for dressing have been developed. Most children at this age are able to pull on or wriggle into their clothing and do the simpler fastening tasks. Help is still needed with tying shoes, with smaller buttons and fasteners, with boots that are snug, and with complex outerwear.

By age five, most children can fold a triangle from paper (if shown how), copy a square or a triangle, and cut along a line with scissors. However, the letters and numbers they write are still large and uneven and very frequently reversed from left to right or from top to bottom. Although still laboring to write his or her name, a five-year-old has often achieved independence in dressing, except for tying shoes. At this age, children still need to see the fasteners they are trying to manipulate, and it is not unusual to see them straining their necks or bending into odd postures to get a view of the zippers on the bottoms of their coats. By age six, nearly all children have mastered ties and fasteners and need visual guidance only with unfamiliar articles of clothing. Try watching children of various ages as they get dressed and note the things that create problems for them.

Six- and seven-year-olds, although they have sufficient small-muscle ability to form all letters, especially with good models and patient instruction, still reverse many letters and numbers and make them large and irregular in size. Some children, however, can easily print letters about one-quarter-inch high that are level with each other. By this age, most have sufficient control of their small muscles to become engaged in writing activities without great difficulty. The child's ability to draw a diamond is often used as an indicator of the development of perceptual motor coordination. To increase your awareness of the development of children's abilities, try exploring what forms (such as the circle, square, triangle, and diamond) or letters children of various ages can copy from a model you make for them, and compare their performances. If children are able to make a particular form, they will usually copy you without any urging on your part.

Six- and seven-year-olds usually perfect skills such as carpentry, clay modeling, painting, and sewing to the point where they can use them to real advantage in creating objects. Their increasing ability and willingness to work on intricate tasks is in significant contrast to their preference for gross motor manipulations when they were preschoolers and kindergartners.

Hemispheric Specialization and Hand Preference

The brain has two **hemispheres** that look like mirror images of each other. There is a great deal of accumulated evidence that the two sides of the brain perform different functions and have differing linkages with the rest of the nervous system. Each side of the body is predominantly controlled by the brain hemisphere on the opposite side. The left brain hemisphere typically specializes in language and serial processing such as that required in reasoning and numerical thinking and controls the right side of the body. The right brain hemisphere, controlling the left side of the body, specializes in pictorial imaging and wholistic processing such as the perception of patterns and melodies. The two hemispheres are connected by the **corpus callosum,** and information is exchanged via the corpus callosum between the two hemispheres. Many tasks, especially complex ones such as reading and writing, probably require the involvement of both hemispheres working in coordinated intricate fashion.

The left and right hemispheres of the brain already have specialized functions in the newborn or, at least, are developed at a very early age (Levine, 1983). Infants' brain activity as revealed by sensors placed on the scalp shows greater activation in the left hemisphere when the baby hears speech and more in the right hemisphere when music is heard (Molfese, Freeman & Palermo, 1975). There is also a tendency for infants to hold their heads more toward one side than the other. This preference is predictive of **handedness.** Typically, this preference is for the right and it is the opposite brain hemisphere, the left, that is the dominant one. It is the left hemisphere that usually develops language and controls the individual's sense of conscious unity (Gazzaniga, 1983). This pattern of language dominance in the left brain hemisphere and right hand preference is true for most of us. For a minority of the population, however, the left hand is the preferred hand (Corballis & Beale, 1976) and presumably significant language function resides in the right hemisphere.

Despite recent advances in our understanding of the relationships between hemispheric specialization of the brain and other behaviors, there is still uncertainty about the cause of these differences. Perhaps damage to the left hemisphere before or at birth requires that the right hemisphere, during the early period of brain **plasticity,** develop dominant functions, including the formation of language. In this case, the left hand becomes the preferred one. Or perhaps tendencies toward a reversed **lateralization** are inherited. More lefties show up in some families than others.

Infants initially use whichever hand comes in contact with an object and reach with the hand closest to a desired object. Most, however, hold a rattle for a longer time in their right hand than in their left (Caplan & Kinsbourne, 1976). By age two, most children have stopped alternating between the use of both hands and have begun to establish hand dominance, the distinct preference for the use of one hand over the other. This preference is typically well set by age five or six (Goodall, 1980).

Handedness is part of a general **lateral** (or sided) **dominance,** which is also evidenced in use of one foot over the other and one eye over the other. Although for most people the preferred foot and eye is the same as the preferred hand, a few adults have a **mixed dominance;** they are, for example, left-eyed, right-handed, and right-footed. It is not unusual to find a child who writes with the right hand, throws a ball with the left, cuts with the right, and sews with the

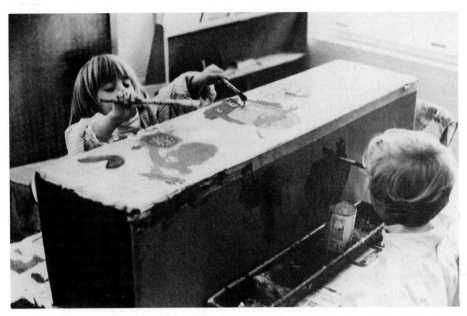

During preschool years, most children develop a hand preference; some do not. *(Lee C. Lee)*

left. In a recent study, Tan (1985) found that in a large sample of five-year-olds, 83 percent were clearly right-handed, 12.5 percent were left-handed, and only 4.5 percent had not yet developed a hand preference. However, the tendency to perform more and more acts with the preferred side continues throughout the school years.

There is no difference between right- and left-handed children in how well they perform motor tasks (Tan, 1985). Nor do they differ from each other in intelligence, despite the fact that their brains appear to be arranged differently.

Being left-handed is not associated, as was once thought, with lower intelligence, achievement, or clumsiness, but it can represent certain problems for left-handed children. If you are right-handed you may never have realized that nearly everything is geared to your preference. Handshaking is just one example; the use of the right hand is the only "acceptable" way. Most scissors and other tools are constructed for right-handed use, and table settings and illumination are usually arranged to benefit the right-handed. Most instruction and modeling of such skills as pasting, cutting, folding, handwriting, and game playing are done with a right-hand perspective. It certainly is to the child's benefit, given these conditions, to be among the majority, that is, right-handed.

Opinions vary on the extent to which children in the toddler and preschool years should be encouraged or urged to use the right hand. According to one point of view, young children should be encouraged to use one hand or the other as the dominant hand. Others, aware of a possible association between forced use of the "unnatural" hand and certain speech problems, especially stuttering, avoid any intervention into hand-use patterns. Because it can be traumatic for a child to be forced to use one hand after he or she has already established some patterns and competence with the other, most preschool teachers permit continued use of both hands.

Nonfunctional Behaviors

In observing children, you may note and wonder about certain motor behaviors that seem to have no particular function. These include body rocking (a rhythmic rocking back and forth in place, usually in a sitting position), grimaces or tics, rapid blinking, nail biting, teeth grinding, thumb sucking, eye rubbing. Among the many potential causes of such behavior are physiological immaturity, emotional insecurity, insufficient opportunity to engage in active purposeful activity, and substitution for other comforts.

Speculation about the causes of nervous mannerisms and programs of preventive action are generally unrewarding for teachers. On the other hand, a teacher may find it profitable to note the conditions under which such behavior increases and decreases and to arrange program circumstances accordingly.

Health and Disease Indicators

An especially difficult problem for teachers is recognizing the onset of a disease condition in a healthy child. In the first weeks and months of contact with children, it is difficult to tell whether they are engaging in natural, healthy "orneriness" when they clown, test, and rebel or whether they are really reacting to some unusual internal state. Since each child's reaction to illness may be highly idiosyncratic, it is usually wise for a teacher to discuss this in initial contacts with the people who know the child best.

Crankiness, unreasonableness, or crying at the slightest provocation may be signs either of chronic or approaching illness or simply of weariness. Fatigue in young children is often very difficult to diagnose because of their tendency to deny it and, in fact, to increase their activity and excitement level. Once a teacher becomes aware of a particular child's early fatigue signs, the later stages may be avoided through diversion into more relaxing and sedentary activity. Some children are attuned to their own bodily conditions and will independently regulate their activity level. As a teacher, you need to become aware of young children's different reactions to their bodily states and to intervene where necessary.

SUMMARY

The newborn's primary mode of interacting with the world is through reflexive actions. The initial reflexes are gradually modified to become schemata, which are more effective for deriving information. It is from these sensorimotor schemata that more abstract thinking processes are derived, according to Piaget's views. Motor and physical development are thus seen to be closely interrelated with other aspects of development from the beginning of the life span.

From the rudimentary skills such as reaching and letting go, developed during infancy, come the more complex motor skills of the three- through seven-year-old. By age three, large-muscle abilities are sufficiently developed to be considered as separate aspects, such as agility, strength, endurance, balance, rhythm, and speed. These abilities develop through processes of differentiation and integration. A sensitive teacher can facilitate repertoire expansion in motor areas by carefully observing and assessing existent abilities in children and by making thoughtful matches with additional activities and experiences.

Physical characteristics of children influence their overall development in two major ways. Their size, posture, attractiveness, hand preference, physical defects, nervous traits, and health all influence the way they interact with the world (both physical and social) and the way they are perceived by the world. As a teacher, you should be particularly sensitive to both influences and, most importantly, to your own reactions to the physical characteristics of the children you teach.

SUGGESTED ACTIVITIES

1 Make a list of things you believe must be supplied to an infant or a toddler to ensure his or her survival and healthy development. Then spend time with someone who is caring for a baby. Observe the child and the caregiver for an extended period (while the child is awake), noting what is provided for the child. Modify your initial list on the basis of what you see.

2 For a period of time, preferably several hours, try to use your nonpreferred hand for all manual activities. Compare your performance on such tasks as drawing circles and squares and writing your name with your preferred versus your nonpreferred hand.

3 Select one area of motor performance, such as stair climbing, and observe a number of children of the same age to become aware of the range in abilities they exhibit.

4 Observe children of varying ages within a family or within a classroom with mixed-age grouping on selected performance areas (skipping, eating, dressing) to become aware of developmental progressions.

ADDITIONAL READINGS

American Academy of Pediatrics. (1987). *Health in day care: A manual for health professionals.* Elk Grove Village, IL: Author.

Begley, S. (1990). Do you hear what I hear? *Newsweek, 117* (26), Special Issue on the Child, 6–9.

Castle, K. (1983). *The infant and toddler handbook.* Atlanta, GA: Humanics Limited.

Comer, D. E. (1987). *Developing safety skills with the young child.* Albany, NY: Delmar.

Julius, A. K. (1978). Focus on movement. *Young Children, 34,* 19–26.

Kendrick, A. S., Kaufmann, R., & Messenger, K. P. (Eds.). (1988). *Healthy young children: A manual for programs.* Washington, DC: National Association for the Education of Young Children.

Orlick, T. (1978). *The cooperative sports and games book.* New York: Pantheon.

Orlick, T. (1982). *The second cooperative sports and games book.* New York: Putnam.

CHAPTER 5

OBSERVING PHYSICAL CHARACTERISTICS AND MOTOR BEHAVIOR

OVERVIEW

This chapter gives you a set of very specific questions about the physical characteristics and motor behavior of individual children you are observing. You will then read sample observations of two young children by a student like yourself. The final portion of this chapter provides suggestions for using information gained through observations as a source of insight in planning programs for young children.

OBSERVING INDIVIDUAL CHILDREN

As an extension of your study of this part of the textbook, we suggest that you arrange to systematically observe individual children. Our recommendation is that you prepare full behavioral assessments, according to the specifications we provide, for as many different children as possible. Ideally, you will arrange to make these assessments for at least three children—one each at three different age levels. This will enable you to gain a sense of age progression as well as individual differences. Each of these behavioral assessments will involve the expenditure of substantial amounts of time and energy, so plan accordingly. We emphasize, however, that preparing a behavioral summary based on a series of observations for even one child is far more valuable than simply studying the materials included in this section without any systematic application.

It is essential that you arrange for several observations of at least ten minutes each for any child you wish to fully assess. It is also important that you are able to observe the child in various kinds of activities and that during some of the observations the child has an option of doing what he or she "wants" to do. It is difficult to get a sense of what children can do if you only see them in situations with limited options. You will need a situation in which you can observe the child and make notes about what you see. If your fieldwork arrangement requires your active participation, you may need to request special arrangements so you can observe for a portion of several sessions without other responsibilities. If this isn't possible to arrange, you may have to make additional fieldwork arrangements for the specific purposes of this assessment activity. You might approach teachers, parents, program administrators, playground directors, or other persons responsible for children, and request permission to observe a child or children in their care. If you offer to share your notes with them, they may be more willing to allow you to make a series of observations. You should emphasize that your major purpose is to develop your skills as an observer and that the reports you prepare are, of course, not yet fully professional. You will need practice and credentials before offering yourself as a professional. Nevertheless, the observations you make will undoubtedly prove very interesting and helpful to the person responsible for the children. Specific guidelines for observing individual children are contained in Part 2 of Appendix 1.

QUESTIONS TO GUIDE OBSERVATIONS

A warning: In providing you with a series of questions and categories to guide your observations of children's development, we do not imply that this is the only way, or even the best way, to organize your investigations. Other equally valid category systems could be devised for investigating these and other aspects of children's behavior. We are simply suggesting that you follow this line of questioning initially as you observe **motor behavior** and that as you become more aware of children's growth and development you should not hesitate to reorganize our questions and categories, especially by adding to or elaborating on them.

Here are the questions. You will note that examples are included to help you interpret the meaning of the question, but by no means should you limit your own entries to our list of examples.

1. Physical characteristics

You may wish to sketch or photograph the child to supplement your verbal responses in this section.

1.1 Is there anything particularly distinctive about the child's body build?

EXAMPLES: ▪ Tiny, small-boned, slim
▪ Heavy proportions, small shoulders
▪ Overheard from peer, "You can't be Superman, you're scrawny"

1.2 Is there anything particularly distinctive about the child's posture?

EXAMPLES: ▪ Reclines or leans on most occasions
▪ Stands squarely; shoulders straight
▪ Swayback; protruding tummy

1.3 Is there anything particularly distinctive about the child's appearance?

> EXAMPLES: ▪ Sallow, pale skin coloring
> ▪ Long lashes framing brown eyes; very appealing
> ▪ Comment from peer, "You look like a witch, you play witch"

1.4 What is the nature of the child's grooming?

> EXAMPLES: ▪ Hair unkempt; face and neck dirty
> ▪ Carefully braided hair; bright ribbons

2. Large-muscle development

2.1 What is the child's action repertoire? What different actions does he or she perform?

Consider the following actions, but also include others as you observe them: crawls, rolls, walks, walks sideways, walks backward, climbs stairs, runs, hops, jumps, slides or shuffles, climbs (trees, ladders, equipment with rungs), swings suspended by arms, swings by legs, falls over (intentionally), swims, flips body over on bars, somersaults, does hand flip on floor.

For each action, note whether it is being differentiated from a more gross activity and is practiced as a new skill requiring the child's whole attention, or whether it has been sufficiently mastered to be performed with little conscious attention and is integrated with other kinds of activities. You may wish to indicate with *D* those actions that are at the differentiation level and with *I* those that are integrated.

> EXAMPLES: ▪ While playing Batman, walks, runs across room, falls over, slides to stop, climbs tree while shouting orders to "Robin" *(I)*
> ▪ Carefully and repeatedly swings self up by arms to flip feet over bars on climbing equipment and then hangs by feet. Goes through whole process several times, then goes to friend Joey and says, "Did you see what I can do?" *(D)*

2.2 How strong is the child? What actions give evidence of body alignment to physically alter the environment?

Consider the following actions, but also include others as you observe them: pushes, shoves, lifts, pounds or hammers, throws, pulls, bends object. Record the object or objects toward which the child is directing his or her strength. Indicate differentiation *D* and integration *I.*

> EXAMPLES: ▪ Loads cart with twenty blocks and alternately pushes it from one side and pulls by rope from other side; adds more blocks and does both again *(D)*
> ▪ Playing Daniel Boone, shouts, "Okay, men, I'll save you. Here's the ammunition," while dragging the wagon filled with blocks across the room *(I)*

2.3 What is the child's ability to balance?

Consider the following actions, but also include others as you observe them: walks on raised beam (indicate width and distance), walks along crack or line (indicate width and distance), balances on inclined plane (indicate width, whether still or walking, distance walked), skates, balances on platform over fulcrum, hops over rocks. Indicate differentiation *D* or integration *I*

EXAMPLES:
- Walks 15 feet along border of bricks (3 inches wide) without falling off *(D)*
- Walks up and down inclined plane (board 6 inches wide) at about 30 degree angle; stops at midpoint; turns around easily, while singing, "Tie a yellow ribbon . . ." *(I)*

2.4 What is the child's ability to use his or her body rhythmically?

Consider the following actions, but also include others as you observe them: skips, gallops, dances, jumps rope, moves to music (in place), uses hula hoop. Indicate differentiation *D* or integration *I.*

EXAMPLES:
- Tries to skip across room, imitating friend Suzy; manages skipping patterns about halfway, simply runs rest of way *(D)*
- Listens to rhythmic music from record player; continues in activity of writing on chalkboard, but performs dance movements in the process *(I)*

2.5 What is the child's ability to move quickly?

Consider the following actions, but also include others as you observe them: runs, climbs, swims, gallops.

EXAMPLES:
- Runs across playground faster than all except two of friends
- When climbing, often delays those behind who are waiting for same equipment

2.6 What is the child's physical endurance? What is the duration of sustained physical activity?

Consider the following actions, but also include others as you observe them: runs, pushes, jumps in place, climbs, skips rope, rides bike.

EXAMPLES:
- Climbs up three steps; walks down to the bottom step and jumps off fifteen times
- Bounces large rubber ball continuously for 15 minutes

2.7 To what extent can the child coordinate several types of large-muscle behaviors into a more complex skill?

Consider the following actions, but also include others as you observe them: runs and catches object that is moving through air; throws to intended target; throws at moving target; runs and slides to base; rides two-wheeler bicycle; roller skates; runs and dribbles ball.

"Just watch what I can do." *(Dunn Photographics)*

EXAMPLES: ▪ Kicks large rubber ball to direct it around other toys and then kicks it to friend who is several yards away
▪ Rides two-wheeler without difficulty once under way, but sways and sometimes must catch self with feet and give extra push from ground before getting off

3. Small-muscle development

3.1 What is the child's repertoire for self-help in areas of eating, dressing, and grooming?

Consider the following actions, but also include others as you observe them: in eating—uses spoon, uses fork, cuts with fork, uses knife to spread, pours from pitcher to glass, serves self from serving dish with large spoon; in dressing—buttons, zips, puts on socks, puts on shoes, puts on tie; in grooming—washes face, combs hair, dries hands, puts toothpaste on brush. Indicate differentiation *D* or integration *I.*

EXAMPLES: ▪ Zips up jacket once lower ends are engaged *(D)*
▪ Puts on shoes; ties first part of bow and then asks for help *(D)*
▪ Drinks from glass without assistance, but allows glass to topple when replacing on table *(D)*
▪ Goes through motions of drying hands, but usually leaves hands wet *(D)*

3.2 What is the child's repertoire for manipulating materials and toys? For using tools?

Consider the following actions, but also include others as you observe them: cuts with scissors, marks with crayon, draws or writes with pencil or crayon, uses hammer, uses saw, uses screwdriver, uses needle, uses pastes, uses pencil sharpener, turns book pages, puts puzzle together, uses games or construction toys with tiny parts. Indicate differentiation (D) or integration (I). You may wish to include examples of children's writing or drawing along with your written notations.

EXAMPLES:
- Removes half-inch wheels from small plastic car and replaces with ease *(D)*
- Takes thumbtack out of bulletin board and replaces in exact spot by inserting into hole made previously *(D)*
- Rips paper while trying to cut *(D)*
- Reverses letters *(s, p); writing otherwise even; letters approximately a half inch in size *(I)*

4. Other characteristics

4.1 Has the child established left- or right-handed preference or dominance? Which hand does the child use? Which foot?

EXAMPLES:
- Uses left hand to scribble

"Climb in. I'll push you 'cause I'm strong." *(Cumberland Hill Associates, Inc.)*

- Uses right hand while eating; transfers fork from one hand to other
- Uses right hand for combing hair
- Uses left foot to kick ball
- Uses left foot to kick blocks out of way

4.2 *Does the child show any evidence of physical disability? Any prosthetic devices?*

EXAMPLES:
- Mouth hangs open; head tilts; drools
- Wears one shoe with heavy sole
- Has hearing aid
- Squints, rubs eyes when looking at book

4.3 *Does the child exhibit any behaviors that appear nonfunctional and that may be indicators of pervasive tension?*

Consider the following behaviors but also include others as you observe them: body rocking, rapid blinking, tics, nail biting, teeth grinding, thumb sucking, eye rubbing.

EXAMPLES:
- Just before session is over, puts thumb in mouth and stands by entrance
- Bites nails while listening to story
- When not involved in muscle activity, rocks body in rhythmic fashion even while looking at books

4.4 *Does the child's behavior or physical appearance suggest symptoms of poor health or disease?*

Consider the following symptoms but also include others as you observe them: runny nose, pallor, coughing, sores, hoarseness, inactivity.

EXAMPLES:
- Complains that head aches
- Sneezes occasionally; coughs continually
- Skin irritation on neck

SAMPLE OBSERVATIONS: STEVEN AND MONICA

The following reports of individual children's physical characteristics and motor development were written by a former student using the guides provided in an earlier edition of this textbook. The student made several fifteen- to twenty-minute observations of two 4-year-olds, Steven and Monica, and then prepared the following reports on their physical characteristics and motor behavior.

Name Steven
Age Four years, two months

Physical Characteristics Steven has a husky build. He is not fat but is built solidly and low to the ground. His height seems to be average as compared to the other children of his age. Steven is round-shouldered and leans forward most of the time, both when standing still or moving around. Steven has blonde hair and blue eyes. His face is freckled. He has sores on his nose and mouth that he picks at, often making them bleed. Steven's clothes are clean although sometimes they are inside out, not color matched, and have little holes in the seams. His hair is usually clean and combed. His body is usually clean when he enters school, but he quickly gets dirty.

Large-Muscle Development When observing Steven, one gets the impression of poor coordination. This observer had the urge to catch him before he fell several times. Steven pulls a cart while walking backward. When he starts talking he stops walking *(D)*. When Steven "runs" it looks almost like slow-motion photography. His run is a slightly accelerated walk with steps of exaggerated length. When walking in a circle, he turns sideways so he is really walking forward. When climbing the four stairs to enter the school, his hands are forward as though he is prepared to catch himself in case he falls *(D)*. He seems off balance if he has to descend the stairs while holding something *(D)*.

Steven does not exhibit much strength. He can pull a wooden cart with two other youngsters in it, but when he comes to a small obstruction, he is unable to pull the cart over it and his friends must get out of the cart. When it is time to pick up the large building blocks, he gets a large riding truck and fills it with six blocks. He then pushes it to the shelf for others to unload. When pulling it, he slides across the floor with the truck next to or behind him. He scoots along the floor in a sitting position. He does not attempt to kneel or squat.

When Steven tries to jump over a piece of wood in the park, he falls on the ground on the other side *(D)*. When he runs, his hands are constantly extended to the front. He looks as if he will fall at any minute. When walking on the sidewalk, his trajectory fluctuates from one side to the other. When asked to stay in line, he seems unable to do so.

Steven exhibits no sense of rhythm or rhythmic movement. He does not participate during song time. He sits and very seldom attends to what is going on.

Steven moves very slowly even when attempting to run. His turns are wide. He continues running activities, however, for as long as allowed and does not seem to get tired. His movements, although taking great concentration, are very slow and deliberate. Steven runs after other children during a chasing game but is caught much more often than he catches someone. When he notices that a child has stopped or has fallen, he will proceed in their direction and attempt to catch them.

Fine-Motor Development Steven's repertoire of self-help skills and manipulative skills is very limited. He has a great deal of trouble both buttoning and unbuttoning. He can unzip his coat but often needs help to disconnect the end. He cannot zip up his coat. When eating he drools, lets liquid flow from his mouth while drinking from a cup, and leaves crumbs all over his face when he is finished eating. He attempts to dry his hands after washing, but they usually remain wet. Often they are also still very dirty. He can put on his own shoes. When grasping an object, he uses his whole hand as opposed to the finger-thumb manipulation. When attempting to use scissors, he inverts his hand so that his thumb points down and away from his body. He was not observed to use a pencil or crayon.

Steven has little hand preference. He cuts with his right hand, paints with his left, eats with both hands, digs in the sand box with his right, pulls a cart with his left, and throws a ball with his right. He kicks a ball or blocks with his left foot.

Except for facial sores, there were no observable physical disabilities, non-functional behaviors, symptoms of poor health, or disease.

Name Monica

Age Four years, seven months

Physical Characteristics Monica is of average body build. She is average height for her age. She stands straight and tall. Her shoulders are square to her body and give the appearance of an easy sense of balance. She has blonde hair, light skin, and brown eyes. She has dark eyebrows and long dark eyelashes. She has petite facial features. She wears clean, well-kept clothing. Mostly she wears dresses; when she wears jeans or slacks, she has coordinated blouses and sweaters to match.

Large-Muscle Development Monica has a wide variety of movement skills. She skips while holding the hand of a friend and talking to him *(I)*. She walks forward and backward with ease. She can do both while talking to others or playing a game *(I)*. While playing a game she stops singing and concentrates very hard in order to walk sideways *(D)*. To accomplish this, she alternates sliding her feet apart and together and crossing and uncrossing her legs. She runs with ease and grace. She can reach out with both arms while running to catch someone *(I)*. She can swing a blanket over her head as she walks across the room *(I)*. She can hop on both feet while imitating a rabbit and a frog.

Monica displayed strength when she picked up her sister who is one and a half years old and carried her across a large room to her mother saying, "Keep her here." Then she proceeded to pick up chairs and push tables to their proper place for storage. She was very intent on this task.

Monica exhibits very good balance. She was observed walking up a very steeply inclined hill while holding the hand of a friend and swinging her outside hand. She also walked on cracks in the sidewalk with her arms extended to the sides with very little swaying from side to side.

There were no actual rhythmic movements observed. Monica did act out the words to the songs, "Itsy Bitsy Spider" and "Nick Nack," during one observation. The motions went along well with the words, but a distinct rhythm was not evident.

Monica was observed running quickly and easily during several observations. During one tag game she was easily able to catch up to the other children in the group even when they had a head start. She was observed making sharp turns and stopping quickly if a child in front of her fell or stopped quickly without notice. She was observed running continuously for four and five minutes. At these times she did not seem to be tired or out of breath.

The only opportunity to observe a coordinated gross-motor skill came during a game in which Monica had to run and catch other children. While doing this she ran with her arms held out and put her arms around the other children, and, if they weren't bigger than she, she would swing them in the air for a moment.

Fine-Motor Development   Monica has many self-help skills. She zipped and buttoned her own sweaters and coats. She was observed trying to tie her shoe. She drank from a glass with one hand without leaving drips on her mouth or around her lips. She was observed combing her hair, but she missed the middle of the back of her head.

Monica put together a twelve-piece wooden puzzle while talking to the teacher who was sitting across the table from her *(l)*. She used scissors well. She cut with ease along an outline drawing the teacher had given her. The lines were straight and accurate. The results were squares, triangles, and circles. Monica was observed painting without spilling or dripping paint off the paper. She put her finger in some paste in order to complete a picture but used too much and made quite a mess. She was also observed using a pencil, a crayon, and finger paint.

Monica has developed right-hand dominance. She uses her right hand for combing her hair, painting, pasting, cutting, drawing, puzzle building, reaching, throwing, and eating. She was observed using her right foot to kick a block.

There were no observable physical disabilities, prosthetic devices, nonfunctional behaviors, poor health, or disease.

FROM OBSERVATIONS TO PLANNING

Although Steven and Monica are in the same preschool group, they are very different in their abilities. Steven is five months younger than Monica, but this probably explains only a part of the differences between them. Steven's maturation rate may simply be slower. Or perhaps there may be experiential differences in their respective histories. Or possibly Steven may have some persistent type of disability. We will not speculate here about Steven and Monica's developmental status. It is obvious, however, that they have differing capabilities for gross-motor and small-muscle involvements. If, as a teacher, you had both of these children in your classroom, what would you plan for them?

The following four guidelines are recommended for matching activities to children based on observations of their physical characteristics and motor behavior. These guidelines may give you insights into what activities might be appropriate for Steven and Monica.

1 Avoid urging the child to engage in an activity that requires more complex behaviors than those you have already observed in his or her repertoire.

2 Avoid urging or encouraging the child to engage in any activity that is already well integrated into the repertoire. Consider cutting. You may observe that a given child can easily cut on a line while carrying on a conversation or while singing along with a record. It would therefore probably be inappropriate to expect the child to be interested in or benefit from a simple cutting task unless it is an integral part of a more complex endeavor; for instance, he or she might be interested in cutting heart shapes to produce valentines. On the other hand, for children who are still just perfecting and practicing the cutting skill, cutting by itself is enough, and they can be happily and profitably engaged in merely cutting pieces of newspaper into strips. For them, if the cutting task is part of a more complex construction activity it might be too demanding, and they might well "tune out" or become frustrated by the less appropriate aspects.

3 Encourage the child to participate in new activities or use new materials that require behaviors quite similar to those you have observed him or her using. Steven enjoys playing chasing games with his friends and moving objects and people about in a cart. These activities may be further enhanced by the provision of stimulating situations and props. Steven's ability to manipulate his body through space, to stop, to turn, to change directions will probably require a great deal of practice. We do not need to urge him to be active, however. We need only to create encouraging circumstances such as the following:

- Construct obstacle courses with running spaces interspersed with blocks or old tires that can be climbed over or jumped from.
- Create spaces on the floor with masking tape for Steven and others to jump into or over.

Climbing up and crawling across playground equipment develops skill and confidence. *(John James)*

- Designate spaces as "safe" areas for tag games.
- Provide balloons for throwing, batting, and chasing.
- Provide large cardboard cartons for climbing in, carrying about, and crawling through.
- Set up a tumbling mat as an airport surrounded by lots of space within which Steven and friends may "fly" between landings and takeoffs.
- Provide a large gym ball that requires force to move about.

In addition to setting up these situations in indoor open space or in an outside play area, encourage Steven with his friends to follow your actions of walking or running to music or drumbeats with the following type of directions:

- Pick your knees up high when you walk.
- Pretend you are walking in sticky mud (or deep snow). You must lift your feet way up.
- Pretend you are picking apples. Go all around the tree. Pick all the apples. Pretend you are putting them in this basket on the ground beside the tree. Reach up high. Put it in the basket. There's a very high one.
- Take giant steps as you go around the circle. Now take tiny steps. Now try giant steps again.
- Pretend you are a big heavy elephant walking through the jungle. Now pretend you are a little kitten walking very softly.

Although these activities would also be enjoyable and worthwhile for Monica, it is likely that she would engage in them only briefly unless she incorporated them into fantasy play or a more complex game structure. In addition, we might arrange the following for Monica:

- Set up a balance beam for intricate experimentation with balance in various postures and directions.
- Provide jump ropes, gym scooters, climbing bars and frames, climbing ropes, and balance boards.
- Arrange for "bowling" games with soft balls and paper pins; targets and bean bags, etc.
- Challenge by modeling diverse animal walks—crab walk, frog jump, lame-dog walk, measuring-worm walk.
- Teach rhythmic songs or chants with movements, for example, Eentsy Weentsy Spider, I'm a Little Teapot, Hickory Dickory Dock, or group singing games, for example, The Muffin Man, Looby Loo, The Mulberry Bush.

It is probable that both Steven and Monica, given sufficient diversity of space, time, and "props," will create for themselves optimal involvements as a normal course of their play activities.

For small-muscle development, we would again need diverse materials and activities to assure appropriate matches for both Steven and Monica. For Steven, small-block play, sand play, and water play with challenging accessories, easel painting with large brushes, and clay manipulation are very appropriate. We could encourage eye-hand control by providing lots of large paper and sturdy crayons or magic markers for scribbling and also a slate with chalk.

For Monica, we might well provide a scrap box with a variety of papers, ribbons, foils, laces, and so forth. Tape, scissors, crayons, and white glue would be needed. Easel painting will continue to be appropriate. She will probably continue to enjoy using such things as commercial puzzles and Lego blocks, but also has the coordination to put her eye-hand skills to work toward her own creative projects. Your goal for the children you teach should be more toward a thorough development of existing skills (using many variants) than toward a speedy introduction of new skills. This thorough development of existent skills is best provided for children by ample opportunities for play in an arranged environment.

4 Provide the opportunity for the child to see others engaged in motor activities slightly more advanced than those he or she has mastered to date. This kind of **modeling** is available because of the developmental differences in almost any group of children. For the more advanced, however, the adult must either provide the model or arrange for older and more skilled persons outside the group to occasionally join them. In all instances, however, avoid making overt comparisons between children's abilities.

If a child voluntarily engages in an activity or voluntarily continues an activity in the absence of adult or peer encouragement, you can feel assured that the activity is appropriate to the child's developmental level. There is something very satisfying to a child (and to an adult as well) in activities that provide a slight challenge, just enough difficulty to require attention and effort but not so difficult as to be impossible. J. McVicker Hunt (1961) refers to this optimal degree of discrepancy as the "match" and to the teacher's task as one of solving the problem of the match. In other words, the teacher's job is to determine for each child what activities or situations will not be too easy or too difficult, but just right. According to Hunt, if "just right" is found, the child will get intrinsic satisfaction from the activity and will not need to be praised, cajoled, threatened, bribed, or otherwise influenced to become and remain involved with the activity.

As a teacher whose task it will be to arrange these child-activity matches, you will first of all need sensitivity to what the child can and cannot do with ease. You are in the process of developing this sensitivity when you observe a child's physical repertoire. You must also be ready to provide the child with a variety of activities suitable to his or her developmental level. This is the business of Part 4.

SUMMARY

In this chapter, a series of questions was posed to guide observations of children's physical characteristics and motor behavior. This system is a combination of the descriptive narrative and category approaches. It requires a focus on specific behavior, yet encourages the collection of detail about behavior within these categories.

Once a series of observations has been done on an individual child, it becomes easier to make decisions about what might be arranged to support his or her learning and development. The program environment needs to be arranged to provide many appropriate possibilities for children's play with each other and with materials and tasks. Within such a context, children with quite diverse abilities find matches conducive to their involvement and learning.

SUGGESTED ACTIVITIES

1 Locate photographs of children that provoke strong feelings in you. Write down your impressions of each photograph, including (a) a report of what you see, (b) inferences about the cause of the actions or conditions depicted, and (c) an evaluation of what you feel is worthwhile or appropriate in the actions or conditions depicted. Ask others to tell you their impressions in the same order and compare their observations with yours.

2 Answer the list of questions posed in this chapter as guides to observation in respect to your own physical characteristics and motor development. Summarize the similarities and differences between your self-appraisal and the appraisals you make of the children you observe.

3 Summarize the similarities and differences between children you have observed using the guides from this chapter. Compare children of differing age, gender, and socioeconomic background.

4 Arrange with a fellow class member to observe the same child, using the guides provided in this chapter, and compare notes on what you both have seen.

5 Summarize your own feelings about the children you have observed while gathering data for this chapter. What in their behavior do you find objectionable? Appealing? Consider the reasons for these reactions and whether they need modification.

ADDITIONAL READINGS

Beaty, J. (1990). *Observing development of the young child* (2nd ed.). Columbus, OH: Merrill.

Brandt, R. M. (1972). *Studying behavior in natural settings.* New York: Holt, Rinehart & Winston.

Cartwright, D., & Cartwright, C. (1974). *Developing observation skills.* New York: McGraw-Hill.

Cohen, D., & Stern, V. (1970). *Observing and recording the behavior of young children.* New York: Teachers College Press.

Irwin, D. M., & Bushnell, M. M. (1980). *Observational strategies for child study.* New York: Holt, Rinehart & Winston.

Lindberg, L., & Swedlow, R. (1976). *Early childhood education: A guide for observation and participation.* Boston: Allyn & Bacon.

Phinney, J. S. (1982). Observing children: Ideas for teachers. *Young Children, 37,* 16–24.

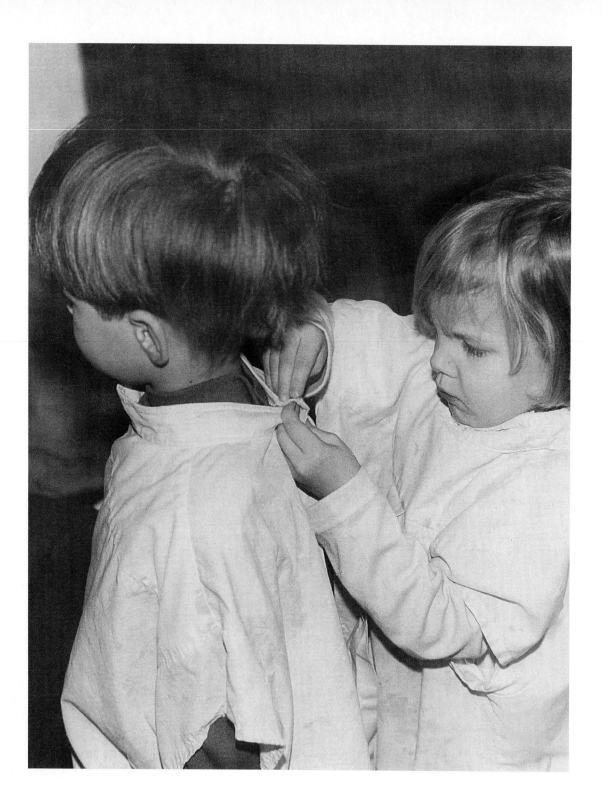

CHAPTER 6

AFFECTIVE AND SOCIAL DEVELOPMENT

OVERVIEW

Consider the following description written by the teacher of Thaddeus, age four, and his conflict with classmate Carl.

> Thaddeus comes toward me looking upset, puckering his face up but not quite crying. He stops and starts back toward Carl, a few feet from him, with his hand held into a fist and raised as if to hit. Carl raises his fist also and takes a threatening step in Thaddeus' direction. Thaddeus turns and runs to me, putting his arms around me as if for protection, looks back over his shoulder at Carl and says, "He hit me. I goin' beat his butt." Carl shouts, "He bump me first."

What in this description would fit the label **affective** (emotional) **behavior?** Social behavior? Cognitive behavior? Physical behavior? Clearly there is anger, fear, and frustration, all affective states. They are evoked in a social situation. If there is to be a solution, however, it will require cognitive input. Thaddeus, Carl, and the teacher must use all of their combined repertoires for talking, thinking, and problem solving if the current state, which appears to be uncomfortable for Thaddeus, and probably for Carl, is to be resolved.

The separation of real-life situations into physical or motor, affective, social, and cognitive or intellectual components is clearly artificial, made for the convenience of studying children's development. Although each of the four components of development is related to the others, affective and social development and cognitive development are often closely aligned. It is far easier to sort out motor development and cognitive development as separate strands than it is to separate affective and social development. We are therefore presenting both affective and social development in this single chapter.

The chapter begins with a discussion of affective development at three age levels: infants and toddlers, ages three and four, and ages five through seven. This is followed by a discussion of social development.

INFANTS AND TODDLERS

A baby's crying is a signal that something is amiss. According to Erik Erikson, who has provided helpful insights into these early periods, if parents attend to and consistently and appropriately respond to their baby's signals of distress, a major contribution can be made to initial affective development. If children's discomfort can be alleviated by caregivers, it is more likely that the children will develop a sense of goodness about the world, a sense that they can depend on their own organisms, their **signaling systems,** and the responsiveness of their caregivers to their needs. Erikson believes this infancy period is critical in developing a healthy balance between feelings of trust and mistrust. A number of research studies (Schaffer & Emerson, 1964; Ainsworth & Bell, 1972, 1974, 1977; Lozzoff et al., 1977) have documented the positive effects of caregivers' prompt response to infant signals on overall competence.

If the baby's signals are ignored or attended to inconsistently, it is likely that the infant will have a mistrustful orientation, will lack confidence in self and others. Most infants do receive sufficient "tender loving care" in this crucial period and do develop the expectation that their world is an "okay" place where their needs will continue to be satisfied.

Of course, this is not an either/or phenomenon. All infants, even with the most attentive and caring parents, suffer from distresses such as feeding upsets, hunger pangs, skin irritations, uncomfortable temperatures, and teething. Also, the best of parenting is sometimes inadequate to provide sufficient comfort for infants. For infants with lower thresholds for these distresses, the infancy period leads to less positive orientations and expectations and often to a reduced level of parental involvement.

It is very easy for the inexperienced teacher of young children (or a parent who has had a happy baby) to look at an edgy, mistrustful three-year-old and think, "If only he had had better parenting." Parents of such children may deserve some assurance that they have had a rough experience through no fault of their own and that their child's initial disadvantage can be overcome at a later age. Although a sense of trust is thought to be most easily and effectively established in the first year, it can be gained at later ages, when the child has full assurance that significant others will care for his or her needs. If basic trust has not been achieved by the preschool age, the teacher's first concern may well be to collaborate with the parents or other caregivers to assure the child that they will care for his or her well-being.

At age five months, infants are becoming aware of themselves as objects that have a continuing existence just as other objects do. Caregivers (mother, father, other family members, or another person consistently caring for the child) are differentiated as objects separate from self. The child, once aware of the distinc-

---

ERIKSON'S STAGES OF DEVELOPMENT

Although many different perspectives on children's affective and social behavior are presented in this chapter, there are recurrent references to the stages of development as described by Erik Erikson. Erikson (1950) writes of eight stages of life, each dominated by a **developmental crisis** around a particular "theme." They are briefly described as follows:

1. Trust versus mistrust

Dependent infants develop expectancies about the extent to which their needs will be cared for by others.

2. Autonomy versus doubt and shame

Early in childhood, children develop expectancies about whether they have the freedom and capability to take certain actions independently of others.

3. Initiative versus guilt

As children "play," they develop expectancies about whether they can initiate their own projects.

4. Industry versus inferiority

During the school-age years, children develop expectancies regarding whether they can perform "real" tasks competently and whether they can persist with activities they do not particularly enjoy.

5. Identity versus identity diffusion

In adolescence, young people develop their own personal identity, imitating, experimenting, and attempting to integrate their views of self.

6. Intimacy versus isolation

Young adults develop expectancies regarding the extent to which and the manner in which they can integrate their lives with others.

7. Generativity versus stagnation (or self-absorption)

The developmental challenge to adults is to become productive and creative and to nourish and nurture the young.

8. Integrity versus despair

In later maturity, there is the challenge of accepting one's life with its disappointments as well as its joys and appraising its relationship to overall human endeavors—past, present, and future.

In each of the stages of development, Erikson sees that there is a central problem to be solved, at least temporarily, if the individual is to proceed with confidence and vigor to the next stage.

---

tion between self and caregiver, forms a very strong emotional **attachment** that becomes the mainstay of feelings of security. Younger infants will accept feeding and care from anyone, but at about eight or nine months they begin to differentiate and may shrink away from unfamiliar persons. They may even suffer a social-emotional setback if their primary person(s) "deserts" them. If this attachment is not abruptly terminated, however, the child can be expected to gradually learn to extend trust and acceptance to other adults as well.

Social interest in peers begins at a very early age. Infants, when in the presence of other babies, are likely to make limited social advances, although these are usually ignored by the potential receiver. These initiations are in the form of looking, smiling, and grasping—behavior that is commonly directed toward almost any object.

As infants grow into toddlerhood, they develop increased interest in the activities of their agemates and often express this interest in conflicts over the use of toys. By age two, toddlers make contact with each other whenever they have the opportunity and appear to prefer being in the company of other children. At this age, most of the children's time together is spent in **solitary play.** They do, however, observe each other and smile and vocalize and imitate each other, as well as struggle over toys. They also sometimes engage in games together such as chase and chaser or ball roller and ball catcher. Social pretend play seems to exceed the cognitive capacity of most toddlers, but by age three and beyond, children verbally recruit each other for pretend play by bids such as, "Let's pretend——" or "I'll be the mother; you be the baby" (Howes, 1985).

In the second and third year of life, the basic affective issue becomes concern about whether one can act autonomously without forfeiting the care and concern of caregivers. In thus asserting themselves, which is a very healthy and positive development, children need assurance that they can do so without alienating those persons to whom they have primary attachments. This can constitute a serious conflict, since toddlers are still very small and helpless and in need of the goodwill of caregivers. If saying "no" appears to be turning adults against them, children may become very distressed. At age two, children may persistently refuse to do things they really want to do, despite an obvious anxiety if a confrontation should occur.

For parents and teachers, this is a difficult time. The two-year-old obviously cannot be given full rein to make decisions about such things as whether to walk in puddles with new shoes on or whether to run across a busy street. Wise adults learn not to provide choices at this age where there really is no choice. They learn that a two-year-old (as well as many three-year-olds) will respond better to a statement such as, "We're going home now" than to "Are you ready to go home?" They learn to give assistance very directly rather than to pose questions

Toddlers enthusiastically participate in cooking activities, especially the tasting part. *(Cumberland Hill Associates, Inc.)*

such as, "Do you need help?" They learn that forced choice questions such as, "Do you want peanut butter or tuna sandwiches for lunch?" is a more effective way to get a two- or three-year-old to the lunch table than asking, "Do you want to have lunch?"

Erikson has helped us to understand that at this age it will be unfortunate if children are led to believe that they are silly or wrong to be so assertive about what they do not want to do or want to have help with. Teasing and shaming children, although often quite effective in stopping "silly" behaviors or arguments, can also have the unintended effect of making them doubt themselves just when they most seek and need confirmation that they are separate, viable persons. The provision of decision-making situations in which the two-year-old can legitimately decide, can acceptably say no or refuse help, are helpful to social-emotional development.

Erikson further points out that adult-child conflicts over toilet training are especially symbolic of this period. The child's ability to control elimination can either provide further evidence of developing autonomy or can become a battle-ground where the adult shames the child for his or her "accidents" and dependency. In this period, which Erikson describes as centering around a favorable balance between autonomy and doubt or shame, toilet training may be but one of the adult-child hassles, but it is a very representative one.

THREES AND FOURS

An interesting phenomenon is the apparent progression of the normally developing child from calm, cooperative, "together" periods to periods of disintegration during which the child's behavior and disposition are very trying to parents and teachers. Adults typically find the two-year-old period a very trying time, thoroughly enjoy their three-year-old, and then again find their patience, understanding, and tolerance put to test as their child turns to four.

If development has generally gone well in the previous years, three-year-olds have a certain delightful sense of assurance about who they are and what they can do. In fact, three-year-olds seem, especially after their "terrible twos" year, to emerge as quite enjoyable people. They are old enough to have well-developed, individual personalities and to have their own ideas and histories but are still young enough to be quite guileless. Their thoughts and passions are easy to read. Teachers of children at this age may become exhausted, but they are seldom bored or disillusioned by the behavior of the children in their charge.

By age three, children have developed a relatively complete and stable sense of self that serves as an influence on further development. Although many of their self-conceptions are still relatively fluid and will be modified by later experiences, many stable views have already been formed that will influence children's involvements, their reactions to various stimuli, and their expectations of others. The child at age three may well have formed a sense of him- or herself as being good or bad, attractive or ugly, weak or strong. All these self-views have developed out of the interactions of the prior three years, and, while they persist, they will strongly influence future interactions. Whereas the child's basic sense of identity is formed prior to age three, it is still quite pliable and susceptible to adult and peer influences during the preschool and early school years. Preschoolers' current **self-concepts** can be reinforced and strengthened, or they can be extended to include additional perspectives.

Four-year-old children typically want to know about the world, what people are like, what they do, and what they themselves can learn to do. They push vigorously into all kinds of activities. This is the stage Erikson describes as centered around the development of initiative, during which children tirelessly question, experiment, and act out various roles in an effort to understand the world around them. If thrusting is not thwarted, children learn that they can do many things. They can paint a picture, do "hard" puzzles, build forts, write, and plan and carry out involved play sequences in which they become daddy, mommy, doctor, teacher, Dracula, or the Cookie Monster. "Let's pretend" is planned and managed with increasing competence, the whole self being thrown into the role. It is not "just play," it is work; and if the child is frustrated in it there will be genuine tears and anger.

Without intending to be difficult, four-year-olds experiment with all sorts of "screwball" actions, such as wearing clothing backward, putting boots on their hands and mittens on their feet, eating with the handle of the fork, and cutting food up into minuscule bits or trying to eat huge pieces. They may cover their whole face, arms, and the mirror with soapsuds when washing their hands, or try out fancy patterns and positions when urinating. They may be full of "What if" questions, such as "What if it snowed for ten years?" "What if we only had spaghetti to eat?" "What if it were always night time?" "What if a big bear came in here?"

Four-year-olds can be frustrating to teachers and parents because their great interest in starting things is not followed by an interest in finishing them or in doing them "well." There is also little inclination among most four-year-olds to clean things up after play. While a three-year-old may cheerfully help adults restack blocks, for example, the four-year-old is much more likely to resist or secretly begin a big new building project while appearing to be sorting the blocks for storage.

At ages three and four, children's social behavior has advanced to increasing interactions with each other. At first, children may predominantly engage in **parallel play,** that is, they play beside each other with the same kinds of materials but with little interaction. This pattern gradually gives way to increased **associative play,** where they exchange materials and take turns by mutual consent.

Preschool children assume that their thoughts and observations are obvious to everyone, and consequently their early attempts to communicate and play with their agemates are fraught with difficulties. Piaget describes this kind of thinking as **egocentric,** that is, assuming that one's perception of the world is shared by all, and that there is therefore no need to explain one's actions or wishes. There is no effort to understand another's point of view because there is no awareness that other views exist. The child's cognitive abilities (or, more accurately, inabilities) directly influence the nature of social exchanges.

Four-year-olds gleefully experiment with all sorts of actions, such as "three on one bike."
(Cumberland Hill Associates, Inc.)

Adults find children's egocentrism frustrating but are usually tolerant and try to find out what the child sees and thinks and then react accordingly. When two children, age three, try to talk and play together, neither can understand the other's egocentric view, and consequently their play involves each child doing his or her own thing and making comments that are quite incomprehensible to the other child. Play and conversations at this stage are often hilarious to listen to, as in the following exchange:

JANE: The baby's hungry. You be baby in a buggy, okay?
SUSAN: Want a ride in my car?
JANE: Here, baby. Here's your bottle.
SUSAN: What's that, gasoline?
JANE: Drink it all up. Then I'll burp you. *(Begins thumping Susan on the back)*
SUSAN: Stop hitting me. I'll have a wreck.

Their contact with peers who do not understand their thoughts or intentions provides children the necessary jolt for moving out of an egocentric view of the world. Children gradually learn that although their signaling behaviors, such as pouting, may communicate a specific message to their mothers, the same behavior has no effect on anyone else, especially preschool friends. Children find that they must learn to grab, ask, barter, or find other ways to communicate what they want.

Children gradually learn to explain ideas and actions and to take into account the views of others so that they can engage in cooperative play ventures. This appears to begin with the agreement to play out particular roles or functions in dramatic play. At the most rudimentary level, one child agrees to be the mother and the other to be the baby. Each may behave quite independently, but each maintains the role, and the net result gives more mutual satisfaction than parallel or associative play. Increasingly, role actions are complementary and coordinated: families go out for a walk together, adults discuss the disciplining of baby, siblings fight, and so forth. From these beginnings emerge highly complex play scenes: moving vans and packers moving a family to California or Texas, or a hospital scene replete with doctors, nurses, a worried mother, scared and injured children, and ambulance drivers. Only with extensive opportunities for interaction can children develop the communication and planning skills needed for such elaborate play scenes. Children who do not attend preschools and who lack play companions in their neighborhoods are often "slower" in developing the necessary social abilities. Such play has affective, social, and cognitive benefits and is extremely important to children's overall personal development.

Children in this age range will voluntarily engage in all kinds of play activity without adult urging. Simply by having materials, equipment, space, and the opportunity available they will become involved in chasing, climbing, dramatic play, building, drawing, writing, constructing, painting, and myriad other activities.

Not all interactions between children of this age are friendly. There may be increases in conflicts during the three- to four-year-old age period in proportion to the increases in interaction. The height of aggressiveness is usually reached at age four, when it appears to be practiced more out of curiosity than animosity. If another activity is offered, four-year-olds can often be easily diverted from aggressive play. For example, one particularly skillful nursery school teacher repeatedly curtails the disruptive activities of groups of marauding four-year-olds by offering such alternatives as participation in a mock wrestling match, complete with cheering, bowing, and bells signaling the end of each round.

Sometimes fights in preschool are the result not of "feeling one's oats" but of real frustration and anger. Just as children of this age are insensitive to roles other than their own during dramatic play, so they fail to perceive the motivation behind the behavior of their peers. Events such as having one's tower bumped over, having to wait for a turn with a cherished piece of equipment, or having one's painting torn, are all taken very personally and may precipitate a battle, even though such actions may have been quite unintentional. This also applies to name-calling. The preschool child does not yet understand that words are simply words and that saying something does not make it so. The child has not sorted out the symbolic function of language and assumes a real connection between the word and its referent. They seem to think they can inflict real, as opposed to psychological, damage with words whenever they are angry. Conversely, they are themselves quite enraged by the words others use to attack them. Many a physical battle among preschoolers has been precipitated by an accidental event (such as a slight bump) followed by an awful name like *baby* or *dummy*. This appears to be a very threatening thing in the child's mind, and therefore is a suitable basis for conflict.

FIVES, SIXES, AND SEVENS

Five-year-olds are usually more settled than four-year-olds. Perhaps by this age most of the antics have already been tried. They have established themselves as "doers" if they have been given a chance, and many, particularly girls, are ready to give up trying everything to focus on doing some things, especially school activities, better and better. Activities last longer and products become more important. Five-year-olds have less need to prove themselves as persons but greater need to improve their skills. They are beginning to look ahead to the progression of their growing up. At this point, the modeling of more advanced behaviors by older children becomes very important. Five-year-olds, when in the company of older children, can take on such grown-up behaviors as sitting

Children are very attentive to modeling by older peers. *(John James)*

quietly, taking turns, or expressing themselves as the older children do, whereas at age four they remained pretty much themselves regardless of the company.

This is an impressionable age. A teacher can easily gain "control" of a five-year-old's behavior, a fact that makes kindergarten teaching both easier and scarier than teaching either older or younger children. Kindergartners often, by mistake, call their teacher mommy or grandma, even if their teacher is male. They generally accept whatever their teacher says. Only occasionally will a strong-willed five-year-old rebel at a teacher's demands, saying, as one did, "You can't tell me what to do. You can't ruin my whole life. Only my mother can do that." If there is a strong influence within the peer group for silliness or misbehavior contrary to the teacher's expectations, many kindergarten children appear to suffer real conflicts in trying to serve two masters. A teacher who tries to rigidly control children's behavior, but without success, would be especially poorly placed as a kindergarten teacher.

Of particular interest in the period from ages three through five is the way in which the child develops **gender-related behavior.** Throughout this period, **gender identification** becomes increasingly apparent. Some of these differences, such as the earlier maturation rate of females, are inborn rather than learned. Other differences, such as the greater activity level of boys, might be both inherited and learned. Boys are typically encouraged or at least permitted to be quite active, whereas girls are usually expected to be quieter and calmer. Boys are more often provided with cars, trucks, and building blocks, toys that encourage activity, whereas girls receive dolls, books, and other quiet toys.

Whether gender-related behavior is a result of the modeling done by adults, older peers, the media, or direct admonition ("Boys don't" or "Girls don't like to"), there is no doubt that children aged three through five learn these lessons well. The gender-related limitations imposed at this age are fewer for girls than boys. If they so choose, girls can play rough, ride tricycles, punch punching bags, and wear dress-up policeman hats and cowboy boots without comment from most adults. Boys, however, are apt to be scolded for crying or playing with dolls and to be told that ladies' hats and purses are strictly girls' things; if they do not engage in active play, they may be prodded to do so. On the other hand, girls at this age may also be learning that since they receive fewer admonitions, they matter less than boys.

Parents, teachers, book publishers, television producers, and toy manufacturers have become increasingly aware of the limiting effects of many gender prohibitions, so behavioral differences in the early years may eventually become less pronounced. However, as long as there remains any suggestions within the culture that certain behaviors are okay or not okay, most children of this age will readily comply with the norm.

At age six or seven, the child makes a very sudden and sometimes traumatic entry into the middle childhood years. A great deal is expected of a child entering elementary school, not the least of which may be boarding and riding a bus to a destination that is relatively strange and far from home. Once in first grade, the six-year-old is often expected to work on assigned tasks for long periods, to follow complex directions, to form letters and numbers, and to remember all sorts of things. At almost no point in the life span are the expectations of the world so markedly altered as when the child makes this transition from the neighborhood or the typical early childhood program into elementary school.

Developmentally, nothing has prepared a child aged six or seven for a sudden increase in sedentary activity. Six-year-olds, especially, retain babyish character- istics such as the desire to be hugged and cuddled. They still cry easily and many of them, particularly boys, would be constantly on the go if left to their own devices. Rather than sit in a straight chair at a table or desk, they prefer to lounge, stretch, sit on the floor, or sprawl out flat.

Most children at this point are eager to learn to read, write, and count, just as they want to learn all the jump-rope rhymes, singing games, and other child- hood customs. Although they are eager, serious learners, many of these children want their lessons served in light doses, preferably intermingled with play activi- ties. The prolonged inactivity that accompanies book learning in many class- rooms can create real tensions. Amazingly, a majority of children make whatev- er personal adjustments are necessary in their school situations. They learn to suppress their feelings of discomfort, to understand that their own wishes are not as important as they once thought, and to accept others' goals instead of their own. Despite such demands, six- and seven-year-olds usually like their teachers and, if the teacher is kind and fair, are eager to win his or her recognition, praise, and special privileges. Going to school becomes a way of life, although recesses, if they are lucky enough to have them, may be the "best thing about school."

School-age children typically enjoy helping to make things go smoothly and are willing to modulate their activities to do so. They begin to have ideas and plans they do not show to the world. Although more difficult to "read," they require less attention from parents, teachers, and other caregivers.

School-age children are not satisfied with mere activity but want to produce something. Just pounding nails into a board is no longer enough; building a table is better. Pretend play, still a very important activity, is often transformed into "doing a play" for an audience.

Much more energy is devoted to projects, both short and long term. Elaborate props may be created for a paper doll or a super-hero play world, or a group may set up a pretend school or hospital in which they play teacher, doctor, or nurse to younger siblings or dolls. Staging and the manufacturing of props for such activities become increasingly important, and the actual playing somewhat less important. Often the fantasizing about the play appears sufficiently satisfying in itself, and the acting may never materialize.

In more active play, time and energy are spent building and arranging forts, space stations, barracks, and helicopter ports. Sometimes boys prefer playing with boys and girls with girls. However, when playing out a currently popular movie, play, or television show, boys and girls often join together to take roles of characters of their own sex.

When not engaged in dramatic activity, children aged six and seven devote much time and attention to practicing skills such as writing, reading, spelling, drawing, jumping rope, bouncing balls, and playing jacks. At first they do these things just to prove their ability, but they soon learn to enjoy using their skills to create something, such as a letter or sign, or to compete with each other.

Six- and seven-year-olds quickly tune into the peer culture in their community and school. They are significantly influenced by the older peer models available to them and eagerly learn and practice the songs, sallies, and superstitions of their age, sometimes to the dismay of adults. This is the age of riddles, knock-knock jokes, elephant jokes, or whatever is in vogue at the time. If children this age hear a joke from older children, they become interested in it, even if they do not quite understand it.

Although grown-up in many ways, the six- or seven-year-old continues to be quite aware of his or her vulnerability. The loss of baby teeth is perhaps symbolic of the age. Having one's teeth loosen and finally hang by a thread is a very momentous happening. Analogous to this sudden loss of baby teeth, the six- and seven-year-old is expected to cast aside all babyish traits. But the skills and experience of grown-ups cannot be accumulated suddenly, so the young school-age child must struggle to maintain the new image, often at the cost of spontaneity, openness, and ease. If parents and teachers can be aware of the nature of these struggles and have patience with the occasional regressions to tears, wet pants, wanting Mommy, wanting help with dressing, and silly fears, then the transition from early childhood to the middle school years can be greatly eased.

Teachers often expect too much of first- and second-graders and thereby unknowingly create tensions that could have been avoided. Children's parents should be asked to inform the teacher if tensions are showing up at home. As one uneducated but concerned mother of a first-grader put it, "Listen here, my boy ain't no genius, and I ain't no genius. But you ain't no genius either. So lay off some." This appraisal of her son's school experience, although roughly stated, was probably far more accurate than the professional teacher's. Six- and seven-year-olds, unlike three-, four-, and five-year-olds, do not openly express their feelings, so the teacher may need help from families in assessing their affective states.

Children experience pressures at home as well as at school, and teachers need to be alert to such situations. Unfortunately, the stereotyped image of the U.S. family, in which loving, mature parents always put their children's concerns first, is often more fiction than fact. There are many happy families, of course, but they too must endure hard times and internal strains that cannot be hidden from their young children. Six-year-old Kim, for example, from a secure and happy family, heard her teacher tell another child, who was trying desperately not to cry, "It's okay to cry. Even grown-ups cry sometimes." Kim came from across the room to confide, "That's right. My mommy was crying a lot last night because daddy goes to meetings all the time and all she ever gets to do is stay home with us kids."

Children usually cannot tell you about their upsets at home. Only occasionally do they have sufficient awareness of their own feelings and enough trust in you to be able to say, as did the following six-year-old, "Teacher, when I was crying this morning, it wasn't because I was mad at you. My mother works and is gone by the time I get home from school every day. I hardly ever get to see her. She was going to stay home today, and I just wanted to stay home with her so badly. I just didn't want to come to school today."

It is impossible for you as a teacher, even in a full-time day-care center, to take on the task of providing parental love for a child. You can provide consistency, respect, praise, physical protection, warm smiles and hugs, and new experiences. You can help the children improve their skills, but you cannot be a parent to the children you teach, and it is important that you become as sympathetic to the plight and dilemmas of the parents as you are to those of their children. Given their view of the world and their resources, most parents do their best to fulfill their conception of "good" people. Although you may disagree with them, you cannot take responsibility for their behavior; your only responsibility is the way you relate to them and their child. If you communicate understanding and optimism about their child along with your concerns, and if you effectively describe what you are trying to do, most parents will cooperate far more than if you make them feel guilty about what they are failing to provide. You must demonstrate to the parents (or caregivers) that you find them worthwhile and acceptable (although perhaps not all their behavior) and that you join with them, rather than compete with them, in seeking the best for their child.

Given the opportunity, children aged six and seven will continue the kind of cooperative, dramatic play ventures described as typical of four- and five-year-olds. If six- and seven-year-olds have not had ample group play experiences previously, it may be important that they be given this opportunity, not just for brief periods under a teacher's active direction but with as much time and autonomy as possible. The value of working cooperatively with peers and independently of adults in decision making, planning, role-playing, and creating props and settings cannot be matched by teacher-directed activities.

Organized group games are increasingly popular for this age group, and children try hard to figure out how to play Spud, Duck Duck Goose, and various other games that they have had an opportunity to learn about. They begin also to participate in skill games such as Four Square, Dodgeball, and beginning versions of such games as basketball and softball. They assume that the rules they learn from older children are givens and tenaciously resist any attempt by adults to simplify or otherwise change them. They may refuse to play at all if things are not done "right." Again, this shows how cognitive abilities (or limitations) directly affect social interaction. They have not, as yet, figured out that rules have not always existed as untouchable entities. They may have no awareness that a rule is a social agreement and that it can be subsequently modified.

Many six- and seven-year-olds also enjoy participating in more formal group discussions, especially those dealing with problems they see as important, such as how to get older kids to stop teasing them, or how to become friends with someone you like who does not seem to like you. The more mature children have sufficient social and self-awareness at this age to enjoy comparing their own ideas and feelings with those of their classmates. Although some children of this age are still more interested in talking than in listening to the other children, there is sufficient other-awareness to make group discussion a satisfying experience for most.

We have referred several times to the relationship between the child's cognitive limitations and his or her social ineptness. Research by Spivack and Shure (1974) into the relationship between cognitive and social functioning disclosed a significant correlation between children's repertoires of ideas for dealing with interpersonal situations and social adjustment. They concluded that children who are frequently involved in interpersonal conflicts, such as how to get a toy from another child, are frequently at a loss as to how this might be accomplished other than through aggression. Consequently, they constructed a program to teach children new ways of behaving. In a series of direct teaching sessions, children were actively involved in learning to use such contrasting terms as *a, some; is, is not; same, different; happy, sad; can, cannot; why, because.* Children were also taught how to talk about consequences (what might happen next), fairness, and alternative solutions. The concepts and vocabulary were practiced in the sessions through games and through the use of stories and simulated problem scenes enacted by puppets. The learnings were also applied to real classroom situations as conflicts arose. The following is an example:

TEACHER: Robert, what happened when you snatched those magnets from Erik?
ROBERT: He hit me.

Associative play: exchanging materials and taking turns. *(Cumberland Hill Associates, Inc.)*

TEACHER: How did that make you feel?

ROBERT: Sad.

TEACHER: You wanted to play with the magnets, right?

ROBERT: Right.

TEACHER: Snatching it is *one* way to get him to give them to you. Can you think of a *different* idea?

ROBERT: Ask him.

TEACHER: *(Calls Erik over)* Robert, you thought of asking him for the magnets. Go ahead and ask him.

ROBERT: *(to Erik)* Can I hold the magnets?

ERIK: No!

TEACHER: Okay, Robert, he said no. Can you think of a *different* way?

ROBERT: *(Starts to cry)*

TEACHER: I know you're feeling sad now, but I bet if you think real hard, you'll find a different idea. You could ask *or* ___?

ROBERT: *(After several seconds)* I'll give them back when I'm finished.

ERIK: *(Reluctantly)* Okay.

TEACHER: Very good, Robert. You thought of another way to get Erik to let you play with those magnets. How do you feel now?

ROBERT: *(Smiles)* Happy.

TEACHER: I'm glad, and you thought of that all by yourself.*

By teaching children additional ways of dealing with social situations (including a more effective vocabulary for thinking about and expressing their desires), Spivack and Shure (1974) found that they were able to reduce children's aggressive behavior and improve their emotional condition. This kind of contribution to children's social competence is clearly within the teacher's sphere of influence.

SUMMARY

Erik Erikson has described the early years as the time for seeking successful resolution of several developmental conflicts—trust versus mistrust, autonomy versus doubt or shame, initiative versus guilt, industry versus inferiority. These have been elaborated on throughout this discussion of affective development. Further, there has been discussion of the individuality of children (even as infants and toddlers), the emergent self-view, the adoption of gender-related behaviors, the pressures of home problems and school expectations, and the influences of the peer group. The activity interests and the typical behaviors for each age level have also been described in considerable detail. Affective development was often directly or indirectly related to social development.

Children's social development was further described as progressing from parallel and associative to cooperative peer interactions. The interrelatedness of all development was evidenced in discussion of the limitations placed upon social

*From Spivack, G. & Shure, M. *Social Adjustment of Young Children* (San Francisco: Jossey-Bass, 1974), p. 62.

effectiveness by preschoolers' egocentric thinking and of the relationship between children's repertoires of ideas for solving social problems and their social adjustment. Clearly, cognitive development directly affects social development. It is only for the convenience of discussion that the aspects of development are separated. As you make observations of individual children and seek programming matches based on those observations, you will recognize how directly one aspect of development can influence the others.

SUGGESTED ACTIVITIES

1 Observe an infant or toddler for a period and summarize the range of behavior and emotion displayed as well as the caregiver's reactions. Especially note your own reactions. What do you consider cute and appealing? What is unpleasant and of concern for you? Why?

2 Recall and list at least three specific incidents that happened to you prior to age seven. Keeping in mind that recall of one's early experiences can be distorted by one's current perspectives and interpretations, recapture the following in regard to those experiences: (a) perceptions of your size relative to other objects or persons, (b) perceptions of competence or helplessness, (c) major concerns in the situation, and (d) the options available to you in the situation. Consider to what extent these experiences are comparable to those described in this chapter.

3 For the early life incidents listed in (2), consider whether any peers or siblings were also involved. If not, consider other incidents in which you were involved with peers at a relatively early age. Try to recall your feelings about these other children, especially if they were older than you. Can you, in retrospect, make any comparisons between your own repertoire for social behavior and those of the older children? If so, consider the personal significance of these differences on those occasions.

ADDITIONAL READINGS

Brenner, A. (1984). *Helping children cope with stress.* Lexington, MA: Lexington Books.

Buzzelli, C. A., & File, N. (1989). Building trust in friends. *Young Children, 44*(3), 70–75.

Chess, S., Thomas, A., & Birch, H. G. (1977). *Your child is a person: A psychological approach to parenting without guilt.* New York: Penguin.

Elkind, D. (1981). *The hurried child.* Reading, MA: Addison-Wesley.

Erikson, E. H. (1950). *Childhood and society.* New York: Norton.

Greenberg, P. (1991). *Character development: Encouraging self-esteem & self-discipline in infants, toddlers, & two-year-olds.* Washington, DC: National Association for the Education of Young Children.

Honig, A. S. (1981). What are the needs of infants? *Young Children, 37*, 3–9.

Kempe, R. S., & Kempe, C. H. (1978). *Child abuse. The developing child series.* Cambridge, MA: Harvard University Press.

McDiarmid, N. J. (1977). *Loving and learning: Interacting with your child from birth to three.* New York: Harcourt Brace Jovanovich.

Mussen, P., & Eisenberg-Berg, N. (1977). *Roots of caring, sharing, and helping: The development of prosocial behavior in children.* San Francisco: Freeman.

Robinson, B. E. (1990). The teacher's role in working with children of alcoholic parents. *Young Children, 45*(4), 68–73.

ALL I REALLY NEED TO KNOW I LEARNED IN KINDERGARTEN

The following material was written by Robert Fulghum, a Unitarian minister. It was presented to his congregation and to other groups as his credo, a simple but comprehensive statement of what he feels is important in life. Its appeal was powerful and led to the publication of a bestseller book in which it and other of Fulghum's writings are featured. Even before the publication of the book, the credo had become well-known via informal person-to-person communication. It was mimeographed, posted on bulletin boards, quoted in speeches on countless occasions. Its appeal serves as evidence to you of how early and how pervasively the basic principles of successful living are learned. What a teacher of young children teaches is important, for always.

All I really need to know about how to live and what to do and how to be I learned in kindergarten. Wisdom was not at the top of the graduate-school mountain, but there in the sandpile. . . . These are the things I learned:

Share everything.

Play fair.

Don't hit people.

Put things back where you found them.

Clean up your own mess.

Don't take things that aren't yours.

Say you're sorry when you hurt somebody.

Wash your hands before you eat.

Flush.

Warm cookies and milk are good for you.

Live a balanced life—learn some and think some and draw and paint and sing and dance and play and work everyday some.

Take a nap every afternoon.

When you go out into the world, watch out for traffic, hold hands, and stick together.

Be aware of wonder. Remember the little seed in the Styrofoam cup: The roots go down and the plant goes up and nobody really knows how or why, but we are all like that.

Goldfish and hamsters and white mice and even the little seed in the Styrofoam cup—they all die. So do we.

And then remember the Dick-and-Jane books and the first word you learned—the biggest word of all— LOOK.

Everything you need to know is in there somewhere. The Golden Rule and love and basic sanitation. Ecology and politics and equality and sane living.

Take any of those items and extrapolate it into sophisticated adult terms and apply it to your family life or your work or your government or your world and it holds true and clear and firm. Think what a better world it would be if we all—the whole world—had cookies and milk about three o'clock every afternoon and then lay down with our blankies for a nap. Or if all governments had as a basic policy to always put things back where they found them and to clean up their own mess.

And it is still true, no matter how old you are—when you go out into the world, it is best to hold hands and stick together.

CHAPTER 7

OBSERVING AFFECTIVE AND SOCIAL BEHAVIORS

OVERVIEW

In this chapter you will find specific questions about the affective and social behaviors of the children you are observing. You will follow the same procedures that you used in making observations and notes of motor behavior and physical characteristics. In the middle of the chapter there are further summaries of the observed behaviors of the two children, Monica and Steven, prepared by a student after making observations using these questions as guides. The chapter concludes with a discussion of how observations of this type are helpful in program planning.

QUESTIONS TO GUIDE OBSERVATIONS

The following questions suggest areas that you can observe when you are in the presence of young children. We would like to point out again that the examples provided are included to help you interpret the meaning of the question and to suggest the range of possible answers that might be given. Your actual responses will undoubtedly be quite different.

1. **Expression of affective states**

   1.1 *What kinds of things give the child pleasure? What things, topics, or activities have particular appeal?*

   EXAMPLES:
   - Grins happily when Melissa says she would save her place while she goes to the bathroom
   - Laughs when going over bump on slide and falls off
   - Smiles when Renee holds her hand and says, "I'm sorry"

- Cuts out all the pictures of lions she can find in magazines and toy catalogs

1.2 What kinds of things cause the child displeasure or discomfort? What things, topics, or activities are particularly aversive?

EXAMPLES:
- Goes and sits alone when Juney calls her "baby"
- Says, "I'm too hot. Turn down the heat," to teacher after vigorous running
- Rips up paper when gets letters in wrong order
- Says, "I don't like you to do that," when Simon kicks his chair

1.3 What kinds of things seem to frighten the child? How is fear expressed? What does the child do about fears?

EXAMPLES:
- Says, "I'm afraid of bees" (in dining room) but enters
- Moves closer to friend when dog comes near
- Cries and hides face when psychologist wants to go to another room "to play some games"
- Goes to adult and says, "That noise scared me"

1.4 What kinds of things seem to make the child angry? How is anger expressed?

EXAMPLES:
- Spits at Donna who said she was stupid
- After shoving Connie for taking her place, notices that Connie went in the bathroom and gagged; follows her and says, "I'm sorry, I didn't know you was about to throw up"
- Says two hours after hitting Shawn, "I hit Shawn. I was real mad"
- Goes up to Sam and gives a shove, saying, "Gimme that!"

2. Orientation of self in world

2.1 In what actions or activities is the child dependent (requires or wishes others to be present, supervise, or assist)? In what actions or activities is the child independent (engages self without help or attention from others)?

EXAMPLES:
- Needs help putting on boots
- Asks teacher to watch after each attempt to perform flip on climbing equipment
- Listens to story on tape with earphones by self
- Plays in sand by self for half-hour

2.2 What actions or activities does the child initiate (participates with no direction or without concurrently seeing others thus involved)?

EXAMPLES:
- Goes to book corner and takes out book when no one else is there
- Tries to touch each finger, respectively, to a different space on chart paper

- Makes obstacles with blocks to jump over
- Makes painting about "me and my mommy chasing our dog"

2.3 What actions or activities does the child appear to sustain or continue to a point of completion (in contrast to engaging in and then stopping without any obvious point of completion)?

EXAMPLES: - Looks all the way through a book
- Does all of puzzle
- Writes note to friend (done in two separate sittings)
- Builds block tower as high as can reach

3. Concepts of self

3.1 What evidence is there in the child's behavior (including self-appraisal) of how he or she views his or her physical appearance? His or her body? His or her size?

EXAMPLES: - Has inaccurate perception of size; tries to crawl into box that is much too small
- Says, "I got ugly hair"
- Admires self in mirror with new shirt on (pleased smile)
- Says, "I'm bigger than you," to Tony

3.2 What evidence is there in the child's behavior (including self-appraisal) of how he or she views his or her worthiness? Goodness or badness?

EXAMPLES: - While waiting to have help from teacher points out, "I'm waiting and not fussing"
- Says, "Ain't I nice?" when shares colander at sand table
- Smiles as says, "Susy thinks I'm mean"
- In reading book about the bad duck Ping, says, "I be bad too"

3.3 What evidence is there in the child's behavior (including self-appraisal) of how he or she views his or her gender identity?

EXAMPLES: - Sorts out boy clothes from dress-ups as own to use, gives others to Jane
- Says to Bryan, "You be daddy and build a house. I'll be mummy and wash dishes. Daddies don't wash dishes"
- When gets pants wet in snow and is looking for dry ones in box of extras, examines each to see if for boys (fly) or girls
- Says, "I can too play with dolls," to other child who says that only girls like dolls

3.4 What evidence is there in the child's behavior (including self-appraisal) of how he or she views his or her skills (motor skills, social skills, thinking skills)?

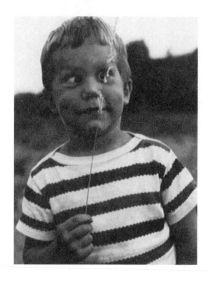

"Want to see me do something funny?" *(Robert Burdick)*

EXAMPLES:
- Says to new child, "Want to shovel? I'll show you how"
- Says, upon making a goof, "I'm so stupid"
- When teacher cannot push open the door, says, "I can do it, let me do it," and tries very hard
- Says to self, "I can climb all the way up there"

4. Social awareness

4.1 *What evidence is there in the child's behavior (including what he or she says about others) of sensitivity to others' feelings and views?*

EXAMPLES:
- Says, "Oh, oh, Neal won't like that" (broken top)
- Asks teacher to help another child who is beginning to cry
- Says to child on other side of chair, "Can you see my feet?"
- Asks, "What are you going to do with that stick, Pam? Are you going to use it to poke Jane?" (fight earlier between two)

5. Social interaction levels

5.1 *In what types of play activities does the child primarily observe others?*

EXAMPLES:
- In the outdoor yard
- Rocking and holding doll

5.2 *In what types of play activities does the child primarily play parallel to others?*

EXAMPLES:
- At sand table
- Playing with toy trucks and cars

5.3 *In what types of play activities does the child primarily play associatively with others?*

EXAMPLES: ▪ Using Tinker Toys
                        ▪ Doing puzzles

5.4 In what types of play activities does the child primarily play cooperatively with others?

EXAMPLES: ▪ Dramatic play (doctor, hospital play)
                        ▪ Building large block house

6. Social leader or follower

6.1 In what different ways does the child initiate contact with others?

EXAMPLES: ▪ Says to Erica, "Come on, let's play house"
                        ▪ Says, "Want to be my friend?"
                        ▪ Just walks over and enters into activity
                        ▪ Says, "Do you want some candy?"

6.2 What kind of ideas or suggestions does the child offer to others?

EXAMPLES: ▪ Says, "Pete, you be the dog"
                        ▪ Says to Kim at lunch table, "Let's not pass her the milk" (mad at Debbie)
                        ▪ Says "Try this one. It's harder" (puzzle)

6.3 What suggestions of others does the child follow?

EXAMPLES: ▪ Follows Sandy when she says, "Want to swing?"
                        ▪ Carries toy tea kettle when friend says, "Pretend this is your purse"

7. Repertoire for solving social problems

7.1 When conflicts or disagreements with peers or adults occur, what does the child do to reach a resolution?

EXAMPLES: ▪ When Ronnie grabs his airplane, says, "You give that back, it's mine," and then, "I'll tell my mommy"
                        ▪ Threatens, "If you don't let me in, I'll rip up your paper" (wants to get in playhouse)
                        ▪ When tips Tim's glass over and Tim is mad says, "I'm sorry. I won't do it any more"
                        ▪ In disagreement over who will feed gerbil, says, "If I get to do it today, you can do it tomorrow"

7.2 If the child is excluded from an activity or group he or she wishes to join, what does he or she do to resolve the situation?

EXAMPLES: ▪ Says, "I won't invite you to my party if you won't be my friend"
                        ▪ Tells teacher, "They won't play with me"
                        ▪ Says, "I didn't want to play anyway," and goes elsewhere

8. Formal (teacher-led) group participation

8.1 What evidence is there in the child's behavior (including what he or she says) that he or she is either comfortable or uncomfortable in group discussions?

EXAMPLES:
- Comes immediately to discussion location and sits waiting
- Tries to hide in lavatory when group assembles
- Spends most of discussion time looking at child next to him and occasionally engages in tickling match
- Listens for about ten minutes and then plays with little puzzle that was in pocket

8.2 *What does the child contribute to group discussion that indicates he or she has heard and understood what another child said?*

EXAMPLES:
- Says, "I went to Florida once too" (Jimmy told about trip to Florida)
- Says to Tom, "What did you do when no one was home?" (in response to Tom's tale of lost cat)
- Says, "My baby sister has the chicken pox" (previous speaker said father had sore throat)

SAMPLE OBSERVATIONS: STEVEN AND MONICA

The following behavioral assessments on affective and social behavior are a continuation of the reports included in Chapter 5 on two 4-year-olds, Steven and Monica.

Name Steven
Age Four years, two months

Affective and Social Behavior Steven shows his pleasure with an activity by smiling and laughing. He smiles while playing in the sand. He smiles and laughs (but does little talking) while he pulls a cart with two friends and pretends they are firemen going to a fire. Steven sits in the middle of a group and smiles while observing the actions of the others in the group.

Steven interacts very little with the children around him. He leaves a play area if the number of other students participating exceeds four or five. Since he is basically an observer, he seems to find this to be too much action to concentrate on at once. Steven exhibits fear around animals. He pulls back and only touches them with one finger after much coaxing from the teacher.

He was not observed getting angry at any time. When others take something away from him or attack him in some way, he does not defend himself. He either ignores the situation or leaves the area.

Steven is never alone. He is usually with a small group of children, but at times will sit with a teacher, aide, or mother when doing a difficult activity. When entering the nursery school, Steven stands and observes the room, seemingly looking for an existing situation into which he will fit. He usually picks an activity in which three to four children are already involved.

Steven engages in puzzle work with the assistance of an adult and smiles often as he does so. He usually completes four to five puzzles before moving on to another activity.

Steven engages in a range of activities without regard to gender stereotypes. He will pretend to cook, take care of a baby, work with blocks and trucks, participate in wrestling matches, and work at the tool bench.

When Steven does anything requiring skills such as cutting, puzzle work, pasting, or finger painting, he requests the presence of an adult. He will tell them, "I can't do it without your help," or "I need you now."

It is very difficult to figure out Steven's feelings. He doesn't seem to interact with others enough to be aware of their feelings either. He always retreats from conflict. He is mostly an observer whose major reaction to activity he cannot accept is to leave the area.

Steven's most regular activity is observing. He may manipulate objects in front of him, but usually this is not actual play, rather a means to blend into the group. Steven plays parallel to others in the sand box or block corner for limited amounts of time with a limited number of others. He plays firehouse associatively with others, but each is involved in his own role-playing activity. This can be noted by their verbal utterances, which have little connection to each other. Steven was not observed playing cooperatively.

Steven is basically a follower. He usually walks over to a group and sits at the edge before trying to blend in with the flow of activity. He will say, "Hey" to another child as he hands him a block. Steven does not offer suggestions but will take the suggestions of others. He pulls others in a cart, puts others' toys away, and moves if asked, when he is in the middle of an activity. Steven avoids all involvement in conflict. He avoids the aggressive children in the group. If a problem arises, Steven leaves.

Although he willingly comes to group-participation activities, Steven has little active participation. He sits quietly and watches the teacher during a teacher-directed activity. He will respond if asked a question directly but his answers are often incorrect. He doesn't interact with others in the group. He does not talk, touch, or look at them.

Name   Monica
Age   Four years, seven months

Affective and Social Behavior   Monica seems to prefer activities in which she can create something. These include painting, cutting, putting together puzzles, and pasting. She requests these activities if they are not already available. She also openly shows her pleasure when chosen to be the teacher's helper during special activities.

Monica refuses to participate in the wrestling activities on the mats. Even when gymnastics are included, she does not join in. She does not like it when other children get into fights or start hitting each other. She tells the teacher immediately when something like that occurs.

Monica seems hesitant when new and strange animals are brought into the classroom. In most cases she backs away and will not touch the animal.

There was no opportunity to observe Monica when she was angry.

Monica needs help when she enters nursery school and must hang up her coat.

Having friends and being a friend are important concerns for preschoolers. *(Steve Sartori)*

The hanger causes her problems. After being shown how to put her coat on the floor and then put the hanger in the sleeves, she did it by herself but looked to an adult for approval. During rest and snack time she has a set of friends she seems to go to for company. During rest time she holds hands with her friend.

Monica goes to the puzzle corner and gets out a puzzle and begins working on it without prompting from an adult or child. While doing these activities she works alone for about five or six minutes without calling attention to her efforts by calling a teacher. She also asks to paint, cut, or paste even though no one else is doing it. Her activities are brought to a logical completion before she leaves them. For example, she completes a puzzle before leaving it, fills in a whole piece of paper with paint before leaving the painting area, and colors in the whole picture she has drawn before leaving the area.

Monica seems to have a very positive self-image. Examples of this are that she walks up to the teacher and says, "See my pretty dress!"; tells an aide, "I just got my hair cut. Isn't it pretty?"; and tells a three-year-old, "I'm bigger than you."

Although Monica never expressed it, she always tried to do what was expected of her. She did not need to be corrected by a teacher for her behavior during any of the observations.

Monica seems to have a very set idea of the things little girls should and should not do. She does not participate in rough activities. These activities include wrestling, gymnastics, and general roughhousing done by the boys. She shows no interest in even watching the organized activities of this type. She does not play at the tool table. Nor does she play with the blocks or trucks. She does not participate in these activities even when asked to join in by a teacher. The closest she came to this type of activity was when the whole group was building a series of tracks to run cars on. She kept her role by taking a car and pretending to go shopping for groceries.

There was no opportunity to observe her views of her motor, social, or thinking skills. The only evidence of these is the confidence she shows when she is involved in new activities that require listening and following new and complicated directions. She seems more than willing to be the first to try things like this.

Monica points out the problems of other children to the teacher frequently. She tells the teacher who did what to whom when a controversy occurs. When she does this, it is usually factual even if it means one of her friends will get in trouble. She was observed telling a teacher, "He feels bad and is crying" and "He hit him and hurt him."

Monica seldom just observes other children, although she seems to be very aware of what others around her are doing. One time she watched several boys and one girl for several minutes as they pounded nails, cut boards, and used screwdrivers. She did not enter into the activity.

Monica plays parallel to other children when she is very interested in the end product of her activity such as during cutting, pasting, and painting activities. Her associative and cooperative play are evidenced in the following activities: sand table play, dramatic play in the kitchen area, puzzle activities that she has mastered, and game playing.

Monica has several different ways of gaining the attention of others and entering into activities, such as when she calls to a younger girl, "Joanne, come here"; walks over to a group playing a game, looks around for an empty spot, and sits down and begins playing the game; and goes up to a teacher and asks a student's name and then proceeds to the student and addresses him or her by name in order to ask a question.

Monica has successful strategies for joining into the activities of her friends. She sometimes just joins a group and starts doing what they are doing. At other times she asks someone, "Do you want to ___?" If a disagreement occurs within a group in which she is a member, Monica will call the problem to the attention of the closest teacher. She does not attempt to solve the problems on her own. Monica seems to avoid the children in the group that are usually involved in problems, and they in turn seem to have little interest in her.

Formal group activities and teacher-directed activities seem to be among Monica's favorites. When the teacher gives her musical signal and asks the children to come to the group, Monica is usually one of the first to arrive. She will enter the group area, sit down quietly smiling, look up at the teacher, and wait for the activity to begin. She sits quietly and listens to a story for ten minutes or more. When a question is asked, she is usually among the first to answer. When others in the group are called on, she sits quietly and looks at them as they answer. She does not interrupt or shout out answers. If a child gets an answer wrong, her hand goes up again. On one occasion she was observed saying, "No," to a boy in answer to his reply to the teacher and then giving the right answer. She watches and listens to others in the group intently. If an activity is started and others need help, she at times starts to give them that help, depending on the child involved. During a discussion about a nest she asked the boy who brought it in, "Where did you find it?" and "Was it up high?"

FROM OBSERVATION TO PLANNING

Following are three general guidelines for facilitating the affective and social development of children.

1   Try to provide opportunities for all children to engage in activities appropriate to their stage of development and avoid involving them in activities that are likely to prove uninteresting or stressful. There is some evidence that pleasure is related not only to emotional well-being in the young but also to other kinds of positive developmental outcomes, such as intellectual achievement. There is general agreement among those who study human development that children who are accustomed to playfully exploring the world of ideas and relationships become more competent than those whose lives are devoid of joy and playfulness. Even if this were not true, most of us still wish to make children's lives enjoyable. Evidence that there may be long-term benefits from fun and playfulness simply make it easier for us to justify making programs pleasurable

"I want my mommy!" *(John James)*

rather than boring and ritualistic. In Part 4 you will expand your repertoire of ideas for providing satisfying experiences for children at different levels.

2   Remember that young children's affective and social behavior, in large measure, is not the product of inborn characteristics and is consistently modified by experience. Although basic orientations and self-concepts are becoming established by age three, they are still amenable to your influence as a teacher, whether consciously or by default.

Imagine Butch, a child in your class who appears to consider himself a bad guy, a real toughie. He teases, attacks, breaks things, and appears to delight in being destructive and feared by the other children. He influences others to do what he wants by threat of physical harm. The children in your group are likely to view Butch just as he presents himself and will further reinforce the limited perspectives he has of himself. As a teacher, will you accept his conception of himself as a mean kid and act toward him as though this were true? Will you only admonish him for being bad, further solidifying his current self-view, or will you also act toward him with the expectation that he is kind, helpful, tender, and sympathetic as well? At ages three, four, and beyond being presented with a new set of expectations about what one is like can be an important influence in modifying one's self-conception. Your behavior toward children can help them extend their view of themselves. For instance, if children have only identified themselves as being good, big, or by similar "positive" attributes, you can help them see that they need not rigidly adhere to these but rather can still be worthwhile persons if they occasionally act bad, little, dependent, or in other "negative" ways.

Undue emphasis on the positive virtues in a developing self-conception is nearly as harmful as conceiving of oneself in only negative ways. Teachers should strive to support a self-conception in a child that is flexible enough to permit a variety of behaviors and states of mind. Children should celebrate themselves as unique, worthwhile persons who do both good and bad things, who sometimes act and feel grown-up but are sometimes babyish, who in some ways are attractive and in other ways not so attractive. The attempt to make young children believe only positive things about themselves is not likely to succeed because so much of their real behavior and thinking will not measure up to it.

As an example, imagine Mike, another child in your classroom. Mike appears to see himself basically as good, helpful, polite, careful, and nice. If Mike were in the same class with Butch he would probably be very aware of Butch's behavior, would probably insist that Butch be punished, and would expect the teacher and other children to like his own behaviors much better than Butch's. If Mike, at age four or so, also engages in aggressive acts, how might you as a teacher respond? Might you quickly draw him back into line by saying, "Why, Mike, that's not the way *you* behave. You're acting like Butch today. That's not the good Mike I know. I'm sure you won't do it again." Or might you say, "I see that you got in a fight today. That's something new for you, isn't it? How did it make you feel?" Of course, there are many other ways to respond. The point is that you, in your teaching role, can act to solidify the child's current self-conception or you can value and encourage explorations into new ways of behaving and feeling.

3   In your role as teacher it will be your responsibility to encourage children to develop, to practice, and to extend their repertoires for social interaction. To a great extent, simply providing opportunities for children to practice different ways of behaving is sufficient. However, the findings of Spivack and Shure (1974) suggest that some children simply repeat again and again the same stereotyped action in critical social situations without being aware that other options could have been tried. You can provide models for alternative ways of behaving and quite directly point out other behaviors appropriate to the situation. If you can determine via your observations what individual children do in initiating social contacts, in trying to influence others, and in trying to resolve social conflicts, you will be able to determine the kind of additional awarenesses, instruction, and practice they need to improve their social relationships. Part 4 offers many suggestions of how specific activities and materials can be used to extend children's social repertoires.

The following recommendations might be made specifically for Steven and Monica. Steven, left to his own devices, will continue to participate as an observer. It may be useful to do some direct instruction and to provide modeling for Steven of how to use some of the classroom materials and how to play cooperatively with another child. A gradual building of repertoire is recommended. Steven's attitudes seem very positive, and he makes maximal use of his limited repertoire. Therefore, the development of repertoire for interaction with peers and using classroom materials appears to be Steven's prime need. The approach should be gentle and playful. It may also be very important for adults to point out to Steven those things that he can do for himself and by himself. A view of himself that includes being capable and independent can be fostered by new learnings and increased recognition of his current abilities.

Monica's affective and social development may also be best served by helping her broaden her concepts of what she can comfortably do. Monica receives a good deal of recognition for her abilities to create with art materials and for her participation in other quiet activities. It may be useful to look for opportunities to reinforce her involvement in traditionally nonfeminine tasks and roles. Praising the involvement of other girls in work with tools, gymnastics, and so forth may be helpful. She may also need help in developing some prerequisite skills for these activities, although, given her existent repertoire, it may be that a change in perspectives about what "girls" do is the key issue. Another area in which Monica may need some help is in the area of problem solving. She can be encouraged to examine the problem situations that she points out to the teacher and to try to figure out some of the alternative solutions that might be tried. Greater self-reliance in social-conflict situations is also a desirable goal.

SUMMARY

If you have observed children, using the questions posed in this chapter as guides, you have undoubtedly increased your sensitivity to children's affective and social behaviors. In moving from observations to planning, you are advised to provide activities for children that seem likely to prove pleasurable to them. The advantages of joy and playfulness to development were stressed. You are also advised to extend children's self-concepts rather than reinforce their current views of themselves, even though those views may be very positive. Providing experiences to help children develop, practice, and extend social repertoire is also part of your teaching responsibility.

SUGGESTED ACTIVITIES

1 Answer the list of questions posed in this chapter as guides to observation in respect to your own affective and social behaviors. Summarize the similarities and differences between your own self-appraisal and those you make of the children you observe.

2 Summarize the similarities and differences between children you have observed using the guides from this chapter. Compare children of differing age, gender, and socioeconomic background.

3 Arrange with a fellow class member to observe the same child using the guides provided in this chapter, and compare notes on what you have seen. Are your reports comparable in terms of amount of detail, objectivity, clarity?

4 For one of the children you have observed, consider the kind of adjectives (e.g., *selfish, shy, naughty, spoiled, good, comical*) that might be evaluatively applied by persons who observe the behaviors you saw. Generate alternative adjectives that might also be as accurately applied to the same behaviors (e.g., *assertive* instead of *selfish; reserved* instead of *shy; spirited* instead of *naughty*). Summarize and compare these two sets of descriptions for this child. How does your view of the child change with the terms that are used to describe him or her?

ADDITIONAL READINGS

Honig, A. S. (1987). The shy child. *Young Children, 42*(4), 54–64.

Pellegrini, A. D., & Glickman, C. D. (1990). Measuring kindergartners' social competence. *Young Children, 45*(4), 40–44.

Riley, S. S. (1984). *How to generate values in young children: Integrity, honesty, individuality, self-confidence, wisdom.* Washington, DC: National Association for the Education of Young Children.

Roedell, W. C. (1985). Developing social competence in gifted preschool children. *Remedial and Special Education, 6*(4), 6–10.

Shure, M. B. (1978). *Problem-solving techniques in childrearing.* San Francisco: Jossey-Bass.

Smith, C. A. (1982). *Promoting the social development of young children: Strategies and activities.* Palo Alto, CA: Mayfield Publishing.

Sprung, B. (1978). *Perspectives on non-sexist early childhood education.* New York: Teachers College Press.

CHAPTER 8

COGNITIVE AND INTELLECTUAL DEVELOPMENT

OVERVIEW

Much can be learned about children's cognitive and intellectual attainments by observing how they respond in situations where they have some freedom to act and talk as they wish. Consider the following situation:

Tina, age four, and Donna, age five, are playing with clay. Tina rolls out a long coil, chops it up into pieces with a tongue depressor, and says, "Three—one, two, three, four, five. One, two, three, four, five snakes." She points to each as she counts the second time. "Oh, oh, too fat," she says. "I'll get you long." She rolls them into a longer and narrower form, aligns them at the edge of the table, and puts a tiny pat of pressed clay by each snake, saying, "Here's some cookie for you. And here's some cookie for you."

Donna, also rolling coils from clay, joins the ends of one piece to form a ring of clay and puts it on her finger, where it hangs loosely. She says, "This thing is too big around. I need to make it littler." She puts the clay back into the ball, rolls it all out again, and puts it into a circular shape. Says to Tina, "Here's a ring for you." Tina puts it on with a smile. Donna makes another ring and puts it on herself saying, "Boys wear married rings. Claudia's brother has a married ring."

As Fred, age seven, walks into the room, Tina takes her ring off and holds it up to show him. "See what Donna made me," she says. Fred says, "What did she make you an O for? You can't read!" Tina replies, "It's no O. It's a ring." Donna says, "Don't show him. He might marry you." Tina looks startled and quickly hides the ring. Fred says, "Show me. I'm not going to marry you, for heaven's sake. You're too little."

Tina's use of clay includes manipulation of shapes, production and alignment of objects, counting, and consideration of proportions. Donna considers size and proportions in producing her objects and is also involved in considering what concrete symbols (wedding rings) actually represent and how this representation occurs. Fred reacts to the younger girls' activities with a different perspective. If the observation of the three children were to continue, there would be further evidence of variations in their internal representation of reality, their current concerns, and the upper limits of their thinking abilities. We might also be able to observe how each of them gradually takes in new information and uses it to modify his or her perspective and transform his or her internal representation of the world.

Events and viewpoints, such as an adult conversation, that are quite out of alignment with a child's current perceptions often appear not to even enter a child's awareness. The views or actions of another child, however, if only slightly different from their own, may be noted with enthusiastic interest and almost immediately cited or included in their activity. It is likely, for example, that Tina will begin making rings of clay and begin to call them Os. Donna may begin to consider how big a person needs to be before marriage rings become something to either seek or watch out for. Thus, accommodations are gradually made in internal representations of reality.

The means by which cognitive and intellectual structures develop are described by Piaget as adaptation. Adaptation is said to consist of the two complementary processes, assimilation and accommodation. The meaning of these terms was introduced and discussed in Chapter 3. You may wish to review that section as these are difficult concepts. They are crucial to understanding the Piagetian view of intellectual development.

It may help to apply the terms *assimilation* and *accommodation* to yourself to give them greater meaning. As you read this chapter, we hope you will engage in the processes of assimilation and accommodation. If you are already familiar with the intellectual development of the infant and the young child, you may simply be assimilating the ideas presented here. That is, you will already have an organized network of intellectual concepts that includes the ideas we are presenting. In short, there will be no need for accommodation to occur; you can simply assimilate the material.

On the other hand, if the ideas we present are not similar to what you already know or believe about intellectual development, you will not be able to conveniently assimilate this information into your existing mental structures. You may then need to accommodate these differences, that is, in some way realign your existing network of concepts and beliefs to take into account the additional perspective or different view.

It may also be that what we offer will be either so discrepant or unmeaningful to you that you will dismiss it as irrelevant and thus will neither assimilate nor accommodate it. Do you think you will be able to assimilate these ideas? Or will you find them irrelevant? For learning, or adaptation, to occur, the mutual processes of assimilation and accommodation must be operating. A change in your mental structure will not occur unless the ideas encountered can be assimilated into your existing mental structure with only a slight need for accommodation.

There are many different views about how and why learning takes place. It was Piaget's view, as well as the view of many others, that the human organism has a built-in (intrinsic) need to function, interact, learn, and grow, that is, to be engaged in processes of adaptation. Satisfaction is derived from situations in which there is a good balance between assimilation and accommodation. The provision of situations with that optimal balance, as was indicated in Chapter 2, is what Hunt (1961) refers to as "the problem of the match." Finding that match for children is the teacher's primary job. You will know that you have succeeded when children are fully engaged without external inducements. Watch any multiage group and note the differences between what engages an infant, a toddler, a preschooler, a school-age child, an adolescent, a young adult, and a mature adult. Note what each one appears to screen out of awareness and what each attends to and responds to.

The human organism responds to external stimulation and instruction according to the internal constructions that have already been developed. There is a "growing edge" at which each person can be engaged fully. Even the brief description of Tina, Donna, and Fred gave a glimmering as to what their "growing edges" might be. To some extent there is a common human progression in these matters, although idiosyncratic differences between individuals do result from personal experiences.

Many psychologists, including Howard Gardner (1983) and Robert J. Sternberg (1985), take issue with the traditional ideas of intelligence. Gardner, for example, extends the usual narrow definition of intelligence to include "the ability to solve problems or create products which are valued in one or more cultural settings." In *Frames of Mind,* Gardner (1983) describes seven intelligences:

- Linguistic
- Logico-mathematical
- Kinesthetic (abilities of dancers, athletes, craftspersons, surgeons)
- Musical
- Spatial
- Interpersonal (abilities to detect moods in others, to motivate, and to lead)
- Intrapersonal (abilities to understand own feelings and use knowledge of self in productive ways)

In this textbook, we have included only the first two of Gardner's list under our classification of cognitive and intellectual development. Other of his items we have discussed as motor, affective, and social behaviors in the prior chapters. Gardner's preference for encompassing all these as intellectual abilities, albeit diverse, may have advantages. Elementary and secondary schools have placed undue emphasis on only the first two of these seven abilities—linguistic and logico-mathematical, and this mistake is increasingly being replicated in early childhood programs. Efforts by Gardner and others to assess and emphasize the development of other abilities as intelligence may help to modify those emphases. As Gardner (quoted by Scherer, 1991) points out, "We have too many compelling problems that threaten our survival for us to put all our money on one or even two intelligences" (p. 25).

Despite our support of Gardner's efforts to redefine intelligence to be more inclusive, in this chapter we have retained the more limited definition. We follow primarily the Piagetian perspectives on common human progression in acquiring cognitive and intellectual abilities. The discussion is separated into sections according to age levels: infants and toddlers, threes and fours; and fives, sixes, and sevens.

INFANTS AND TODDLERS

Researchers have recently established that the human fetus does a great deal of learning prior to birth. Newborns, for example, have been found to respond differently to sounds they have heard before birth. Still, as you observe infants, you will note that much of what is going on around them appears not to be within their sphere of awareness. This is not necessarily due to an undeveloped sensory apparatus. The organs for seeing, hearing, touching, smelling, and tasting are all functioning well. In fact, prior to birth (by the seventh month of pregnancy) the fetus's eyes have opened and can perceive light. It is simply that infants have not yet had sufficient interaction with the environment to develop mental structures that transform meaningless sensations into meaningful perceptions. As Piaget put it, according to Flavell (1963), "It is a remarkable thing that the younger the child, the less novelties seem new to him" (p. 105). Infants appear, nevertheless, to possess from birth an amazing ability to process information and to develop expectations about their environment.

During infancy and the toddler years, organized patterns of behavior develop, enabling children to meaningfully perceive more and more of what surrounds them. Piaget referred to these patterns as *schemata*. To study a person's cognitive and intellectual status is to inquire into their level of perception or awareness, which in turn stems from the schemata that have been developed in the ongoing adaptation process. According to Piaget, schemata are developed in the following sequence during the sensorimotor period:

1 Use of reflexes only (such as sucking, swallowing, and grasping).

2 Modification and coordination of reflexes (for example, something grasped becomes something to suck).

3 "Intentional" repetition of actions that at first were chance occurrences. For instance, the infant may squeeze a rubber duck as it is placed in its hand, hear a quack, squeeze the duck again. If the quack is repeated, the infant may continue to make it happen, laughing delightedly at each repetition.

4 Coordination of two schemata to make things happen (for example, reaching for a desired object and moving obstacles out of the way to do so).

5 Trying new actions to see what will happen; experimentation.

6 Use of symbolic representation (signs) to invent solutions instead of just engaging in trial and error (for instance, how to keep a rolling object where it is placed, how to open a box, and how to get in a more convenient position for performing actions).

Once children are able to **symbolize** objects or events (by representing them in some way in order to mentally manipulate them), Piaget described them as passing from the sensorimotor period. Piaget (1952) gave an example of how **symbolic action** is initially attained. His child, Lucienne, at age one year and four months, was given a nearly closed match box containing a watch chain. She unsuccessfully tried to open the box using two schemata she had previously discovered through active manipulation of other objects. She first tried to turn the box over in order to empty it of its contents, and she then reached inside the box with a finger. Neither action was successful, because the opening was too small. Looking intently at the box, Lucienne opened and shut her mouth several times, at first slightly, then wider and wider and then unhesitatingly put her hand in the slit, and instead of trying as before to reach the chain, she pull[ed] so as to enlarge the opening." Piaget interpreted this mouthing action as Lucienne's use of a motor symbol, or sign, that gives the same kind of assistance to her thinking about a problem situation that words and other imagery will later provide.

PIAGET'S STAGES IN THE DEVELOPMENT OF INTELLIGENCE

Jean Piaget's views of the child are presented throughout this chapter, as well as in other portions of this book. The picture of the development of intelligence that emerges from Piaget's studies is one of continuous transformations in the organizations, or structures, of intelligence. The sequence of stages described by Piaget is as follows:

1. Sensorimotor period (birth to eighteen or twenty-four months)

During this stage, the inborn sensorimotor reflexes (such as crying, sucking, and grasping) are generalized, coordinated, and differentiated through direct action on "reality" to form the elementary operations, which begin to be internalized.

2. Preoperational period (eighteen or twenty-four months to seven or eight years)

The first phase within the preoperational period, sometimes referred to as the *preconceptual* phase, is when symbols are constructed in which children imitate and represent what they see through actions and language. This phase lasts to about age four. During the second

phase, sometimes called the *intuitive* phase, children are extending, differentiating, and combining their action-images and correcting their intuitive impressions of reality.

3. Concrete operations period (seven or eight years to eleven or twelve years)

During this period, children's thinking becomes *decentered,* that is, less dependent on either actions or immediate perceptual cues. Internalized thinking operations facilitate classifying, ordering in series, numbering, grouping, and subgrouping of action-images.

4. Formal operations (eleven or twelve years to fifteen or sixteen years and beyond)

At this stage, children begin to systematize classification, ordering, and numbering, and to consider the logical extension of these systems beyond action-images. The central thinking processes become sufficiently autonomous to permit consideration of all possible instances, that is, beyond those present in any actual situation.

These early motor imitations (mimicking actions with the body) may become the signs or **images** that allow initial internal constructions of reality. As the child becomes able to construct, through motor imitation, some rudimentary signs that can be mentally manipulated in problem situations, there is less dependence on motor schemata. Piaget described how the various types of representations invented by children help them move toward more and more reliance on symbols and less on actions. For Piaget's child, a piece of paper was made to represent food and a piece of cloth was made to represent a pillow. These objects were then reacted to with all the actions and emotions usually reserved for eating or going to bed.

According to Piaget, the acquisition of language is made possible by children's experience with these early motor representations and the rudimentary internal manipulation of these symbols. The first use of objects as symbols is a very private invention on the part of individual children and has little meaning to others who have not had close association with them. Similarly, a child's first words, even though they are imitated from language that is heard, will have very private and unique connotations that may not coincide with the "public" meaning. A word like *mama* may be used by the child to refer to many things, such as wanting to be held, an opening door, or food, as well as the presence of mother.

Vygotsky, the Soviet psychologist, differed with Piaget in some respects regarding these ideas. The parent's involvement in a socially shared encountering of the infant's world is gradually taken over by the child, Vygotsky insists, and the parent's representations gradually become the child's. Language and other learnings are thus centered in social interactions, as Vygotsky sees it. This is a difference in emphasis from Piaget's idea that representation and subsequently, language, are provoked from sensorimotor interactions with physical objects during the first months of life.

Many children by age one use several words whose meanings may or may not match the public usage. The task of gradually modifying the private meanings of words to coincide with their public meanings continues throughout the life span. Many of our jokes are made possible because of the errors that occur when a person misuses a word. We remember with a chuckle the child with a much older sister who said, "I used to have a sister but she's a grown-up woman now."

From the time when a child first begins to use words as signs that represent something repeatedly experienced (whether or not that usage matches the public meaning), there are rapid increases in efforts to represent more and more experiences with words. At ages eighteen months to two years, children appear to become keenly aware that everything has a name, and they set about busily trying to learn the names for everything. At about this time, children also begin to use words in combination. The phrase, "What's 'at?" is one of the combinations acquired relatively early and used constantly thereafter in the energetic quest for word symbols; the child begins to assume that these symbols exist as an integral part of every object.

Many multiword utterances, such as "all gone" or "go bye-bye," are often learned by children as though they were single words. They are later differentiated and separated into word components. In a family where formal terms were used for toilet functions, the youngest of three siblings had among her first "words" an understandable version of, "I wanna urinate." The referent matched that of the older siblings and the grammatical intent was appropriate, but the child had no awareness of the words as separate entities.

It is amazing how easily children produce language to serve different functions, such as speaking of the present versus the future or the past, asking questions, making statements, giving commands, or indirectly requesting particular behavior from others. Linguists vary in their explanations of how these abilities are achieved. Behaviorists such as Skinner (1957) emphasize the acquisition of language through reinforcement. Other linguists point out aspects of language learning that are not well explained by reinforcement principles, for instance, new forms appear suddenly, not gradually, and then are used extensively, even being overgeneralized and used in inappropriate ways, whether or not they are reinforced. The child having begun to use *-ed* endings to denote past will apply the new learnings to irregular verbs producing, "He wented home," and so forth, even though previously the verb had been used correctly.

Lenneberg (1967) believed that there are inherent human propensities toward the acquisition of language structures and that these are simply triggered when children hear language being used. This view is supported by the remarkable success with which nearly all children learn whatever language they hear at certain developmental levels, even when it is only occasionally heard. Lenneberg proposed that language acquisition is due to a specific maturational schedule that is similar to, but separate from, motor development. Exposure to language, even minimal exposure, provides the stimulus for the acquisition for all basic grammatical constructions.

Linguists Chomsky (1965) and McNeill (1970) further describe the process of language acquisition as follows: (1) as children mature they become increasingly able to hear language forms, (2) they make sense out of what they hear according to their level of maturity, (3) they intuitively derive rules in accordance with the language they hear, and (4) they produce speech that is in accord with these generalizations. Chomsky and McNeill, like Lenneberg, believe the human mind is uniquely designed or "prewired" to detect and use the rules of language.

Other linguists, on the other hand, place greater emphasis on the interactive nature of language learning. Children's earliest talk seems to match what they are experiencing in the environment. Universal sentence structures (subject-verb-object) are said to be explained by the universality of early experience with actions on objects rather than by innate brain structures. These interactionists also point to the mistakes that children make as evidence that they are extracting syntactical rules regarding what they hear. It is certainly clear that children are not just repeating what they have heard when they say things like, "Me no go bed" or "See the mouses." If the child is acting on and experimenting with what is heard and is actively involved in the process of figuring out the rules that govern appropriate and inappropriate expressions, then this activity has implications for adults who work with children. The adult must be attuned to the constructions the child is already using and, above all, allow the child ample opportunity to practice and receive feedback concerning the invented rules.

Whatever the processes of learning, almost all children show amazing progress in language development prior to age three. By that age, children can have a vocabulary of some 1,000 words, and most of what they say is intelligible even to strangers. The grammatical complexity of utterances is roughly that of everyday, spoken adult language, although many mistakes still occur.

Although motor activity remains critical to learning, the three-year-old has long since ceased to rely *only* on sensorimotor schemata for thinking and learning about the world. Language is now used to represent and manipulate reality, including the reconstruction of previous experiences.

THREES AND FOURS

According to Piagetian formulations, the **preoperational period** begins with the early use of signs and symbols in the thought process at around age one and a half or two and continues to age seven or eight. During this period, the child is "transformed from an organism whose most intelligent functions are sensory-motor overt acts to one whose upper limit cognitions are inner symbolic manipulations of reality" (Flavell, 1963, p. 151). Three- and four-year-olds develop an extended capacity to form mental symbols that stand for or represent absent things or events. They create and manipulate mental substitutes for the real thing. Much of this happens through imitation. Just as the one-year-old handles things, looks at them, and tries to act like them, thus gaining information and tools for thinking, threes and fours are mentally imitating and creating internal symbols of the outer world. Development of language to represent reality is part of this process. Language, thus, becomes a tool for thinking processes.

Children understand and use an amazing number of words. However, even after children begin to use certain words regularly, they are still deciphering the exact meaning in relation to other similar words. Experimentation with words continues in various settings over long periods and results in gradual refinement of meanings. Children hear words and phrases and try out what they think is the appropriate use until either their communication fails or new listening experiences lead them to revise their initial usage.

The process of language acquisition often requires the simultaneous refinement of concepts along with mastery of words. The toddler may call anything that has four legs "a doggie." He or she not only must learn specific words such as skunk, fox, kitten, cat, puppy, and lion but must also learn the characteristics that distinguish one animal from the other. The process of learning what is *not* "a doggie" is incomparably more complex than the initial acquisition of the word. The sorting out of appropriate meanings is, of course, necessary for each word acquisition. Many three-year-olds still consider all women mommies and all men daddies. We know of a toddler who wanted cold water when hot was coming from the faucet, and said, "Turn it to the other channel." Why not? We also chuckled over the words of another toddler whose father was going to

Pictures can support learning if children have had prior first-hand experiences. *(Permission of Bernice Wright Cooperative Nursery School)*

accompany him to the cooperative nursery school for the morning to do a stint as a parent assistant. The child's mother asked, "Daniel, do you think Daddy will know how to behave at nursery school?" Daniel thought it over and then replied, "I think he will be a little hāve." Again, why not? Learning the common usages of words is, indeed, a complicated task!

Preschool children, however, are very concerned about learning the right names for things; they do not like to be wrong. For them, there is nothing arbitrary about words; they believe the name to be an intrinsic part of the object. When Piaget asked a child how people knew that the sun was called the sun, he was told, "They say it was called the sun because they could see it was round and hot." This is a typical response. A four-year-old told one of the authors that she was named Michelle because she looked like a Michelle.

To acquire new vocabulary and learn appropriate meanings, it is helpful for children to interact with verbally mature persons. Those children, for example, who benefited most from watching the educational television program "Sesame Street" were found to be those whose parents watched with them and talked about what they had seen (Ball & Bogatz, 1970). The amount and richness of face-to-face language interactions appear to be critical in promoting language development.

Adults' understanding of children's efforts to expand their language abilities is rather limited. They have little theoretical awareness of the complexity of language acquisition but, despite this lack of formal knowledge, may provide highly useful corrective feedback. For instance, if the child says, "It isn't any more snow," the adult will almost automatically correct, "There isn't any more snow," and may add, to be conversational, "It all melted, didn't it?" If the child says, "What does this does?" the adult will probably repeat, "What does this do?" changing inflection for emphasis and then giving the answer.

By such verbal interactions, adults provide a child with just the kind of help many linguists feel benefits children most—simple talk, slightly more complex or correct or different from what the child said. This help is typically intuitive; the adults involved are usually unable to describe the nature of their corrections, the kinds of sentences they have modeled, or the kinds of sentences the child produced.

As a teacher, you will do well to emulate what the parent does naturally. However, you can also benefit from systematically studying children's language and selecting the kind of help that seems most appropriate. It is important to acquire the ability to listen and to appraise children's language—what they are trying to say, their syntactical usage, and their vocabulary. We will try to help you do this by identifying some of the more typical language changes that occur. The questions we offer as a guide to your observations of individual children also pose certain very specific things for you to look for.

Between the ages of two and a half and four, children begin using longer sentences (more words per sentence) and also begin including particular word structures that make their communication more specific. Some of the changes most typical of this period can be summarized as follows (Pflaum, 1974):

1 Increasing use of *-ing* with verbs, as in "I mak*ing* coffee," "He go*ing* up ladder," and I work*ing*."

2 Increasing use of auxiliary verbs to express tense, to indicate questions and negatives, and to show the passive voice, as in "Me *have* this one," "Daddy *did* it," "I *am* too cowboy," "*Want* take this?" and "I *been* good."

3 Acquiring the forms of the verb *to be,* as in "Doggie *is* here," "That'*s* a clock," "He'*s* going up the ladder," "There'*s* a fire and here'*s* a ladder," and "He *isn't* coming."

4 Developing greater facility with negative sentences, as from *"He no bit you,"* or *"I no want it,"* to *"I don't want cover on it," "They not hot," "He didn't caught me," "I didn't did it,"* and *"I am not a doctor."*

5 Developing greater facility in asking questions, as from *"Who that?"* or *"Ball go?"* to *"Where my mommy go?" "What you doed?"* and *"Did I saw that in my book?"*

6 Acquiring word parts that make nouns plural and produce noun-verb agreement. As they become aware of rules for this they may overgeneralize and make mistakes with words they had previously said correctly.

By age four, many children will use the following constructions:

Main clause conjunction, as in *"Mary sang and Mary danced"*
Conjunction with deletion, as in *"Mary sang and danced"*
Relative clause, as in *"The man who sang is old"*
Because sentence embedding, as in *"You come here 'cause Mommy said so"*
Particle separation, as in *"Put down the box"*
Reflexive, as in *"I did it myself"*

Although many four-year-olds use the following constructions, they are much more common among five-year-olds.

Imperative, as in *"Shut the door"*
Passive, as in *"The boy was hit by the girl"*
If sentence embedding, as in *"You can go if you want to"*
So sentence embedding, as in *"I gave it to him so he won't cry"*
Compound of nominal, as in *"baby chair"*

The ways in which children group and label objects are highly indicative of their conceptual abilities. Limitations in thinking are revealed when children are presented with an array of objects (or pictures) and asked to put together all the things that go together or, alternatively, are presented with one object within an array and asked, "Which of these other things goes with this?" Very young children usually group objects according to their momentary fancy, with little or no attention to common characteristics. By age five, however, they can sort the objects according to similarities such as size, color, shape, or, less frequently, function. However, they may change their grouping criterion from one choice to the next; that is, they might first match a white toy rabbit with a white mitten *(color)*, then put a hat with the mitten because both keep you warm *(function)*. In general, three- and four-year-olds tend to sort more by color and size and less by form than do older children.

By the time children are age three or four, they have usually become aware of counting and try to learn how to do it. Even though they haven't yet grasped the concept of numerals representing an invariant quantity, they are interested in trying to say the series of numerals in the way they have observed others do it. They do know that there is an order to be learned and do their best saying, "1, 2, 6, 10." Not many at this age will be able to match the saying of the word in one-to-one correspondence with touching or pointing to each object in a group that is being counted. Interestingly, though, they may have learned that the last word said in counting a set of objects tells how many objects there are in that set. Once they have learned this rule, which is in mathematical terms called "the cardinality rule," they apply it when they count, whether or not they can accurately count the set (Fuson, Pergament, Lyons, & Hall, 1985).

Children aged three and four generally have little interest in the explanations of physical causality for the happenings about them. They want to know how things work but not why. They egocentrically assume that causations are linked to themselves—either caused by or for them—and consequently find further

Classification of shape and colors can be encouraged by providing small objects and a muffin tin. *(Permission of Department of Early Childhood Education, Syracuse School District)*

investigation irrelevant—the car is there to give them a ride; the rain comes to water their plants. Or, the child may assume that events happen because they are needed, they are "supposed to happen"—the tree just knows it is supposed to grow apples, the cloud wanted to send down rain. The possibility of impersonal causes is seldom considered.

Children's concept of space is developed during the early years by their own actions. Their perceptions of space stem more from their tireless clustering and separation of objects than from merely viewing objects in space. The child must learn to "see" space and spatial qualities such as distance and position; this ability is not the product of simple visual maturation. A child who has not had opportunity to actively manipulate objects may have delayed or distorted space perception and faulty orientations.

By age three, children's spatial awareness is often reflected in the use of terms such as *up, down, off, come, go, here, there, on, at, in, way up, up in, in here, in there, far away, back corner, over from, by, up on top,* and *on top of.* At age four, the following terms are likely to have been added: *next to, under, between, way down, far away, in back of, under, out in, down to, way up there, way far out, way off,* and *behind* (Ames & Learned, 1948).

The space concepts mastered by children bear a clear relationship to their own bodies. Only later are objects perceived in relation to other objects. Four-year-olds may know that both you and a particular object are far away, but will not be aware of whether the object is behind, beside, or in front of you. They will especially not be able to perceive how an object might look from some vantage point other than their own and will totally ignore any expectation that they should even try.

Children's concept of time develops from the experience of regular sequenced events that are accompanied by time-oriented descriptions. The youngster learns through repeated experiences that breakfast is followed by "Sesame Street," or play time by the mail delivery. As adults and older siblings talk about the events as "Know what you can do next?" "Not until after Sesame Street," "Did the mail come yet today?" the child gradually begins to anticipate the regularities of happenings through time and is assisted in this process by learning and using the vocabulary that others model. By age three, children may correctly use terms such as *now, going to, in a minute, today, after, morning, afternoon, some day, one day, tomorrow, last night, all the time, all day,* and *at lunch time.* They may also refer to what they will do tomorrow or at Christmas or that they are three years old (Ames, 1946). It is difficult to determine in many instances the actual meaning of time references for them. By age four, they may use many past and future tenses accurately and will use terms such as *for a long time, for years, a whole week, two things at once, it's almost time, in a month,* and *next summer.* They will often make errors in trying to describe time, such as "the next tomorrow" or "I'm not going to take a nap yesterday." However, they seem at this age to have a clear understanding of the sequence of daily events.

In the minds of many, the three Rs—readin', 'ritin', and 'rithmetic—are the primary work of school, and often specifically of first grade. They mistakenly assume that most of the learning in these areas is accomplished through formal lessons. This is not the case. A great deal of progress in these areas is made by children at younger ages without formal instruction, as is illustrated by the record of Tommy's experiences on pages 150–151. When children are in a language-rich environment with adults who are responsive to their queries and efforts, they attain most of the essential concepts and learn to read easily and successfully in the primary grades—and often before.

Given the opportunity to observe writing and to experience the functions and values of the reading process, young children will very early become interested in producing writing and will gradually give their scribbles more of the appearance of writing-horizontal lines of connected or closely arranged markings. They will move from scribbling to drawing to attempts at copying letters to production of names and other words (but not necessarily read as words). By age three, children are likely to be making good progress in differentiating writing from pictures, and by age five, they probably have learned to differentiate letters from letterlike forms that are not letters. It is also likely that they will have figured out some of the conventions of English written language—directionality (from left to right) and the way letters are arranged in groupings with spaces in between to denote separations between words.

These awarenesses have resulted from many experiences with print (signs, cereal boxes, books, notes, lists, and TV ads, and so on) and may also be attributed to their own efforts to create writing that is recognizable to others. Gibson and Levin (1975) and others who study the psychology of reading point out how children's attempts at copying and making letters help them figure out which features are critical in making each letter recognizable. They, thus, learn to disregard irrelevant irregularities and flourishes. With the accumulation of experience in examining and attempting to make letter and word forms, children gradually become proficient in attending to those details in words and letters that are useful for discrimination and ignoring those aspects that are irrelevant.

Learning to make increasingly finer discriminations that hone in on the relevant visual detail while ignoring the less relevant is the same process as in all earlier discrimination learning. The infant learned to discriminate between kinds of foods, between his mother and others, between his own stuffed toy and other objects. The toddler makes further detailed discriminations, such as between dogs and cats and squirrels, between bowls and plates, between happy faces and sad faces. The number of discriminations mastered by this age is phenomenal. The preschooler continues to develop finer and finer discriminations, including such fine points as the differences between dump trucks and cement mixers, between Porsches and Volkswagens, between zebras and horses, between kinds of seashells, between kinds of leaves, between the individual letter forms, and between a number of word forms.

FIVES, SIXES, AND SEVENS

Children at ages five, six, and seven are usually still in Piaget's preoperational stage. They largely rely on what is often called preconceptual or intuitive thinking. The preoperational child is dominated by the perceptions of how things appear at the moment and has an apparent inability to consider how they appeared previously or how they can be anticipated to appear. This is sometimes referred to as the child's inability to **decenter.** The child seems to have little capacity for keeping one thing in mind while considering another and, consequently, has no way to make comparisons that might lead to greater understanding. In the following discussion, we give many examples of the characteristics of children's thinking at this stage.

Prior to age seven or eight, children are unlikely to be able to engage in **multiple classification,** the ability to align or sort objects according to several dimensions simultaneously. Thus, children given large and small triangles and circles of red and blue cannot sort them into separate piles, such as large red triangles or small red circles, without intermediary sorting operations. With the assistance of an adult, young children can successfully sort according to any one dimension at a time; for example, they can classify color, putting red and blue in different piles, and can then sort each of those piles into large and small, and

Most kindergarteners can use geoboards with nails and rubber bands to make triangles, squares, and rectangles of all sizes. *(Lee C. Lee)*

each of those into triangles and circles. If they concentrate on one dimension (shape, size, color, or function) they appear to become oblivious to all other dimensions. They can switch and attend wholly to another dimension but will then forget the first.

An early step toward numerical competence is the ability to align objects in one-to-one correspondence. This simple task is far more difficult than it appears from the adult perspective. If you ask a very young child to put two different kinds of objects in lines so that there are just the same number in each line, you may be surprised to find that he or she cannot do so or, at least, cannot continue to do so. Attending to the extension of the lines detracts from attending to their proper alignment. Conversely, the child can arrange two lines of objects but may have quite a different number in each line. Many five-year-olds and some six- and seven-year-olds still have difficulty with this kind of task.

Even when children have developed the ability to align objects in one-to-one correspondence, they may not be aware that the lines continue to have the same number even when the objects are rearranged. They may agree that each has the same number of objects after placing them out in matching one-to-one rows, but if you either spread or bunch the objects in one row, thereby making it longer or shorter than the other, the child may say that one row now has more or fewer objects than the other.

Watch a kindergartener aligning toy cars on top of blocks that they call garages. They line them up carefully, one car on each block, never two on a block, never an empty block. They are aligning them in one-to-one correspondence. If you were to ask them if there are the same number of cars and blocks, they would count both cars and blocks to prove it. If you then helped them clean up at the end of the period, putting cars in one box and blocks in another, and asked as you finish, "There are just the same number of blocks as cars, aren't there?" they may look at the two boxes and say, "No, there are more blocks." They do not keep in mind or even consider that they just finished setting them out one to one. They now confuse volume and number because the blocks, being larger, take up more room.

You may wonder whether children even understand you, since the terms *same* and *more* are difficult but essential to mathematical thinking. However, they will choose a dish with a spread-out array of Cheerios rather than one that actually has more cereal but in a more closely grouped arrangement. "I got the most," each declares as they devour them. Again, they were guided and fooled by "looks" without regard to number.

Piaget calls this the inability to conserve on number. Later, when the children are seven and eight, they will evidently have accumulated enough experience with operations such as counting, rearranging, and recounting to no longer be fooled by appearances. At that point, once they have aligned or counted a group of objects, they will "know" how many there are regardless of how they are subsequently arranged. At this stage, children can be described as having accomplished **conservation** of number, an early indication of movement from preconceptual to operational thinking.

Conservation of number is essential to the development of mathematical abilities. Effective number computation demands an awareness that the number of objects in any grouping remains the same regardless of how radically they are rearranged. A child must comprehend that a given grouping of, for instance, nine objects, remains stable in number whether they are arranged as six and three, as two and seven, or as three, three, and three. For direct instruction in addition, subtraction, and other computational processes to be beneficial, the child must comprehend this concept of invariance of number.

Seriation is the ordering of objects or events according to a given dimension (such as size, weight, or distance from a given point). Just as children spontaneously engage in classification and one-to-one alignment activities, so they also spontaneously align objects according to such criteria as height and width. The difficulty of simultaneously perceiving two or more aspects of things is just as evident in the seriation efforts of preoperational children as in their **classification** efforts. Five-year-olds find it relatively easy to place a series of blocks of differing lengths in sequence from the tallest to the shortest, or vice versa, if allowed to build from one extreme to the other. It is likely that they will have great difficulty, however, in finding the proper slot in an existing sequence for a single, mid-point block. By age seven or so, children will be able to make the bidirectional comparison necessary for such a placement, but before that time this kind of problem just leads to frustration. The task simply demands a cognitive feat of which they are not yet capable.

When using a material such as clay, children younger than age seven or eight often confuse quantity with other physical attributes, such as height, length, or width. They may form two balls that they declare to be "just the same," but on rolling one to be longer or squashing it to be flatter, they will often insist that one or the other contains more or less clay. They lack conservation of mass, according to Piagetian terminology.

Similarly, when children pour liquids from one container to another, they may insist that the volume changes as the surface level falls higher or lower in relation to the proportions of the container. "Here, let's make it more," the children may say, as they pour from a soup-size can into a taller, thinner vial. As they pour it back, they may say, "Now there's not so much." They lack conservation of liquid quantity.

In each of these instances of nonconservation, children fail to see any need to account for what they had previously observed. The **invariance** of given amounts of things is not their concern. Only after repeated experience with **reversibility** (changing from one form to another and back again) will they doubt appearances and begin to conserve, that is, to hold in mind the previous states while viewing the current one.

Children in kindergarten and primary grades, when quizzed about familiar phenomena, describe what they see and assume that this is a sufficient explana-

Creating effects through their own actions is an essential aspect of learning for children. *(Robert Burdick)*

tion, even though there may be contradictions in their statements. For example, in regard to the buoyancy of objects, a child may declare that a leaf floats because it is light, a ship floats because it is wood, a chair sinks because it is wood. Any consideration of the inconsistencies of these explanations is not long lived. The concept of general principles that can be derived through experimentation may still be beyond their comprehension.

Spatial abilities become increasingly differentiated for fives, sixes, and sevens. Terms such as *left, right, opposite from,* and *across from* may not be acquired until age six or seven, however. Children younger than six or seven have little interest in or ability to consider the physical perspective other than their own. One of the authors once tried to read what she considered to be a fascinating book to a group of bright kindergarteners that depicted how a mouse might view a cow differently from various positions within the barn—from above, behind, front, and side. They were totally disinterested. What young children see from their own perspective is of interest to them, and they consequently learn to recognize objects from whatever perspectives they might have used, but the hypothetical appearance of an object from a different position is of little interest to children aged five, and often to older ages as well.

Only a very few children at age six or seven actually use clock hours to regulate or describe their activities, although they are very interested in clocks and watches and in learning to tell time. They are more apt to regulate their time by the passage of regularly occurring events, such as the time between television commercials, than by clock hours.

The number of words understood in others' talk and the number of words mastered sufficiently to be used in one's own conversation continues to grow. Once children recognize that words represent classes of actions, objects, or events, the existence of a new word signifies to them the possibility of something to be learned. After encountering an unknown word, a child is able to seek the referents for it and thus to acquire abstract ideas that might otherwise have been overlooked.

There is considerable evidence that language, or lack thereof, influences thinking modes and behavior. For example, the work of Spivack and Shure (1974) referred to in Chapter 6 suggests that specific language concepts are prerequisite to a child's awareness of alternatives in problem situations. The terms *and, or,* and *not* are prime examples. A child who wants the toy another has but who does not have the language facility to tell herself, "I can grab it, or I can ask for it, or I can wait until he finishes," also does not have the means for considering alternative behaviors. Without the words *or* and *not,* the child cannot consider, "Should I do this *or* this?" or "Should I do this *and not* that?" By learning these rudimentary language concepts, the child gains the means for considering actions as choices rather than as necessities.

Spivack and Shure (1974) suggest that children's awareness of words that are closely related to their behavioral decision making (such as *same, different, happy, sad, mad, if, then,* and *but*) can be developed by initially teaching their meanings in regard to the physical world. They recommend language modeling, such as: "Who is holding the hat? Who is *not* holding the hat?" "Is Carol standing, *or* is she sitting?" "Is a hat the *same* as a flower?" "Is stamping my foot the *same* as patting my head, or is it *different*?" Once such concepts are clearly understood in reference to the physical world, their meanings can be transferred to social behavior, and children can be taught to think in terms of the alternative behaviors available to them. Without such words in their vocabulary, children appear unable to deal with *if-then* relationships such as, "If I do this, then what might happen next?"

Teachers of young children sometimes overestimate children's capacities for understanding language, often by assuming that if children use a word "correctly," their meaning must coincide with the adult usage of the same word. In one classroom, for example, a kindergarten teacher discussed with the children an upcoming parents' meeting that was to be held in their classroom. There was eager discussion of what various children thought parents would like to see when they came for the meeting. Someone even volunteered to make a sign for the rat cage warning the parents that the rat had once bitten someone. However, when asked to take a note to their parents announcing the meeting, several children looked puzzled and asked, "What's a parent?" Investigation showed that the children's meaning for the word *parent* ranged from "some kind of teacher" to "bigger kids like teenagers." Only a few children were sure that a parent is a father or mother. Given the language exposure of this current television generation of children, who talk glibly of ranges, porpoises, Hawaii, the year 2000, and so forth, it is easy to be misled into believing that they know and understand far more than they actually do.

In assessing children's language development, teachers need to be aware that what may appear to be incorrect forms of expression can be quite correct within the dialect used by the child's subgroup. The language patterns of Black English, for example, should not be regarded as incorrect even though they differ from the standard English spoken in schools and in the business and professional world. Children learn the structures of the language they hear. The irregularities that a standard English speaker hears in the Black English dialect are actually quite regular and follow consistent, if somewhat different, language rules.

There is no doubt that the speakers of dialects, whether Black English or others, will benefit from learning the standard English forms. However, according to many linguists, these standard forms should be learned as a language alternative, that is, not to replace the original speech but simply to expand it through a new and different language pattern. Within the black community, the language used by the speakers of Black English will be far more functional and correct than standard English. Children must learn when to say "Susy is sick," "It's his book," or "He's over at the school," and when to say, "Susy, she be sick," "He book," or "He over to the school." A child who feels comfortable with both speech patterns will be able to move easily and competently in either social environment.

Despite early interest in writing and concomitant visual familiarity with written language, most children even at five and six years have little awareness of

AN EXAMPLE OF A YOUNG CHILD'S PROGRESSION INTO READING AND WRITING

To study children's gradual progression from listening and talking to reading and writing, consider the following notations made by teachers in a child-care center about one child's language development from age three to five. These observations illustrate how many small, personalized steps children take in developing their reading and writing skills.

Tommy made some scribbled lines on paper and said, "What's that spell?" He then said, "That's a little monster. He's friendly though."

I wrote Tommy's name. He grabbed some other chalk and made a dozen or so *T*'s. Tried to make the letter *m* but couldn't seem to get the parts together to satisfy himself that they looked right. Kept saying, "Oh, oh, made a goof."

Tommy wrote his name on paper. When I asked if he knew the name of letter *T* he said, "Me."

Played with Alphabet Bingo cards after watching older children playing it. Easily matched most of the letters—except confused *b*'s and *d*'s.

Found all letters in his name from box of wooden letters. Also found *B* for Bobby's name and *J* for Joey's. Asked what the name of their letters were.

Wrote on chalkboard *T, R, B, C, H, I* (made *C* backward).

Tommy looked at my pad and said, "My name's on there." Points to *Tommy*. Says, "Me and Tim have a *T*."

Tommy talked about the names of other children, which all began with *T*—Tim, Terry, Tammy, Tina. Interested in how much Tammy's name looks like his. I also showed him how Tim's name looks when it is written out as *Timmy*. He paid close attention and went to get Tim to come and look too.

Matched *T, H, K, s, f, m, u, y, o, b, q,* and *j* on the letter form board. Asked the name of *q* and whose letter it was. Very interested that we don't have anyone in our group who has a *Q* initial. Evidently had thought there would be a name for every letter.

Wanted me to write on his picture "This is a house." Indicated the left side when I asked him which side of paper the writing should start on.

Tommy asked me to write *Happy Birthday* on the picture he painted for his mother. I said the names of the letters as I wrote them. He commented, "It has two of those, huh?" pointing to the *p*'s, and then added, "I got two the same too, right?"

Used the typewriter. Said his mother has one at home. Found and typed *T* for *Tommy*, *B* for *Brenda* (sister), *M* for *Mother*. Made rows and rows of

periods.

He drew a picture of his mother. Eyelashes first and then *lots* of hair. He then told me to write, "This is Tommy's mother." He spoke slowly waiting for me to write the word before saying the next.

As soon as Tommy saw the alphabet he went over and started putting letters in. Said names of some of the letters as he did so but seemed to pay no attention when I said names of others.

Told me that I make the letter *m* wrong (means different from his mother, she makes it as capital letter—writes his name in all caps). I explained that both ways are right ways and that he can make it either way.

Asked, "Will you read me a story?" He went and got *Rabbit and Skunk and the Scary Rock* and said, "Hi, all you rabbits! What do you do?"

Found his own name and Joey's name on list of children who would ride together in car on the way to the fire station visit.

When he saw *ABC* book said, "Oh, ABC books." Read *A,B,C* and then said *book*.

Tommy dictated story about fight he had had with his brother the night before. Wanted it read to him several times.

Tommy asked me to write a note to his mother and tell her that "I doed hard puzzles."

Found letters for last name from alphabet box (while looking at written model on card). Scrambled all the letters and rearranged in order. Took frequent looks at model as put back in correct sequence (started left, went right).

Wrote whole name looking at model of last name. Resaid each letter after all written.

Played Alphabet Bingo with two cards at once! Says that's how his mom plays Bingo.

Asked if he could have a notebook (loose leaf) for his papers (like Roger's). We found one for him and he made four sheets of "writing" to put in it, full of his name and other letters and pictures.

Tommy found the word *strawberry* on his ice cream cup lid after I showed him how the word *strawberry* looked where it was written on my cup lid. Checked other cup lids to see if they said some other flavor.

Tommy was telling an incident about how he got lost and then "founded." I started to write it down as story. He slowed down to my writing speed. Seemed pleased with the story. Wanted to read it to Joey.

After I read *Billy Goats Gruff* to Tommy and several others, he "told" it all the way through with great dramatic flourish. Kept his audience interested all the way.

Sat with books for forty-five minutes. Asked questions and very involved. Noticed in one picture that the man's feet were facing the wrong way.

Discovered all the places in *Green Eggs and Ham* where it says *Sam.* He differentiated between *Sam*, *see*, and *so*, saying, "Starts like *Sam* but it ain't *Sam*" or "That there ain't *Sam*," or "That there is *Sam*."

Actually read several pages of *Little Bear* using some context to help him figure out words; asked me for help with others. Reread these pages at least three times today.

The preceding notes about Tommy's progress toward becoming a reader and writer are, of course, but a sampling of the many instances in which he had involvement with words and books over two years. These notes are sufficient, however, to represent some principles common to the experiences of many children.

the component sounds of their own speech. They listen and talk, concerned with the meanings of what is said, but give little attention to the structural phonological aspects of language. Although they can and do rhyme words, producing great strings of *goo, doo, poo, roo, soo, moo-moo, poo-poo,* and can detect differences in sound of syllables and words, they have little awareness of the way these sounds are varied to constitute different words or even the separate words within the speech flow. Most children do not become involved in analyzing spoken language into phonemic elements without adult involvement, and it is often difficult for school beginners to understand and comply with an adult's request to do so. Turning something sensible (that has meaning) into something without meaning, as is the case with the isolated **phoneme,** is usually resisted. Meaning is what children naturally search for in oral language, and adults who understand this look for ways to let the meanings in reading materials engage children to recognize words instead of directly trying to teach letter-sound correspondence. Smith (1977), insists, "Children will not learn by trying to relate letters to sounds, partly because the task does not make sense to them and partly because language does not work that way" (p. 387). The relationship between phonemes and letters appears to be easier for children to grasp when they are trying to **encode** their own words into writing than when they are trying to get meaning from print.

The process of learning to read both requires and contributes to a linguistic awareness that language is different from and separate from the actual things and events being represented. When the child becomes aware that what a thing is called is not a feature of that object but instead an arbitrary symbol and that a written symbol (unique arrangement of letters) represents the spoken symbol, the search for patterns of correspondence between the written and spoken symbols is facilitated. The ability to **decode** (derive meaning from print) independent of adult help is greatly accelerated when the child becomes aware, through repeated exposures, that there is some degree of systematic reliability in the way in which letters in combination are used to represent spoken words. Discovering this code and having it confirmed by the meanings that are then derived from print is a great joy to the "new" readers.

The following kind of interchange becomes usual between adults and children learning to decode:

CHILD: I know this word says *egg* because what else could a hen lay? *The hen lays an egg.* Isn't that what it says?

TEACHER: Right! How did you know it was a hen?

CHILD: Well, it has that part (designating *en*) like when I write *The End* when I make those stories, and so I just figured it out.

TEACHER: How did you know that this word is *lays?*

CHILD: Oh, you know. It is the same as your name *(Lay)* with that (points to *s*) on it.

TEACHER: And how did you know what *the* was?

CHILD: I just remembered, and it sounds right.

TEACHER: Good thinking! You figured it all out. Want to read it through again?

Having parents or teachers who prompt, share, enjoy, and confirm their discoveries moves children into reading success. Vygotsky's "zones of proximal development" (as discussed in a prior chapter) are useful to consider in this regard. Vygotsky argued that children's cognition can benefit from interaction with more experienced members of their culture only if the level of interaction falls within the range between what the child can do independently and what can be done with guidance from someone more advanced. Vygotsky spoke not just of literacy acquisition but of all kinds of cognitive development, and learning to read seems to provide a prime example. Admittedly, there is both pleasure and utility for children in discovering independently how letters represent sounds and how letter combinations (such as phonograms *ook* and *ing*) dependably represent word elements. However, myriad pleasurable interchanges with others, such as parents, teachers, or a slightly more experienced peer, talking about "how print works" and about the messages that print conveys are at the heart of the learning to read process. Sometimes adults go beyond the child's "zone of proximal development" to systematically teach the minutiae of the adult conception of phonics and spelling rules as formal systems, forgetting that the child's goal is to convey or get meaning using print.

Encouraging children from the beginning to expect meaning in printed materials and to encode meaningful ideas through drawing and writing makes sense. What we want to do is to help children become successful users of a written language. Nicky, a resourceful kindergartner who found himself in a situation that stretched his meager writing ability to the limit, provides an example. When Nicky arrived home from kindergarten, he found that his mother was not there. He had been given prior permission to go to a friend's house to play but had been told to come home for lunch with his mother first. He waited a while, but when his mother still did not arrive, he fixed and ate a peanut butter sandwich for lunch. When his mother arrived home somewhat later, she found the remnants of Nicky's lunch and a message that used three words. The note said, "I go. Nicky."

SUMMARY

According to Piaget, adaptation through mutual processes of assimilation and accommodation occurs across the life span. The rate of adaptation, however, is particularly rapid in the early years. Cognitive and intellectual development is accelerated, according to Piaget, when the child from age one and a half to two years and upward discovers ways to symbolize aspects of sensorimotor experience so that it can be internally represented. Vygotsky emphasizes the parent-child communication processes, rather than the child's discoveries and inventions, as the roots of thinking and language.

The child, according to the Piagetian view, progresses to the use of language and visual imagery to construct and incorporate mental representations of external reality. Only to the extent that there is a matching internal construction can aspects of the surroundings be meaningfully perceived. Across the preoperational years, children gradually become capable of more effectively representing to themselves the things they experience. They gradually become able to go beyond their immediate perceptions to consider a phenomenon from other perspectives. Also, they begin to take into account what has been previously only perceived. This decentering process occurs within several areas of cognitive and intellectual activity including classification, use of number concepts, seriation, understanding of mass and liquid quantity, causality, space concepts, time concepts, and language usage. Only to the extent that you as a teacher can accurately assess children's current thinking abilities in these areas will you be able to determine the kinds of learning experiences and the kind of demonstrations and verbal interchanges that might further enhance this functioning.

SUGGESTED ACTIVITIES

1 Observe children in restaurants, laundromats, parks, buses, and other common settings within which you find yourself, noting what they notice and how they investigate what they notice. Also, note the reactions of adults to children's attempts to investigate the phenomena around them.

2 Observe adults in interaction with children and note, in writing, all of the instances where it becomes obvious that the adult is not in tune with the child's thinking level. Note, for example, when the adult says something that confuses the child or asks that the child do something of which the child is not capable.

3 Interview (talk with) children of different ages asking the following types of questions. Inquire as to why they give one explanation versus another.

   a Where does the rain (or snow or fog) come from? Why does it rain?
   b Are trees alive? Are people alive? Are chairs alive? Are cars alive? Are airplanes alive? Are birds alive? How do you know?
   c Are dreams real? What are dreams? What happens to dreams when you wake up?
   d What happens to the sun at nighttime?
   e Why aren't children as big as grownups?
   f Where does the water come from that comes out of your faucet?
   g When you see people on TV, where are they really? What happens to the pictures on TV when you turn off your set?
   h Why is it that some grownups are teachers and some are doctors and some are firefighters? Can teachers change and decide to become firefighters?
   i Why do people look so different from each other? Why is it that you don't look just like your friend?
   j Who made this building that we are in right now?

ADDITIONAL READINGS

Bruner, J. S. (1983). *Child's talk: Learning to use language.* New York: Norton.

Caruso, D. A. (1988). Play and learning in infancy: Research and implications. *Young Children, 43*(6), 63–70.

Cazden, C. B. (Ed.). (1981). *Language in early childhood education* (Rev. ed.). Washington, DC: National Association for the Education of Young Children.

Dombro, A. L., & Wallach, L. (1988). *The ordinary is extraordinary: How children under three learn.* New York: Simon & Schuster.

Flavell, J. H. (1985). *Cognitive development.* Englewood Cliffs, NJ: Prentice-Hall.

Forman, G. E. (1977). *The child's construction of knowledge: Piaget for teaching children.* Monterey, CA: Brooks/Cole.

Genishi, C. (1988). Children's language: Learning words from experience. *Young Children, 44*(1), 16–23.

Kantowitz, B., & Wingert, P. (1989, April 17). Special report: How kids learn. *Newsweek, 13*(16), 50–57.

CHAPTER 9

OBSERVING COGNITIVE AND INTELLECTUAL BEHAVIORS

OVERVIEW

This chapter provides very specific questions about the cognitive and **intellectual behaviors** of children you are observing. Follow the same procedures that you used in making your observations and notes on the other aspects of development. You may find that many of the questions posed cannot be answered as readily as those in the other chapters—the children you are observing simply may not behaviorally demonstrate their cognitive abilities within the limited time span you have for observing. You must be especially attuned to the cognitive processes that our questions probe and to the physical and verbal behavior of the children relative to these processes.

In this chapter, as in Chapters 5 and 7 you will find behavioral descriptions of the two children, Steven and Monica, as prepared by a student who used the questions as guides to observation. At the end of the chapter there are recommendations for program planning to facilitate children's cognitive development.

QUESTIONS TO GUIDE OBSERVATIONS

In your observations relative to the following questions you may find that both simple and complex behaviors are present. If so, record only the complex ones. For example, if a child can match word forms, it would be irrelevant to also record that he or she can match identical toys or other objects since the more advanced ability would not be possible if the simpler ones had not been mastered first.

Record all behaviors that might be indicative of the child's thought processes, even if you question whether the child actually understands the actions or words. You may also wish to record in your notes your doubts about your interpretation of the behavior. For this area of development, it will also prove useful to record observations that demonstrate the child's *inability* in a particular area of thinking. For instance, in response to the question regarding the child's performance with one-to-one correspondence, you might wish to note something akin to the following: *Starts to line up pairs of red and black checkers, placing a red one beside each black, but soon loses track of that and simply makes two uneven lines, one red and one black, without one-to-one correspondence.*

1. Classification

1.1 On what basis does the child note objects or situations to be alike or different?

    EXAMPLES:
- Sorts poker chips into red, blue, yellow piles
- Puts animals in barn and people in house while playing with blocks
- Puts all of what he calls "girl stuff" (purses, aprons, dolls) outside of housekeeping corner before he begins to play there
- Finds all words on page that begin with *t*

2. Number

2.1 What is the child's ability to align objects in one-to-one correspondence?

    EXAMPLES:
- Aligns red checkers and black checkers in two lines
- Fastens single dot (from the paper punch) on each of lines she had drawn on paper
- Counts out even amounts for herself and friend by saying, "One for you; one for me; one for you" as she places them in one or other plate.

2.2 What is the child's ability to count objects?

    EXAMPLES:
- Counts pieces of carrot at snack time: "One, two, three, four, five, eight, ten"
- Asks for cotton balls and when asked "How many?" says, "Five," and counts them correctly as placed in her hand
- Counts how many baby chicks have hatched; counts six instead of actual five when one moves to different place

2.3 On what basis does the child make comparisons in total number between groups of objects?

    EXAMPLES:
- Rolls two dice and decides which one she wants (it has more dots) without counting; only visual inspection
- Says, "We got five chairs and only three kids. Wanta sit down?" (to me)

- In comparing his baseball cards with Rob's, puts them out in one-to-one correspondence to see who has more

2.4 Does the child show recognition that different subgrouping arrangements may be made without changing the total number?

EXAMPLES:
- When playing Candyland game with two dice, says, "You got the same as me," when Sue throws the numbers three and three right after he throws four and two
- Shows me that eight glasses can be arranged as four groups of two or two groups of four, but seems unaware of other possible arrangements
- Puts out five Tinker Toy pieces and sings, as she alternately takes some away and replaces them, "Now there are three. Now there are five. Now there are two. Now there are five . . ."

3. Seriation

3.1 On what basis does the child appropriately order objects or events? How many?

EXAMPLES:
- Lines up six bottles according to height
- Says correctly that she is older than Tod and he is older

"Hands on" translates into "I do and I understand." *(Cumberland Hill Associates, Inc.)*

than Benjie; looks puzzled when I ask if she is older than Benjie
- When given an array of six sandpaper sheets of varying roughness, discriminates between two with greatest contrast, but says others are "just the same"

4. Mass and liquid quantity

4.1 How does the child appear to think about mass and liquid quantity?

EXAMPLES:
- Says everyone will "get the same" while pouring juice, and then fills all glasses to comparable heights even though there are glasses of quite different diameters
- When playing with salt clay makes "pancakes" for everyone at table; squashes one down very flat and gives to Tina, saying, "Here, you can have the biggest one."
- Carefully measures out two cans of water for animals into their watering dishes so they will "all have the same"

5. Causality

5.1 What, if any, explanations does the child either seek or give for physical phenomena? For his own or other's behavior?

EXAMPLES:
- "I've got to wear my raincoat because it's raining"
- "It's raining today 'cause the sun got so tired of shining all the days"
- "It broke 'cause she was too rough and it's fragile" (teacher used *fragile* earlier)

6. Space concepts

6.1 What evidence does the child give of awareness of space, position, location, or spatial perspectives?

EXAMPLES:
- Says to self upon standing back and looking at opening she has made in block construction, "That wagon ain't goin' to git in there"
- Asks, "Why you put my pictures up so high? I want them down here"
- Says, at sharing time, "We going to visit Grandma out in Wyoming. It's so far we'll stay in a motel two nights"

7. Time concepts

7.1 What evidence does the child give of awareness of time perspectives (past or future) or of the duration of happenings or activities?

EXAMPLES:
- Says, "I liked that swimming yesterday. Can we go today?"
- Says to Robin, "I will call you up when `Mr. Roger's' done" (meaning after the "Mr. Rogers" TV program)
- Says, "Who was borned first, me or my mother?"

8. Spoken language

8.1 Vocabulary

8.1.1 What is the child's use of relational and opposing terms? (Consider terms such as and, or, not, same, different, more, less, instead, if, then, because. Cite sentences in which terms are used.)

EXAMPLES:
- When asked whether he wanted fork or spoon, says, "I want a fork *and* a spoon"
- When hat is misplaced, cries because one offered to replace it is said to be "not the *same*—it's too big"
- Says indignantly, "I'm *not* little"

8.1.2 What words in the child's vocabulary appear to represent the greatest degree of differentiation regarding the following categories? (Cite the words that the child uses.)

EXAMPLES:
- animals: *dog, cat, rat, chipmunk, alley cat, Siamese cat, cougar*
- people: *grown-up, kid, baby, mommy, daddy*
- family relationships: *sister, brother, grandma, auntie, uncle*
- colors: *red, black, yellow*
- space: *big, little, over here, right there, someplace*
- time: *now, today, yesterday, when I'm big, at three thirty*
- shape: *round, circle, square, triangle*
- containers: *box, cup, dish, suitcase*
- machinery: *lawnmower, vacuum, mixer, fire engine pump*
- vehicles: *truck, car, jeep, boat, jet, helicopter, Ford*
- clothes: *coat, shirt, pants, socks, shoes, jacket, hat, raincoat, leotards*
- weather: *raining, hot, cold, sleet*
- foods: *apple, milk, ice cream, hot dog, catsup, chili*
- furniture: *chair, table, bed, rocker, bean bag chair*
- body parts: *arm, leg, head, eyes, nose, mouth, knee, hand, fist*
- body movements: *run, walk, jump, go away*
- feelings: *happy, don't like, like, mad, fun*
- toys: *ball, doll, blocks, gun, Steiff bear*
- liquids: *water, milk, orange soda, juice, drink*
- plants: *tree, flower, leaf, poinsettia*

8.2 Sentence complexity and variation

What is the evidence of the child's ability to use language in functionally varied ways? (From records you make of the child's oral expression, select examples of differing types of sentence structure and syntactical forms to show the variety of language the child is capable of producing.)

EXAMPLES:
- I'm going to be a nurse.
- What's that?
- The girl who came here is my sister.
- He got too heavy, so I left him there.
- Put that down.

9. Written language

9.1 *What evidence is there of the child's knowledge of left-to-right orientation in written language?*

EXAMPLES:
- When copies words (his own or other's names) starts at left and goes right
- Points to left when I ask him where to start writing
- Asks, "Where you start?" when starting to write

9.2 *What evidence is there of the child's abilities in auditory discrimination? (Does the child note or produce rhyming words or sounds? Does the child note whether words begin, end with, or contain similar sounds?)*

EXAMPLES:
- Says "pop, hop, slop," laughs and says it several more times
- Supplies rhyming endings when I pause at the end of the line in reading poetry
- Says, "You can hear that `s-s-s` when you say *Miss*"

9.3 *What evidence is there of the child's ability to make visual discriminations? Between objects? Two-dimensional forms? Pictures? Letters? Numerals? Word forms?*

EXAMPLES:
- Sorts shells according to similar appearance
- Correctly finds all the *w*'s on the page
- Confuses *q* and *g* in Alphabet Bingo game

9.4 *What evidence is there of the child's awareness of how written words represent spoken words?*

EXAMPLES:
- Asks, "What does that say?" about sign on the door
- Asks me to write on his painting, "This is Jimmy with his baby sister," and points to each word as he "reads" it back to me after I have written it
- Says to child who is looking at pictures and telling story, "Are you reading the words or making it up?"

9.5 *What evidence is there of the child's awareness of how letters represent sounds?*

EXAMPLES:
- Writes letter *v* and says, "Does that say *m-m-m*?" and when told that it does not, says, "What letter is for *m-m-m*?"
- Tries to figure out the word *pop* by saying to self *p-p-p*
- When asked how to write *car*, I tell him *c* and *a* and then suggest that he could figure out the last letter by

Some children write more easily when they use typewriters or computer keyboards. *(Steve Sartori)*

the way the word *car* sounds, and he writes *r* (very pleased with himself)

9.6 *What evidence is there that the child recognizes (or can quickly figure out) some word forms? What words (or types of words)?*

EXAMPLES: ▪ Goes through several pages of *Cat and Dog* book finding all the places it says either *cat* or *dog*; also identifies *I, see, can, go, and, to,* and *the*
  ▪ Reads several pages of *Are You My Mother?* and only asks for help with *will* and *with*
  ▪ Knows most words from high-frequency list; only confuses *what, who; that, was, saw; there, where; with, will; did, put*

9.7 *What evidence is there that the child is able to obtain messages (meanings) from written language?*

EXAMPLES: ▪ Laughs as reads funny parts of story to herself
  ▪ Asks for clarification when things do not make sense to him—asks, "What does that mean?" about the line *Look into my eyes*
  ▪ Looks at sign on the classroom door that says, "Don't forget to put Jell-O in the refrigerator" and says to friend, "Oh, oh. The Jell-O!"

SAMPLE OBSERVATIONS: STEVEN AND MONICA

As in the prior two chapters, the case studies are from reports on observations of two preschoolers in the same classroom, Steven and Monica.

Name   Steven
Age   Four years, two months

Classification   Steven can sort by color but not by shape or size. He knows the color name for red and frequently says, "Dat's red." When making pudding, the teacher asked if two of the cups were the same (a cup and a quarter-cup). Steven pointed to the cup measure and said, "Higher."

Number   When counting, Steven said, "five, eight, two." In passing out crackers at snack time, he left out some people and gave more than one to some.

Mass and Liquid Quantity, Causality, Seriation   There was little opportunity to observe Steven's abilities with seriation, mass or liquid quantity, or causality. He arranged stairsteps with the large blocks putting them in seriated order. His interaction with water, salt, clay, and sand, among other substances, were seemingly primarily sensory experiences. There was no obvious representation or comparison by amount, weight, or other criteria of that type.

Space Concepts   Steven's concepts of spatial relations are indicated by the following: After snack he said to the teacher regarding replacement of extra cups, "That one don't go there," and in response to a question from the teacher about where the bike could be parked out of the way, he said, "Put it over there under the tree."

Time Concepts   Steven's understanding of time concepts is hard to judge due to his very limited verbal skills. He was observed saying the following, however: "We have snack now?" to teacher after nap time (correct assumption) and "We go home now?" to the teacher at the end of the day (again correct). There was no evidence of a concept of yesterday, tomorrow, future, or past.

Spoken Language   Steven's spoken language is, as previously noted, very limited. It sometimes appears that he is communicating with others in the group more than is actually the case since he seems to speak rather often. In reality, he often is echoing the talk of others. He often imitates their voice fluctuations and makes noises but does not use real words. He does use communicative language periodically as well, mostly in three- to four-word sentences. Examples of Steven's speech are as follows:

"I go now."
"My mommy here?"

"Me want that."
"Me not do it."
"We play fireman."
"I burning."
"I caught in fire."
"Come on you, Mark."

Steven primarily observes during teacher-directed activities. When asked a question, his answer is more than likely to be, "Because," "Yes," or "No."

Written language   Steven was not observed to examine or comment on written language during the periods of observation.

Name   Monica
Age   Four years, seven months

Classification   Monica showed several different ways of classifying objects during my observations. She sorted dishes and pots and pans in the kitchen area and put each type of article in its proper place. She sorted blocks according to size and shape so that they could be put away properly. She sorted some blocks according to color and made a tower out of each color. All these skills seemed to be well integrated into her repertoire.

Number   Monica was noted to count as high as thirteen. It is not known if she can count higher as she ran out of objects to count. When looking at a picture a teacher held up, she told the teacher that there were three girls and two boys in the picture. She put fifteen blocks in groups of three and then in groups of four, obtaining an additional block for the final grouping of four. She counted the fingers of others during story time. She seems very comfortable with number concepts and frequently comments on the number of objects present or how they are arranged within a group.

Seriation   Monica arranged the miniature dinosaur figures from largest to smallest. She also discussed with a friend which child in the group is "tallest," "next tallest," and "next tallest."

Mass and Liquid Quantity   When making pudding, Monica commented when the measuring cups were full. During snack time she commented on the fact that her friend's cracker was "bigger" than hers; her friend's cracker was broken up into bits.

Causality   The following statements were recorded as indicating Monica's awareness of causality in differing situations:

"I had to wear my coat today because it's cold."
"I wore my good dress today 'cause I'm goin' to the doctor."

Ordinary objects found in nature stimulate interest and inquiry. *(Barbara Daley)*

"Why is the grass wet out here?"

"That (paper) bends because it is not strong. You should have cardboard." (In speaking of a stand-up paper doll that kept buckling over)

Space Concepts   Monica uses the concepts of *over there, far away, close, here, between, next to,* and *in back of* correctly.

Time Concepts   During observations Monica showed the following under-standing of time:

"My mother is coming to help tomorrow."

"After rest time is snack time, right?"

"I was late today because Mommy had the washer going and we had to wait for it to finish."

"I want to paint later today."

Spoken Language   Monica uses the spoken word very effectively in order to meet her needs.

Expressing needs: "I am hungry." "I am tired." "I have to go to the bathroom."
Expressing feelings: "I like you." "This is fun."

Expressing curiosity: "What is this used for?" "What are we going to do next?" "What is in the box?" "Where is Mrs. Nolan?"

Expressing command: "You go over there." "Come here right now." "Put that down."

Monica uses language and grammatical forms with ease. As illustrated above, Monica can use speech as a tool for description, explanation, and questioning.

Written Language   There is some evidence that Monica is aware of print and its use. She asks, "Where does it say___?" when listening to stories. She was also observed making letters, some reversed, unconventionally formed, and without horizontal alignment, on her drawing. She said to me as she noticed that I was looking at her paper, "That's the story about it." The letters were *H, M, O, L,* and *E.* There were a lot of *E*'s.

FROM OBSERVATION TO PLANNING

On the basis of your observations of children's cognitive and intellectual behaviors, you will be able to make some initial judgments about the tasks and problems that will interest and satisfy them and about the kind of instruction you might provide in your interactions with them. It will increasingly become second nature to take in information about children's behavioral repertoires from which you can draw inferences about the kind of experiences to provide for them. In making transitions from the assessment of children's current abilities to deciding about the experiences and instruction you as a teacher might provide, there are four guidelines you should consider (or reconsider):

1 Instead of trying to push the child on to more advanced functioning, provide new contexts, new "twists" for the application of his or her existing repertoire. The opportunity to adapt what has already been mastered to a variety of situations leads to consolidation and confidence. Ample opportunities to use current abilities should usually precede expectations for further achievement.

2 Most children younger than age seven or eight benefit far less from following adult directions than from structuring their own actions. Adults can use children's initiations and activities as the basis for developing vocabulary, concepts, and insights. Children are more likely to attend to and profit from such interactions than from more formal instruction.

3 Children will benefit from opportunities to observe and interact with peers who are operating at a slightly more advanced level than theirs. The modeling of a child with a more advanced thinking and language pattern and with skills that are almost, but not quite, within the ability level of the less advanced child provides a potent stimulus to cognitive and intellectual development.

4 The preoperational child's intellectual and cognitive development will proceed better if there is an abundance of zest, joy, pleasure, surprise, and fun in learning situations. This is in contrast to monotony, boredom, and grimness.

Play and gratification are the basis for all growth, including growth in cognitive functioning. For a child who is really learning there is no separation of work and play. There is no need for and, in fact, great disadvantage in equating learning with the absence of pleasure. The more playful the child can be while learning, the better the learning will go. Perhaps this is also true of adults. What do you think?

Steven appears to have a significant start in a number of cognitive areas even though his development is clearly delayed in comparison to a norm group. Giving him more opportunities to do what he is known to do successfully will be desirable—he can be asked to sort by color (with various materials), asking him to pick out everything red and allowing him to tell some of the numbers for counting.

His abilities to use puzzles (with help) as noted in Chapter 5 and his awareness, however limited, of spatial arrangements as recorded in these observations may suggest the desirability of using easy variations of activities that require the manipulation of materials. Parquetry blocks, cylinder set-ins, and giant Tinker Toys may be successfully used.

Capitalizing on Steven's interest in observing and imitating the other children seems promising. It may be useful to use some simple echo games in which more mature expression plus some new vocabulary are used. He will probably enjoy this, and it may help in language repertoire building. Talking with Steven as often as possible about the people and things around him is also very desirable.

Monica's concepts and skills will be enhanced by involvement in a wide range of activity possibilities (sociodramatic play, art, music, and natural and physical sciences). If the adults with whom she interacts are skilled in active listening and descriptive feedback (see Chapter 15), she will likely flourish in her cognitive development. Opportunities to interact with others in concept attainment activities will also be useful. She will benefit from opportunities to observe "talk into print" activities. A continued exposure to excellent children's books will be important for Monica. Opportunities to observe, even if only occasionally, slightly older children who are beginning to read books and other material independently should also prove beneficial.

SUMMARY

This chapter has presented questions on cognitive and intellectual behaviors. Obtaining behavioral indicators of functioning in these areas is difficult within the span of a few brief observations. Nevertheless, the observational effort has attuned you to the dimensions that should prove useful as you have more extensive contacts with children. You probably were particularly aware of the differences between Steven and Monica in cognitive abilities, as illustrated in the behavioral summaries. Accommodating the needs of both of these children within the same classroom would be difficult in a program designed for uniform performance. Instead, the program must accommodate diversity and provide the opportunity for each child, regardless of his or her functioning, to use existent repertoire in new ways and in new contexts. It is likely that such a program would have multiple ages grouped together and would provide options for children to structure their own actions. An abundance of zest, joy, pleasure, surprise, and fun are essential components for cognitive growth. Observations of children's interests and performance levels are useful in planning a program that promotes play and gratification, the basis for all growth, including growth in cognitive functioning.

SUGGESTED ACTIVITIES

1 Summarize the similarities and differences between children you have observed using the guides from this chapter. Compare children of differing age, gender, and socioeconomic background.
2 Arrange with another class member to observe the same child, using the guides provided in this chapter, and compare notes on what you have seen.
3 Combine observations made of the same child using guides from Chapters 5, 7, and 9 and summarize in a full case study. Include evaluative statements and recommendations for programming for this child. Also consider the following questions:
   a How do you personally feel about the child's behaviors? Would you enjoy having the child in your classroom? What aspects of behavior would you find appealing? difficult? How would you react to the behaviors if you were the child's teacher?
   b What experiences do you feel would be most beneficial for the child?
4 Discuss the case study you have prepared from your observations with your own parents (or others who were responsible for your care as a child) and ask for their reactions to the child's behaviors. Their handling of you as a child will probably parallel what they recommend for this child. If so, consider whether there are insights for you into your own orientation.

ADDITIONAL READINGS

Kamii, C. (1982). *Number: In preschool and kindergarten.*Washington, DC: National Association for the Education of Young Children.

Kamii, C., & DeVries, R. (1978). *Physical knowledge in preschool education: Implications of Piaget's theory.* Englewood Cliffs, NJ: Prentice-Hall.

Mehler, J., & Fox, R. (Eds.). (1985). *Neonate cognition: Beyond the blooming buzzing confusion.* Hillsdale, NJ: Erlbaum.

Piaget, J. (1951). *The origins of intelligence in children.* New York: Basic Books.

Piaget, J., & Inhelder, B. (1969). *The psychology of the child.* New York: Basic Books.

Tudge, J., & Caruso, D. (1988). Cooperative problem solving in the classroom. *Young Children, 44*(1), 46–52.

PART THREE

CLASSROOM ORGANIZATION AND MANAGEMENT

As a teacher, you will have responsibility for organizing and managing a classroom, including the arrangement and use of space, the organization of time segments, the selection and use of equipment and materials, and the establishment of ground rules for children's behavior. Organizing all these elements can be likened, in some respects, to the work of an orchestra conductor, who must coordinate and bring harmony out of various musical elements. Different educational effects are achieved through different arrangements of the basic program elements. Organizational skill depends on the ability, first, to create a plan and, second, to implement that plan to achieve particular educational goals for a diverse group of children with varying backgrounds and needs. Excellent communication skills are necessary to work with children, coworkers, and parents in the implementation of a coherent plan.

Chapter 10 discusses three different orientations to child development—behaviorist, maturationist, and constructivist—and the types of program features favored within each orientation. Chapter 11 describes five specific program models that are currently popular and that represent differing perspectives about what programs for young children should accomplish and how they should be conducted. From these two chapters you will gain a sense of the alternatives available for consideration and their supporting rationales.

Chapters 12, 13, 14, and 15 focus on your own preparation for classroom teaching responsibility. In Chapter 12, techniques are discussed for establishing the physical environment of the classroom, the schedule, and guidance and discipline techniques. Strategies for teaching, in lesson format and in informal dialogue, are presented in Chapter 13. Chapter 14 will help you appreciate the diversity of children for whom you will have responsibility and to assist them in understanding and learning about human differences and commonalities. In Chapter 15, skills for communication are further elaborated so that you may practice, master, and apply them in work with children, their parents, and your coworkers. The value of developing these skills and perspectives *before* you begin to teach cannot be overemphasized.

CHAPTER 10

DIFFERING ORIENTATIONS TO EARLY CHILDHOOD EDUCATION

OVERVIEW

For each historical period, for each different society, for each individual family, the view of the child held at a particular time usually feels "right and natural" to those who hold it. Some of these differing perspectives were presented in Chapter 2. Contrasting views produce feelings that range from vague uneasiness to outright rejection or hostility. Yet if the contrasting views are added to one's original conception, they usually enrich one's appreciation and understanding and make possible more flexible and intelligent decision making.

In the following discussion, we urge you to become familiar enough with the perspectives concurrently held so that you can understand how the adherents of each arrive at their conclusions about the type of program most advantageous for young children. Three contrasting orientations to child development—behaviorist, maturationist, constructivist—will be presented. Some program characteristics associated with each orientation are also discussed. In the latter portion of this chapter, program models are presented to illustrate how varied the experiences concurrently provided for young children can be.[*]

BEHAVIORIST ORIENTATION

One orientation, often referred to as **behaviorist** or **environmentalist,** can be historically traced from John Locke to Edward Thorndike and subsequently to B. F. Skinner, the formulator of the principles of operant psychology. As pointed out

---

[*]Specific guidelines for doing classroom interaction observations in a fieldwork setting are provided in Part 3 of Appendix 1.

in Chapter 2, John Locke viewed the human infant's mind as a tabula rasa, a blank slate upon which a variety of experiences could be imposed to create quite different sorts of development. The view that external influences can **shape** the developing child and therefore should be carefully arranged to create desired outcomes is central to the tradition of environmentalism.

Behaviorists are primarily concerned with determining how environmental influences shape particular kinds of behavior in an individual. They have traditionally examined how events that either precede or follow particular behaviors appear to increase or decrease the occurrence of those behaviors. Their goal is the better arrangement and management of those events so that desirable behaviors can be encouraged and undesirable behaviors eliminated or decreased.

Behaviorists' views of the child seldom include attention to such factors as the child's self-concept, physical maturation patterns, or internal thinking processes. Behaviorists tend to think that it is irrelevant to try to infer how a child feels or how he or she is viewing the world, that only observable behavior is worthy of study. They feel quite justified in this emphasis, since it has been demonstrated that behavior-management techniques are effective in bringing about and maintaining specific behavior changes. B. F. Skinner and his colleagues, in studies of both animal and human behavior, have repeatedly demonstrated that to influence behavior you need only have knowledge of (1) what is rewarding or reinforcing and (2) how to systematically schedule these reinforcements according to empirically derived principles. No knowledge of feelings or motivations is necessary to alter behavior, they point out, only knowledge of behavior.

A particular person's reinforcements are determined by observation, by noting those stimuli (events or objects) that seem to increase the desired behavior. For example, if it is noted that a child tends to persist with an activity after receiving a smile or verbal praise, it is thought likely that these social acts are reinforcing for that child. Or perhaps a food or trinket reward or a special privilege is more effective in maintaining or encouraging a given behavior.

According to Skinnerians, there are two kinds of behaviors. The first are *reflexive behaviors* (such as knee jerk or eye blink); these behaviors are not under volitional control. The second are **operant behaviors;** these are engaged in voluntarily, presumably to bring about some effect on the environment that is considered desirable and rewarding.

Consider the following example: Jimmy, age three, is hungry. At first he cries and fusses but is ignored by his mother. He then tries unsuccessfully to reach into the cookie jar for a cookie. Finally, he says, "I want a cookie." His past experience has taught him that *all* these behaviors will lead to his being given a cookie. In this instance, only the asking behavior proves effective in achieving his cookie goal. Since the asking was instrumental in producing food, he is more likely to use verbal requests when next hungry and is less likely to attempt the other strategies. If, on the other hand, the crying and fussing had proved successful in bringing forth attention and food, the frequency of these behaviors would then be maintained or increased.

Thus, according to Skinnerians, it is not preceding stimulus conditions (in this case hunger) but rather the effects brought about in prior situations under similar conditions that lead to the particular choice of behaviors. The frequency with which one engages in any behavior, according to this line of thinking, depends on the effects that have been produced by the same or similar actions in the past. This is a critical point: What must be studied in understanding the behavior of others is the effects that follow the behavior.

From this perspective, a teacher, knowing this, can systematically lead a pupil to desired behaviors or learnings. Whatever the child finds reinforcing must be made **contingent** (dependent) on the desired behavior. The child's behavior is thus shaped by denying something he or she wants or enjoys (reward) until a desired behavior (teacher objective) is made or approximated.

The implementation of these principles requires four steps. The first is clarification of the desired behavior. The second is the determination of the closest approximation to the desired behavior that the child is already exhibiting. The third is the determination of what is reinforcing to the child. And the fourth is making those reinforcements contingent on the child's behaving in the desired way. If these four steps are successfully completed, the principles of **behavior modification** can be applied toward specified behaviors, including learning goals.

Several models that are behaviorist in orientation have become well known and are widely used. These include the Direct Instruction Model (also referred to as the Academic Preschool, DISTAR, and Engelmann-Becker Follow Through Model), Behavior Analysis, and PEP-Primary Education Program.

Programs most compatible with the behaviorist view of development often have the following five characteristics:

1 There is a focus on very specific objectives.
2 Disciplines or subject fields are viewed as sources of knowledge that must be simplified (broken into pieces) and carefully graded or sequenced for transmission to children. The sequence is "preprogrammed" so that each step provides a gradual transition from simpler to more complex tasks.
3 The teacher very actively directs children's activity. Intensive training, especially in areas where children seem "retarded" or weak in comparison with their age peers, is seen as especially necessary. It is the teacher's role to direct, correct, and reinforce behavior in desired directions.
4 The learner is shaped by the teacher through reinforcement. It is the teacher's role to control reinforcements to the children, thereby directing them into desired learnings and behaviors.
5 Children are moved as quickly as possible from concrete (involvement with real materials and actions) to abstract manipulations of subject matter. Much of the instruction is verbal, either oral or written. Language is seen as synonymous with thought, so training in correct language usage and logical statements is viewed as the main avenue for promoting intellectual development.

PRINCIPLES OF REINFORCEMENT

An understanding of principles of reinforcement will prove helpful in analyzing behavioral forces at work in family interactions and in classrooms.

Positive reinforcement

A **reinforcement** is defined as anything that increases the frequency of a given behavior. **Positive reinforcement** often consists of rewards such as attention, praise, and recognition. These social reinforcers are most effective for young children whose family lives have connected these rewards with the gratification of primary needs (such as feeding, affection, and warmth). Where these associations have not been formed, as in chronically disorganized or deprived families, smiles or praise from a teacher may have little, if any, effect on child behavior. In these cases, physical materials such as food or toys are more likely to serve as effective positive reinforcers. One should not assume that what is reinforcing for oneself or for most other people will necessarily be reinforcing for everyone. Only careful observation of the rewards that actually increase the frequency of a given behavior can produce dependable information regarding reinforcement possibilities.

In addition to food, objects, and social acts, positive reinforcements can come from the opportunity to engage in particular kinds of activities. This principle, as expressed by Premack (1959; 1965), states that voluntary, high-frequency behaviors can be used to reinforce low-frequency behaviors. Thus, a child can be influenced to spend more time practicing writing skills, an activity that he or she would not normally engage in, if rewarding activities, such as outside play or access to toys, are made contingent on demonstrated accomplishment in writing. To apply the **Premack principle,** a teacher must carefully observe a child to determine his or her preferred activities so that they can be used to reinforce other, low-frequency behaviors the teacher considers desirable. To illustrate: If a second-grader uses Lego blocks, the teacher could increase the child's involvement in writing by making opportunities to play with Lego blocks contingent upon writing involvement. A child's preferred activities can thus be used as reinforcers just like food, trinkets, social approval, or other privileges. Proof that a reinforcer works is determined by whether or not it increases the specific behaviors made contingent on it.

Negative reinforcement

Negative reinforcement has also been demonstrated to alter the frequency of behaviors. Negative reinforcements involve the cessation of some undesirable stimulus (such as pain or teacher scolding). For example, if you want children to walk in straight lines, you might scold them whenever they do otherwise, until they do as you wish. If they find your scolding unpleasant, they may conform to your expectations of walking in lines because they are reinforced by the cessation of scolding. You should be aware, however, that just as individual children vary in what is positively reinforcing, so they vary in what is negatively reinforcing. To some children, scolding may not be particularly aversive; a few may even be positively reinforced by the attention scolding produces and may therefore be led to increase rather than decrease their objectionable behavior.

Nonreinforcement

When a behavior brings no reinforcement, it will gradually be dropped. Thus, the prime advice is: *Ignore undesired behavior. Pay no attention to it.* To eliminate undesired behaviors most effectively, however, you should also positively reinforce any opposite and desirable behaviors. If a child's whining behavior is to be reduced, for instance, it is best ignored (without scolding or otherwise giving any attention). At the same time, any cheerful positive acts by the child should immediately and consistently be followed with attention, privilege, or whatever is reinforcing to the child.

Punishment

Punishment refers to the application of something aversive (such as scolding, spanking, or deprivation of a privilege) as the consequence of particular undesirable actions. You may find the difference between negative reinforcement and punishment difficult to understand. Think of punishment as an aversive consequence of a child's noncompliance with parents' or teachers' wishes and of negative reinforcement as the child's ridding him- or herself, through compliance, of something he or she finds aversive. The latter is more dependably effective than punishment.

For punishment to be effective, it must be severe and applied immediately after the objectionable act. Although the effects of punishment on subsequent behavior are not totally clear, there is agreement that the use of positive or negative reinforcement and nonreinforcement are far more effective. Unless punishment quickly modifies the undesirable behavior, there is little likelihood that its continuation will eventually produce the desired modification.

Schedules of reinforcement

The other important aspect of reinforcement technology is the **scheduling of reinforcements.** If a reinforcement is applied to every instance of the target (desired) behavior, it is described as **continuous reinforcement.** To most effectively bring about behavior change, continuous reinforcement is initially more effective. This requires great vigilance on the part of the teacher when attempted in a classroom. If, for example, you wished to use reinforcements to get a child to pay attention to your presentations, you would try to note and reward each instance of the desired attending behavior. In practice this is difficult. Nevertheless, continuous reinforcement is generally more effective than **intermittent reinforcement** in initiating a modification in behavior. Skinner and his followers have also thoroughly investigated the effectiveness of different schedules of intermittent reinforcements.

The first aspect of intermittent reinforcement is the interval of time between reinforcements. One approach is to have reinforcements occur according to a **fixed interval schedule** (such as every two minutes, two days, or two months). An example of fixed intervals might be the teacher who each afternoon gives out "stars" or praise for the day's accomplishments. In contrast would be the teacher who at varying, unpredetermined intervals throughout the day praises or otherwise rewards children's work efforts. The latter is called a **variable interval schedule.**

The second aspect of reinforcement schedules involves the number of responses or behaviors necessary for each reinforcement to occur—this is referred to as a **ratio schedule.** Instead of reinforcing according to a particular time schedule, the teacher may give out gold stars or praise on the basis of some predetermined amount of accomplishment, such as a finished puzzle or a correctly done row of number problems. This is called a **fixed ratio schedule.** If the ratio of responses necessary for reinforcement keeps changing, this is called a **variable ratio schedule.** For example, the teacher would initially praise each correct response and then would gradually begin to reserve praise until successively larger groups of correct responses were made.

The varying interval and ratio schedules have predictable effects that are important for you to understand. To bring about behaviors that will persist across time, the most effective reinforcement schedules will be those with variable intervals rather than fixed intervals and variable ratios rather than fixed ratios. Thus, although continuous reinforcement of specific behaviors will most rapidly bring about initial modifications, varying reinforcement schedules (interval and ratio) have proved more successful than fixed reinforcement schedules in maintaining those behaviors. The basic reinforcement principle is to make rewards contingent on behaviors in a person's current repertoire that are closest to the desired behavior, and simultaneously, to avoid reinforcing actions that are incompatible with the desired behavior.

Most behaviorist programs have a traditional academic focus and are directed toward success in traditional schools; however, this is not necessarily the case with all program developers of this persuasion. Others may emphasize the early or remedial acquisition of social skills, foreign languages, musical skills, or athletic skills. The common view is that the child's own interests and inclinations are not as important in constructing a program as the adult conceptions of what the child can become, given appropriately structured and managed experiences. Although behaviorists may not always agree on what the child should become, they would agree that it is the adult prerogative and responsibility to make that determination and then to find the most effective and efficient means for structuring programs to bring about the desired state.

MATURATIONIST ORIENTATION

The **maturationist** orientation contrasts sharply with that of the behaviorist. The focus of maturationists is on those aspects of development that are least influenced by environmental forces. They emphasize regularities with which all humans develop, and they argue that what comes from within the child is the most important aspect of development. Although environmental forces are seen as possible supporters or inhibitors of internal growth potential, the primary direction of that growth is seen as coming from within. Parental, educational, and societal influences are consequently viewed as aiding or facilitating growth rather than as directing it.

The maturationist sees a child's behavior at any particular time as primarily reflecting one stage in a continuing and largely unalterable unfolding process that is universally experienced. Faulty development, as evidenced by a child's unhappiness or maladjustment, is attributed to interference with the child's capacity to develop according to his or her own timetable and according to his or her own needs. The French philosopher Jean Jacques Rousseau, cited in Chapter 2 as a believer in the basic goodness of human instincts, was an early maturationist. His expectation was that children, if given the opportunity to grow in natural ways, would develop to their full potential and that teachers or parents should therefore primarily avoid impeding a child's natural inclinations.

This orientation has often been expressed by using the analogy of the growing plant. Unless it lacks basic life supporting conditions, the plant will sprout and thrive and grow to its maximum potential. The gardener must simply respond to evidence of its needs for water and sunshine, and the plant will become what it can become. There is no need for the gardener to try to alter or hasten its growth; the consequences will either be unsuccessful or undesirable. Educators of the maturationist persuasion liken themselves to the gardener caring for the plant's basic needs but leaving the growing process to the plant and the universal growth forces within it.

Sigmund Freud and many of his followers in psychoanalysis can be considered proponents of a maturationist orientation. They viewed the primary influences on development as coming from within the child and as being universally experienced. Erik Erikson, for example, examines the way the child is able to face a series of **psychosexual conflicts** that are thought to be central to the maturational process. Particular discrete behaviors would not be seen by psychoanalysts as important, except as they reflect a person's conflicts at a particular growth stage.

Although very general guidelines can be derived from the maturationist's view of the child, there is little direct and immediate action proposed for altering or influencing children's development. The educator is advised to care for the child's expressed or observed needs rather than attempting to directly and systematically alter those behaviors that might be viewed by some as evidence of faulty developmental progress.

Some within the maturationist tradition, such as Arnold Gesell and his coworkers at Yale University, have focused on the regularities of children's growth and development across time. Over many decades, they have sought to determine, through observation, testing, and parental interviewing, what children can do at various ages. From these studies have come carefully derived **norms** that describe children's characteristics and abilities at various age levels.

dren as they show interest and readiness, but instruction that is poorly timed and imposed on an unwilling child is considered not only likely to fail but also to have a negative effect. When programs are provided, therefore, maturationists prefer to foster the development of the "whole" child in directions inherent within him or her, rather than toward specific isolated objectives, academic or otherwise.

Maturationists are in relative agreement about the following general principles:

- Children will spontaneously select activities appropriate to their developmental level if given a range of options and a minimum of adult intervention.
- A variety of materials should be available for children to use to nourish their development. Adults should provide materials that are appropriate to the child's interests and stage of development. If children do not use the materials provided, this is an indication that the materials are inappropriate to their particular developmental level.
- Specific types of activities should be available at regular time periods each day, with a balance between active and inactive, group and individual, directed and nondirected activities. The particular balance is determined by age, the amounts of group and directed activities increasing with age.
- Children should not be pressured or enticed to perform beyond their current level; if they are given an unpressured, nurturing atmosphere, they will gradually develop their capabilities in all important areas.
- The optimum placement for children is with a group of peers at the same developmental level. When maturational readiness indicates successful participation at the next level, the child should be advanced. Children who are developmentally delayed or are suffering from handicaps that limit their functioning are best grouped with others like themselves.
- There should be only a minimum of correction of children's efforts in work or play. Actions or responses are "right" given the child's developmental level and experiences. Additional real experiences can be provided to correct erroneous impressions or to develop more advanced skills. These, however, should be presented as possibilities rather than as requirements. What the teacher does not do in directing children's actions is often viewed as more important than what the teacher does. Acceptance, gentle guidance, and facilitation of children's wants and interests are desirable, but directing, correcting, or actively modifying behavior are questionable or undesirable.
- Children primarily respond to growth forces within themselves. It is the teacher's role to help them understand and accept themselves. Given a nurturing and accepting environment, outcomes for children will ultimately be positive even though particular phases may be experienced as difficult.
- Experiences seen as desirable and feasible for children should be provided for them without explicit contingencies. Attempts to sway children from their natural inclinations by systematically providing reinforcements is shortsighted and counterproductive to overall development.

Many maturationists assume that quality education depends on classes organized around similar developmental levels—the key to effective schooling is to place each child in a class with others who are ready for similar learnings. According to Arnold Gesell and his successors at the Yale Child Study Institute, the greatest teaching-learning problems stem from inappropriate class placement. Ilg and Ames (1964) said

> Possibly the greatest single contribution which can be made in guaranteeing that each individual child will get the most out of his school experience is to make certain that he starts that school experience at what for him is the "right" time. This should be the time when he is truly ready and not merely some time arbitrarily decided by custom or the law (p. 14).

In addition, they indicate:

> A child needs not only to go at his own pace, but also benefits from the stimulation of others who are progressing as he is. He thrives on an environment geared for him. When he is in a group that is operating more as a unit, his own adjustment is more easily discerned (p. 13).

Although placement by age appears to this group to be preferable to an "ungraded" or mixed-age group, they prefer the use of developmental tests to ensure that a child is placed with those learners most like him or her in overall development. The use of age alone, they feel, is likely to lead to some misplacement due to individual differences in development rates.

Unlike the programs developed from the behaviorist perspective, maturationist programs lack specificity. Faith in the inherent goodness of humankind sustains the efforts of the maturationist teacher. There is a pervasive expectation that children's growth will be positive in a setting that supplies predictability, trust, and warmth. What is actually done in the classroom, however, depends on ongoing judgments about what will best meet children's needs.

CONSTRUCTIVIST ORIENTATION

A third group can be referred to as **constructivists** (or **interactionists**) to differentiate their ways of viewing children from the other two major orientations.[*] The constructivists are concerned with how children derive the concepts through which they make sense of the world, what means they use in their explorations

---

[*]The relationship between the terms *constructivist* and *constructive play* may be confusing. Constructivists are early childhood educators who are concerned about how children derive the concepts through which they make sense of the world—what means they use in their explorations and thinking and, especially, how their interactions with the environment help them move toward more complex states of development. Children involved in constructive play often reveal their mental constructions, and they use materials in ways that help them test out and extend those mental concepts. For example, as children attempt to represent an airplane with blocks, they choose those attributes of the airplane that characterize it and, in the process, learn about the similarities and differences between airplanes and other things such as cars, houses, and helicopters. Thus, constructive play helps children develop more complete and satisfying concepts. Also, children engage in problem solving as they invent ways to use the materials at hand to represent their concepts. Constructivists value all types of play, not just constructive play, but the use of the same root word in the two phrases is not a mere coincidence. The meanings are closely associated.

Constructivist teachers arrange for new experiences to challenge existing concepts. *(Dunn Photographics)*

and thinking, and, especially, how their interactions with the environment help them move toward a higher state of development. Constructivists assume that children's own active functioning guides their development; thus in viewing children, they note primarily the nature of the child's transactions with the environment.

Whereas the maturationist generally emphasizes age as leading to a new developmental stage regardless of experience at previous stages, the constructivist emphasizes that appropriate experiences are essential to progression. The richness and appropriateness of the stimulation encountered at each point of development are felt to have a direct bearing on how well a child moves through a series of developmental stages to the next level of functioning.

The constructivist is thus less concerned than the maturationist with attributes of a particular stage of development and seeks instead to understand the dynamic process by which the child builds on one stage to reach another. Both orientations accept the notion of a progression through a series of stages. The constructivist, however, does not see this progression as an "unfolding" process generated from within the organism due simply to innate and/or genetic patterning, but as the result of the child's own activity. A child's characteristics, at any particular time, are the result of the constant interplay between environmental stimuli (encountered through exploratory behavior) and the intellectual structures through which those stimuli are filtered.

Constructivists contrast with behaviorists in that they do not see children primarily as shaped by reinforcing stimuli that lead them to perform particular behaviors. Nor do they see children as simply emerging "good and whole" as maturationists tend to do. They see children as active agents constantly engaged in figuring out who they are and what the world is all about and, since many experiences are universally encountered, going through some rather predictable developmental patterns and stages in the process.

Each of the three perspectives also differs regarding its ultimate expectations for human development. Maturationists simply assume that the upper limits of human capacity are genetically determined. Behaviorists, on the other hand, can only consider shaping children to levels of development that parallel the behaviorists' own current functioning—but not higher. Constructivists assume that by improving children's early interactions with the environment the children will ultimately reach a higher level of functioning than the current generation. They assume that the upper limit of potential in any given individual is not likely to be attained; however, they hold that an enriched experience throughout the life span will foster higher levels of development than would otherwise have been achieved.

Within these definitions, John Dewey would be considered a constructivist. His views of knowledge and learning were concerned with the processes that would lead children to more effective inquiry and problem-solving strategies. Central to his philosophy was the human quest for knowledge. Children who learned to think and investigate were expected to ultimately make discoveries that would benefit society.

The work of Jean Piaget, the Swiss psychologist, is cited throughout this book. Piaget's extensive studies of children's thought processes have led to a clearer perception of how the child's own activity can be central to his or her understanding. Piaget describes how a child's motor explorations are gradually transformed into more sophisticated means of exploration and eventually into representational thinking via abstract manipulation of symbols and language.

Constructivists assume that development, behavior, and learning are substantially influenced by both external influences and maturational processes. They, however, strongly emphasize the activities of individuals in constructing a view of the world, which then serves to regulate further learning and development. Life encounters are seen as crucial to constructivists, in contrast to maturationists. And unlike behaviorists, constructivists assume that learning depends on the activity of the learner and cannot be effectively prestructured or appreciably accelerated through direct instruction.

For constructivists, development consists of successive transformations of internal **cognitive structures** that are the basis for the individual's behavior. Each individual is constantly engaged in cognitive restructuring based upon the evidence gained from operations performed on the social and physical environment. Intellectual, social, affective, and perceptual-motor experiences are inseparable. According to this view, significant changes in behavior occur because of cognitive extensions and elaborations (the development of new and more adequate schemata) gained through operations on the environment. Schemata are modified into increasingly complex and internalized operations. The child's behavior gradually becomes less dependent on new incoming perceptions and more influenced by logical internal manipulations of objects and events.

Constructivists do not expect that any specific learning (such as letter recognition) or any small modification of behavior (such as frequency of "attending" behavior) will significantly influence long-term development. The acquisition of particular bits of knowledge or specific academic behaviors is generally assigned a lower priority in programming than is involving the child in finding order and relationships through operations such as classification, seriation, and generalizations.

The cognitive structures that form the basis of all specific knowledge are thought by constructivists to be acquired through experience with phenomena of the physical and social world. The fullest and richest development stems from a broad range of child-initiated experiences, coupled with encouragement, guidance, and constant interchanges with teachers and peers. Through alteration between student-initiated activities and inputs from teachers, children develop increasingly varied and functional schemas.

The program conditions constructivists favor for young children can be summarized as follows:

1 All kinds of experiences should be available, not merely those labeled *academic*. Learners are provided with many possibilities for active hands-on involvement with physical materials, which is the basis for later abstract thought processes.

2 Long, unstructured activity periods should be provided so that children can engage in the independent planning and execution of projects.

3 A variety of peers should be available for social interaction so that personal views can be validated or modified.

4 Beyond providing the learning environment, adult input is largely provided on a one-to-one basis or through small groups formed for a specific purpose (for example, to compose a group story or to learn to set up a terrarium) and disbanded immediately thereafter (in contrast to being maintained over time).

5 Adults frequently request input from children that requires recall, synthesis, conjecture, estimation, demonstration, and experimentation.

6 There is a constant focus on better conceptualization of the physical and social world.

A document prepared by the Education Products Information Exchange Institute (1972) describes goals compatible for constructivists as follows:

> Students should understand differences in amounts and sizes of things in the physical world, establish a basic framework for orientation in space and time, develop a concept of numbers through handling of sets of objects and the study of relationships,

extend their understanding of numbers through carrying out measurement operations, learn to communicate through graphs, charts, and numerals.

Students should develop facility with abstract symbols (numbers, letters) through familiarity with the physical and human environment, achieved by exposure to participatory experiences and active symbolic similarities in objects, functions, personal roles, and personal feelings.

Students should develop a repertoire of actions to perform on objects; an ability to predict regularity of cause and effect, and to figure out means towards ends; language to communicate precisely, knowledge of language conventions, and ability to see others' points of view; an ability to classify on similarities and differences; increased mobility of thought; ability to sort by comparing differences among objects, in the structuring of space and time, in representation ability; symbols and signs (pp. 31–32).

Constructivist programs have a strong emphasis on children's activities. They pay particular attention to those portions of a child's behavior that indicate the extent of his or her involvements and the nature of his or her conceptualizations. It is not assumed in these programs that placing the child in a nurturing and age-appropriate environment will be sufficient for optimal development, nor is it assumed that a systematic presentation by teachers of skills and knowledge will suffice.

To constructivists, it is important that the things a child encounters mesh with the child's mental constructions. The ultimate source of the curriculum for the constructivist teacher is therefore the active child engaged with aspects of the environment that appear to intrigue him or her. The behavior and language expression of the child then provides the teacher with cues regarding what further explanations or materials are needed to extend the child's understanding. As Dewey (1897) expressed it in his pedagogic creed:

There is, therefore, no succession of studies in the ideal school curriculum. If education is life, all life has, from the outset, a scientific aspect, an aspect of art and culture, and an aspect of communication. It cannot, therefore, be true that the proper studies for one grade are mere reading and writing, and that at a later grade, reading, or literature, or science, may be introduced. The progress is not in the succession of studies, but in the development of new attitudes towards, and new interests in, experience. Education must be conceived as a continuing reconstruction of experience; the process and the goal of education are one and the same thing (pp. 11–12).

SUMMARY

Three contrasting orientations to child development are described in this chapter. Major concepts from Locke, Skinner, Premack, and other reinforcement psychologists were presented as the behaviorist orientation. Views of Rousseau, Freud, Erikson, Gesell, Ilg, Ames, and the Moores were cited relative to the maturationist orientation. The ideas of Dewey and of Piaget were presented as the constructivist orientation. We hope this examination of contrasting orientations and program approaches for early education has helped you clarify your own views. You should be forewarned, however, that it may be difficult to find any "pure" representations of these orientations, as we have presented them, in the local programs to which you have access. You are much more likely to find eclectic programs that combine a number of different approaches according to the fancies of the teaching staff. You may find programs that tend more toward one of the orientations than the others, and the knowledge of the pure contrasts as presented in this chapter will prove helpful to you in analyzing what you see.

SUGGESTED ACTIVITIES

1 Ask any assortment of people available to you what they believe to be true about how children should be reared and educated, and why. Decide whether their views generally reflect the orientation of behaviorists, maturationists, constructivists, or some combination of these, or whether they have other views that are quite different from any of these categories.

2 Make a collection of comments on child rearing and education from a variety of sources. Look at editorials, letters to the editor, and newspaper and magazine features. Listen to talk shows and opinion programs. Try to categorize the opinions you hear according to the orientations they express.

3 Recall your own early schooling. Consider how you would characterize the orientation of those programs. On what basis do you identify them as behaviorist, maturationist, constructivist, or eclectic?

4 Consider the program characteristics of those early childhood education programs with which you are most familiar. On what basis do you identify those programs as behaviorist, maturationist, constructivist, or eclectic?

5 Prepare a statement of your own beliefs about children's development and learning. What is your orientation and why? Compare your beliefs with those of others in your class.

ADDITIONAL READINGS

Ames, L. B., & Chase, J. A. (1981). *Don't push your preschooler* (Rev. ed.). New York: Harper & Row.

Dewey, J. (1963). (Original edition, 1938). *Experience and education.* New York: Collier.

Elkind, D. (1976). *Child development and education: A Piagetian perspective.* New York: Oxford University Press.

Engelmann, S., & Engelmann, T. (1966). *Give your child a superior mind.* New York: Simon & Schuster.

Forman, G. E., & Fosnot, C. T. (1982). The use of constructivism in early childhood education programs. In B. Spodek (Ed.), *Handbook of research in early childhood education.* New York: Free Press.

Hymes, J. L. (1955). *A child development point of view.* Englewood Cliffs, NJ: Prentice-Hall.

Ilg, F. L. & Ames, L. B. (1964). *School readiness.* New York: Harper & Row.

Kohlberg, L. (1968). Early education: A cognitive-developmental view. *Child Development, 39,* 1013–1062.

Maier, H. W. (1978). *Three theories of child development* (3rd ed.). New York: Harper & Row.

Moore, R. S., & Moore, D. N. (1977). *Better late than early.* New York: Reader's Digest.

Moore, R. S., & Moore, D. R. (1973). How early should they go to school? *Childhood Education, 50,* 14–20.

Moore, R. S., & Moore, D. N. (1979). *School can wait.* Provo, UT: Brigham Young University Press.

Peters, D. L., Neisworth, J. T., & Yawkey, T. D. (1985). *Early childhood education: From theory to practice.* Monterey, CA: Brooks/Cole.

Skinner, B. F. (1953). *Science and human behavior.* New York: Macmillan.

Weber, E. (1984). *Ideas influencing early childhood education: A theoretical analysis.* New York: Teachers College Press.

CHAPTER 11

PROGRAM MODELS

OVERVIEW

There are many different program **models** available for early childhood educators to consider. The term *program model* refers to a distinctive configuration of components, such as objectives, teachers' roles, time scheduling, space arrangement, equipment, materials, and the like. In this chapter we present five program models: Cognitively Oriented Curriculum, Direct Instruction, Bank Street, Montessori, and Constructivist Primary. There is a significant contrast among these five models, and they are somewhat representational of the existing program diversity.

All may be used during the age range from preschool and kindergarten into the elementary grades. As you read through each of the five descriptions, look for evidence of orientation. Are they purely behaviorist, maturationist, constructivist, or some combination?

THE COGNITIVELY ORIENTED CURRICULUM

The Cognitively Oriented Curriculum, developed by David Weikart and associates at the High/Scope Institute in Ypsilanti, Michigan, is an attempt to translate Piaget's theory of development into an education program. Initially called the Perry Preschool, the program includes a strong emphasis on children's cognitive development or, stated more specifically, on the way children organize and interpret relationships between objects and events in the environment.

The physical arrangement of a classroom using the Cognitively Oriented Curriculum typically has a central open area for group meetings and action games and has work areas (art area, block area, quiet area) around the perimeter of the room. The elements of the daily routine are presented in Tables 11-1 and 11-2. Learning the order of the daily events is considered important, and, therefore, teachers are expected to follow a consistent routine.

Children's planning efforts are of central concern in the Cognitively Oriented Curriculum. During a period referred to as Work Time, children make and post their own plans and must identify them by placing their symbols (a two-dimensional shape with the child's picture and name) on a board used for that purpose beside each work area. As children move from area to area during the work period, they take their symbols with them and place them on the planning board in the new area.

During a period designated in the schedule as Recall, Snack, or Small-Group Time, small groups of children, five to eight in number, meet with an adult to recall and share their work-time activities. This is often done while children are having a snack. After the snack, the children usually work with materials chosen by the adult to allow an opportunity to observe the children's actions. For exam-

TABLE 11-1   SAMPLE DAILY ROUTINE FOR A HALF-DAY PROGRAM

8:30–8:50 A.M.	Planning time
8:50–9:45 A.M.	Work time
9:45–10:00 A.M.	Cleanup time
10:00–10:30 A.M.	Recall, snack, and small-group time
10:30–10:50 A.M.	Outside time
10:50–11:10 A.M.	Circle time
11:10–11:20 A.M.	Dismissal

Source: Mary Hohmann, Bernard Banet, and David P. Weikart, *Young Children in Action,* © 1979, p. 61. Reprinted by permission of The High/Scope Press, Ypsilanti, MI.

TABLE 11-2   SAMPLE DAILY ROUTINE FOR A FULL-DAY PROGRAM

7:30–8:30 A.M.	As children arrive, adults plan with them and get them started on a short work time.
8:30–9:00 A.M.	Breakfast and brush teeth
9:00–9:20 A.M.	Planning time
9:20–10:30 A.M.	Work time and cleanup
10:30–10:50 A.M.	Recall time
10:50–11:20 A.M.	Outside time
11:20–11:45 A.M.	Circle time and preparation for lunch
11:45–12:30 P.M.	Lunch
12:30–1:30 P.M.	Nap time. Children either sleep or lie quietly with a book.
1:30–2:15 P.M.	Small-group and snack time
2:15–4:00 P.M.	Some children leave. Adults plan with the remaining children, who then work until they leave.

Source: Mary Hohmann, Bernard Banet, and David P. Weikart, *Young Children in Action,* © 1979, p. 61. Reprinted by permission of the High/Scope Press, Ypsilanti, MI.

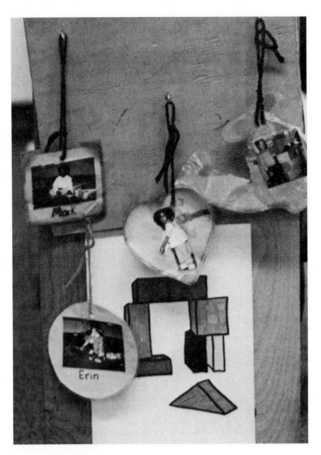

In the cognitively oriented curriculum each child is provided a symbol.
(High/Scope Educational Research Foundation)

ple, the children may make individual batches of play dough or be given a set of materials to explore and manipulate. This is not a teaching time; instead, it gives teachers the opportunity for observation and introduces children to experiences and materials that they might not otherwise encounter.

The Cognitively Oriented Curriculum focuses on the following: active learning, language, experiencing and representing, classification, seriation, number, spatial relations, and time. Each of these is emphasized throughout the program day and key experiences have been identified by the program developers in *Young Children in Action: A Manual for Preschool Educators* (Hohmann, Banet, & Weikart, 1979) as follows.

Active Learning
- Exploring actively with all the senses
- Discovering relations through direct experience

- Manipulating, transforming, and combining materials
- Choosing materials, activities, purposes
- Acquiring skills with tools and equipment
- Using the large muscles
- Taking care of one's own needs

Language

- Talking with others about personally meaningful experiences
- Describing objects, events, and relations
- Expressing feelings in words
- Having one's own spoken language written down and read back
- Having fun with language

Experiencing and Representing

- Recognizing objects by sound, touch, taste, and smell
- Imitating actions and sounds
- Relating models, photographs, and pictures to real places and things
- Role-playing
- Making models

Children indicate their plans by placing their symbols on the board by the area where they choose to work. *(High/Scope Educational Research Foundation)*

- Making drawings and paintings
- Observing that spoken words can be written down and read back

Classification

- Investigating and describing the attributes of things
- Noticing and describing how things are the same and how they are different; sorting and matching
- Using and describing objects in different ways
- Talking about the characteristics something does *not* possess or the class it does *not* belong to
- Holding more than one attribute in mind at a time
- Distinguishing between "some" or "all"

Seriation

- Making comparisons
- Arranging several things in order and describing their relations
- Fitting one ordered set of objects to another through trial and error

Number

- Comparing amounts
- Arranging two sets of objects in one-to-one correspondence
- Counting objects

Spatial Relations

- Fitting things together and taking them apart
- Rearranging and reshaping objects
- Observing and describing things from different spatial viewpoints
- Experiencing and describing the relative positions, directions, and distances of things
- Experiencing and representing one's own body
- Learning to locate things in the classroom, school, and neighborhood
- Interpreting representations of spatial relations in drawings, pictures, and photographs
- Distinguishing and describing shapes

Time

- Understanding time units or intervals
- Sequencing events in time

The Cognitively Oriented Curriculum, as developed and implemented by Weikart and associates, is only one of the many programs based on Piagetian theory. Although there are many differences among these Piagetian programs, they are similar in emphasizing an active involvement by children with materials and events arranged in an appropriate setting.

THE DIRECT INSTRUCTION (ACADEMIC PRESCHOOL OR DISTAR®) MODEL

Described as an academically oriented preschool program, the Direct Instruction Model was initially developed at the University of Illinois by Carl Bereiter and Siegfried Engelmann. It is described in considerable detail in their book, *Teaching Disadvantaged Children in the Preschool* (Bereiter & Engelmann, 1966). The program was based on the idea that waiting for academic readiness to develop in children is a highly inappropriate educational practice, especially for the disadvantaged population. To quote Engelmann, "When you say a kid's not ready, you've decided that he's not going to learn and you're blaming him for it. That's irresponsible" (Divoky, 1973). Bereiter and Engelmann emphatically made the point that the maturationist's practice of following children's inclinations and patterns in a play-oriented program was a disservice, since these children could be led to greater achievement in academic settings where reinforcements were reserved for work-related behaviors.

When first developed, this program was highly controversial and received a great deal of publicity. It was further developed and elaborated for commercial distribution by Siegfried Engelmann and Wesley Becker as DISTAR®. This approach was selected for use in two major projects commissioned to evaluate various approaches for teaching young disadvantaged children—Head Start Variation and Follow Through. At that point, it was renamed the Englemann-Becker Model, and its implementation was coordinated from the University of Oregon.

The program emphasizes instruction in three areas—reading, language, and arithmetic—and its goal is to provide children instruction for very specific skills. In reading, children are to look at written symbols (letters) and quickly say the sounds in a series of letters from left to right, the goal being the blending of letters into words.

In language, they are to answer the question "What is this?" in regard to pictures of objects and symbols, in both the affirmative and the negative. They are taught to use oppositional terms and relational concepts—*if-then* statements and the terms *not* and *or*—in making deductive statements.

In arithmetic, they are taught to count forward and backward and to count in groups. They are taught the functions of symbols such as +,−, and =, and to answer questions about numbers that are expressed with these symbols.

Children are organized into groups for instruction. Group sizes vary from three to eight children and are arranged according to ability. In a classroom group of twenty-five children in the primary grades, ideally at least one teacher and two aides are available to conduct the program. Children attend three classes of twenty minutes each—one in each of the subject areas—within the daily session. During the teaching session, they sit in a semicircle around the teacher, who follows the very specific directions provided in a handbook. The distinctive characteristics of the program are (1) a fast pace, (2) strong emphasis on total group verbal responses from the children, often in unison, (3) carefully planned instructional units with continual feedback, and (4) heavy work demands during the sessions, with little tolerance of nonwork behavior.

The program implementer must get the children to make the right responses in the presence of the right stimulus, so that these can be positively reinforced. Rapid-fire questioning by the teacher regarding a page of pictures, letters, or figures held up in front of the group brings shouts in unison as a typical response. Questions are carefully sequenced to facilitate correct responses from the children, and there is much ado, especially at first, over correct responses. The teacher gives cookies, praises, shakes hands, tells the children how smart they are, and so on. Incorrect responses are not accepted, and the question is posed again until the correct response is forthcoming. It is then reinforced before the teacher proceeds further. "Good!" is probably the most frequent pronouncement of the able DISTAR® teacher. Tight control is achieved through carefully specified objectives for children's conduct and learning. Children are rewarded for attending and responding.

The Direct Instruction Model uses few of the play materials seen in many early childhood classrooms. It is considered desirable to minimize environmental distractions that could tempt the children to run about and explore. Acoustical arrangements to reduce distraction between instructional groups meeting concurrently are considered very important, but there are few other requirements for the facilities. The tendency to overstock the classroom is warned against by Bereiter and Engelmann (1966). Toys are limited to form boards, jigsaw puzzles, books, drawing and tracing materials, Cuisenaire rods, a miniature house, barn, and set of farm animals, paper, crayons, and chalk.

The schedules recommended for four-year-olds by Bereiter and Engelmann for the Academic Preschool (with a one-to-five adult-child ratio) are shown in Tables 11-3 and 11-4.

Note that, with few exceptions, the time periods are labeled with the specific subject matter to be taught during that time. The program schedules proposed for longer days (six hours or more) include more unstructured and semistructured activity periods, but these are arranged so they provide maximum support for the instruction periods.

In the Direct Instruction classroom, children are expected to be quiet and restrained, even during the unstructured periods. It is felt that "letting off steam" during free periods does not pacify children but, rather, makes it more difficult for them to get back to work during the next study period. At the end of the unstructured periods, the children are expected to terminate their activities promptly and are rarely granted permission to finish nonacademic work such as drawings. Cleanup periods are brief. If cleanup will take more than two minutes of the children's time, teachers are expected to do it later. The teaching schedule clearly has a higher priority than cleanup or other nonacademic involvements.

Children are required to walk single file, without pushing or crowding, as they move from one location to another. They sit in assigned seats during the instructional periods, leaving their places only with the teacher's consent. They are required to participate, answering the teacher's questions in a loud, clear voice, and to work hard at the tasks presented them. They are not allowed to

TABLE 11-3   ACADEMIC PRESCHOOL TIME SCHEDULE FOR A TWO-HOUR DAY

	Group 1 (5 Children)	Group 2 (5 Children)	Group 3 (5 Children)
Period 1 (10 min.)		Unstructured activity	
Period 2 (20 min.)	Language	Arithmetic	Reading
Period 3 (30 min.)		Toilet, juice, and music	
Period 4 (20 min.)	Arithmetic	Reading	Language
Period 5 (20 min.)		Semistructured activity	
Period 6 (20 min.)	Reading	Language	Arithmetic

Source: Carl Bereiter and Siegfried Engelmann, *Teaching Disadvantaged Children in the Preschool,* © 1966, p. 67. Reprinted by permission of Prentice-Hall, Englewood Cliffs, NJ.

TABLE 11-4   ACADEMIC PRESCHOOL TIME SCHEDULE FOR AN EIGHT-HOUR DAY

	Group 1 (5 Children)	Group 2 (5 Children)	Group 3 (5 Children)
Period 1 (10 min.)		Unstructured activity	
Period 2 (20 min.)	Language		Semistructured activity
Period 3 (20 min.)	Semistructured activity	Language	Semistructured activity
Period 4 (20 min.)	Semistructured activity		Language
Period 5 (40 min.)		Toilet, juice, and singing	
Period 6 (60 min.)		Unstructured activity and lunch preparation	
Period 7 (60 min.)		Lunch, cleanup, and toilet	
Period 8 (20 min.)	Arithmetic		Semistructured activity
Period 9 (20 min.)	Semistructured activity	Arithmetic	Semistructured activity
Period 10 (20 min.)	Semistructured activity		Arithmetic
Period 11 (20 min.)		Toilet and rest	
Period 12 (20 min.)		Music	
Period 13 (20 min.)	Reading		Semistructured activity
Period 14 (20 min.)	Semistructured activity	Reading	Semistructured activity
Period 15 (20 min.)	Semistructured activity		Reading
Period 16 (50 min.)		Unstructured activity	

Source: Carl Bereiter and Siegfried Engelmann, *Teaching Disadvantaged Children in the Preschool,* © 1966, p. 96. Reprinted by permission of Prentice-Hall, Englewood Cliffs, NJ.

interrupt and are discouraged from relating personal experiences or otherwise interjecting ideas irrelevant to the teacher's presentation. Only when the teacher signals children to express their own ideas may they do so.

The means for establishing these ground rules are based on reinforcement theory. Several principles are recommended by Bereiter and Engelmann (1966):

- Reward the child who tries.
- Try to avoid rewarding undesirable behavior. For example, the teacher should avoid holding the misbehaving child or taking him aside and talking with him.
- Avoid shaming and coaxing. The teacher matter-of-factly tells children what to

do and expects that they will perform and work hard, that they will be "smart," and that he or she will be proud of them.

- Preserve the spirit of the group. Teachers avoid children's rejection of each other through tattling. Teachers only act to correct behavioral offenses that they personally see, not those reported by other children. In response to tattling they may say, "If he did that, he broke a rule," but they avoid encouraging children to turn against each other. The group should never be punished for the offense of any one child.
- Emphasize the rules of behavior that must be maintained, not the child's adequacy.
- Exploit work motives rather than play motives.
- Provide the child with a realistic definition of success and failure. Teachers are not to approve incorrect or inadequate responses. If the child works hard, he or she is rewarded for doing a good job but is not led to believe his or her incorrect responses were correct.

The children are rewarded according to whether they follow the established rule for the situation, and the teacher is careful to communicate that both he or she and the children are governed by the rule, and that rewards are not related to the teacher's feelings about a child. During the first month of the program, punishment is sometimes used to clarify the rules. Punishment is used only for behavior that is unthinking and automatic; isolation is used for behavior that is more calculated. Two warnings are given before a child is placed in isolation. Rewards include verbal approval, and, to strengthen their rewarding power, verbal praise is initially paired with concrete rewards such as cookies, toys, games, and special privileges.

THE BANK STREET "DEVELOPMENTAL INTERACTION" APPROACH

The Bank Street approach; as developed for Head Start and Follow Through implementation by Elizabeth Gilkeson and associates, focuses on the development of confidence, inventiveness, responsiveness, and productivity. From these general goals, many specific objectives are drawn. The approach reflects a philosophy developed over more than half a century at the Bank Street College of Education in New York City. The term *developmental interaction* is often used to describe the approach. *Developmental* refers to the Bank Street concern that the curriculum be individualized in relation to each child's stage of development. *Interaction* refers to the premise that children learn best through interaction with peers and adults in an environment designed to provide rich and varied involvements.

The approach requires teachers to continually assess children's progress and to offer the children activity options in accord with the assessment. The curriculum requires that teachers make decisions regarding the experiences individual children need to gain mastery in necessary areas of skill. Elaborate assessment systems have been developed for these purposes.

The Bank Street method requires a learning environment that allows children to choose from a large variety of activities, including a wide range of sensory and motor experiences. Materials such as play blocks, dress-up clothes, dolls, sand toys, pets, books, games, and counting objects are provided. Both teacher-made and child-made materials supplement those commercially obtained. Figure 11-1 illustrates the diversity of the environment recommended by Gilkeson and Bowman (1976) for a second-grade classroom. Note the emphasis on storage space for materials to be brought out for special uses.

All areas of the curriculum are integrated through the development of themes or units, for example, seeds, building a house, community helpers. In selecting themes, Bank Street teachers attempt to meet the following criteria:

- It is something in which they are personally interested.
- It has resources available.
- It will lead to activities and discussions.
- It has relevance for children and is understandable by them.
- It will assist in the development of children's conceptual learning of "large ideas."
- It is suitable for the children's age level.
- It has potential for children's independent learning.

Once a theme has been selected, teachers decide what concepts can be built with the theme. One activity is expected to lead naturally into another, and several kinds of learning involvements result from a single activity. A group project, such as making applesauce, might lead to counting, measuring, weighing, observing, reading, and writing in the various subgroups that become involved in some aspects of the activity.

Motivation is supplied by the pleasure inherent in the activities themselves—extrinsic rewards are not systematically used to influence children's learning, choice of activities, or behavior. It is also anticipated that the teacher will gain the children's cooperation through consistently showing concern, care, and support. The teacher-child relationships are key to the program implementation.

The daily schedule is carefully structured to provide a balanced set of involvements. There is, however, a high degree of flexibility, and teachers may bend the schedule to take advantage of unexpected opportunities. Children often work independently or in small groups, with or without adults. Many activities go on simultaneously. There are, in addition, some whole-group meetings when the nature of an activity calls for everyone's participation.

Reading and writing are considered just two of the many activities that may be enjoyed in the classroom. They are closely linked to children's individual expressions and choices as well as theme-related activities. Children write their own books and read from books that other children have written. Teachers read to children daily, and a wide selection of picture books and simple readers are used for individualized reading instruction. Children accumulate a reading vocabulary through charts, labels, stories, games, and writing prior to being pro-

FIGURE 11-1 Example of a Bank Street classroom environment for second grade

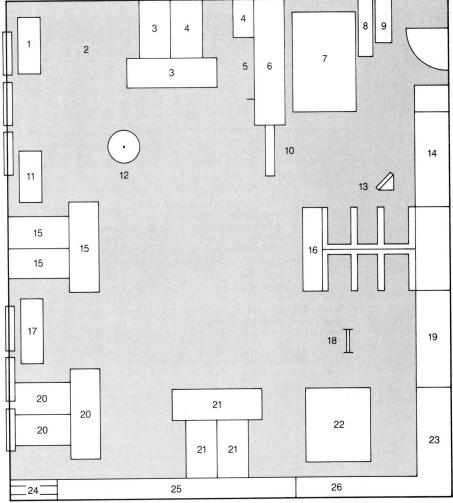

1. Block storage
2. Block building area
3. Table, multimedia purpose
4. Cooking area
5. Cardboard wall
6. Cabinets, books—displays
7. Rug, reading library area
8. Book cabinet
9. File cabinet
10. Book display
11. Game cabinet
12. Rotating diary shelves
13. Stand-up chart
14. Clothing cabinet
15. Table, multipurpose
16. Cubbies
17. Science cabinet
18. Easel
19. Clothing cabinet
20. Science table
21. Table, math materials
22. Art table
23. Storage cabinet, sink area
24. Math books
25. Math materials/counter
26. Storage cabinet

Source: From E. C. Gilkeson, *The focus is on children: The Bank Street approach to early childhood education as enacted in Follow Through.* New York: Bank Street College of Education.

vided with a preprimer, which they usually find they can read through, with a little assistance, from beginning to end.

Achieving two-way communication with parents is important to the Bank Street approach. Home visits, the provision of parent resource rooms, and other outreach efforts promote parental involvement.

THE MONTESSORI METHOD

At the turn of the century, Maria Montessori, the first woman physician in Italy, developed ways of working with children that contrasted markedly with previous practices. Although her initial work was with children who were considered mentally deficient, she derived and proposed general principles of education that had wide appeal and were adapted for use with normal children. As pointed

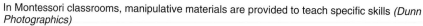

In Montessori classrooms, manipulative materials are provided to teach specific skills *(Dunn Photographics)*

out in Chapter 2, Montessori programs became very popular in many parts of the world, including the United States, during the early 1900s but were then gradually dropped in the United States as a total approach. Some aspects of the Montessori methods were broadly incorporated into other early childhood programs, however, and there was a rebirth of interest in Montessori programs during the 1960s. At the present time, Montessori programs, or adaptations, have again become prominent as a viable alternative in early education.

Montessori believed that the child's development consists of an unfolding of inborn characteristics, but she also insisted that certain environmental conditions must exist if these inborn traits and abilities are to develop normally. Unlike Arnold Gesell, a contemporary of Montessori, she did not believe that normative behaviors at given ages should be accepted as necessary behaviors for that age level. She especially disagreed with the maturationist view that periods of disruptive behavior are simply a "stage" that, if tolerated, will naturally disappear as the child matures. She pointed out that whenever children are provided with appropriate activities, their "disturbed" behavior changed to concentration, self-confidence, and self-acceptance. Her entire effort, therefore, revolved around constructing environments within which children would have opportunities for appropriate "occupations." Montessori proposed that children should choose their own activities in the classroom and believed it was the educator's job to provide choices appropriate to the abilities of the individual child. She wrote, "The child, left at liberty to exercise his activities, ought to find in his surrounding something organized in direct relation to his internal organization which is developing itself by natural laws" (Montessori, 1964, p. 70).

Montessori became skilled at designing special apparatus whose educational appropriateness for children was measured by the children's degree of concentration as they interacted with the materials. It is the Montessori equipment that is best known by educators and is sometimes mistakenly considered as the whole Montessori method. The materials are of four types: (1) materials for daily living (such as personal grooming, cooking, and cleaning); (2) sensory materials (visual, tactile, auditory, and olfactory); (3) academic materials (language, reading, writing, and mathematics); and (4) cultural and artistic materials. Some of the sensory and academic materials are designed to be self-correcting, so the child can tell whether his or her use of the materials is appropriate. Variations are carefully introduced to provide a gradual transition from simple to complex manipulations.

Once a child has learned the precise use of a material—in a brief, individualized session called a **fundamental lesson**—the child is then invited to use the material whenever he or she wishes. Children are taught how to take the materials from a shelf, how to arrange them on a mat provided for that purpose, and how to return them for use by the next person. After the initial instruction, the child does not usually require the teacher's assistance. According to Montessori (1964):

> The child not only needs something interesting to do, but also likes to be shown exactly how to do it. Precision is found to attract him deeply, and this it is that keeps him at work. From this we must infer that his attraction toward these manipulative tasks has

an unconscious aim. The child has an instinct to coordinate his movements and bring them under control (p. 179).

Montessorian educators believe that if the activities correspond to the inner development of the child, he or she will delight in the repetition of these activities and will continue to use them as a self-directed learning tool. The children are not required to use the materials unless they wish to. After the child has fully absorbed the possibilities inherent in particular equipment, the teacher introduces the vocabulary that represents the concepts the child has been exploring. First, the names are provided; then it is determined whether the child associates the names with the appropriate concepts; finally, it is determined whether the child correctly uses the new vocabulary.

Less well known than the equipment are some of the other program emphases. Montessori stressed the interest of the child in the natural environment. She also emphasized the growing sense of community that evolves from including children of differing ages in each classroom. Each child in the Montessori classroom has full dominion over his or her own activity, unless it

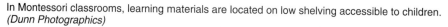

In Montessori classrooms, learning materials are located on low shelving accessible to children. *(Dunn Photographics)*

interferes with the activities of the others. Children are not allowed to join "the work in progress" of another child unless that child extends a specific invitation to do so. There are few teacher-planned group activities in the Montessori system, and children need not share their individually chosen equipment until they desire to do so. According to Montessori teachers, children gradually begin to seek each other out and work together.

The role of the teacher in the Montessori program contrasts markedly with that in other program approaches. There is no effort, for example, to establish a close relationship in which the child will wish to please the adult. Nor is there any effort to systematically reinforce children, thereby accelerating and directing their learning and development. The design and maintenance of appropriate environments, based on careful observation of the children, is the Montessori teacher's concern. The teacher serves as a model for the children in extracting learning experiences from the environment, but ideally this is done without intruding too much of the teacher's personality into the situation. The child's autonomous functioning is the goal, and it is considered unfortunate if the child's attention is drawn away from his or her own interests and occupations by a desire to relate to or receive approval from the teacher.

A quite different view of classroom facilities can be seen in Montessori classrooms. Essential to the Montessori approach is the prepared environment. Maria Montessori believed that the environment must be a nourishing place for children. As cited earlier, she believed that the environment should be matched to the child's potential, thereby leading to a fruitful interaction. Montessori (1964) identified her philosophy in the following statement:

> Plainly the environment must be a living one, directed by a higher intelligence, arranged by an adult who is prepared for his mission. It is in this that our conception differs both from that of the world in which the adult does everything for the child and from that of a passive environment in which the adult abandons the child to himself. . . . This means that it is not enough to set the child among objects in proportion to his size and strength; the adult who is to help him must have learned how to do so (p. 224).

There is no time structuring for most of the Montessori sessions, but there is a definitive space structuring. Materials must be located in a known place (although this place may be changed) and must be continuously accessible to the child in that place (unless they are being used by another child). Materials are grouped according to similarity of function and are arranged in sequence according to degree of difficulty.

The Montessori environment is also designed to bring the child into closer contact with reality and away from his or her fantasies and illusions. Therefore, toys such as replicas of furniture or dress-ups are not included. Children use real things instead of playthings, real tasks are performed, and in modern Montessori classrooms a real refrigerator, stove, sink, and telephone are available. Silverware is polished when it is tarnished; shoes are shined; nourishing food is prepared, with sharp knives available for cutting; a heated iron may be used for ironing. A child is not encouraged to play being an adult in the Montessori setting; instead, he or she is provided with the tools for doing tasks that adults do.

There is in Montessori classrooms only one of each type of equipment. Children must wait until another child is finished if the equipment they want is in use. The intent of this is to help them to learn to respect the work of others and to cope with the realities they meet in daily life.

Many of the Montessori materials are **self-correcting,** affording children far greater autonomy and freedom to pace their own learning efforts. Materials are expected to be treated with respect, however, and never used improperly. When a child decides to use a particular exercise, he or she may bring all the materials and arrange them on a mat or rug. The child is not interrupted while using the materials, either by other children or by the teacher. When the child is finished, he or she returns the materials to the storage location, usually a low shelf, in good order for the next child.

Some of the Montessori equipment is thought to develop the skills necessary for future academic work. An example of this is the materials for handwriting preparation. Children are shown how to lift and manipulate knobs on metal stencils, developing finger and thumb coordination as they do so. They are then provided paper and pencil and shown how they can use the stencils to guide their pencils in drawing basic forms. They are next provided sandpaper letters to develop a "muscle memory" of letter patterns. Thus, it is believed, by the time they are motivated to write they will have abilities that allow them to do so without failure or frustration.

The Montessori environment is typically an evolving one. Rather than having all the equipment available from the start of the program, new pieces are gradually introduced in response to the children's developing abilities. The appropriateness of materials is measured by the degree of concentration, involvement, and satisfaction the child experiences. When the child begins to experiment with possible new uses or begins to use an apparatus in fantasy play (such as using the rods as airplanes), it is time for the introduction of a similar apparatus that presents greater difficulty.

THE CONSTRUCTIVIST PRIMARY MODEL

As the name implies, the Constructivist Primary Model is designed for kindergarten and primary grade children (preferably grouped in multiage arrangements) and is based on a constructivist orientation as described in Chapter 10*. A

---

*This model, unlike the other four described in this chapter, is not a model that has a representative implementation located in one particular site at the present time. It is, instead, a composite of various features of programs that have been implemented over the years in various locations. We cannot tie this model to any particular developer or promoter. In many respects, it is like the Open Education Model of the Education Development Center, a Follow Through model modeled after the British Infant School's Integrated Day Approach. It is similar to a number of programs the authors have personally developed or visited in the past.

great deal of advance preparation by the teacher is necessary to implement this model since it requires knowledge of the kinds of activities that are likely to be of interest to the particular age range to be enrolled. Materials are provided for a broad array of activities, including an ample supply of expendable raw materials and a well-organized system for access and replacement of materials. The activity centers include areas for art expression (clay, painting, scrap box), music expression, drama (stage, curtain, dress-ups), writing, displaying, and reading books, math and science investigations, live animals, a woodworking bench and tools, and child-size building structures that can be transformed into various theme representations. There is open space for group gatherings, movement activities, and construction activities and tables and chairs for sedentary activities.

The following schedule is typical of Constructivist Primary programs:

News time Sharing out-of-school life in various ways

Quiet work time Choices of quiet activities such as drawing, painting, writing, sewing, listening center

Sharing Showing or talking about the experiences and products of quiet work time

Recess Outdoor play with various options

Book time Looking at books and other print/picture materials, reading to self or another, writing, making books

Math time or writing time Individual and small-group activities with intermittent large group discussion and sharing

Lunch

Story time Teacher-read or told stories or individual reading or looking at books

Noisy work time All the quiet work time choices, as indicated here, plus additions of dramatic play, carpentry, clay, musical experimentation, dancing, and other noisier alternatives

Sharing Showing or talking about the products and experiences of noisy work time

Unit or theme activities Group and individual activities related to interest themes such as museums, changing seasons, occupations

This schedule is characterized by the predictable diversity of activity options provided for children within consistent time arrangements. The name of the time period refers to the kind of activities the children are expected to engage in rather than a specific subject matter. Choices between activities in any particular time period remain fairly constant. As was described in the Cognitively Oriented Model, planning and decision making are important parts of children's responsibilities. The sharing periods provide the opportunity for children to reflect on what decisions were made and what their outcomes were.

Teachers in the Constructivist Primary Model must communicate to children that they are expected to become constructively engaged in learning and in creative efforts, and that they are to use time, materials, and other resources in a responsible fashion. Children who make responsible decisions and become very productively involved in doing and learning, whatever direction that may be, are subsequently given additional options. On the other hand, children who do not become productively involved (who interrupt others, waste materials, and so forth) are provided greater structure and fewer options. The continuing goal for all children is to increase their abilities to make and carry out their own plans and to seek the knowledge and skills necessary to those plans.

During the various activity periods, teachers in the Constructivist Primary Model interact with children in individual conferences (both informally and as scheduled) and in small groups brought together on a one-time or few-times basis because of a common interest (to hear a story about a space flight) or a common need (to learn how to count money in making change for the group's "movie theater" ticket sales). There are no set ability groupings as in many other primary programs.

A central feature of the Constructivist Primary Model is teacher-child dialogue, which has as its intent encouraging and helping children reflect on their experiences and their understandings of the phenomena they have encountered. In talking with children, the teacher tries to avoid asking questions to which he or she already knows the answers ("What color is that?" "How many do you have now?") and instead asks questions that encourage children to tell about something they have seen or done at another time or are currently thinking about. The teacher asks many *why* questions and accepts the answers, whether or not the thinking appears adequate from an adult perspective. "Why do you think . . . ?" is frequently heard. Peer discussion is encouraged, and cooperative endeavors toward trying to figure out how to do something or the answer to a tough question are facilitated by the teacher. Constructivist primary teachers are aware that adequate understanding requires the learner to build and then to discard many partial and unsatisfactory explanations. They also recognize that memorized "right" answers only partially understood discourage the pursuit of understanding.

Constance Kamii (1985*a*, 1985*b*) has clarified in her demonstration projects and her writing how constructivist teachers can work with children in the traditional academic areas of reading, writing, and arithmetic. She emphasizes activities in arithmetic, for example, "(a) situations in daily living such as the counting of votes and (b) group games such as dice and card games" (1985*a*, p. 6). She also emphasizes the exchange and coordination of points of view among peers, saying that the coordination of viewpoints is essential for the development of "logico-mathematical knowledge" (1985*b*, p. 163).

In the Constructivist Primary program, extensive individual records are kept for each child that indicate the nature of the child's involvements and accomplishments, including, but not limited to, the conventional academic areas. These programs assume that learning is not complete unless children actually use concepts or skills in their self-initiated activities. The records on accomplishment are limited to what the child actually does voluntarily, not how they respond when asked during an interview or conversation or when tested. The categories you used in assessing individual children in Part 2 are examples of the framework used in such records. Parents are encouraged to contribute to these records through their observations of the activities their children initiate at home that demonstrate learning and skill development.

SUMMARY

The five program models we presented in this chapter vary in the degree to which they are easily identified as fitting any one of the three orientations described in Chapter 10. Nevertheless, each of the five models—Cognitively Oriented Curriculum, Direct Instruction, Bank Street, Montessori, and Constructivist Primary—has an identifiable configuration including time scheduling, space arrangements, facilities, teacher-child relationships, and objectives. You will find, however, that a program that identifies itself as one or another particular model may differ markedly from the ideas of the originator. A program model is typically modified each time it is implemented. Such modifications often reflect the preferences of staff members who unconsciously interpret a given program to fit their own personal teaching philosophy. Thus, you may find several types of Montessori programs. You may find programs that say they follow the Bank Street model that look quite dissimilar to what we have described. Nevertheless, it should be useful for you to have the reference points of the three orientations and the five models as a basis for making comparisons among the programs you encounter, most of which will be eclectic. Eclectic early childhood programs are more common than any other kind.

SUGGESTED ACTIVITIES

1 Consider how you would respond to job offers in which you would be expected to develop skills and attitudes necessary for the successful implementation of any given model described in this chapter. Assuming that all the other aspects of the job offer were similar and desirable, how would you feel about accepting classroom teaching responsibility in a Cognitively Oriented Curriculum classroom, a Direct Instruction classroom, a Bank Street classroom, a Montessori classroom, or a Constructivist Primary classroom? Summarize your reactions.
2 Observe in classrooms that are attempting to implement any of these models and analyze how they are like or different from each other and from other programs that are not identified as following any particular model.
3 Interview experienced early childhood educators about the early childhood program models they favor and have attempted to emulate. Find out the reasons for their preferences and discuss any problems they have encountered in trying to implement these models.
4 Interview parents of children enrolled in a particular type of preschool about why they have chosen this preschool rather than others available in the community.
5 Develop a comparison chart that contrasts the five models described in this chapter or other prototypic models on the basis of such variables as program objectives, teacher

role, time scheduling, equipment and materials, expectations for children's involvement, and expectations for parental involvement.

ADDITIONAL READINGS

Bereiter, C., & Engelmann, S. (1966). *Teaching the culturally disadvantaged child in the preschool.* Englewood Cliffs, NJ: Prentice-Hall.

Boegehold, B. D., Cuffaro, H. K., Hooks, W. H., & Klopf, G. J. (Eds.). (1978). *Education before five.* New York: Teachers College.

Chow, S., & Elmore, P. (1973). *Early childhood information unit: Resource manual and program descriptions.* San Francisco: Far West Laboratory for Educational Research and Development.

Cryan, J. R., & Surbeck, E. (1979). *Early childhood education: Foundations for lifelong learning.* Bloomington, IN: Phi Delta Kappa Educational Foundation.

Day, M. C., & Parker, R. K. (Eds.). (1977). *The preschool in action: Exploring early childhood programs* (2nd ed.). Boston: Allyn & Bacon.

DeVries, R. (with Kohlberg, L.). (1987). *Programs of early education: The constructivist view.* New York: Longman.

DeVries, R., & Kohlberg, L. (1987). *Constructivist early education: Overview and comparison with other programs.* Washington, DC: National Association for the Education of Young Children.

Evans, E. D. (1971). *Contemporary influences in early childhood education* (2nd ed.). New York: Holt, Rinehart, & Winston.

Gilkeson, E., & Bowman, G. (1976). *The focus is on children: The Bank Street approach to childhood education as enacted in Follow Through.* New York: Bank Street College of Education.

Hohmann, M., Banet, B., & Weikart, D. P. (1979). *Young children in action: A manual for preschool educators.* Ypsilanti, MI: High/Scope.

New, R. (1990). Excellent early education: A city in Italy has it. *Young Children, 46* (6), 4–10.

Rambusch, N. (1962). *Learning how to learn: An American approach to Montessori.* Baltimore, MD: Helicon.

Roopnarine, J. L., & Johnson, J. E. (Eds.). (1987). *Approaches to early childhood education.* Columbus, OH: Merrill.

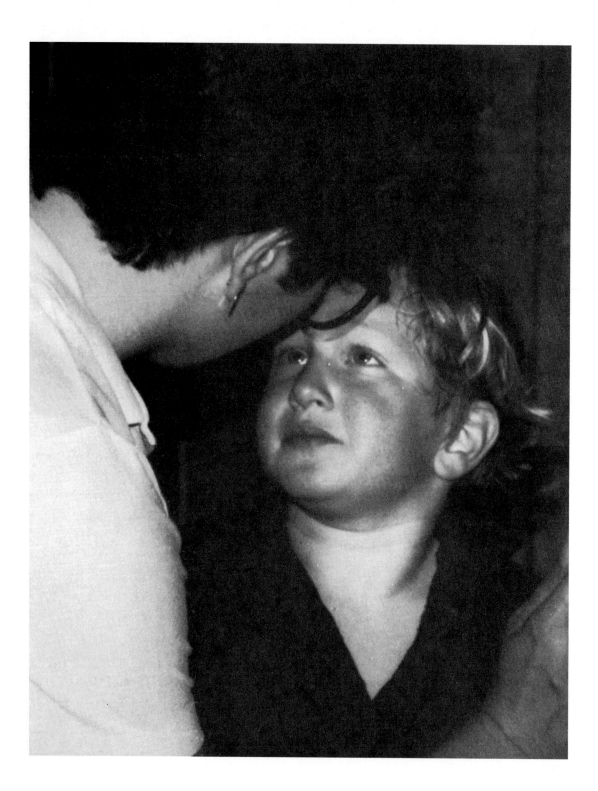

CHAPTER 12

CLASSROOM MANAGEMENT AND DISCIPLINE

OVERVIEW

Classroom management refers to what a teacher does to keep children constructively engaged in activities that are developmentally and educationally appropriate. **Discipline** refers to the actions of the teacher when a child, despite management efforts, continues to engage in behavior that is not considered acceptable. If a teacher is skilled in classroom management, there is far less need for discipline. Thus a teacher who is having discipline problems will likely benefit, not from better methods of discipline, but from improved management skills. Although the terms are sometimes used interchangeably, there is an advantage in distinguishing between them and focusing energies more on management than on discipline.

There are at least three aspects of classroom management to be considered: the physical environment, daily routines, and guidance strategies. These are presented in the first part of the chapter. Discussion of discipline is in the latter portion of the chapter.

THE PHYSICAL ENVIRONMENT

As a teacher, you may find that the space assigned to you for your classroom is one large room or two or more smaller adjoining rooms. It is likely that you will have little choice in this matter. The way the classroom space is to be arranged, however, will usually be left up to you. Unfortunately, there is often insufficient time for leisurely consideration of these matters in an actual teaching situation. Sometimes teachers are expected to have their classrooms all set and ready for children after only a day of preparation. It therefore behooves you to study various classroom spaces now and to make some advance decisions about the kind of arrangements that are possible under various constraints of space and equipment provision.

The way in which you plan the program day and your supervisory activities must take into account such factors as whether children will be in one large space or in several small ones, whether toilet facilities are close, and where sinks or other water sources are located. In planning for the physical environment in the classroom, a great many decisions must be made, including:

What areas shall be created?
Where shall the areas be placed in relation to each other?
What shall be placed in the areas?
What display space can be created? How shall display spaces be used?
What storage spaces are needed, and how shall they be arranged?
How can the environment be made aesthetically satisfying?

As you go through this chapter, visualize yourself in the role of teacher, and consider the management decisions you would personally make for a classroom in which you have primary responsibility.

PLANNING FOR SPACE ARRANGEMENT

In making the decision about areas to be created, you need to consider the kind of participation you wish children to have. The orientation to child development, as described in Chapter 10, is influential in this respect. If you want children to uniformly attend to instruction, the most functional arrangement may be the one often seen in elementary schools in which rows of individual desks and chairs are arranged across the available space. If instruction is often directed to a small group, an arrangement of chairs in a semicircle facing a teacher's chair in the center is desirable. Few objects, such as toys or personal possessions, would be present to detract from the messages presented by the teacher. These two arrangements best fit the kind of teaching planned by behaviorists.

If, as is usually the case with maturationists and constructivists, you want to arrange an environment to stimulate children's interaction with each other and with equipment and materials, you should place a number of activity centers within the available space. The following centers are often arranged: block play, dramatic play, art, water play, sand play, listening, puzzles and manipulatives, books, nature, discovery, writing, printing, woodworking, climbing, puppet plays, and cooking. Full descriptions of many of these centers are included in Part 4, along with recommendations for their use.

In making the decisions about placement of the centers, you may find it helpful to visualize the classroom as four sections based on a wet versus dry dimension and a quiet versus noisy dimension (see Figure 12-1). Within the wet-quiet quadrant are many art activities. Wet-active activities include water play, sand play and sometimes sociodramatic play, cooking, and real-life activities such as

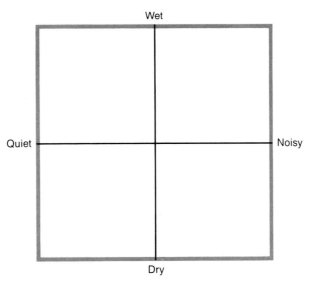

FIGURE 12-1 Conceptual schema of classroom space

scrubbing and shoe shining. Examples of activities for the quiet-dry quadrant are a book center, a listening center, and a manipulative material (table toys) center. Active-dry areas include block play, large-muscle play, music, puppet areas, and movement and group-meeting spaces. Many classrooms, of course, are not square like the one in the figure. Whatever the shape of the room or rooms devoted to the program, conceptualizing the space in terms of these dimensions should prove useful. It avoids having materials such as books ruined by wetness or paint and reduces the extent to which the most boisterous play must be "shushed" to accommodate those needing quiet concentration.

Traffic patterns between areas must also be carefully arranged. The important issue is whether the space arrangement helps or hinders the transition of children from one activity to another. In planning the placement of classroom areas, visualize the location of children at various points throughout the program day, and think about what space and equipment will be needed at each point. If there is to be a sharing time after an independent work period, for example, consider whether there will be space available for placement of work products before and after each child has the opportunity to report on and show their efforts. Or, if children are going outside for a playtime immediately after a story, will the necessary play equipment and the children's outside clothing be easily accessible?

When planning the physical arrangement of the classroom, you should also try to visualize where you will position yourself at each point. If, for instance, during the free activity period, you will wish to spend a portion of the time in the art area labeling children's paintings, the art area needs to be placed so that it has visual access to most of the other activity areas. Or, as another example, if

Sprouting plants and lively polliwogs are attractive educational features in this prekindergarten classroom. *(Ursula Moeller)*

snack time is to proceed smoothly, you may need to position that area so you can simultaneously monitor the late arrivals from toileting while carrying on a conversation with those already at the snack area. If each point during the day, especially the transitional periods between one type of activity and another, can be visualized and provided for in the room arrangement, the result will be far more satisfactory.

Planning for Placement and Storage of Materials

As previously indicated, guidelines for what to put in specific areas and for the use of the areas are included in Part 4. There are, however, some general pointers that may prove useful. Where possible, materials should signal an invitation to the children, and their placement should signal where they are to be stored after use. Bins with markings, taped shapes on shelves, and pull-out storage crates all invite independent action in acquiring and replacing materials. The amount of material to put out at any one time depends on the total number of

Children who have observed polliwogs carefully feel confident in creating their own representations using tempera paints. *(Ursula Moeller)*

children, their ages and stages of development, and to some extent, on the program philosophy. For example, in behaviorist programs very little would be placed on open shelving for children to manipulate independently. In a Montessori program, on the other hand, although very little will be placed on shelves at the start of the program, materials will be gradually introduced and, once introduced, will be consistently present. In other programs, certain basic materials will be present from the start and others introduced as special features during certain time periods. Despite these variations, an overall rule of thumb is to place in open storage only those things that you wish children to use. Store other materials not currently intended for children's use in other locations.

An early childhood program requires a great deal of storage, both open accessible storage within the classroom and closed storage. Although programs differ in what and how much they put out in open storage, there are certain general principles:

- Plan carefully for storage at the start of the program and avoid rearrangement thereafter.
- Have an array of standard items always available in low open storage.

- Insist that children learn the storage techniques and expectations.
- Reserve some storage space for short-term "special" needs.
- Show how and where things are to be stored, used, and then replaced in storage. Bins, boxes, and baskets help with this delineation. Symbols such as a sample piece in a plastic bag attached to the storage bin are helpful.
- Avoid crowding materials together on the shelves.

If closed storage is not immediately accessible for art supplies, books, picture files, accessories for dramatic play, water play, block play, sand play, musical instruments, manipulatives, cleanups, snacks, and so forth, settle for a more distant location but acquire a wheeled cart for daily transportation needs. It is usually preferable to have a more distant storage site than to try to keep all supplies in open storage within the classroom.

There is also need, regardless of program orientation, for each child to have an individual storage space. For primary-age children this is often a desk, but there are other viable alternatives that take up less classroom space. Bins, "cubbies," and boxes are sometimes substituted. For young children, a cubbie with several shelves—one for possessions and one for shoes, books, and the like— and a space (within which the child can also sit) for hanging outer garments creates a sense of personal ownership that seems very positive.

Planning for Aesthetics

In addition to planning for the physical arrangement of the environment, you will need to give attention to the creation of an aesthetically satisfying environment. Teachers and children spend a great deal of time in classroom settings, yet spaces designated for children's programs are often located in hard, bland environments, without carpeting, draperies, or other such accoutrements of home or modern office living. Teachers, in these situations, whatever their orientation, sometimes acquire soft and colorful items such as area rugs, cushions of various sizes, fabric wall hangings, and cork wall coverings. Any modification that creates a more aesthetically pleasing environment for children and for adults may have surprisingly positive consequences in overall classroom management.

Some teachers create a station for themselves in the classroom that is not only functional but also creates an aura of comfort and beauty. They bring to this space art work, weavings, artifacts, and personal touches such as photos of family or pets. Attractive baskets or other colorful containers can be used to organize diverse supportive supplies such as felt pens, scissors, and tape.

The environment can also be enhanced through the use of attractive plants, soft background music, or a tinkling mobile. Alternative olfactory experiences may be introduced periodically by such strategies as heating cinnamon in water, putting peppermint extract in playdough, or acquiring fragrant flowering plants. Modifications in lighting can change the mood of the classroom. The installation of dimmer switches, as suggested by Marion (1981), allows greater lighting flexibility. Although these suggestions may not be in keeping with the orientation of many programs, the underlying message to you is to put thought into creating an aesthetically pleasing environment that you will enjoy sharing with children and their parents.

Planning for Display Space

You also have to make decisions about display space. Here, too, the orientation of the program is a factor. Numerous materials on display may be distracting to children in instructional situations. In behaviorist classrooms, there will probably be limited display space, mostly devoted to posting children's best efforts. These displays are best positioned so that they are not in view of the children during instructional periods. In Montessori classrooms, highly aesthetic use of color and arrangements is emphasized. In most early childhood programs, however, bright arrays of children's creative expression predominate, sometimes in quite unsightly profusion. In maturationist and constructivist programs, the following items are considered particularly appropriate for displays: children's artwork, such as paintings, drawings, prints, collages; charts, graphs, stories, and photographs developed with children's participation; informational materials such as "how to" charts, work assignment lists, and so on.

Most classrooms have bulletin boards for displays. If these are not available, there are many other ways to create display space. Cupboards or screens, used to subdivide space into activity areas, can also provide surfaces for mounting charts or children's artwork. Screens of this type can be constructed with minimal carpentry skills using pegboard sheets purchased at building supply houses. Other possibilities include mounting taut lines between classroom walls and using clothespins to attach materials or arranging a fishnet decoratively between doorways and using paper clips to attach display materials. And, of course, in some situations attaching materials directly to the walls is acceptable. In creating bulletin boards or classroom displays that are aesthetically pleasing, the following guidelines are useful:

- Display "busy" artwork, photographs, and the like on a plain background. A textured material such as burlap may make an attractive backing. The color may be neutral or bright, but beware of floral or striped background coverings that visually detract from the featured exhibits.
- Limit the number of items you try to mount on a given surface.
- Leave ample uncovered space.
- Keep in mind basic design principles of balance on horizontal and vertical planes.
- Tie together various areas of the classroom through coordinated use of color on display backgrounds.
- Use children's own art rather than commercially prepared holiday symbols such as Santas. When adult art is displayed in the classroom, use works of excellent quality, such as reproductions of masterpieces to which children might not otherwise be exposed.

DAILY ROUTINES

Opinions vary on the type of time schedule that is preferable for children's programs. As discussed in Chapter 11, the daily schedule is determined in large measure by the orientation of the program planner. There is general agreement, however, that there are benefits in establishing children's expectations for a daily pattern of events, whatever those may be. Regularity of events is believed useful in helping children develop a sense of time. Also, by knowing what to expect, children become more secure and autonomous in their actions. They need not be as dependent on an adult to tell them what to do. When a program's daily routine is carefully planned and consistently implemented, there is a more positive atmosphere and fewer clashes resulting from discrepancy between teacher expectations and child behavior. Although some teachers may prefer to be flexible and creative in their scheduling sequences, there is good reason to question the wisdom of so doing. The younger the children, the more likely that schedule modifications will prove difficult for them. When changes are to be made in the regular schedule, it is wise to prepare the children by carefully explaining how the day will be different. In one nursery school we visited, there was a good deal of discussion about the upcoming "backward" day in which outside play time would be first instead of last to accommodate the schedule of a special set of visitors. With this kind of talk and advance preparation, the children adjusted to the changes rather easily.

Advance Planning

The results of a number of studies of elementary teachers as classroom managers suggest that a key factor in managerial effectiveness is detailed advance planning of how the classroom environment is to be used throughout the program day. This advance planning allows the teacher to concentrate, from the first day, on communicating to children about expected behavior. According to Emmer, Evertson, and Anderson (1980), the more effective managers among the third-grade teachers they studied established themselves as classroom leaders from the start and worked intensively on classroom socialization during the first weeks of school. Poor managers failed to have well-thought-out procedures, were vague and inconsistent in their expectations, and failed to take constructive action through reteaching when children's behavior signaled misunderstanding of procedures. Management, viewed in this light, is primarily a matter of deciding about classroom procedures and then effectively teaching those procedures to the children. To think through daily routines for a classroom program, you need to consider the following:

Where will I locate myself as children are arriving?
What will children do as soon as they arrive?
How will I show children how to obtain and replace materials?
How will I alert children to the availability of help should they need it?

What will I do with other children should one child be ill or in great distress? How will I serve snack? Where do I expect the children to sit?

What are my expectations for children's behavior as they go outside the classroom?

Where and when will it be okay for children to be very active—to run, jump, and tumble?

How will I signal to the children that I want to talk with them as a group? Where will I and they be situated for a group meeting?

GUIDANCE STRATEGIES

The goal of positive management is to keep children constructively involved with activities that they enjoy and that will help them learn. By now you must be well aware that we favor the constructivist perspective and assume that children engaged in learning will be active and sometimes noisy. They will be

Teach and reteach until the appropriate behaviors are clearly within the child's repertoire. *(Cumberland Hill Associates, Inc.)*

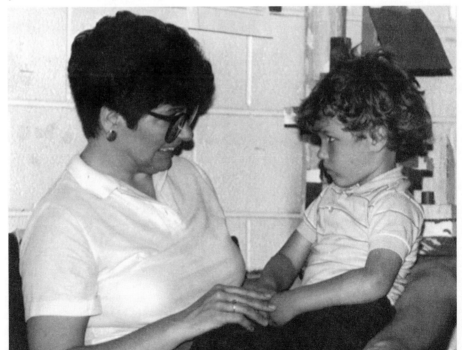

silly as they engage in linguistic play, saying such things as "Goopy, gloopy, droopy, soupy, poopy. . . ." But they are also quiet and serious. The good manager of classroom behavior is so well prepared for childish behavior that there is little concern about the natural ebb and flow of giggling, crying, shouting, and whispering.

Ten General Strategies

Beyond setting clear expectations that are taught and retaught as necessary, to be an effective classroom manager, you should also do the following:

1 Be alert to what everyone in the group is doing. Take visual snapshots of the classroom frequently. Even when you are involved with a single child or small group, position yourself so that you can see as much of the room as possible.

2 Use frequent eye contact with individuals and communicate nonverbally (with smiles, nods, quizzical looks) your involvement with their activities.

3 Listen attentively to each individual to whom you give your attention. Identify the child's concern accurately, and respond in such a way that the child's concern is addressed.

4 When you give directions and instructions, make sure that they are clear, and help children follow them through if necessary. Give directions one at a time, if possible, and no more than two at a time. In general, the younger the child, the fewer the number of directions he or she can remember and follow. When possible, give children directions for specific activities at the time and place when you want the behavior to occur, not in advance of the situation and setting. For example, give playground directions on the playground, not inside the classroom.

5 Use a variety of methods and materials. (See the alternative teaching strategies discussed in the following chapter.)

6 Develop a sense of how the children perceive the classroom. Look for any misconceptions and gaps in their thinking about how to participate in the classroom activities.

7 Keep group times short, lively, and interesting.

8 In praising or reprimanding, be very specific about what the child is doing well or failing to do.

9 Give advance notice, as much as ten minutes ahead, of the end of activity periods.

10 Expect interruptions or problems to occur, and develop strategies for dealing with them. Examples of frequently recurring problems are children's tardiness or absence and return from absence; classroom visitors, administrator, or parent interruptions during class sessions; children's illness; power failures; inclement weather; lost possessions; uncomfortable temperatures.

Communicating Expectations

Although inexperienced teachers know the behaviors and attitudes they want to develop in children, they lack a repertoire for how to communicate these expectations to children. This is especially the case for those who are concerned that children develop into autonomous, not merely obedient, persons. The goal, it would seem, is to speak to children about their behavior in ways that sensitize them to the need for standards and that communicate your confidence and help in acquiring these behaviors. You do not want to convince them by what you say or do that they are bad or stupid. Different ways of verbally reacting to a problem situation draw very different reactions from children. Consider a scene in which four-year-old Ronnie has bumped into Carla while walking about holding an easel paintbrush. He has made a huge orange paint splotch on her pink blouse. As a teacher you might say any one of a number of different things:

"Ronnie, you've got to be more careful with your paintbrush or you won't be able to paint anymore."

"Ronnie, can't you watch what you are doing?"

"Ronnie, tell Carla you are sorry. And watch what you are doing from now on."

"That's all right, Ronnie. I know you didn't mean to bump into Carla."

"Ronnie, why don't you ever use your head. You are so careless. Now look at what you've done."

"Carla, let's see if we can sponge off some of that paint. And, Ronnie, as soon as I'm finished helping Carla, let me show you about putting your brush down before you move away from the painting easel."

Only in the last statement was Ronnie given a cue as to what to do to avoid such incidents. Consider what conclusions he might reach from the other statements. Of course, it is easier to recognize a constructive response than it is to generate one on the spot when something unfortunate or discrepant has just occurred. It pays to think ahead how you will respond in various situations. Think through some of the following six guidelines, and consider how you might incorporate them into your own management repertoire.

1 Use positive suggestions. Tell children what to do rather than what not to do:

"Sit on the chair," rather than, "Don't sit on the table."

"Turn the book pages by the top corner like this," rather than, "Don't be so rough with the books."

"Wipe your brush on the jar," rather than, "Don't drip paint on the floor."

2 Emphasize the desirable aspects of behavior and communicate that you have confidence in children's ability to use them:

"Jane knows how to clean up."

"Jimmy knows how to carry scissors."

"Mary is remembering to keep the sand in the sandbox. She knows about sand."

(About spitting) "Herbert is still learning about keeping spit in his mouth. He knows, I think, that he can spit in the toilet or in a tissue if he needs to."

(About biting) "Yvonne is still learning about when to use teeth. We use teeth to chew carrots and meat and other food."

3 Give choices only when you are willing to accept the children's decisions:

"It is time to clean up now," rather than, "Do you want to clean up now?" or "Will you help me clean up, okay?"

"Two people can use the wagon. One can pull and one can ride in it," rather than "Wouldn't you like to share the wagon?"

4 Explain the reasons behind your expectations:

"Place the blocks in the cupboard like this. If we throw them in, they become chipped and broken and hurt our hands when we build with them."

"Blocks are for building and balls are for throwing."

"I can't let you hurt other children, and I can't let anyone hurt you. School has to be a safe place for everyone."

5 Try to explain children's behavior to each other. If a child complains about another who is not following the class routines or is not sharing, you might say, "I think he is still learning about that. Maybe he will be able to do it tomorrow." This explains the child's behavior and yet, lets him feel there is progress and expectations for the future. You might say:

"John thought you were through with the truck."

"I think Margaret is trying to be friendly."

I think he is trying to tease you. Acting silly."

"Wayne is tired and wants to rest awhile."

6 Use a variety of methods to communicate about an expected behavior. If a first request is not successful, word the second request in a different way. Try to use ingenuity rather than confrontation to make situations go smoothly. To stop a particular type of behavior that is objectionable, provide an alternative. Children are more responsive to new suggestions than to reprimands. Help the children establish patterns of happy performance instead of negativism.

DISCIPLINE

It is particularly important to make sure that limits to be imposed are both necessary and developmentally appropriate. A good rule of thumb is to have as few rules and "don'ts" as possible. It may be wise to start with two or three rules that are absolutely necessary to maintain a safe and functional environment. Use positive methods like the guidance strategies just discussed, and make sure that the rules are followed. Add others that seem absolutely necessary at a later point.

Setting and Managing Limits

Many children will test limits, especially in initial contacts, to see if the adult is serious and to discover the consequences of noncompliance. Some continue to test limits for the sake of getting adult attention. In being clear about limits, it is also useful to make the consequences for overstepping them explicit, predictable, and logical. For example, if children know that initiating use of a new table toy depends on replacing material previously taken, there will probably be compliance after some initial testing. This is especially likely if the task of replacement has been made simpler by clear arrangements and if the reasons for the rule are clearly understood. For instance, "We put the toys back on the shelf so they don't get all mixed up and broken." If, on the other hand, the consequences of noncompliance are infrequently and unpredictably enforced, continual testing and noncompliance are likely.

If some children, despite all efforts at constructive group management, continue to break rules and ignore limits, you should make sure they have actually learned the appropriate behavior and when it is expected. Find out through inquiry or observation whether the children know what to do as well as what not to do. Teach and reteach until appropriate behaviors are clearly within each child's repertoire. When there is evidence that this learning has been accomplished but inappropriate behavior continues, the following three strategies (mostly derived from the reinforcement principles described on pages 178–179) may prove effective.

1. Ignore the misbehavior   Give attention to the child's other behaviors that are desirable. This is sometimes referred to as the "catch them being good" strategy. With most kindergarten and primary grade children it works rather magically to remark, "I like the way Maria has———." Most of the children will look to see what Maria has done well and will follow suit. As you praise or otherwise reinforce appropriate behavior in other children, be sure to be very specific about what they are doing that you approve of. This is a useful strategy for children whose problem behavior appears to be a means for getting attention.

It is important to keep in mind here that reinforcement differs for different individuals. For one child, teacher attention is reinforcing, but for others access to special activities or materials is more potent. By determining the kind of response the particular child finds reinforcing, it becomes possible to more systematically influence the child through making reinforcements more contingent on desirable behavior.

2. Scold the child   Even though this way of dealing with a child's misbehavior may often be observed and may, in fact, result in immediate compliance, typically the undesirable behaviors soon reoccur. Children normally find scolding aversive and, consequently, cease whatever they are doing and are reinforced by the termination of the scolding. This strategy is an example of negative reinforcement. Negative reinforcement, as is pointed out on page 178, is reinforcement that comes from termination of some noxious condition. Although behavior can, to some extent, be controlled by negative reinforcement, the climate that is created is not one that contributes positively to children's development and learning.

3. Remove the materials the child is using and/or remove the child from the situation   These approaches have the advantage of being logically related to the misbehavior. It is possible to explain to the child who is throwing blocks, "You must stop playing with the blocks now because you are throwing them. Blocks are for building, not for throwing." Do not engage in a discussion about the matter. Be brief and emphatic, dealing with it as unemotionally as possible.

Removing the child from the situation should be done as infrequently as possible, since it becomes less and less effective as a deterrent. Porterfield, Herbert-Jackson, and Risley (1976) describe the removal of the child from the situation as asking the child to "sit and watch." The child is told to sit on the sidelines for a brief period so that he or she can watch how other children are playing appropriately. After a few minutes, when the child is sitting quietly and actually watching others without crying or whining and appears to concentrate, the child is asked whether he or she can now do whatever it is that is expected. The child is then allowed to begin to play again. As soon as he or she is appropriately involved, the teacher comments positively about the activity.

Discipline approaches such as scolding, taking materials from the child, and removing the child from the situation are most effective when they are used infrequently. Carefully planned classroom management and clear communication about reasonable expectations within a program designed to be involving to children greatly reduces the need for discipline strategies. Resorting to discipline techniques, even positive ones, may be a sign of management failure and often impedes the progress of the class. Disciplinary actions usually have broader effects than the immediate modification of the behavior in question. As a teacher scolds one child, all others within earshot are absorbing the message and the attitudes of the teacher and the target child. This effect has been systematically studied by Kounin (1970) and designated by him as "the ripple effect." If children observe disrespect from the teacher for other children in the class, they may also learn to disrespect each other. If they observe physical punishment, they learn that it is okay to use physical force to get others to comply with their own wants. It is therefore very important that teacher management and discipline behaviors provide suitable models for children to emulate.

SUMMARY

Classroom management and discipline are complementary processes. The teacher well skilled in management has infrequent need for discipline techniques. Those poor in management, however, are found to increasingly engage in disciplinary actions.

Scheduling, space arrangements, and environmental maintenance all contribute to program involvement and must be carefully planned. Children need to be systematically taught how and when to use equipment and materials and what behavioral expectations are in the program setting.

Positive management strategies are usually very effective in promoting a constructive program environment. It is sometimes necessary, however, to enforce limits through discipline techniques such as planned ignoring, scolding, material removal, and removal of a child from a situation. The overall atmosphere is affected by the frequency and type of discipline used, and there are advantages in maintaining a positive classroom milieu for all concerned—for individual transgressors, for the larger group, and for the teacher.

SUGGESTED ACTIVITIES

1 Create a diagram of the spaces, indoor and outdoor, of an early childhood education program where you observe or participate. Note whether there is a separation of noisy from quiet areas and wet from dry areas. Also note any other factors that may explain the placement of particular areas or pieces of equipment such as patterns of traffic flow or concern for supervision.

2 Observe in classrooms and compile a list of strategies teachers use to keep the program operating smoothly. Also compile a list of the situations within which management problems seem to arise. Consider alternative management strategies that might prevent the occurrence of such problems.

3 Interview experienced teachers about how they organize and manage their classrooms and how they handle discipline problems of various types (tattling, aggression, destruction of materials and equipment, discourteous behavior, improper language).

4 Record on video- or audiotape your own interactions with children in a situation in which you have some responsibility for their safety, welfare, or learning. Analyze the points at which problems seem to arise and consider how they might have been avoided. Next consider what alternatives might be as desirable as or preferable to the one you took in handling the situation.

5 Make a list of the common behavioral guidelines teachers provide in classroom situations and state each as a negative statement. Rephrase in a positive form.

ADDITIONAL READINGS

Alger, H. A. (1984). Transitions: Alternatives to manipulative management techniques. *Young Children, 39*(6), 16–25.

Allen, K. E., & Hart, B. (1984). *The early years: Arrangements for learning.* Englewood Cliffs, NJ: Prentice-Hall.

Charles, C. M. (1985). *Building classroom discipline: From models to practice* (2nd ed.). New York: Longman.

Clewett, A. S. (1988). Guidance and discipline: Teaching young children appropriate behavior. *Young Children, 43*(4), 26–31.

Drawbaugh, C. C. (1984). *Time and its use: A self-management guide for teachers.* New York: Teachers College Press.

Harms, T., & Clifford, R. M. (1980). *Early childhood environment rating scale.* New York: Teachers College Press.

Haswell, K. L. (1982). Techniques for dealing with oppositional behavior in preschool children. *Young Children, 37,* 12–17.

Marion, M. (1987). *Guidance for young children* (2nd ed.). Columbus, OH: Merrill.

Morrison, J. W. (1991). The art of redirection. *Day Care and Early Education, 19*(1), 4–7.

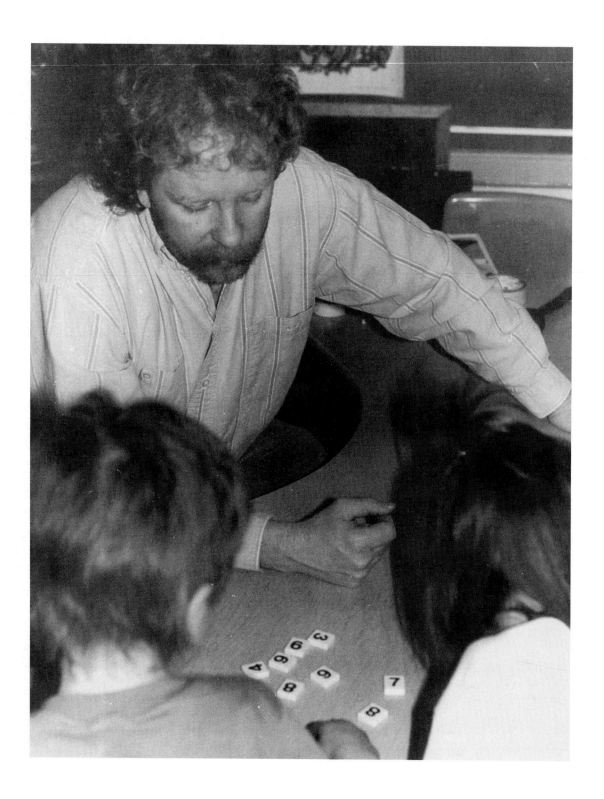

CHAPTER 13

TEACHING TECHNIQUES AND STRATEGIES

OVERVIEW

This chapter focuses on the alternative means teachers of young children use as they plan and provide for children's learning. Although teachers develop their own individual styles, there are many common techniques and strategies, whose mastery is an important aspect of preparation for teaching.

In the first section of this chapter, there is a general discussion of planning in which two contrasting approaches are presented. Strategies teachers use in dialogues with young children and in planning lessons for children are then discussed in two separate sections.

PLANNING FOR TEACHING

Kate and Erica are the teaching team for eighteen prekindergarteners. As we join them to observe their planning session, we see them on a Thursday afternoon in April seated at a small round table near their classroom teacher station. Both have their shoes off, feet propped up on another chair, and cheese, crackers, and glasses of tomato juice at hand. The following excerpts are taken from their planning conversations.

KATE: How did you think the pulley activity went today?

ERICA: Just great. Kim really got into it. Did you notice? And when Timothy discovered that he could lift that heavy load of blocks so easily, he kept giggling to himself. That was a great activity.

KATE: What did they say about it? I couldn't hear what they were saying from where I was.

ERICA: Timothy didn't say much of anything. Kim kept commenting, "I bet you can't lift that much," and then would pile on more blocks. Peter made a couple of interesting comments. He said, "We couldn't do this, you know, without those wheels and rope." Then he said, "You know that thing over there has wheels and ropes too." And he pointed to the construction crane across the street. Even though we had talked about pointing that out to the children, I really didn't think any of the kids would notice on their own. It was much more effective for Peter to point it out than for me to.

After a similar discussion of several of the week's activities, Kate initiated a discussion of the upcoming week by showing Erica the written plan she had prepared. (See Figure 13-1.)

KATE: Here's your copy of what I'm thinking about for Monday, Erica. I've selected a number of activities that should make the children more aware of the seasonal changes going on right now. Here are the activity cards for the activities you'll be responsible for: manipulatives 5; active play 3; songs 7, 18, and 15; fingerplays 3 and 2; movement 6; art 5; dramatic play 7. Keep track of how often you are able to work in the targeted teaching activities. Is there anything else you want to add? Or anything to change?

ERICA: I wonder whether movement 9 might not be a better choice. It's almost

FIGURE 13-1   Completed planning grid for full-day kindergarten for teaching team (head teacher, Kate; assistant, Erica)

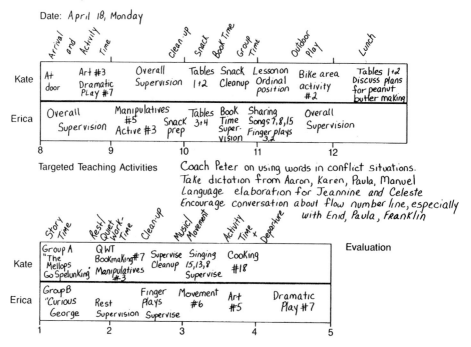

the same but requires less following of directions. I don't think this group is ready for that yet.

KATE: That's probably true. Let's make that switch. I'm concerned about that though. I hope we can make some improvements in the children's ability to follow directions. Now let's look at Tuesday's plan. I have movement 8. It's that imitation game. That requires following several directions also. Let me try it, but would you please watch carefully during that time? Perhaps you can tell if there is a breakdown in communication with just a few kids or whether I'm missing the mark with a large number of them.

ERICA: Yes, I'll do that. If I'm going to observe them though, we need to change the next activity to one that requires less preparation.

KATE: Oh, sure!

The teachers in this scenario use a daily planning form to coordinate their efforts. Some teachers use a weekly planning form that is far less detailed than the one that Kate follows. It is not unusual for experienced teachers to list only the name of each specific activity or lesson they intend to include on a weekly planning sheet. Kate, however, prides herself on using a system that is detailed enough so that assistants, substitutes, visitors, and administrators can easily understand what is to happen. The activities referred to by numbers are from an index file of activity plans that Kate has prepared over a number of years. She browses through her collection and selects the activities relevant for a given week. She prepared some of the activity plans while she was an undergraduate, and although she has modified and expanded many of them, she is still using the same file cards during her tenth year of teaching. She also has a card file of objectives with suggestions for lessons to fulfill these objectives.

Activity Plans

Kate uses both **activity plans** and **lesson plans.** She predominantly relies on activity plans, however. Her orientation is the one described in Chapter 10 as constructivist. The kind of plan Kate prefers is one that features an event, happening, or involvement. Note such an activity plan in Figure 13-2. The plan specifies the equipment, materials, and advance preparation required, the suggested procedures, and the possibilities for learning presented by the activity. Each activity plan provides for children with a range of abilities and has sufficient complexity to permit numerous ways for children to become involved. Various types of learning are expected from each activity. Teacher planning focuses on finding ways to stimulate and encourage children to connect new with previous experiences, to experiment, to categorize, to theorize, and to draw inferences. Each activity and set of materials is analyzed in considerable detail by the teacher as part of the planning process. Possibilities for children's involvement and learning are considered with little expectation that any of the particular items listed as possible learnings will actually occur. With various possibilities in mind, the teacher is more alert and flexible concerning ways in which the children might become involved.

FIGURE 13-2   Example of an activity plan

Name of Activity:

Soap bubbles

Equipment and Materials:

Detergent, water, drinking straws, disposable cups, measuring spoon ($1/4$ teaspoon), two small pitchers, paper towels or wipe-up cloths, Ping-Pong ball or other light object, shallow box.

Advance Preparation:

Set up bubble activity in an area where spills will not be disastrous. Protect table and floor surfaces with newspaper, plastic, or toweling if necessary.

Suggested Procedure

1. Put some water in a small pitcher and make it available to the children to pour into glasses. Emphasize that they are to fill their glasses half full, demonstrating how much water that will be. Distribute straws and suggest that they experiment with sucking in and blowing out.
2. Demonstrate putting in a fourth teaspoon of detergent and stirring to make soap suds. Also demonstrate blowing a bubble, emphasizing that you are being very careful to blow out and explain why. Demonstrate how, upon completion, the soapy water is to be placed in a pitcher in a set location for later use in washing some object during daily clean-up.
3. Before giving each child the measure of detergent ask them to show you that they understand what blowing out means by blowing on a Ping-Pong ball or other light object placed in a shallow box and moving it about with their blowing.
4. Give verbal description of sequence even though the children will undoubtedly know what to do. Emphasize their actions with words such as "First, dip the straw in soapy water. Second, put straw between your lips. Next, blow out air and see if you make a bubble."
5. Encourage children's experimentation. Comment and or explain in pace with the children's involvement.

Possible Learnings

1. Word awareness of terms such as *drip, drop, small(-er, -est), break, pop, bubble, double bubble, triple bubble, straw, detergent, soap, near, far, out, in, blow, air, dip, breath, blow, fragile.*
2. Exhalation control (differentiation of breathing in vs. blowing out; impulse control—intentionally blowing strongly or gently).
3. Sequence awareness.
4. Measurement concepts such as half full, full.
5. Science concepts: Air takes up space. We breathe air in and out of lungs through nose and mouth. Soapy water around the bubble of air makes it slightly heavier than the surrounding air and so it drifts to the floor. Other moving air may deflect the bubble as it falls. When bubble hits another object or the floor, it bursts because weak surface tension makes it very fragile. It is so fragile that sometimes it bursts without striking anything. Light shining through water creates rainbow effects, that is, is bent to display component colors. Water by itself has less surface tension than soapy water making it more difficult to blow bubbles in water without soap or detergent.

Possible Variations

1. Set up as an outside activity on a warm windy day.
2. Use soap bubble rings like those provided with commercial bubble mix.
3. Encourage children to experiment with adding various other substances to see if they create sufficient surface tension for bubble making. Provide salt, vinegar, soap flakes, sugar.

Evaluation:

Record the kind of involvements the bubble-making activity engendered in individual children. Note verbal and motoric learnings and social exchanges during the activity. Also record any evidence of vocabulary or other learnings observed later in the day or on subsequent days.

The following characteristics are examples of what should be considered in preparing activity plans:

1 The physical characteristics of available objects

   Size   What are the size relationships between objects? Which is larger? smaller? wider? taller?

Head teachers have primary responsibility for the coordination of planning. *(Lee C. Lee)*

Shape What is round? square? rectangular? cylindrical?
Color What is red? yellow? brown? dark? light?
Texture What is smooth? rough? bumpy?
Transparency What can be seen through?
Reflectivity What reflects light, serving to mirror objects?
Weight What are the weight relationships? Which is heavier? Which is lighter?
Mass What is the area or volume of objects?
Composition Which objects are metal, glass, wood, plastic, paper, fabric, manufactured, natural?
Symmetry Which objects are symmetrical, nonsymmetrical, have symmetrical aspects?
Patterns Which objects display patterns or, together with other objects, form a pattern?

2 The potential uses of available objects

Containability What can hold or contain other objects or substances?
Combining ability What can be combined, and with what else?
Malleability What can be molded, folded, or bent into different forms?
Changeability What can be changed into different states (evaporated, melted, frozen, dissolved, burned)?
Reversibility What changes can be reversed, returning objects to their original states?
Sound production What can be used to produce sounds or variations in sounds?
Marking What can make marks on other surfaces?

3 The language requirements of specific situations

Vocabulary needs   What words are necessary for naming and describing various objects and actions?

Grammar and syntax needs   What will involve the child in language expression of various kinds?

4 The written communications already available and the potential for introducing new writing activities

5 Imaginative associations

Movement   What movement activities are suggested by objects and situations?

Emotion   What emotional tones or expressions are suggested by objects or situations?

Human roles   What human roles are suggested by objects or situations?

Literature   What stories or poems are suggested by objects or situations?

6 The social possibilities within situations

Interactions   What interactions might the situation foster? What social repertoire is necessary?

Cooperation   What possibilities for cooperative endeavor are present in the situation?

Conflicts   What kinds of conflicts might the situation engender? What alternatives can be modeled for conflict resolution?

This list does not exhaust the possibilities that might be considered in mentally preparing for an activity with young children, but it does provide a broad base and considerable variety.

Once the activity card is prepared it can be used again and again, with modifications made from time to time as new possibilities are noted.

The preparation of activity plans is akin to the idea of "extension" as described by Cazden (1971) after visits to schools in England and Wales. Cazden cited Margaret Roberts of the University of London Institute of Education as describing good teaching as "sensitive observation," a "mental companionship" between teacher and child, which in turn leads the teacher to extend the child's ideas and language.

Cazden (1971) also cited comments of Mr. Norfield, head of a primary school in London, as follows: "If the teacher is not aware of particular aspects of experience, she can't pay attention to them; if she's not aware of the intellectual skills and concepts in the simplest activity, she cannot nourish those skills and concepts in the context of children's play" (p. 121).

Lesson Plans

Behaviorists and others who see the task of the teacher as providing direct instruction to children favor lessons as the preferred planning form. The lesson plan consists minimally of four parts: (1) objectives to be accomplished, (2)

equipment, materials, and advance preparation necessary for the lesson, (3) procedures to be followed in conducting the lesson, and (4) follow-up activities to provide further practice. There is also often an evaluation of whether the objectives have been accomplished. See the example of a lesson plan in Figure 13-3.

Objectives are normally the starting point in the construction of a lesson. Once the teacher has decided what is to be accomplished, the next step is to consider how the objectives might best be met in the specific situation. Activities are then selected based on how effectively they will contribute to the accomplishment of the objectives.

In formulating objectives, it is advisable to think in terms of performance. Note in Figure 13-3 that each objective begins with a verb that indicates what children are to do. Specification is also given of how they will perform when the objective is accomplished. Action words such as *write, choose, touch, say, cut,* and *mark,* are further examples of recommended beginnings for objectives. When objectives are stated in performance terms, it becomes possible to deter-

FIGURE 13-3   Example of a lesson plan

Goal:

To develop awareness of positional terminology

Objectives:

The children will become able to:
1. Place objects near or far from themselves according to verbal directions
2. Use the terms *near* and *far* correctly to describe the position of objects in relation to themselves

Equipment and Materials:

Variety of toys and other small objects; snapshots of objects in the classroom; chart easel, chart paper and felt pens

Advance Preparation:

Position some of the toys or other objects around the room at a distance from where the lesson will be conducted. Mount photographs of classroom objects on large sheet of chart paper.

Procedure

1. Introduce *near* and *far* by discussing which toys or objects are near and which are far away. Ask individual children to move certain objects. If the object is near, ask them to place it far away and vice versa. Explain as children move the objects, "The airplane was near. Now it is far away." "The bear was far from us. Now it is near."
2. Show a large chart paper that has on it snapshots of

classroom objects (aquarium, painting easel, flag, and so forth). Discuss each and allow volunteers to draw a circle around those objects that are *near* to where the group is sitting.

3. Make a written list of words on another piece of chart paper of the things that children name as being *far* away. If they name objects or people outside of the classroom, make separate columns of those that are far (but in the classroom), farther (in the immediate area but outside the classroom), farthest (out of the community, in other states, nations, continents, and planets).

4. Distribute a toy to each child and ask them to follow directions such as: "Put the toys near to me." "Put the toys far away from this circle." Then ask each child individually to tell whether they will place their toy near to the circle or far away. Have them make the placement and repeat for them, "Yes, you said you would place it far away and you did place it far away." Finish this phase by asking all children to bring the toys near and place them in the box. Refer to the box as also being near but then ask a couple of the children to take it to the storage cabinet at the far side of the room.

Evaluation:

Observe whether children are appropriately using the terms *near* and *far* to describe their action in the last activity. If not, provide further experiences and instruction.

mine the extent to which a lesson is successful. If objectives are not accomplished during the lesson, an alternative lesson plan may then be developed using a different strategy or mode of presentation. Or in some cases, objectives may be broken down into component parts to be accomplished in a series of lessons.

Many commercial materials—kits, workbooks, media packages—come with established objectives and prepared lesson plans. As one publisher's advertisement states, "teacher's editions keep you two steps ahead of the class. . . . what a convenience." The most useful of these published materials are those that suggest a number of alternatives so that the teacher can select what best fits the particular children and situation.

ALTERNATIVE STRATEGIES FOR DIALOGUE

Thus far, in this chapter, general planning processes and two types of plans (activity and lesson) have been presented. In the remainder of the chapter, the discussion will focus, first, on alternative strategies for teacher-child dialogue outside of a lesson situation and, second, on alternative lesson strategies.

During activities, daily maintenance situations (lunch, toileting, dressing, and undressing), or quiet periods of teacher-child conversations, there are many opportunities for teachers to develop and use dialogue strategies that promote children's understanding, motivation, and self-confidence. Among these dialogue strategies are active listening; descriptive feedback; directing, telling, explaining; question asking; modeling; and prompting and coaching. Each of these will now be briefly described.

Active Listening

One only needs to observe a teacher skilled in **active listening** in dialogue with children to conclude that it is the most powerful tool available for promoting involvement and learning. Such teachers situate themselves so that they are on the child's eye level. This may require kneeling or sitting on the floor or on a small chair. Eye contact is very important. Beyond this, the child must be made to feel that what he or she is saying is of the greatest importance. Note the following dialogue:

C: Look at what I made.
T: *(Kneeling beside C and looking seriously at the object and then back at C)* You've been working on that for a long time, haven't you?
C: *(Nods)* I put this here and this here *(points)*.
T: You put this here and this here *(points to the same places)*. *(Pause)*. What else did you do?
C: A lot!
T: I'd like to hear about it.
C: Well, I got this circle thing and made it stick on here.
T: Oh, yes, I can see how you attached that circle. How did it work out?
C: Fine. I'm quite good at doing this, right?

T: That's what I think. What else are you planning to do with it?

C: This one is finished. But I'm going to make another. If I can find another circle, that is.

T: How do you think an oval piece would work? *(Moves to the scrap box, retrieves oval-shaped paper, and then returns to kneeling position)*

C: *(Examining oval)* That offle [*sic*] will be good. Looks like an Easter egg.

T: Easter eggs are oval shaped, aren't they?

In this exchange, the teacher did a minimum of praising. She has learned that praise from her, although pleasing for the child to hear, is more likely to close down on the child's verbal sharing than to lead to an elaboration. Instead of saying, "That's very good," she comments on the behavior she observed—a long period of effort. She makes use of rephrasing to make the child aware that she has correctly understood. She often asks open-ended questions. She waits patiently for a response each time. She also supports the child's planning through material provision, and she does a bit of informal teaching in the process. Through active listening the teacher helps the child engage in an elaborated verbal communication. The skill of active listening is described in greater detail in Chapter 15.

Descriptive Feedback

To help children better understand and appreciate the activities in which they are engaged, teachers often use a form of dialogue called **descriptive feedback.** There is some overlap between active listening and giving descriptive feedback. In the first instance, the teacher responds primarily to what the child says. With descriptive feedback, the teacher emphasizes verbal descriptions of the child's actions. For example:

(Observing C painting at the easel) "You let your colors mix here in the middle of your painting, didn't you? And at the top and the bottom, the red and the yellow colors are kept separate."

"You are waiting very patiently for your turn with the new puzzle, aren't you?"

"The doll is certainly dressed up now—a vest, a coat, pants. Is he all ready?"

Such comments help children note certain things that they might otherwise have only dimly perceived and expose them to vocabulary that describes their experience. Quite often words used casually by teachers during this kind of descriptive talk are soon incorporated into the children's own vocabulary. You may have noted that none of the descriptive feedback questions are open-ended. They serve a different purpose, that of modeling the use of language and concepts, and are not intended necessarily to engender further conversations about the topic.

Directing, Telling, Explaining

During activities, teachers sometimes get involved in directing, telling, and explaining. When they do, they often try to link their message to children's previous experiences. Note the way these teachers give their directions, telling and explaining in terms that are meaningful to the children:

"Remember how you always take turns outside in riding the bikes. You can play this game (pick-up sticks) by taking turns too. First, Peter, let John pick up all the chopsticks he can without moving any of the others. And then, John, you let Peter do it next."

"This bowl is different from the ones we usually use. It is very fragile. That means it may break unless we are very careful. That's because all parts of it—the sides and bottom (pointing) are so thin. Notice how thin this glass is and how thick it is in a regular cereal bowl. It isn't very strong. Let me show you how to handle such a fragile thing. Watch how to do it."

Question Asking

One of the most potent methods teachers can use to foster cognitive growth is to ask children questions in a way that activates their thinking. Certain kinds of questions are much more educationally useful than others. For example, it is helpful to ask about cause-and-effect relationships:

"What do you think will happen if you ___?"
"How did you do ___?"
"Can you do something to make ___ happen?"
"Why does ___ happen?"

To respond in each of these instances, children must focus their attention on transformations and the causal events behind those transformations. Possibilities for this kind of questioning are abundant in activity situations.

It is also useful to ask questions that require what Siegel and Saunders (1979) called **distancing** in order to provide an answer. Distancing refers to the linking of immediate behaviors or events with similar ones that are outside the immediate environment. An example of a distancing question is "We had a good trip to the zoo today. Where else do people sometimes go to see animals?" Such a question allows many different responses, may raise an issue intrinsically interesting for the child to contemplate, and puts the cognitive responsibility on the child for coming up with an adequate answer. To move from actual happenings to possible alternatives requires distancing. Also helpful are questions that start the child thinking about alternatives to what he or she has proposed. The child says, "I want hot dogs for lunch." The teacher may reply, "Does that mean you don't want to have an apple for lunch," or "Does that mean that you don't want to have hot dogs for dinner?" Such teacher intervention, judiciously used, challenges the child toward greater linguistic and conceptual precision.

After posing a question during dialogue with children, it is important to wait patiently for an answer. When an answer is given, it should be accepted without posing other alternatives. It is desirable to show approval of thoughtful answers even though they may not be the correct ones. Pursuing the thinking behind incorrect answers is advisable since both the teacher and child benefit. The

Children often initiate opportunities for teachers to engage them in dialogue. *(John James)*

teacher learns more about the child's thinking, and the child is encouraged to give the matter more thought.

Modeling

Teachers sometimes engage in the activities they provide for children for the purpose of modeling new or more appropriate behaviors. Teachers may, for instance, play in the water at the water table, using the various props and responding enthusiastically to the effects that are created. Or they may, in a dramatic play setting, say, "I'm going to pretend I'm the grandmother and will get some food ready to eat," or "I'm going to be a doctor. Let's see. I'll need the stethoscope and some tongue depressors and a pad for writing down what I find out about the patients." By this behavior, teachers are informally modeling possibilities for involvement as well as the vocabulary needed for communicating about the activity.

Prompting or Coaching

Teachers use many informal prompts to stimulate children's involvement. They also influence the nature of that involvement by what they say to children. Prompts may consist of such comments as:

"This is a book I thought you would like, Rob."
"I think the family needs a big sister, Ellen. Would you like to be a big sister?"
"There's a space for one more person here."
"Ask Raymond if he needs help."

Other comments serve to coach children about how to engage in an activity so that they find it more satisfying and successful.

"Would you like these foam pieces for your block house?"
"If you put the block of wood into the vise, it will be easier to saw it. Let me show you how."
"Would it work better sideways?"

Although children learn a great deal through their own activity without adult intervention of any kind, their learning is often enhanced by the judicious use of prompts and coaching statements.

In summary, the skilled teacher uses combinations of active listening; descriptive feedback; directing, telling, and explaining; question asking; modeling; and prompts and coaching statements. When you have the opportunity, analyze the behaviors of experienced teachers during informal periods and note how they use these categories of behavior in various combinations.

ALTERNATIVE STRATEGIES FOR LESSONS

Whenever there are specific objectives to be accomplished by a group of children, a lesson plan is needed—at least a mental one. Although those with a behaviorist orientation do more of this kind of teaching than constructivists or maturationists, there are times when lesson plans are used regardless of orientation. For example, even in the most maturationist of programs, children must be taught what to do during a fire drill or about safety rules on the playground. Given these kinds of lesson objectives, the teacher decides which of several alternative strategies will be most effective. Among these strategies are direct instruction lessons, structured inductive lessons, structured modeling lessons, advance organizer (reception) lessons, repertoire-building lessons, and cooperative learning lessons.

The younger the child, however, the less likely it is that lesson formats, particularly group lessons, will be appropriate. In determining the wisdom or folly of presenting lessons to preschool or kindergarten children, consider the following questions:

Do the children experience a significant degree of success during the lessons?
Do the children participate with a minimum of coercion?
Do the children "catch on" to most of what is taught?
Do the lessons result in positive attitudes toward peers?
Do the children use what is presented during lessons in nonlesson situations?

If the answers to the above questions are *yes,* feel assured that the lessons are appropriate and useful. If not, there is reason to restructure the lessons, try a different strategy, or reconsider whether any type of lesson format is desirable for these children at this point in time.

Direct Instruction Lessons

Direct instruction lessons are appropriate for learning objectives aimed at a particular discrimination and/or vocabulary increment. These lessons have many variations, but generally include four sequential steps. The sequence may be repeated a number of times throughout the session as new bits of information are introduced.

1 *Tell:*
   This is a ___.
   This is how to ___.
   This is what to do first.

2 *Ask for identification, using several examples and several nonexamples:*
   Is this a ___?
   Is this how to ___?

3 *Ask for discrimination among alternatives:*
   Which is ___?

4 *Ask for recall:*
   What is ___?
   Show how to do ___.
   Tell how to do ___.

The direct instruction lesson often emphasizes contrasts as in step 2 above. The presentations of nonexamples begin with extreme contrasts and move toward finer and finer discriminations. The child is to learn the "right" response, and the teacher's role is to sequence the presentation and questioning so that children will be right most of the time.

Direct instruction is primarily identified with the Direct Instruction program model described in Chapter 11. Some of the characteristic features of the direct instruction approach are: use of attention signals, instances and noninstances, response signals, feedback, reinforcers, pacing, pauses, rhythm, response rates, volume variations, body language, enthusiasm, stimulus change, surprises, intentional mistakes.

Attention signals may consist of the teacher's raising a hand and saying, "Listen!" or "Look!" or, possibly, sounding a buzzer or bell. The signals should be taught and practiced before using them during instruction, and teachers should be careful to reinforce only those children who attend properly. Children must learn response signals as well. They may be taught that when the teacher points to an individual child, only that child should respond and that a sweep of the hand is a signal for a group response. Responses are never accepted from a student when a signal has not been presented. When a signal is given and an accurate response is forthcoming from a child, the teacher immediately reinforces by saying, "good" or "correct" or using any one of a variety of reinforces, such as handshakes or touches. If the child's response is incorrect, the teacher says, "No, the answer is ___" and immediately reasks, "Is it ___?" thus preparing the child through this prompt for a correct response that can then be reinforced.

In direct instruction, teachers vary their pacing from rapid-fire to slow-rate questioning, inserting strategic pauses for emphasis and attention. They plan in advance how and when to do this, creating a rhythm of loud, soft, fast, slow, pause, and so forth. A high rate of questioning and responding is attempted, with each child being expected to respond individually or with the group. A high proportion of these responses should be correct; if not, the teacher is remiss in choice and sequence of questions.

For each fifteen minutes of instruction, the focus of attention should be changed three times, that is, different activities at least every five minutes. Surprises such as dropping a book or slapping a desk or table are planned, one for each fifteen minutes of instruction. In addition, many teachers plan to make two or more intentional mistakes during each lesson, such as placing a picture or letter upside down or giving a wrong answer. Catching the teacher's mistakes is fun for the children and keeps them alert.

The success of direct instruction in accomplishing specific academic objectives has been well documented in a number of studies (Bereiter & Engelmann, 1966; Becker & Gersten, 1982; Rosenshine, 1978).

Structured Inductive Lessons (Concept Attainment)

The traditional differentiation between inductive and deductive teaching is that *induction* moves from specific instances to the formation of a generalization whereas *deduction* starts with a generalization and then moves to specific instances. **Concept attainment** lessons use the inductive approach. It is a particularly useful strategy for developing an awareness of similarities between objects or events that constitute a concept. Bruner (1956) used tasks labeled concept attainment to study children's thinking strategies. In these tasks, an assortment of examples (items that fit preset criteria) and nonexamples are presented to children. The children are then invited to figure out whether each item, pointed out one at a time, is "right," that is, fits the criteria the adult has in mind.

The concept attainment lessons, which are very appealing to children, are of two general types, each having several variations. In the first, the teacher selects a **concept** to be discovered and presents both examples and nonexamples, one at a time, placing them in one of two groupings. Children try to guess the underlying concept that determines why some items go into one group and some into the other. They are encouraged to explain their choices and to discuss them with each other. Examples of sort criteria are circles versus squares, plants versus animals, indoor versus outdoor articles of clothing, happy faces versus sad faces.

A variant to this is to have the teacher accept only "right" items into a single collection. Thus, everything red would be accepted by the teacher for placement in a particular collection, but any picture without red would be said not to fit. Children try to guess the underlying concept rather than being told what it is; they guess what the criterion may be and test out their hypothesis by applying it

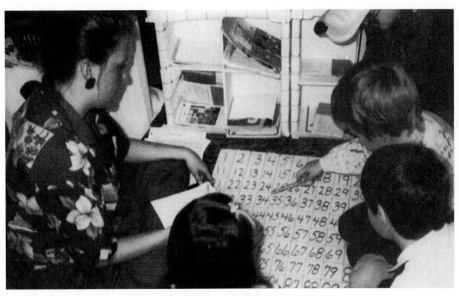

"All in this row have 'four' in them." *(Cumberland Associates, Inc.)*

to later instances. The teacher uses familiar materials such as small objects or pictures in this type of concept attainment lesson and presents many examples and nonexamples of the concept. Children are given ample opportunity to test out their own ideas and are encouraged to discuss their guesses with each other.

This kind of concept attainment lesson can be used for teaching in many subject areas. For example, a teacher using the two-group format arranges such a lesson to help children learn the concepts of triangle versus square. She uses a flannel board and, one by one, places flannel-backed cutouts in one of two groupings—triangles and squares, of various sizes and colors. As each is placed, she says, "Let's see, this goes here," or "And this goes here." After placing three or four in each grouping, as she holds up the next form she asks, "Where does this go? Why do you think so?" She presents a great many more, asking about the placement of each and pausing for discussion. As the discriminating characteristics become well recognized by the children, the teacher says, "All these are called squares, and all these are called triangles." She then includes the use of these terms repeatedly in her comments as she places additional examples of each and encourages the children to use the words as well.

In the second type of concept attainment lesson, the children are shown a full mixed array of pictures or objects that can be sorted according to a variety of characteristics they share (for example, tools that could be classified according to size, mechanical versus electrical, kitchen versus garden, or color). The teacher does not predetermine a "correct" sort dimension but invites the children to share with each other their differing ideas of which things go together and why. Inductive lessons follow the pattern of natural learning observed at all ages and are usually fun activities for both teachers and children.

Structured Modeling Lessons

The research of Bandura and associates (1971, 1975) has helped us to understand the power of modeling as a teaching device. The behavior of persons children like and respect is often imitated and incorporated into their own patterns of behavior. Charles (1985) outlines procedures developed for modeling lessons that are appropriate for many early childhood settings. Although the teacher may qualify as a model, a more potent model is often a respected child a year or two older than the group in focus, one who incorporates traits the children see as desirable and who is able to demonstrate well the target behavior. Admired children within the group may serve as models if they are taught the desired behaviors in advance of the lesson and have, in fact, mastered them. Adult males may also be especially effective models for some preschool and primary children. The recommended procedures are to:

1 Have the model correctly perform the desired action as the group watches. This action may be repeated several times. Preschoolers will benefit from having verbal labels connected to what they see. This helps them to remember. Either talk through the process as the model performs or ask the children to tell what they see at each step.
2 Call for verbal recitation (in unison) to describe what was modeled. Repeat two or three times making sure all participate.
3 Ask for volunteers (at least two) to repeat the action individually.
4 Draft two nonvolunteers to repeat the action individually.
5 Have the children meaningfully apply the action to a realistic situation.

This type of lesson is effective for teaching children procedures to follow, such as fire drill behavior, shoe tying, cleanup and storage procedures, use of new equipment, and appreciative handling of books.

It is important to emphasize the correct behavior of the model and of the children who then reenact that behavior. When mistakes are made, have the model go through the action again and emphasize the portions of the action that have not been learned.

Advance Organizer Lessons (Reception Learning)

The ideas of Ausubel (1963, 1968) have led to the development of lesson formats (Lawton & Reddy, 1983) that begin with general ideas and then proceed to develop more specific variations of these ideas. This is described as particularly important for young learners, since they consider only one aspect of a problem or situation at a time and often jump to erroneous conclusions from limited experience. Thus, they may conclude through induction based on their experience that only men can be doctors or that only women can be teachers.

In the **advance organizer** lesson, children's discovery or invention of knowledge is deemphasized. Instead, the teacher's role is to present accurate content in meaningful ways within a hierarchical framework. Preplanning for this kind of lesson consists, first, of decisions about the hierarchical sequencing of the presentation. The teacher tries to decide what the most general concepts are that have already been mastered by the children that could serve as linkage for new information to be presented. Once the format from general to specific is set, the teacher locates appealing props or pictures to go with the lesson. During the lesson presentation, the teacher constantly tries to determine what information the children already fully understand so that new discriminations can be linked to those more general ideas.

In such a lesson on the themes of gender and occupation, for instance, the teacher may begin with a discussion about what it means to have a job or be employed or "work for pay." Once the general understanding is set, children are encouraged to talk about the jobs they know about. At this point, the teacher might present photographs of people in particular job roles. Among the photographs might be female doctors and male preschool teachers. Finally, real objects (stethoscopes, felt pens, thermometers, children's records) related to various jobs might be examined and discussed with conversation directed toward questions of what objects Paul might use at work if he were going to be a teacher and Cynthia might use if she were going to be a carpenter.

Through this process, the children's general understandings are corroborated and then discriminations gradually added; in this case, the added discriminations include nonsexist orientations. Proponents of the advance organizer lesson strategy believe that learning proceeds most efficiently with this approach since new information is linked to the learners' existing conceptual framework.

Repertoire-Building Lessons

In **repertoire-building** lessons, a problem situation is typically used as a focus. It may be a social problem (such as how to get a turn with a cherished but scarce resource such as a playground bike) or another type of problem (such as how to find a lost article). The problem may be a simulated one described to the children or demonstrated via role-playing, or it may be an actual problem of concern to one or more members of the group. The goal is not necessarily finding a "right" or "best" answer but instead to build a repertoire of possible alternatives for problem situations.

As children generate ideas in response to the question posed by the teacher ("How can ___ so that ___?"), responses are acknowledged and listed on a chart or chalkboard (even for nonreaders). After each addition, the teacher repeats it as well as all previous suggestions and asks, "Who's got a different idea?" Only serious responses receive attention. The lesson continues as long as children are attentive and as long as the ideas continue. Teachers, as well as children, contribute ideas.

This kind of lesson is used in the Spivack and Shure Interpersonal Problem-Solving Curriculum for four- and five-year-olds cited on pages 112–113 (Spivack & Shure, 1974; Spivack, Platt, & Shure, 1976; Shure, 1980). The Spivack and Shure lesson scripts include the initial development of essential vocabulary and concepts for the consideration and discussion of problem-solving alternatives.

"Do you remember the size of the carrots we pulled out of the garden yesterday?" *(Permission of Bernice Wright Cooperative Nursery School)*

Once children understand and use terms such as *and, or, other, not, same, different, if, then, why, because,* they have the prerequisite concepts and language to engage in a repertoire-building lesson. Spivack and Shure include in their writings sets of detailed scripts for lessons on social repertoire building. The basic strategies, however, can be used in any problem-focused group discussion.

Cooperative Learning Lessons

Cooperative learning has become a very popular lesson approach in recent years. The approach has been researched by Roger and David Johnson (1989) at the University of Minnesota; many other educational leaders also champion the approach as contributing both to social goals and to learning goals.

Cooperative learning lessons are appropriate for all subject areas and many kinds of problem solving. In using a cooperative learning approach the teacher emphasizes social skills with the children as well as the learning task. Social skills include such things as knowing the task, listening to one's partner, calling one's partner by name, talking in quiet voices, taking turns, asking for help, complimenting the partner's participation, avoiding "put-downs" of the partner. During lessons teachers monitor whether children are using the social skills and make sure that children know that these are as important as the lesson tasks.

Primary grade or younger children usually work in pairs rather than in groups of three or more. Heterogeneity of assignment to pairs is seen as very desirable in supporting students' acceptance of differences, including differences resulting from disabilities. The effectiveness of the strategy for promoting learning is believed to come, in large measure, because of the concentrated "time-on-task" which results from working intensely with another or others and from the cognitive benefits of talking through one's thoughts. As Ellis and Whalen (1990) state it: "To learn, we need to talk about what we are thinking and to adjust our thinking as we hear ourselves saying things that don't quite make sense. Through talking, we discover what we know and what we don't yet understand" (p. 20). Working with someone on another achievement level does not detract from the benefits of talking through and explaining one's own thinking to the other person.

An example of a cooperative lesson task, as presented to children, is provided by Ellis and Whalen (1990), as follows:

> Your pair has two jobs. One job is to find six objects in the room that begin with the sound of your group's letter. Each time you find an object that you both agree starts with the sound of your letter, you will tape one of your group's paper letters to the object, so we'll all know which ones you found. Your other job is to remember to take turns taping the letters. As I watch each group working, I'll be listening to see if you check with your partner to be sure you both agree that an object starts with the sound of your letter, and I'll be looking to see if you take turns taping the letters (p. 27).

Students' behavior is evaluated by the teacher and by the children themselves according to the general criteria for cooperative group behavior and for the particular lesson.

For younger children of kindergarten and primary age, cooperative group tasks may be of a type described by Wasserman (1990) as "play-debrief-replay." In this kind of cooperative lesson, the children are first given an opportunity, in small groups, to play with a set of objects carefully selected to support the learning of a particular curriculum concept. The kinds of observations to be made during the play are suggested. For example, for one social studies lesson, the materials suggested were "a collection of shoes (rain boots, sneakers, running shoes, sandals, sports shoes, work boots, [many more listed]" (pp. 128–129). Children working in a small cooperative group were to use these to make observations, e.g., "How are these shoes different from each other? How are they alike? What similarities and differences can you find? . . . Which ones belong together? Why do you think so?" (p. 129). After the children have had opportunity to play with the materials and discuss their observations, they engage in a "debrief" session with their teacher and other groups during which questions are asked with the intent to give the inquiry a new focus, perhaps an extension into another curriculum area. The group is, over a period of time, often several days, given the opportunity to again play with the materials, sometimes with new additions, and add to their initial observations.

The play-debrief-replay sequence is only one example of the way in which cooperative learning lessons may be used with young children. Activities such as making group terrariums, making group murals, cooperative block building, cooperative puzzles, and so forth were cited by Kohlberg and Lickona (1987) as appropriate activities for cooperative learning. Other examples of learning tasks for kindergartners are learning colors or tying shoes. Whatever the task or activity, in cooperative learning, individuals in small groups work together and are expected to assist each other in the process.

SUMMARY

Planning is very important to successful programming for young children and should include reflections on the prior experiences of the group as well as projections into the future. When teachers work in teams with the same group of children, it is important that planning be done together. Even though one of the teachers on a team may take the lead, the other members of the team should also be involved.

Two approaches to planning were described in this chapter. The activity plan is an open-ended approach that, in addition to specifying how an activity is to be presented, requires teachers to give considerable thought to the various possibilities for learning contained in the activity. The lesson plan, on the other hand, is a more closed approach that focuses on how to accomplish specified objectives. Both strategies are useful, but neither one taken alone is sufficient for the complex planning needed in early childhood education.

During both planned and informal (unplanned) classroom activities, teachers make use of the following teaching strategies: active listening; descriptive feedback; directing, telling, and explaining; modeling; question asking; and prompting and coaching. A teacher skilled in the use of these dialogue strategies can infuse learning experiences into virtually any school activity. When planning lessons, there are also a number of different instructional strategies to consider. These include direct instruction lessons, structured inductive (concept attainment) lessons, structured modeling lessons, advance organizer (reception learning) lessons, repertoire-building lessons, and cooperative learning lessons. Each of these lesson formats is useful for certain purposes, and using a combination of them increases the involvement of children. General guidelines for determining the suitability of these or any lesson format for young children were presented. In general, we emphasized that learning results from pleasurable and successful involvement. To the extent that lessons and activities result in pleasurable interactions and success for all involved children, they are likely to result in desirable outcomes.

SUGGESTED ACTIVITIES

1 Evaluate the environment in which you are currently located (at the time of this reading) in terms of its teaching potential. List all the aspects of the environment that suggest teaching-learning possibilities. How might each aspect be useful?

2 For any set of curriculum goals, generate ideas for how these goals might be accomplished through lesson strategies or through teacher-child dialogue during activity sessions.

3 Observe in classrooms and try to determine whether teachers are using lesson or activity plans. Evaluate effectiveness in terms of children's involvement and learning.

4 Analyze the teaching you observe in activity 3 and determine which dialogue and which lesson strategies are used.

5 Prepare a series of lesson plans and a series of activity plans. If possible, have them critiqued by your instructor or experienced teachers. When the plans are well formulated, try them out with a child or group of children. Evaluate your plans and make notes on how they might be revised on subsequent occasions.

6 Ask practicing teachers if you can see their written plans for their current program day or week. Also ask them questions to learn about the additional details of what they intend to do but do not include in their written plans.

7 Observe several different teachers during activity sessions and list the various dialogue strategies each uses. Note the repertoire differences among teachers and consider whether the teachers' repertoire for dialogue affects children's involvement and learning.

ADDITIONAL READINGS

Blank, M. (1973). *Teaching learning in the preschool: A dialogue approach.* Columbus, OH: Merrill.

Bos, B. (1983). *Before the basics: Creating conversations with children.* Roseville, CA: Turn the Pages Press.

Brown, J. F. (Ed.). (1982). *Curriculum planning for young children.* Washington, DC: National Association for the Education of Young Children.

Hart, B. (1982). So teachers can teach: Assigning roles and responsibilities. *Topics in Early Childhood Special Education, 2,* 1–8.

Katz, L. & Chard, S. (1989). *Engaging children's minds: The project approach.* Norwood, NJ: Ablex.

Lillard, P. P. (1972). *Montessori: A modern approach.* New York: Schocken.

Krogh, S. (1990). *The integrated early childhood curriculum.* New York: McGraw-Hill.

Rowe, M. B. (1978). *Teaching science as continuous inquiry* (2nd ed.). New York: McGraw-Hill.

Schickedanz, J. A., Chay, S., Gopin, P., Sheng, L. L., Song, S.-M., & Wild, N. (1990). Preschoolers and academics: Some thoughts. *Young Children, 46*(1), 4–13.

Sparling, J. J., & Sparling, M. C. (1973) How to talk to a scribbler. *Young Children, 28,* 333–341.

Wasserman, S. (1990). *Serious players in the primary classroom.* New York: Teachers College, Columbia University.

DIVERSITY

OVERVIEW

Chapter 14 will assist you as a prospective teacher in planning for the kind of classroom which is a welcoming and facilitative setting for *all* children and their families. That we live in a diverse world is well-illustrated in Peter Spier's (1980) magnificent picture book *People.* The diversity of humankind is presented in full visual array. In the author's words, "More than 4,000,000,000 people . . . and no two of them alike." One panel portrays forty-two shapes of noses! Another panel shows types of housing; another, pets; and so forth. The book concludes with two double-spreads of a world—the first is uniform and drab, and the second includes color, variation, and glorious diversity. The text asks, "Aren't you glad that we are all different?"

As you read this chapter on diversity, you will be asked to identify and celebrate your own uniqueness and to prepare yourself to celebrate and support the uniqueness of the children for whom you have responsibility. In the upcoming years you will teach children of diverse races and diverse cultures who speak in different languages, who have differing patterns of abilities and disabilities, who have differing family composition and life-styles. Your responsibility will be to enthusiastically include all children in your classroom programs in ways that respect and value their differences as well as their common needs.

PERCEPTIONS OF TEACHERS

As a teacher you have an important role in fostering appreciation of human diversity. Your first step in preparing for this task is an introspective examination of your own physical, ethnic, and racial characteristics and background and your feelings about those who are different from you. In our college teaching, we have sometimes asked individuals in groups who are meeting together for the first time to identify and share with each other some single thing that they think may set them apart from all the others in the group. We ask, "What is unique about you?" Most students immediately produce some aspect of their physique or background or experience and pose it as possibly being unique within the group. In doing this, we learn interesting and amazing things. One student may have been born on a train, another may claim to have more siblings than others in the group, another may point out that she has an artificial limb, another may cite his ability with three languages. As a get-acquainted exercise, this is usually very successful. Amazingly, though, there are some college students who claim not to be able to think of anything unique about themselves. They insist that they are very ordinary and that they are not in any way different from their peers. Are you such a person? We propose that unless you are able to identify and freely share the aspects of yourself which set you apart from others, you may also be less likely to value unusual aspects of others. Therefore, we urge you to spend some time thinking about the question: "In what way am I different from other humans with whom I've interacted today, and in what ways are we all alike?" Among the dimensions of difference that you might consider are height, weight, body type, facial features, skin color, hair color, eye color, gender, temperament, disposition, language, political beliefs, dietary habits, dress, and religious beliefs. You might also consider economic background, housing, possessions, family composition.

Also, ask yourself this question: "In what ways do I feel myself to be superior to others, and on what dimensions do I feel inferior?" People consider themselves to be better or worse than others for a number of reasons. Many of these reasons may reflect unconscious attitudes that nevertheless affect behavior and communicate to others very clearly.

Perhaps you are saying to yourself, "I just don't notice differences at all. I am very accepting." If this is what you believe, beware! Continue your self-examination, asking yourself about the irritations you sometimes feel toward others and the basis for that irritation. Ask yourself with whom you associate for extended periods and with whom you do not associate. Become aware of the extent to which you are inclusive or exclusive of those who are different in some ways from what your cultural subgroup considers to be the norm. Two quotations seem to encapsule these twin aspects of the acceptance of diversity: Thomas Merton (1955) pointed out in *No Man Is an Island:*

> If I cannot distinguish myself from the mass of other men, I will never be able to love and respect other men as I ought. If I do not separate myself from them enough to know what is mine and what is theirs, I will never discover what I have to give to them, and never allow them to give me what they ought (p. 247).*

---

*The use of the word *men* in Merton's expression instead of the more gender-neutral *humans* is a reminder of how well hidden our biases may be. Certainly Merton did not intend to present himself as a gender-biased person. Awareness of bias about the relative status of men and women, as communicated and reflected in language, is of more recent origin than the 1950s.

The other aspect of actively moving beyond difference to encompass others through our common humanness is captured by Edwin Markham's metaphor in this verse:

> He drew a circle that shut me out—
> Heretic, rebel, a thing to flout
> But Love and I had the wit to win;
> We drew a circle that took him in![†]

Teachers need to "draw circles" which warmly embrace the diversity which may be found in any group of young children and their families. Even if you have been personally rejected because you are from a less (or more) privileged background, are from a different race, speak differently, or some such thing, as a teacher you need to be able to find the common ground upon which successful relationships may be built.

"I'M IN YOUR CLASS."

As you consider how you will organize your own classroom as a teacher and how you will provide for children's (and their families') identification with you and with program activities, consider who may show up as your pupils. You may have an entire class composed of children from white middle-class families looking as though they were replicas of the families of Dick, Jane, and Sally of the old Scott-Foresman readers. However, it is more likely that your class will have considerable diversity. You might have the following in your class:

- Yoshi Nagaguchi is the child of professional Japanese parents. She speaks both Japanese and English very fluently. Her mother speaks very little English, but her father has command of several languages. Yoshi loves to paint, dance, and often demonstrates her abilities in paperfolding. She also loves birds and can identify many kinds. Her parents are eager to be supportive of school activities. They do, however, express some dismay at the impetuosity of U.S. children they encounter in the classroom and are concerned when they see any of this kind of impatience in their own daughter.
- Becky Norew is the daughter of a teenage single mother, Sandy Norew. Sandy and Becky reside with Sandy's mother, also a single parent with many other younger siblings (some of whom are close to Becky in age). Becky loves TV and movies and knows a great deal about actors and various programs, films, etc. She is very sophisticated in interpersonal relations, having learned to tease and wheedle to make sure that her needs are met. Becky, like 2.5 million other U.S. children, has asthma.
- Ronnie Moniewski is the son of Steven and Elaine Moniewski. They are adoptive parents, mid-forties in age, and have one other adopted child, a daughter

[†]*The Home Book of Quotations* (3rd ed.) (p. 273) by Burton Stevenson (Ed.). New York: Dodd, Mead & Co., 1937.

two years older than Ronnie. Ronnie is an interracial child with dark skin, brown eyes and blond curls. Ronnie has a severe hearing disability. He wears a hearing aide and does a little lip reading but still seems to miss much of the content of classroom interaction. He either keeps to himself or concentrates a great deal of attention and energy on trying to comprehend what is being said by those around him, especially the adults. Ronnie likes to play with blocks and spends long periods at the water play table. He also enjoys looking at books and has many books of his own which he brings to share with the other children.

- Junie Brown is the child of Sam Brown and Jane Zimmerman. Jane's eight-year-old daughter and ten-year-old son from a prior marriage live with Junie, Sam, and Jane. Sam also has children from both of his previous marriages who often are with the family on weekends and during part of summer vacation. In addition, Sam's stepchildren from his second marriage are often welcomed to the family for extended stays. Jane is a surgeon, and Sam is a pediatrician. Junie is very independent and very enthralled with dramatic play, stories, animals, and ballet (for which she has frequent lessons).

- Anne George is the daughter of Karen George, an executive in a local social service agency. She is also the adopted daughter of Gail Cramer, an artist who creates prize-winning stained glass creations. Karen and Gail are very open about their lesbian relationship, and Anne calls them both "Mom" or by their first names, depending on the situation. Anne is fascinated by any kind of art media. She is very verbal and often sings to herself as she works and plays. She is fascinated with Broadway show tunes. She adores "The Phantom of the Opera," which she, along with her two moms, has seen three times.

- Stacy Robinson is the first child of Clark and Dorothy Robinson. The Robinsons are African-American. Both are newly employed professors at the nearby university. Stacy has traveled abroad a great deal with her parents over the past two years as they pursued studies which required their residence in the Netherlands and France. The family has recently returned from abroad and is in a new home. The parents have new demanding jobs and a new younger sibling will be born in a few weeks. Stacy is full of smiles and becomes involved in dress-up and other activities when one or the other of her parents is present. When they attempt to leave the program, however, she goes to her cubby, holds tightly to some of her possessions, and hides her face. Sometimes she cries softly to herself. Her parents report, however, that she tells them a great deal about what has happened at school. Although she converses freely at home, she says very little at school even when her parents are present.

- Juan Perrone is the child of Puerto Rican parents, Maria and Jesus Perrone. He is the youngest of eight children and shares a room in their small flat with three of his older brothers. The family has recently moved to your state from Puerto Rico. Juan speaks only Spanish. His parents are struggling economically and work at various part-time jobs; they are unable or unwilling to come to meet with you or to see Juan's classroom.

- Maggie Endicott is a victim of birth trauma resulting in cerebral palsy. She has stiff jerky movements and some balance problems. She is able to walk, albeit awkwardly. She has severe speech problems, and understanding what she says is almost impossible. Maggie evidences great interest in books, in other children, and in many nature areas, especially insects. She has a tremendous will to learn, to achieve, and to be accepted by peers. Her parents seem to differ in their reaction to their daughter's disabilities. Maggie's mother seems totally dedicated to compensating for her daughter's disabilities, and Maggie's father appears distant and alienated. Mrs. Endicott confides that they are considering a trial separation.

Quite realistically, children with the mix of profiles listed above are not at all likely to be in the same group. There is a very good likelihood, though, that any teacher of young children will encounter many children and families with highly variable characteristics. Unless teachers of young children develop their understanding and appreciation of diversity along with a broad repertoire of skills in relating to such diversity, they will not do their jobs adequately.

TYPES OF DIVERSITY

Race

Many adults believe that young children are not aware of racial differences, and the adults therefore try to behave as though they were color-blind. However, a great deal of evidence indicates that children by age three do categorize others on such dimensions as skin color, ways of speaking, hair color, and eye color. By the time children enter first grade racial awareness is well-established (Katz, 1982). This is a very normal developmental occurrence. Young children trying to learn about their world constantly engage in a sorting process. To develop the concepts required for human functioning, they must "clump" like objects and beings together and learn to label and to discriminate between what does and does not fit into each classification. That racial identifications develop during preschool is not surprising and may be considered a positive occurrence in the child's development. What needs to be of concern to the early childhood educator, however, is what meaning or valuing is related to the classifications. The development of appreciative views of racial diversity or the development of prejudice also occur during the preschool years. Although children are predisposed to notice differences, they are not predisposed to reject differences. As declared in the lyrics from the musical *South Pacific:* "You have to be taught before it's too late, to hate all the people your relatives hate. You have to be carefully taught." If, instead, children learn, by the age of seven or eight, to value those who differ from themselves, we have more hope for the next generations. The work of parents and of preschool teachers is to help children honestly and appreciatively discuss and enjoy racial differences.

Although few teachers intend to teach racial bias, many do quite inadvertently by consistently avoiding any mention of differences and diverting children from any curiosities which touch on differences. Sometimes adults are embarrassed when children make comments, ask questions, or nonverbally show curiosity regarding racial characteristics in the presence of a racially different

Singing songs together is fun and supports both acceptance and learning. *(Cumberland Hill Associates)*

person. From such behaviors, children learn that there must be something terribly wrong with such differences which are so unspeakable. Children then may begin to place a negative evaluation on their own racial characteristic or the characteristic of the other race.

The book *Anti-Bias Curriculum: Tools for EMPOWERING Children* (Derman-Sparks et al., 1989), an excellent guide for teachers, recommends that children be encouraged to talk about their own and others' physical characteristics such as skin color, hair texture, and eye shape. Only as children talk about the differences they note can teachers become involved in guiding their thinking toward interracial acceptance. Derman-Sparks and colleagues believe that teachers should seize these opportunities and promote such conversations rather than to cut them short.

Consider the following:

- Charles says, "I'm more brown than you are" to his friend, Eddie. Eddie looks down at his skin and looks doubtful. His teacher says, "Yes, your skin is a beautiful color, Charles, and your skin is beautiful too, Eddie. We have wonderful skin colors in this group, don't we?"

- When Enid says to Michelle, "Why are your hands pink but your arms are brown? Why don't you wash your arms?" their teacher waits. Michelle says, "That's just the way my skin is. It is brown skin." Enid says, "It sure looks dirty to me." Their teacher says, "Michelle is right, Enid. Her arms are not dirty. I bet that you are thinking of the times when you get some mud or something like that on your arms and when you washed it, the brown spots came off. Is that it?" Enid nods. The teacher says, "I can see why you thought that, but Michelle's skin color is a lot different than dirt. Take a closer look and I think you can tell that. And it is interesting that persons with dark skin have lighter colors on their hands. Pretty, isn't it?"

- Dominique says to Hai, a biracial child of a black father and a Vietnamese mother, "I can make my eyes like yours" as she pulls her eyes down by the corners. "That hurts. Do your eyes hurt you?" Hai turns away without answering. The teacher says to Dominique, "Are you wondering why Hai's eyes look different from yours?" Dominique nods. The teacher says, "Everyone is born with the same kind of eyes as others in their family. Hai's eyes have that beautiful shape because her mother's eyes are like that. You have lovely eyes too. Are your eyes shaped like your mother's too? It's good that everyone doesn't look just alike, isn't it?"

- Tim, an African-American child, is drawing a picture of a boy. He is coloring the circle representing the face with an orange crayon. Wilson, also black, says, "Why is he making his picture [of a person] like that? He ain't that color, he be black." The teacher turns to Tim, "Why did you decide to color your boy's face with that color, Tim?" Tim says, "This ain't me; this is some white guy." The teacher says to Wilson, "I guess that right now Tim wants to make a picture of a person with skin that color and probably another time he will want to make someone with another color of skin. His pictures will look like our classroom with lots of different colors, right?"

- The teacher observes Nan, a child of northern European descent with blond straight hair gingerly touching the many tiny braidlets of Erica, an African-American child. Nan is obviously curious and fascinated. Erica says, "Stop that. I don't want you touching my hair." Nan persists and the teacher says, "I heard Erica ask you to stop touching her hair, Nan. It is pretty, isn't it? You can look at it without touching, okay?"

- "Why do those kids say that I am red?" asks William, a native American child of the Onondaga tribe. "Jim and Evelyn call me 'redskin.'" The teacher responds, "'Redskin' is a very old fashioned name for native Americans, but most people think that it is not a very good name. Your skin isn't red, is it? It is a light brown color. Jim and Evelyn are still learning about these things. I guess they haven't learned that yet. But they will soon."

- David, a child of African-American descent, is playing with his Mexican-American friend, Carlos. He says in an admiring voice, "When I grow up more, I'm going to be Chicano too like you, and then I can speak Spanish with you." Carlos looks doubtfully toward the teacher and asks, "How do you get to be Chicano?" The teacher says, "You are Chicano because you were born to

Chicano parents. David is black because he was born to black parents. Some things about you change when you grow up like getting taller and stronger, but you both will look very much the way you look now when you grow up. Your skin will be about the same color, your eyes will be the same color." The teacher continues, "But, David, you can learn to speak Spanish if you want to. Lots of people speak Spanish who are not Chicano. Would you like to learn some Spanish?"

- Jean asks, "Why does her mother call my mother a person of color?" The teacher says, "I think she means that your mother has a little darker skin color than some other people." Jean says, "My mother says that we are black. We don't really have black skin though." The teacher says, "Your whole family has beautiful skin color. I like the color of my skin too. Some people call it white but it really isn't white, is it?"

To overcome your own inhibitions about open discussion of race, you may find it helpful to talk with other adults of various racial and socioeconomic background about their childhood memories of learning about racial differences and the valuative implications. Probe into your own and others' recollections to determine what values were incorporated from the behaviors and talk of those early years. Try to figure out what inferences were made from what was said or not said by others which led to your own belief structures and ease or lack of ease in interracial company.

Cultural Background

Since cultural diversity is less obvious than racial, it may be overlooked by teachers, assuming that everyone shares their own respective cultures. **Culture** was defined by Levine (1984) as "a shared organization of ideas that includes the intellectual, moral, and aesthetic standards prevalent in a community and the meaning of communicative actions" (p. 67). Only when something becomes blatantly discrepant in another's behavior based on a nonfamiliar "organization of ideas" does awareness of culture develop. Children are not likely to be aware, for example, of their Jewish identity or their Italian parentage or their Swedish heritage. Nevertheless, differences relating to cultural membership continuously affect both children and adults in the extent to which relationships and settings feel comfortable and welcoming or awkward and forbidding. It has been noted by Washington (1989), for example, that many children from culturally and linguistically different backgrounds seem to "disappear" into corners of classrooms and only reappear at lunch or recess, settings which are informal and feel more hospitable.

The scope of this chapter does not allow enough space to give even an adequate sampling of the nature of these differences. Let's consider just a few. There is the matter of personal proximity and touching. Persons with different cultural experiences have different expectations about the extent to which close proximity and touching are considered comfortable and desirable. Washington (1989) points out that interactions between African-Americans include much more touching than many European cultures. Hall (1959) described the discrepancies in the distance which feels comfortable to persons of differing cultures. He recounts a scene in which a U.S. businessman is backed into a corner as he tries to create what is for him a comfortable space for interaction while his Arab colleague moves closer and closer in pursuit of what for him is a more comfortable distance. There are differences between cultures in the pacing of conversations, in the use of nonverbal gestures, in the extent to which eye contact is considered appropriate or impolite, in tolerance for conflict, in degree of deference shown to others, and so forth. The list is seemingly endless.

A relative, now nearly eighty, still vividly recalls being rejected as a child growing up in a poor rural neighborhood because the stylish clothing she had acquired while visiting her grandmother was seen by her peers back home as "stuck-up" and "hoity-toity." Only when she switched back to shabbier garb was she accepted again. Until she had received the new clothing, she says she had no awareness of the kind of clothing locally worn. We are all like the goldfish who doesn't know that it is in water until it jumps out of the fishbowl and discovers a difference. We are unaware of our own culture until we encounter different cultures. Young children are just beginning this long journey of learning who they are and how they and their families are like and different from others. As a teacher of young children, part of your job is to learn about and value the backgrounds of the children you teach as well as their families and to assist them in valuing their own special heritage.

Let's consider one example of cultural difference. You are likely to have a number of Vietnamese children in your class, given the massive migration of Vietnamese families to the United States and Canada after the Vietnam war. If you are to teach Vietnamese children, you will do well to learn about themes and values in Vietnamese culture by reading basic reference materials and current articles, by interviewing others who know the culture, or by visiting and observing settings in which Vietnamese people are present. You may learn the following kinds of information from such research:

- Vietnamese names consist of three parts, in this order: family name, middle name, and given name. Terms such as "honored teacher" or "little sister" are used instead.* *Nguyen* became a very common Vietnamese family name about 1225 A.D. when the Nguyen dynasty overthrew the Ly dynasty and forced all Vietnamese with the name of Ly to change to Nguyen. It was also not unusual for subjects of a king to adopt their ruler's name. Nearly half of all Vietnamese currently have Nguyen as a family name. Many Vietnamese given names are used for both males and females. Names which are definitely male (e.g., Van) or female (e.g., Thi) are often used as middle names. The family name is seldom used by itself as for example, Mr. Nguyen. Instead, all three

*Information on the varying traditions regarding names of Vietnamese, Cambodians, Laotians, and the Hmong may be obtained from Morrow (1989).

names are more typically used (i.e., Mr. Nguyen Van Vinh). Given names are seldom used by Vietnamese when addressing another in conversation as it is considered impolite except for close friends.

- Vietnamese place a high value on harmony in interpersonal relationships as part of the continuing search for harmony in life.
- Vietnamese value behavior that avoids shame for themselves or their families. Appearing "cool" is important, and in a difficult situation, they may giggle or laugh to suppress emotion rather than display an outburst of anger or frustration.
- The Vietnamese may hesitate to answer directly in a negative way. Instead, they may avoid a response or give a polite response of agreement. This is not seen as dishonest, merely tactful.
- Vietnamese consider it inappropriate to look directly into the eyes of those they respect.
- Handshaking is seen as acceptable, but otherwise touching a stranger is not considered appropriate.
- Familial relationships are very structured. Elder siblings have considerable influence and authority over younger children in the family.
- Once a relationship is established, the Vietnamese expect it to continue.

Although background information on cultures of the children you teach may prove insightful, beware of forming incorrect expectations (**stereotypes**) for the behavior of the children you teach or their families. Remember that great cultural variations occur within even one country. Consider our differences from region to region. A child growing up in Manhattan or in the suburbs of Boston has a different cultural milieu than the child in an isolated "hollow" of West Virginia or the reservation in New Mexico. These kinds of differences may also be found in other national groups. Assuming great similarity within the cultures of all Asians, all Africans, all South Americans, all central Americans, and so forth is particularly inappropriate. The 3.5 million Asian-Americans in this country, for example, comprise at least eight distinct ethnic groups. And, of course, the appearance of being of Asian, Central American, and so forth does not necessarily imply new immigrant status. As Chen (1984) emphasizes regarding Asian-Americans: "We are a diverse group—some born and acculturated in Asia; many first, second, or third generation Americans—born knowing no language other than English" (p. 11). The best resource, of course, about the cultures of the children you teach are their parents. You can learn most of value about a particular family's cultural background and expectations from your opportunities to be with them and to talk with them about their family experiences (with an interpreter, if necessary). You may find from such direct contact with Vietnamese families, for example, that some statements such as those listed above are stereotypes and inappropriate for the particular families with whom you are having direct experience.

In learning about the characteristics of children from different family backgrounds, hold in abeyance generalizations about specific cultural differences until you have had the opportunity to consider the particular children you teach.

You may read, for example, in Bowman & Brady (1982) that Vietnamese children may need a highly structured curriculum, since obedience and dependence are important family values. A book by Hale-Benson (1982), listed at the end of this chapter, suggests that for black children highly structured and verbal-based programs are ineffective, since their cultural background tends to be nonverbal and people-oriented with an emphasis on individualistic values. Hadley (1987) suggests that modeling and imitation are particularly important strategies to use with Hispanic children. Such general guidelines are certainly valuable to consider; you need to keep in mind, however, that they may not be useful for specific Vietnamese, black, or Hispanic children you teach.

Some generalizations, however, should be heeded by teachers who wish to respect the cultural and religious background of all children. Devoting large amounts of program time, for example, to the celebration of Christmas and Easter, which are linked closely to a Christian heritage, even though the majority of families are of this religion, is a case in point. In programs with children of differing traditions and religious faiths, such focus is especially inappropriate. The better practice is to encourage all children to talk about and share the customs of their family holidays with a minimum of hoopla devoted to any. Thus, all children would learn from each other the traditions of Christmas, Halloween, Thanksgiving, Passover, Ash Wednesday, Kwanzza, Tet, Chinese New Year's, Valentine's Day, Rosh Hashana, Yom Kippur, and so forth. Although this advice runs counter to common practice in early childhood and elementary programs in this country, a newer perspective suggests that home and religious centers are the more appropriate settings for celebrations of religion-based holidays.

Language

In a multicultural society communication with persons of differing languages, although difficult for many adults, is often necessary. It is of particular interest that, given the need, young children relatively easily acquire second (or more) languages. Especially impressive to adults who struggle with pronunciations and language flow—and still never get the different language patterns quite right—are young children who learn language with ease. The young child has the "built-in" brain potential for hearing and reproducing many diverse speech sounds. Only those brain cells which are activated as language abilities develop are maintained and become part of the organizational structure which facilitates communication. At later stages of development, this learning capacity is less available. Little wonder then that the three-year-olds of foreign-speaking parents in our early childhood programs learn to speak English perfectly and rapidly simply by hearing others' language while their parents listen in amazement.

Being immersed in a second language in a social environment would likely be an ideal learning experience for every preschooler as long as the heritage language is also maintained and enhanced. As children play with each other, argue, negotiate, boast, and so forth, they become more and more competent in their use of the second language. In arguments, particularly, children are pushed to learn and use language effectively. Lein and Brenneis (1978) reported the following example of an argument in English between two 5-year-old Chinese newcomers to English:

B: My father bigger your father.
C: You father big big big big big.
B: My father, uh, bigger you father.
C: My father, my father like that! [stands, reaches high]
B: My father stronger your father.
C: My father like that![arms wide]
B: Don't talk for—I hit you!

The motivation is strong in such an argument for using every nuance of meaning at one's command to best the other. The effectiveness of peer modeling and feedback for second language learning in childhood is strongly emphasized by linguists such as Ervin-Tripp and is illustrated in the following example:

The children were playing a game with repetitive turn cycles. At the end of each cycle the alternate child got to start the next cycle. The French-speaking child said to the

"¡Hoye, dame un poco de barro!" *(Cumberland Hill Associates)*

American: "Tu commences," as she set out the materials for the next round. The American child looked puzzled at the new word but began the round. At the end, she did the same, saying "Tu commences" to her partner (1991, p. 89).

As Ervin-Tripp points out, who knows whether the child thought the phrase meant "It's your turn" rather than "You begin." From such beginnings, however, children learn increasingly complicated expressions and compare and infer the meanings. They are highly motivated and ready to acquire language in such encounters. The presence of speakers of different languages may well enhance the experience and learning of all the young participants in program settings.

Although language immersion is a means for rapid language learning, it is important for children to know that teachers and others are also appreciative of their existing abilities with their heritage language. A teacher of non- or limited-English-speaking children can learn and use some words and phrases from the child's language, thus showing them that their own expression, an integral part of their identity, is valued. The presence in the classroom of adults, if only as occasional visitors, who communicate in the first language of each of the children in that classroom is very desirable.

Developing an awareness that one's own language is just one of many is an important learning experience. In multilanguage cosmopolitan settings such learning is a natural occurrence. For children in every classroom, whether or not there are foreign language speakers enrolled, learning that many different words represent the same things has cognitive benefits. Comparisons can be made between the different names that are used for grandmothers—grandma, nana, grandmother, grammie, oma, babka. Teachers can point out that some of us say *hat,* others wear *caps.* Non-English words can be offered as a further extension of English variations: chapeau, čiapka, and so forth. Even very young children can be told that many of the words used in their native tongue were taken from other languages. This is especially the case with English. Children can understand that knowing lots of different ways to talk is valuable and fun. When these children encounter speakers of other languages, then, they may be more likely to find it interesting rather than simply strange.

The value of immersion experiences is much less certain for schoolage children who must receive adult instruction in a nonfamiliar language. We believe that it is advantageous for children to develop literacy in language in which they have well-developed and very comfortable speaking and listening abilities and, likewise, to have communication as easy as possible regarding basic concepts of number, science, social knowledge, and so forth.

The issue of language is actually more controversial than the above paragraphs suggest. Some strongly support an "English-only movement" which would declare English as the official language of the United States and would discourage use of other languages or the development of bilingual abilities under public auspices. An alternative movement is for an "English-plus" alternative which advocates that all citizens of the United States acquire and use the English language and that increased emphasis be given to second-language training for English speakers. This later position is supported by research suggesting that bilinguals who develop full competency in both languages are superior to those who have only one language "in areas such as cognitive flexibility, metalinguistic awareness, concept formation, and creativity (Padilla et al., 1991, p. 125)."

Ability

An estimated 10 to 12 percent of children in the United States have disabling conditions. The prevalence of children with disabilities is growing in this country for a variety of reasons: births to mothers who have HIV disease or AIDS, have substance-abuse histories, or were exposed to toxic substances, and medical advances which now regularly save the lives of tiny premature babies who grow up with disabilities which require special intervention services and programs. These are new trends which add to the incidence of handicaps from other causes. What differences in abilities you will encounter in your teaching is unpredictable, but you certainly will have children who need special services.

The past decades has seen a revolution in beliefs and practices regarding the appropriate educational placement of children who have identifiably different patterns of abilities resulting from genetic influences, prenatal or birth traumas, disease, or injury. Perhaps you remember participating in some of the classrooms which were part of the sometimes traumatic early transitions toward the integration of students with disabilities into "regular" classrooms. Do you recall the rationale which led to federal legislation in support of **mainstreaming?** Part of that rationale was moral and legal, namely, the indefensible social inequality of segregated services. In addition, the achievements of persons educated in segregated settings did not show benefits from "special" education. Quite the contrary, persons with disabling conditions operating in integrated settings were found to benefit from observing and learning from the behaviors of their nondisabled peers and, through processes of modeling and imitation, to improve their functioning.

In 1975 Public Law 94-142, the Education for All Handicapped Children Act, was passed by Congress and signed by then President Gerald Ford. This legislation mandates access to public education for children with handicapping conditions. The provisions of PL 94-142 provide special services as a part of public education for the following groups: mentally retarded, hard of hearing, deaf, speech or language impaired, visually handicapped, seriously emotionally disturbed, orthopedically impaired, or other health-impaired children, or children with **specific learning disabilities.** Public Law 94-142 mandates the **least restrictive environment,** that is, that "to the maximum extent appropriate, handicapped children . . . are educated with children who are not handicapped" (Education for All Handicapped Children, 1975). Only when the needed services cannot be arranged in the regular classroom is segregation in other settings (i.e., special classes or institutions) appropriate. For many students with the disabling conditions, the least-restrictive environment in which special services can be provided is not the "special education" classroom but, instead, the regular school program.

Even before the landmark PL 94-142 legislation, 10 percent of the children included in Head Start programs, according to a 1972 Congressional mandate, had one or more of the following conditions: physical, speech, hearing, visual, intellectual or emotional impairments ranging from mild to severe. Other early childhood programs, both public and private, emphasized mainstreaming as well. That mainstreamed programs work effectively for both the children with and those without disabilities was repeatedly demonstrated throughout the 1980s (Bailey & McWilliam, 1990; Guralnick, 1990).

The early years may be even more important to the development and learning of the disabled child than they are for the normally developing child. This fact was recognized by the major legislation passed in 1986, PL 99-457, Amendments to the Education of the Handicapped Act. These amendments made incentive funding available to state, local, and private agencies to develop improved services for young children with special needs and their families. Part H of this legislation provides for a discretionary early intervention program for eligible disabled infants and toddlers from birth through three years of age and their families. All states initially elected to provide this program, although some have already cut their programs, citing budgetary deficits. Any cut in the provision of services to the youngest disabled children is believed to be indeed unfortunate and short-sighted by those who are most knowledgeable about the effects of early intervention in infancy (Guralnick & Bennett, 1987; Odom & Karnes, 1988).

Another part of the PL 99-457 legislation requires all states to provide a free appropriate public education to all eligible three- to five-year-old disabled children. There is no requirement that preschool programs mandated by this legislation be mainstreamed. The mainstreaming principle, however, is being implemented in many situations, and preschool programs supported by the enrollment of children with disabilities also often include other children as well. What is sometimes called "reverse mainstreaming" is increasingly common as more and more preschool and day-care programs created to accommodate the handicapped do, by design, admit children with normal abilities. The successful integration of children with special needs due to disabilities depends upon the creation of a classroom which responds to the diversity among all the children's needs, not simply those of the handicapped versus the "typical" child. As Hobbs (1975) pointed out:

> In schools that are most responsive to individual differences in abilities, interests, and learning styles of children, the mainstream is actually many streams, sometimes as many streams as there are individual children, sometimes several streams as groups are formed for special purpose, sometimes one stream only as concerns of all converge. We see no advantage in dumping exceptional children into an undifferentiated mainstream; but we see great advantages to all children, exceptional children included, in an educational program modulated to the needs of individual children, singly, in small groups, or all together. Such a flexible arrangement may well result in functional separations of exceptional children from time to time, but the governing principle would apply to all children: school programs should be responsive to the

learning requirements of individual children, and groupings should serve this end (p. 197).

A great deal has been learned about the integration of children with differing abilities in a regular program setting through experimentation across recent years. We have learned that simply placing a differently abled child in a mainstream setting does not, for example, ensure peer interaction nor does it ensure optimal developmental progress. The teacher's actions are often needed as a catalyst if the benefits of mainstreaming such as modeling are to be realized. To illustrate, Bailey and McWilliam (1990) suggested that the development of children with communication deficits is enhanced by a teacher who:

> (a) actively engages children in communicative exchanges by using lead-ins, openended questions, or gestures to draw children into interactions; (b) comments on activities or events in which children are engaged to provide a linguistic model; (c) prompts children to elicit more advanced levels of communication; (d) responds immediately and contingently to children's verbal and nonverbal attempts to communicate by acknowledging the child's intent, answering, reinforcing, or imitating the child; (e) gives children adequate time to respond, not preempting their opportunities to communicate; (f) expands children's utterances to provide models for more advanced communicative behavior; (g) promotes peer interaction through environmental structuring . . . and teacher prompting; (h) prompts appropriate communication skills to replace or prevent undesirable or inappropriate behaviors; and (i) uses environmental modifications such as violating routine events, withholding objects or turns, violating object functions, or hiding objects so the child is prompted to comment, protest, correct, or request (p. 40).

Research reports reviewed by McLean and Hanline (1990) and our own experience suggest that teachers need on occasion to intervene in the social and environmental encounters of the child with disabilities to facilitate successful interactions with nonhandicapped peers. One teacher, for example, structured the play of a blind child and his nonhandicapped peers during an enactment of "The Three Bears." By giving verbal descriptions of the actions of the peers and prompts to the nonseeing child, a routine was developed which allowed pleasurable engagements for all. Cooperative learning strategies, discussed in Chapter 13, are often used to foster such peer interaction.

In welcoming children with special needs into your classroom and demonstrating to them and to their peers that such placements are right for all of you, consider the following:

- Analyze the physical environment from the perspective of the disabled child's needs and make whatever modifications are necessary to make activities accessible.
- Think through the experience of each disabled child during each regularly scheduled period and decide how to maximize that child's participation, especially in social activities.
- Expect the disabled child to adhere to the ground rules set for all children. In those situations where this is not possible, describe to the child and to the other children why you are making an exception.

- As advised previously in relation to racial differences, encourage children to talk openly about differences in appearance or behavior of the disabled child. Make sure that children know that the child with special needs has just another kind of difference not unlike all the other differences that exist within any group.

When working with children with disabling conditions, most of your teaching activities will not differ markedly from your work with any other child. First, be sensitive to what the child can already do, even though it may differ from what his or her agemates can do. Second, provide for the ample use of existing abilities as well as for a gradual expansion into additional areas of functioning. Handicapped children, like all children, primarily need full acceptance as growing, valuable human beings. They also need encouragement to behave as "normally" as possible and the expectation that they will develop their abilities to the fullest extent.

Family Life-Styles

Perhaps in reading the prior section about the children who could be part of your class, you may have been reminded of the great diversity in life-styles which are commonly present in our society. You and the children you teach can together develop an awareness of the differences represented in your immediate group. There may, for example, be differences in housing. Some children may live in a one-family house with a yard around it, others may live in apartments, in rooming houses, in trailers, in condominiums, in tents, in duplexes, in shanties, or in cabins.

Family composition will differ as well. Some children may live with lots of uncles and aunts and cousins, others may live just with their parents and siblings or with one parent only. Exploring these differences in nonjudgmental ways leads toward greater self-understanding and acceptance.

Recent compilations of statistics reported by Hymes (1991) and the Children's Defense Fund (1991) include the following:

- Nearly one-fourth of all children under age five live in poverty. Over 40 percent of black children live in poverty.
- One in eight marriages ends in divorce.
- Millions of divorced, separated, or never-married mothers raise their children without help from fathers.
- Over 12 percent of children born in 1986 had teenage mothers.
- By the year 2000, 70 percent of preschoolers will have working mothers. In 1989, about 60 percent of mothers of children younger than six were in the labor force.
- During a recent year approximately 250,000 children lived in foster care, in group homes, in residential treatment centers, and in other institutions.

Clearly you as a teacher should expect to encounter great differences in the life experiences of the children and families you teach. Some of these differences may be due to economic considerations, but others are less easily explained.

GUIDELINES

In your efforts to prepare yourself for the challenging job of teaching the diversity of children who may be assigned to your class group, certain guidelines may prove helpful. Consider the following:

- Children need to learn about and talk about the differences they observe between themselves and others. Conversations about differences may often be initiated by teachers. The presence and involvement of the child with the characteristic in question is appropriate. There can be no secrets about differences; secret conversations about others lead to suspicions, regardless of the words spoken, that there is something very wrong with those persons.
- Use the diversity within the classroom group to build multicultural understanding, interracial acceptance, integration of the differently abled, and so forth. Do not single out the "minority" child's culture as a focus of group study. Instead, help children and their parents understand that everyone has a culture to share which is of interest to others. Extend these learnings by arranging further diversity beyond the immediate group milieu for the children to experience.
- As the children explore differences they will also learn about human similarities. Emphasize the needs and habits that all people have in common.
- All children, whatever their characteristics, need to see many persons like themselves in pictures, in books, in toys, in role models.
- All children need to be encouraged to be independent and to meet the same behavioral standards as others. Whether children are differently abled, use a different language, are of a different race, or have other exceptionalities, they need to learn that they can accommodate to the routines and agreements for group living in the classroom. When they cannot yet manage this, communicate a clear expectation that even though they now cannot do certain expected things, they are learning to do so.
- Develop the clear expectation that it is never OK to say you won't play with someone because they are of a particular gender, of a particular race, of a particular ethnic group, of a particular religion, or other such identity. If such rejection happens, intervene and point out that such a reason for not wanting to play with another is not acceptable. Model to the rejected child, if necessary, how to say that such a reason for rejection is not liked. If there is objectionable behavior from the rejected child which has led to the incident, encourage the discussion of what that was about. For many children, one such confrontation is sufficient. If not, a planned series of experiences may be necessary to root out the reasons for the child's bias and to replace whatever has caused it with other images and learning.

For further explanation of these and many other similar guidelines, we advise that you carefully study the aforementioned antibias book by Louise Derman-Sparks and the A.B.C. Task Force (1989). This book, readily available from the

National Association for Young Children, is full of anecdotes which poignantly illustrate how to successfully foster other-acceptance in young children and, in all likelihood, self-esteem.

SUMMARY

A good place to begin the preparation for teaching children from diverse backgrounds and with diverse characteristics is to assess your own uniqueness and the commonalities between yourself and others. The children you will teach will vary in many respects including diversity of race, cultural background, language, ability, and family life-styles. This chapter has focused mostly on the recognition, study, and celebration of human diversity, but also included has been a recognition of the more prevalent commonalities. Norman Cousins (1983), in the book *Human Options,* spoke eloquently to that issue:

> Education prepares us superbly for a bird's-eye view of the world; it teaches us how to recognize easily and instantly the things that differentiate one place or one people from another. But our education sometimes fails to teach us that the principal significance of such differences is that they are largely without significance. We fail to grasp the fact that beyond the differences are realities scarcely comprehended because of their shattering simplicity. And the simplest reality of all is that the human community is one—greater than any of its parts, greater than the separateness imposed by actions, greater then the divergent faiths and allegiances or the depth and color of varying cultures (p. 36).

SUGGESTED ACTIVITIES

1 Create an informal consciousness-raising group (possibly from your own class group) which represents some diversity of characteristics and backgrounds, and get together several times to discuss some of the following types of questions:
   - How do you describe your own racial/ethnic identity? How do you describe other aspects of yourself which are part of your unique background (ableness, religion, language, family composition, and so forth)?
   - What experiences, pleasant or unpleasant, have you had related to your racial/ethnic identity (or other differentiating characteristic)?
   - When and how did you first become aware of your own racial/ethnic identity (or other differentiating characteristic)?
   - What are the views of your family members about persons of other racial/ethnic identities (or with other differentiating characteristics)? Do you share those views? In what ways do you agree or disagree?
   - How would you like others to view and behave toward persons of your racial/ethnic group (or persons with other differentiating characteristics like yours)? What do you find objectionable about the way your group is treated or viewed?

2 Write a profile of a child who contrasts with your own characteristics in two or more respects—for example, race, cultural background, language, ableness, family composition. Using the perspective of this child, examine the books in an early childhood

classroom (and/or the public library) and determine whether you can find portrayals of people like yourself (in the role of this child). Prepare a report on your findings.

3 Select any minority culture (but not your own) which is likely to be represented in the population in a location where you may wish to work as an early childhood teacher. Learn as much as you can about this subculture through reading, interviews, and/or observations, and summarize that knowledge for your fellow students.

4 Observe in classrooms, and note the extent of diversity in the student body and in the teaching staff. Note interaction patterns between children, between staff members, and between staff members and children. Summarize your observations, and from your findings try to generate some guidelines for yourself which you will wish to put into practice in your own classroom.

ADDITIONAL READINGS

Comer, J. P. (1988). *Maggie's American dream: The life and times of a black family.* New York: New American Library.

Derman-Sparks, L., and the A.B.C. Task Force. (1989). *Anti-Bias Curriculum: Tools for EMPOWERING Young Children.* Washington, DC: National Association for the Education of Young Children.

Dimidjian, V. J. (1989). Holidays, holy days, and wholly dazed: Approaches to special days. *Young Children, 44*(6), 70–75.

Hale-Benson, J. (1982). *Black children: Their roots, culture and learning styles* (rev. ed.). Baltimore, MD: Johns Hopkins University Press.

Heitz, T. (1989). How do I help Jacob? *Young Children, 45*(1), 11–15.

Kagan, S. L., & Garcia, E. E. (Eds.). (1991). Special Issue: Educating linguistically and culturally diverse preschoolers. *Early Childhood Research Quarterly, 6*(3), entire issue.

Kitano, M. K. (1989). The K–3 teacher's role in recognizing and supporting young gifted children. *Young Children, 44*(3), 57–63.

Ramsey, P. (1987). *Teaching and learning in a diverse world: Multicultural education for young children.* New York: Teachers College Press, Columbia University.

Sholtys, K. C. (1989). A new language, a new life. *Young Children, 44*(3), 76–77.

Vazquez, A., & Ramirez-Krodel, A. (1989). *America's Hispanic heritage: An overview of Hispanics in the United States.* Ann Arbor, MI: Program for Educational Opportunity, Michigan University. ERIC Reproduction Service Document No. ED 316 370.

Wardle, F. (1987). Are you sensitive to interracial children's special identity needs? *Young Children, 42*(2), 53–59.

Wolfle, J. (1989). The gifted preschooler: Developmentally different, but still 3 or 4 years old. *Young Children, 44*(3), 41–48.

York, S. (1991). *Roots and wings: Affirming culture in early childhood programs.* St. Paul, MN: Redleaf Press.

CHAPTER 15

COMMUNICATION

OVERVIEW

How you communicate with others is central to your success as a teacher. Although the most important persons to whom you relate are the children in your classes, it is also very important that you effectively relate to their parents. In early childhood settings, where teaching usually involves a team effort, you will also need to successfully communicate with co-workers. There are some aspects of communication that are different for each of these groups, but many of the most important principles are common to all. The first section of this chapter focuses on generic guidelines, and the latter sections specifically discuss communication with children, parents, and co-workers.

Any honest discussion of communication principles and strategies must also consider the personal dimension. Much of your communication is intimately connected to who you are as a person. You are who you are—that special mix of genetic endowments and environmental learnings constituting the unique you. As you live your life and have additional experiences, the way you communicate as well as the substance of your communication will undergo some modification. There are, however, some general strategies you can learn and put immediately into practice. These strategies fall into three categories—active listening, assertiveness, and problem solving.

ACTIVE LISTENING

To listen effectively, you must put energy into getting the other person's message. You must be active in attending to the other person, in encouraging that person to fully express his or her ideas, and in letting the speaker know that you have comprehended the message including its emotional content.

Helpful Conditions

Effective communication requires that you give your full attention to the speaker and that this attention be perceived by that person. Keep comfortable eye contact with the speaker. Although a fixed stare is not effective, you should avoid glancing around the room or looking at papers or objects in your hands. If you are squarely facing the speaker and leaning slightly in his or her direction, your interest is more evident. If you cross your arms over your chest, turn away, or move about, you may inadvertently be communicating rejection or disinterest.

Certain environmental factors affect your ability to give your full attention and to communicate your interest. Try to keep physical barriers such as desks and dividers from separating you and the speaker. Remain comfortably close to the speaker, keeping in mind that people of different subcultures and experiential backgrounds may differ in what they consider a comfortable distance. If the other person backs away from your "comfortable" distance, respect that as a nonverbal message and maintain that distance. In fact, an excellent principle to follow is to match your speaking behavior to the behavior of the person with whom you are conversing. If, for example, the mother of five-year-old Susan reaches out and taps or touches you as she talks, she would likely find it reassuring if you reach out and place your hand on her arm as you speak. If your co-

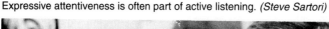

Expressive attentiveness is often part of active listening. *(Steve Sartori)*

worker, Annette, speaks very rapidly, you may find it more effective to speed up your own speech rate to the extent it is possible for you to do so. Experts in the field called **neurolinguistic programming** advise that matching the body positioning of the other person enhances communication. Thus, as Mrs. Johnson, your supervisor, puts her hand to her forehead and then shifts her body forward as she speaks to you, following suit may lead to her perception of you as tuned in to her concerns.

Neurolinguistic programmers also emphasize the importance of identifying the mode by which the other person processes information. According to this perspective, people differ in preference for visual, auditory, or kinesthetic modes of taking in information. We are told that preferences can be detected by listening to the expressions that appear in one's talk. A person who prefers visual processing will emphasize such expressions as "the way I see it," "from my perspective," "from my point of view," "do you get the picture?" and "look here." The auditory person will, on the other hand, say such things as "sounds good to me," "let's hear that again!" "from what I hear," "listen here." The kinesthetic person will say things like "I like the way that feels," "from where I sit," "for a person in my shoes," "that gets right next to me," and "I feel."

According to the neurolinguistic programming perspective, using words that are compatible with the words the speaker uses will enhance communication. At the very least, you might do well to avoid mismatches such as those in the following conversation between parents of two young children:

MRS. T: I feel Cara's crying may be related to her need for affection. She misses the hugs and kisses she gets at home from me.

MRS. J: I don't see it that way. The way I look at it, it appears quite different. I see her looking around at school and not finding anything familiar looking. That's how I view it. Do you see what I mean?

MRS. T: Well, maybe, but somehow that doesn't feel quite right to me. Do you ever get the feeling that no one can sense what a child needs except its mother?

MRS. J: From my perspective, I see you missing the mark on this one. Look at it this way. Even children have an image of the way things should be. Then if they look around and nothing looks right, they can't cope.

MRS. T: I can't get a grasp on what you are trying to lay on me here.

MRS. J: I don't see what the problem is with what I just said. It seems clear to me. See, here. . . ."

Neither Mrs. J nor Mrs. T are aware that their word patterns may increase their communication difficulties. If Mrs. J occasionally said, "I feel . . ." or Mrs. T said, "The way I see it is . . ." the other might more readily receive the content of the message.

Effective Responses

To attend to such details of communication requires a very active listener. The active listener also encourages the expression of the other's ideas and feelings

Skilled teachers note children's nonverbal expression and then encourage them to use words to describe their feelings. *(Cumberland Hill Associates, Inc.)*

both through inviting remarks and questions and through acknowledgement responses. The most effective communicators are not necessarily the people who talk a great deal. Instead, they may set the stage for others to talk and then really listen to what others have to say.

There are a number of useful ways to invite others to express themselves, including:

"I'd be interested in hearing how you feel about that."
"You seem happy."
"You seem upset."
"Tell me about ___."

When the other person shares information or feelings with you, acknowledge what they have said with brief statements or nonverbal gestures. Saying "Um-hmm," "I see," "Interesting," "Right," "Yes," "Is that so?" "That's amazing," and the like indicates your interest. It is also effective to nod, smile, frown, or use hand gestures appropriate to the message. Sometimes attentive silence enables the other person to go on in greater depth on the same topic. Asking open-ended questions also supports the speaker in further exploring the topic he or she has initiated. Note how Mrs. K uses open-ended questions, acknowledgement responses, and silence to help her friend think through a problematic situation.

MRS. K: You are looking distressed. What's happening?

MRS. L: Does it show? I've been worrying about Eric's temper tantrums.

MRS. K: What kind of things have you been concerned about?

MRS. L: Well, the tantrums seem to be happening more frequently and at the most difficult moments. I've just totally lost my patience. Something's got to change. But I don't know what to do.

MRS. K: Do you have any ideas on that?

MRS. L: I sometimes think that keeping a more regular schedule with more consistent expectations might help. Other times I feel we've just spoiled him with too much tolerance and that I should punish him severely enough so that he knows I mean business. *(Silence)* But then I realize how terrible he must be feeling to be acting that way. *(Silence)* Yes, that's really the important issue to consider. How is he feeling and what is he thinking when he has the tantrums? That's a more useful way to consider it, I would expect.

MRS. K: So you think that understanding his perspective will give you some guides to how you should react?

MRS. L: That's it. I never thought about it just that way before. It certainly has been helpful to talk it over with you. Thanks.

The way you respond to other's communication directly determines the extent to which they continue the interchange and initiate further talk with you on other occasions. While some sharing about your own comparable experiences is useful, it may be more effective to draw out a more complete commentary from the other person. This is illustrated by Mrs. K's dialogue with Mrs. L, prior to shifting the focus of the conversation to you. There are several ways to do this—paraphrasing the other's major points and reflecting the other's feelings.

In paraphrasing, the listener shows an accurate awareness of what the other has said by stating the central message back to the speaker using slightly different wording. The following is an example of paraphrasing:

JAN: I have been running around all day trying to get all these details cleared away, but I haven't actually accomplished anything yet.

RAY: You've been running around but nothing gets done, hmm?"

JAN: Yeah, first I went to the bursar's office and tried to figure out why they keep billing me. And after waiting for a half hour, I'm told that they can't tell me anything because my account representative is off sick today.

RAY: After waiting for a half hour, you weren't able to get any information at all?

JAN: Well, yes, I did get some information. I found out that the whole system is screwy.

At this point, Ray may want to also make use of a second responding strategy, reflecting feelings. For example:

RAY: You sound very fed up with everything.

JAN: For sure! I am so angry!

RAY: Really gets to you. I can see that.

JAN: One of the reasons I'm so angry is that I took the time I could have used to finish off that report for my psychology class. I really should have made an appointment instead of just going on in and waiting.

RAY: So you've figured out how to avoid some of that hassle the next time, I guess.

JAN: Yeah, you're right. I guess I at least learned something from the experience. And, Ray, thanks a lot for listening.

Paraphrasing and reflecting feelings are very important responding strategies. Contrast the previous scenario with this one.

JAN: I've been running around all day trying to get all these details cleared away, but I haven't actually accomplished anything yet.

RAY: I've had the same kind of day. Tried to call my mother and got no answer. Guess I'll have to write a letter.

JAN: Well, see you around.

It takes practice to feel natural in using paraphrasing and reflection-of-feeling responses. The effort, however, is well rewarded. For one thing, the process of listening for the speaker's content, necessary for paraphrasing, keeps the listener very actively involved. It is easy to nod and say, "Hm-mm," but paraphrasing requires activity on the part of the listener to really understand what is being said with sufficient clarity to use the content in the paraphrased response.

ASSERTION

A very important part of effective communication is asserting one's own personal needs to others in such a way that they can be met without damaging personal relationships. Whether the assertion of needs is directed toward children, coworkers, or the children's parents, the same positive approaches are most successful.

There is always risk involved in assertion, but there is also risk in nonassertion. When needs are not met in a situation, resentment often builds and may be inadvertently expressed, often indirectly and nonverbally. By asserting your needs, you create the possibility of finding a mutually satisfying solution. Although it may not be comfortable to tell another person about something that requires a change in his or her behavior, it is essential in promoting positive long-term relationships. The ability to be assertive about your needs is essential if you are to continue a close association with the other person.

Example

Perhaps you are concerned about being seen as aggressive or about alienating others. Although there is always that possibility, if you can state your needs without blame, alienating the other person is far less likely. Consider the following example:

Mary Greene, a day-care teacher, is becoming upset over the repeated instances in which Bill and Betty Bloser fail to arrive at the day-care center at closing time to pick up their son. As the person responsible for the center at closing time, Mary must remain there with the child until the Blosers arrive. They have shown no awareness of the problem even though Mary has on a couple of occasions stated flatly, "Our final pickup time is at 5:30."

Mary has a number of options. First, she can continue to be patient, denying her own needs. This, however, will probably lead to a coolness in her interaction with the Blosers. Worse yet, it could possibly create a subtle negativism in her response to their child. Second, Mary could point out to the Blosers that their behavior is inconsiderate and warn them that she will no longer put up with such selfishness. This may seem justifiable to her and, in fact, may lead to a change in their habits. It is unlikely, however, that a healthy climate for further communication would result. The first option is too submissive. The second is too aggressive. The third option, assertion, has greater probability of changing the behavior while at the same time maintaining and improving the relationship.

In assertion, I-messages are the key. Mary, in a nonblaming way, would simply tell the Blosers of her problem. She might say initially, "I need to talk with you about something that is of real concern to me. Do you have time now or can we arrange a time?" Given the assurance of their attention, she might then state, "My problem is that when you come late to pick up Jackie, I am not able to catch my bus, and I end up being late to my evening class. I feel resentful about that because it makes me appear irresponsible to my instructor, and I'm always feeling rushed. I really need to leave here each day shortly after 5:30."

This kind of straight talk leads to a full discussion and the high probability of solving the problem. Note that Mary did not blame the Blosers for their past behaviors. She focused instead on her own situation and feelings and needs. She used I-messages, not you-messages. To successfully assert, the speaker faces the other person and looks directly at him or her. It is important that facial expression, posture, and voice match the seriousness of the message. An earnest statement of one's own needs without casting blame for prior wrongdoings on the other is the essence of assertion.

PROBLEM SOLVING

Problem solving with others for everyone's mutual benefit requires full use of the powers of both active listening and assertion. More is required, however. All parties must have the sincere desire to find or invent an alternative that meets most, if not all, of the respective parties' needs. Also, all parties must give up their claim to being "right" in the interest of finding an alternative that suits others' needs as well as their own. The process of problem solving frequently involves the following five phases:

1 **A full review of the perceptions and needs of all participants**   It is in this phase that skilled listening and honest assertion are essential. Paraphrasing and summarizing the perspectives that are expressed by others creates a positive climate and ensures that all that needs to be taken into account in devising and selecting a solution is known. As a final part of this step, each participant should state the needs of the others in such a way that the others are assured that they have been correctly understood.

2 **Brainstorming for possible solutions**   Once the essential information from all parties has been fully presented and satisfactorily restated by all parties, it is useful to engage in brainstorming for possible solutions. During this phase, any idea, no matter how absurd it may appear, is voiced. All parties refrain from evaluating their own or others' initial suggestions. Instead, they are accepted and perhaps listed so that they may be remembered for later consideration.

3 **Selection of alternatives for implementation**   Once a full set of ideas has been developed, they are appraised as to which meet all or most of the needs of those concerned.

4 **Implementation plan**   The next step is to decide how, where, and in what manner the solution will be tried and for what period of time.

5 **Evaluation**   An agreement is reached as to when the solution will be reevaluated and the matter reconsidered. One or more of the parties takes specific responsibility for initiating a follow-up discussion.

These problem-solving steps are as relevant to one's own personal relationships as to professional situations. In fact, the best way to practice and master the skills necessary to be an active listener, a skilled asserter, and a problem solver is to constantly practice them in your everyday encounters. Like any new skill, they will feel strange and awkward at first, but if you practice until you can do them without self-consciousness, you will be pleased with the consequences and will also be well prepared for their application in your professional life. Specific examples of these skills are provided in the following sections on communication with children, parents, and co-workers.

COMMUNICATION WITH CHILDREN

All the general guidelines for communication apply to communication with children. You will do well to reread the first section of the chapter, visualizing a child in the role of "other." With children, the adult may need to stoop, kneel, or sit during interchanges to be at the child's eye level. Eye contact is very important, as is body positioning and other nonverbal communication. Much of what a child gets from an exchange is the nonverbal message. Children often have an awareness of when adults are uneasy, irritated, or angry. Thus, learning the "scripts" for talking with children is not enough. You will need to internalize a view of children in which they are valued as unique persons—each with valid feelings and ideas (even though behavior may sometimes be objectionable). There are a number of excellent guides for communicating with children mentioned in the Additional Readings section of this chapter. Try to use the examples given in these guides to extend your own repertoire of specific strategies. Look beyond the specific wordings, however, to the attitudes that the words express.

Respecting Feelings

Children have many very real problems and concerns. They also have lots of eager plans and happy feelings. The most effective communication with children tunes in to these feelings, whatever their nature. For example, children may sometimes be genuinely sad for good and real reasons. As an adult listener, you will do well to accept a child's genuine grieving and encourage its expression. There is a tendency in all of us to try to deny distress in others, particularly children. We evidently feel threatened by sadness and immediately act to cheer the child and, in the process, may discount the validity of the concern. We make jokes or interject distractions. These actions cut off communication and teach the child to suppress feelings. Instead, we would do better to use active listening skills much as we would with another adult. Invite expression of feelings with remarks such as "You really seem unhappy." That may be enough to encourage a child to talk about a concern. Validate feelings with remarks such as: "That does sound sad"; "Now I can understand why you were looking so upset. It must make you feel awful"; "I'm glad you could tell me about it."

Making Suggestions

Being a good listener, even to a child, does not require solving the problem, although you may ask about how the child has attempted to deal with the problem. Some problems are just not solvable. For the kind of problems that may be resolved, such as rejection by a friend, a teacher may suggest possibilities to the child. It is important to make sure that possibilities are presented as that—as a possibility or alternative that could be tried. You can be a helpful listener to a child if you respect feelings. You do not need to necessarily become emotionally involved, taking on to yourself the sadness or other emotion. The most important role you can play is a listening and reflecting one. For effective communication of this kind, however, you need to establish with the children that you really do want to listen to their ideas and feelings.

A LETTER FROM THE CHILDREN

— Dear Teacher,

It seems like everyone is always telling us what to do. We expect you to do this, teacher, since you are big and know a lot about kids. But sometimes it sure would be nice if you would listen to us kids a little more. Please, teacher, try to remember that —

— we need to be respected and valued as people

— we need to learn that it is safe
to love and to trust you

— we need to have you
share in our delight
of the world's many
small pleasures

— we need to learn by experimenting in many different ways

— we need to have experiences that lead to wondering, questioning, and understanding

— we need to learn how to solve the problems that arise in our lives

— we need to learn about the joys of reading and the joys of friendship

— we need to play at
doing what we see
adults do

— we sometimes need
to reflect quietly
by ourselves

— we need to become
responsible for ourselves

— we need to learn to value both ourselves
and those different from ourselves

If you remember
our needs, we will
be yours forever.

Love,
The Children

COMMUNICATION WITH PARENTS

A prime rule in successfully relating to parents is to communicate a lot. Talk, write, smile, signal, meet, confer, and visit. Use many different modes of communication, and use them often. As a professional responsible for a child's program, you are also responsible for developing a partnership with the child's parents. Being professionally responsible, though, does not mean being formal. You should strive to make parents feel comfortable with you and in your program setting.

Creating a Sense of Partnership

To set a tone of partnership, encourage parents to use your first name and avoid arrangements that tend to create formality, such as sitting behind a desk or table when you talk with them about their children. There are times when you will want a quiet setting for lengthy conversation, such as during a scheduled conference, but you can arrange it with confortable chairs over a cup of tea rather than in the kind of forbidding atmosphere that sets you off as the sole source of knowledge and authority.

Types of Contact

In addition to opportunities for conferencing, parents also need ongoing brief opportunities to give or receive information about their children. If you are positioned at the door during children's arrivals and departures, you can in many early childhood situations greet both the child and the parent on a regular basis. You cannot, of course, become involved in lengthy conversations at such times, and it will sometimes require assertion on your part to terminate contact with parents who simply want to chat. You will find, however, that you can learn a great deal about the parental concerns and the child's state through brief exchanges and through careful observations of nonverbal communication and feelings.

There are other ways to make sure that home-school communication occurs. In some programs, a loose-leaf notebook is provided with a section for each child in which both teachers and parents record information for each other, creating, in effect, a written dialogue. In other settings, there is a mailbox or a bulletin board where each parent has a reserved space. For situations in which parents are not proficient with written expression, it is necessary to arrange staff duties so that two teachers are available as greeters, one greeting children and the other concentrating on parents. This arrangement, of course, limits the activity options available to children early in the program session, but communication with parents may be a more important consideration.

In many situations, children arrive at the program site via group transportation, thus increasing the difficulty of maintaining ongoing home-school exchanges. When this is the case, the telephone can be used more frequently. Many brief phone calls prove more useful than a single extended conversation. To prevent phone calls from becoming simply social calls, it is important for a teacher to be able to say, "I can only talk for a minute more now. Is there anything else I need to know?" If telephoning is not a possibility, home and school visits by teacher and parents are desirable. In one way or another, it is essential that there be continuous contact between home and school. Only if there is a comfortable pattern of exchange already established between home and school will devices such as periodic parent-teacher conferences, open-house events, newsletters, and social gatherings be worthwhile.

Parent-teacher conferences provide opportunities for teachers and parents to take stock of children's programs in a more leisurely fashion. It is important that parents know the purpose of the conference and come prepared to contribute from their unique knowledge of the child. Some teachers send parents advance questions such as: "Which school activities does ___ talk about at home? What does she say?" "Which children does ___ seem to particularly like?" "Does ___ have any favorite books, stories, or songs?" "What kinds of activities does ___ enjoy most at home?"

In a conference, parents usually want to learn that program personnel are knowledgeable about their child's abilities and interests. Parents want to know what the teachers are trying to accomplish and how their child fares on these objectives. Parents will often have concerns about academic abilities, since they have so frequently heard or read that an early start is important to later academic success. They may be concerned about their child's likelihood of successful participation at the next level of schooling as well as at the present one. It is, therefore, important that teachers be able to speak to these issues—not just in general but also in relation to the individual child. Parents will welcome comments that suggest that the teacher is focused on helping their child learn and develop and is aware of their child's current status. Illustrative materials such as written anecdotes, narrative descriptions of children's behavior, collections of expressive and task work, photographs and videotapes of children's program involvement, and results of any formal testing or informal assessments help to stimulate discussion of the child.

Maintaining a Problem-Solving Focus

When parents seem critical of school practices, it is difficult for a teacher not to become defensive. Criticism of schools by parents is not unusual. It would be surprising if this were not the case. It is also easy for parents to become defensive when teachers seem critical of the child's behaviors or abilities. Consequently, it is helpful to use all the skills at your command to keep the focus of the discussions on problem solving rather than on blaming or defending. Identifying a problem need not put blame on anyone—parents, teacher, or child. By keeping the focus on problem solving in contrast to fixing blame, constructive communication is more likely to occur. Try to reach some agreement on what steps will be taken by both the teachers and the parents to accomplish important goals or to resolve problem situations. Set a time for follow-up discussion of the outcome by saying, "I would like to talk with you again in about three weeks to see whether the nervous signs you're noticing in Patrick have lessened. In the meantime, we'll both try some of the strategies we've just talked about." Of course, having set up such a plan, it is very important to actually carry it through.

Given the many perspectives that exist about schooling and development, it is impossible to reach agreement with all parents on the important issues of their children's program. Nevertheless, it is the responsibility of the professional teacher to persist in communication efforts for as long as the child is enrolled in the program.

COMMUNICATION WITH CO-WORKERS

In nearly all preschool situations and in many kindergarten and primary classrooms, the teaching is done by a team rather than a single individual. The team will often have a head teacher and one or more assistants, and sometimes include volunteers, student teachers, parents, and older pupils. Even in situations where there is not a teaching team with joint responsibility for a single classroom, teachers must work cooperatively with other professionals who at one time or another share responsibility for the children. Communication skills, as discussed in the initial part of this chapter, are very important to success in these situations. The ability to actively listen to the ideas of other people and to attend to their expressed needs is important in the decision making and problem solving in which professionals must engage cooperatively.

Being Explicit

Success in communicating with co-workers requires clarity of expression, tolerance for differences, and cheerful ease. Clarity is very important. You must say all of what you want others to know. Do not expect them to read your mind. Think about how to say things so that your message will be understood. Think about what the other person already knows that will help them understand what you are trying to convey. Rather than saying, "Let's put the kids in a circle for butter making," for example, you may find it more effective to give some reference points, such as, "Remember how we had the children in a circle last week for the firefighter's visit? They did so well in passing those materials to each other. If we had them in that same sort of circle for butter making they could each have a turn to shake the jar of cream." This kind of clarity usually requires a more extended communication. To work well with others, you need to frequently make the extra effort to put your thoughts and plans into well-formulated words and to make sure that your co-workers do the same.

Being Assertive

In any group endeavor, it is easy to become irritated over the ways in which co-workers do things differently from you. Since children are very sensitive to tensions between their teachers, it is important for all concerned to resolve such conflicts. The use of assertion regarding problem situations is very important. Even small problems, if left unaddressed, expand in seriousness and may balloon into full-blown conflicts. For each irritation, then, it is important to consider how important to you it really is. Let's consider an example. Your co-worker insists that children hang up their coats, yet she consistently tosses hers in a corner. How important is it? You may decide it is not a matter of great import and not of sufficient concern to you to necessitate a discussion. If, on the other hand, you find that it is a definite barb for you, you may wish to engage in some assertion. Perhaps something like this would ensue:

YOU: May I talk with you about something that's been bothering me? It seems like such a small thing that I've hesitated to mention it. I've decided though that it is important enough to talk with you about it. It's this. When you put your coat on the floor there, I just cringe because it seems such a bad example for the kids.

JAN: I guess you're right. The reason I do it is because I really don't have time to go into our coatroom at that point, and I don't like to have it dragging among the kid's clothes on those low hooks.

YOU: I can see that you wouldn't want your coat hanging there.

JAN: Yes, and I don't have time for anything else.

YOU: Right, it is rushed then, for sure. Maybe we could get a higher hook put up here. How would you feel about that?

JAN: That would do it. I agree that it isn't a good model for the kids to do what I've been doing. I'll bring in a coat hook if you'll help me put it up.

Notice that there was no blame in the conversation. There was, instead, assertion, active listening, and constructive approaches to problem solving. You will find that some co-workers lack skills for constructively engaging in dialogues such as the one just cited. The more you can model these behaviors, however, the more likely they are to respect you and cooperate with you in problem-solving efforts.

SUMMARY

In this chapter, guidelines have been presented for three aspects of communication—active listening, assertion, and problem solving. Each of these must be consciously practiced before they can be usefully integrated into your daily routines. Once they are mastered, however, they assist professional encounters with children, parents, and co-workers. Even though initial practice in everyday situations may seem awkward and ineffective, you are urged to persist until these skills are a part of your communication repertoire.

SUGGESTED ACTIVITIES

1 Observe others' interactions with children or their own peers, and determine which aspects of their behavior contribute to or detract from the effectiveness of their communication.

2 Prepare audio or video (preferably video) recordings of your interactions with children or peers and determine which aspects of your behavior contribute to or detract from the effectiveness of your communication.

3 Select target behaviors you wish to incorporate into your communication repertoire, and consciously practice those in "safe" situations with friends and family until they feel less strange and unnatural.

4 Keep a diary on the success or problems you have in communication and the outcomes of your conscious efforts to incorporate ideas gained in this chapter into your interactions with children and with other adults.

5 Identify situations in which you feel very comfortable in interaction with others and situations in which you are very self-conscious or awkward. Consider the nature of the contrasting situations. From this analysis derive guidelines for structuring your own communication to provide comfortable communication with parents of the children with whom you will work and with co-workers.

6 Attend a parent meeting at a school, day-care center, or nursery school, and make a list of the various concerns you hear parents express. Note the reactions of the teachers to these concerns and consider what alternative responses could have been made.

7 Role-play or write out scenarios of effective problem-solving behavior in the following situations:

   a Mrs. Smith is concerned that her daughter, Karen, comes home from school with paint spots on her clothing.

   b Your co-worker, Alicia, feels that teachers should not have responsibility for cleanup of messes created by children. You disagree.

   c Mr. Carroll, father of four-year-old Tim, punishes his son for using "bad" language. He insists that you must do the same at school and each day stops by to ask whether you are following his instructions.

ADDITIONAL READINGS

Berger, E. H. (1991). *Parents as partners in education: The school and home working together.* New York: Macmillan.

Bos, B. J. (1983). *Before the basics: Creating conversations with children.* Roseville, CA: Turn the Pages Press.

Faber, A., & Mazlish, E. (1980). *How to talk so kids will listen and listen so kids will talk.* New York: Avon.

Gordon, T., & Burch, W. (1974). *Teacher effectiveness training.* New York: Hyden.

Greenberg, P. (1989). Parents as partners in young children's development and education: A new American fad? Why does it matter? *Young Children, 44*(4), 61–75.

McLoughlin, C. S. (1987). *Parent-teacher conferencing.* Springfield, IL: Thomas.

Nedler, S., & McAfee, O. (1979). *Working with parents: Guidelines for early education and elementary teachers.* Belmont, CA: Wadsworth.

Powell, D. R. (1989). *Families and early childhood programs.* Washington, DC: National Association for the Education of Young Children.

Swap, S. M. (1987). *Enhancing parent involvement in schools.* New York: Teachers College, Columbia University.

PART FOUR

FOUR

TEACHING
RESOURCEFULNESS

Teaching resourcefulness is the ability to provide children with experiences and instruction relevant to development that matches their needs, interests, and capabilities. The ability to assess these factors was the focus of Part 2. This part is designed to extend your repertoire for (1) providing activities for children and (2) posing questions and making comments that advance their learning. The more extensive your repertoire for providing varied activities and instruction, the greater the likelihood that you will be an effective teacher.

The first chapter in this part, Chapter 16, focuses on the development of literacy and the role of teachers in fostering this development through a number of activities, including the sharing of literature. The remainder of the chapters highlight the following types of activities: (1) manipulative materials such as sand, water, clay, and blocks; (2) art activities; (3) pretend play; (4) music activities; (5) sharing activities. These are the kinds of activities that are included in many early childhood programs from the toddler years through the primary grades, especially those that hold to a constructivist or maturationist perspective. The activities discussed in Part 4 are premised on the ideas, emphasized in Chapter 3, that children's play is valuable, especially when adults have the resourcefulness to augment children's play as a medium for learning.

LITERACY AND LITERATURE

OVERVIEW

This chapter begins with a review of research findings on how **literacy** develops across the early childhood years. In addition, in this chapter, you will find a description of the **whole-language** approaches which are compatible with what is now known about **literacy acquisition.** Chapter 16 provides an amplified description of what you as a teacher will need to be able to do and to provide to help children acquire the skills and joys of literacy. Also included are recommendations for sharing with children the special literature which is their heritage.

THE DEVELOPMENT OF LITERACY REVISITED

Children begin figuring out reading when they first notice written language. At some point during the toddler years they begin to understand that there is meaning connected to those squiggles called print and that figuring out that meaning may be worthwhile. If toddlers have the opportunity to observe readers getting messages from written language, they may begin to model what they have seen and "read" by making up messages and saying them in a "reading" voice, inflections differing from normal speech. Also children notice those examples of written language which appear to have particular utility. Some of children's early knowledge of word-message correspondence may be of commercial symbols and signs. Thus, a three-year-old may look at the word configuration of MacDonald's along with the arches sign and say, "That says, that's where to eat."

Most children acquire a great deal of information about writing as toddlers (Gibson & Levin, 1975; Lavine, 1977). They, for example, learn a great deal about the visual features of written language units—letters and words. The letter *L,* they become aware, has the features of a horizonal line and a vertical line. They learn the difference between the way the letter *O* looks and the way *U* looks. Even very young children often show their awareness in their scribbles, which begin to include forms with features which resemble letters even though they are not precisely the letter symbols of the alphabet they have seen.

Children learn the general form of writing long before they have the specific knowledge or physical coordination to produce what adults would consider writing. Three-year-old Shauna recently drew me a page of scribbles of varying colors. Before presenting it to me she made first one row of little dots and lines from left to right and then, directly underneath, another row. She said in a cadence which differed from her normal talk and approximated an adult reading aloud as she made her rows of marks, "I made this picture for you because I love you. You can keep it and put it on your refrigerator." None of Shauna's marks resembled letters or words but she definitely has the idea of writing as recording meaningful messages, and she seems to be aware that our language system arranges writing in rows from left to right and from top to bottom. Since she is interested in this process as well in lots of other things, she will continue to observe and inquire and experiment. Before long she will probably note **text features** which differentiate letters (written correspondence) from grocery lists, paragraphs as in books from newspaper columns, cartoon "balloons" from maps, traffic signs from recipes, and so forth. Not all children acquire awareness of left to right as easily as Shauna has. (Six-year-old Clark writes "real" sentences with well-formed letters and words but is likely to arrange them in a reverse order from right-to-left or in some confused directional mixture. He has learned many things but still has directionality to master.) While learning these discriminations, young children also begin to apply their abilities to recognize and form the features of the letters of the alphabet to embellish their drawings with their own and others' names and with labels.

Marie Clay (1975), a sensitive observer of young children's progression toward literacy, has noted that prewriting children often produce pages of letterlike forms. The intent of the children seems to be to fill the page. The child may or may not intend to communicate an actual message in a page of such writing, but the activity itself appears to be very important and satisfying.

By examining young children's scribbles and "writing" and listening to their accompanying talk, one can sometimes determine whether children are aware of how letters grouped together make words and of how a stream of words conveys longer messages. Researchers have given us some insights into when and how this happens. Part of the early learning process requires discriminating among pictures, designs, and writing. The three-year-olds studied by Ferreiro & Teberosky (1982) and Lavine (1977) were able to quite successfully sort words and nonwords into two separate piles. Many of the three-year-olds believed, however, that only one letter or two letters together could not be a word. According to what they believed, there needed to be at least three letters to make a word. First graders, on the other hand, identified one- and two-letter configurations as word if they knew them to have some meaning.

At an early stage of building familiarity with letter forms, young children conceive of certain letters as belonging to or representing particular people. Our precocious two-year-old neighbor Tommy makes many letters and looks for representations of letters he knows in the environment. All kinds of round things look like *O*s to Tommy, and all sorts of up- and down-slanted lines are identified as *M*. He thinks that all these letters are his (in his name), but he is particularly thrilled when he makes or sees his very special letter *T*. It is going to be a big surprise to him at some point to realize that there are other uses for these letters and that they do not belong just to his name! As an introduction into literacy, however, Tommy's letters are serving him very well.

Early writing, which to the casual observer may appear to be only scribbling, often has configurations matching the orthography of the child's culture. At age four, children in Saudi Arabia scribble differently from children in the United States. Harste, Woodward, and Burke (1984) point out how the American four-year-old places wavy lines from left to right and creates a whole page of such lines starting at the top of the page and finishing at the bottom. In contrast, a four-year-old in Saudi Arabia uses a series of very intricate curlicue formations with lots of dots over the script, and an Israeli child makes shapes that look like Hebrew characters (mostly) and moves from right to left. The authors also point out that young children who have not yet had any formal instruction in reading and writing format their "writing" on the page in the traditional manner of their cultural orthography, according to whether it is a letter, list, story, or map. Children try to make their writing conform closer and closer to the print they observe about them; as they do so, children in this culture make a series of discoveries which may include the following:

- Writing uses the same shapes again and again.
- Writing consists of a limited number of letters used over and over in different combinations.
- The same letters can be written in different ways—manuscript, print, cursive writing, and type-style variations.

Children's knowledge that supports literacy evidently grows and changes over a span of years. Contrary to what some believe, literacy does not begin at the point at which reading instruction is received. Instead literacy emerges and becomes more and more functional and elaborated across the preschool and primary years. Most children figure out long before they are first graders that there is a one-to-one correspondence between spoken words and written words. Learning that each word they see written will, when read, be heard as a separate spoken word is an important milestone. The development of this idea is facilitated by myriad experiences of seeing print being transformed by a reader into spoken words and, conversely, seeing spoken words being transformed by a writer into print. Part of this learning requires awareness that the space between words is the indication of where one word ends and another begins.

Learning about written word–spoken word correspondence would likely be much easier if all words had only one syllable. Since this is not the case, children are often puzzled by multisyllable words as they try to determine these relationships. The difference between syllables and words is a tough one. It's fairly universal that children trying to read try to match spoken syllables to written words instead of spoken words to written words. Thus, a child in trying to make sense of the writing on the greeting card that they have been told says *happy birthday* may have some difficulty. She may say *"hap-"* while pointing to *happy* and then point to the *birthday* and say *"-py."* The child then wonders where the two words are that should match with *birth* and *day*. As Schickedanz (1981) points out, children sometimes then say things such as, "Hey, this book isn't working right."

Eventually children discover how multisyllable words match print. This is facilitated by many experiences of hearing and seeing how spoken words are written by an adult or older child who does it in a manner in which the written word–spoken word correspondence is obvious.

As children engage in scribbling and the writing of letters at their own volition, they make many useful discoveries about print. They gradually build their ideas about how print works by watching others write and by looking at print in books, on signs, and so forth. They try out their guesses as they produce writing. It is of some surprise to educators who have traditionally assumed that learning to read should come before or simultaneously to learning to write that this is often not the case. Given the support of responsive adults in a **print-rich environment,** many children become quite facile writers (producers of original text) before they tackle and become proficient readers of print (either their own texts or the texts of others). Adults who work with children in the early stages of producing writing which resembles conventional print become very aware that reading and writing, although interrelated, are far from identical. Young writers are often unable to read the words that they write.

When children are in environments where there is a great deal of print to be seen, they quite naturally are curious about what it is and how it works. Print is just one other aspect of the interesting world. They ask questions, and if the answers are given promptly and with pleasure, they ask more questions. When adults point out and remark about the features of print on the page being read, children begin to wonder about how to make sense of it. As in all aspects of their lives, they are eager learners when they are able to initiate inquiries and control the rate of information received. Adults sometimes err in using a minor inquiry as an opportunity to expound on the alphabetic principle and phonic relationships beyond the interest of the child. The point to keep in mind is to respond very briefly and directly with interest, warmth, and pleasure to each question that is asked and then to wait for the next question. When adults let children know that they like to engage in dialogue about print, questions and talk about text, signs, writing, and so forth follow.

From myriad experiences observing and experimenting with print, children derive the following principle of encoding and decoding:

Letters represent sounds, and there is a consistency between words in that regard; that is, when a letter has been determined to represent a certain phoneme in one word, it can be used to represent that same phoneme in another word.

What a significant discovery! Based on this conceptual breakthrough, children experiment with using the letters for which they have derived a sound correspondence (often starting with the letters in their own names or the names of their family members) to create **invented spellings** of words they want to write. They do so very tentatively at first, but as they find that their attempts are often successful in producing words that others can successfully decode, they usually step up their efforts with zest. Once children discover that there is an alphabetic principle which writers can use to decide which letters to employ in creating a particular message, they become more focused in their experimentation with print. Examine the children's writing shown in Figure 16-1 and see if you can determine the basis for some of their invented spellings.

At some point in the process of learning about the features of print, every child who is to become successfully literate develops an additional level of awareness. This is the principle of *uniqueness of word forms*. This principle is as follows:

A particular set of written-down letters put together in a particular sequence is always the same spoken word.

Children do not, of course, articulate the words that express this (or their other print discoveries) either aloud or to themselves. They do develop, however, the working awareness that each spoken word is represented by a unique configuration of letters invariably used for that word. Since most adults have no need to think about this principle and since it is not easily communicated by words in any case, children are on their own to figure this out for themselves. For some children, this realization comes very early. Others, with fewer experiences with print to support the emergence of such an idea, may proceed into the primary grades with only a vague sense of what it is that people do when they recognize and "read" words. They may assume that a reader always must sound out each word as it is read. That works and so it is a logical conclusion. Even children who have a sense of the alphabetic principle may not for some time become aware of the uniqueness of word form. These children produce letters that encode their own messages with invented spellings but seldom try to decode their own or others' messages. The task of "sounding out," they find, is arduous and unlike what they see real readers doing. They therefore stick to writing, which seems more manageable, and leave the magical reading process to adults.

Consider the following examples of children with no understanding of uniqueness of word forms. Five-year-old Rebecca dictated the following words for her teacher to write:

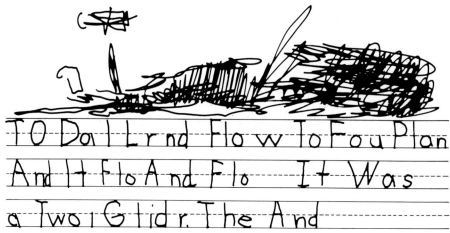

TO Da I Lrnd Flow To Fou Plan
And It Flo And Flo It Was
a Two Glidr. The And

The translation is: Today I learned how to fly a plane. And it flew and flew. It was a toy glider. The End.

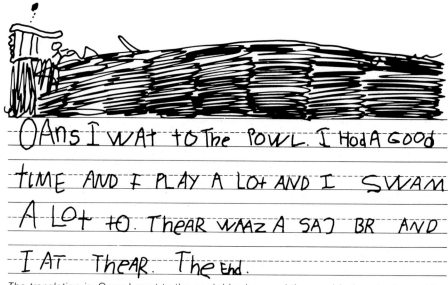

OAns I wAt to The POWL. I Hod A GOOd
tIME AND I PLAY A LOt AND I SWAM
A LOt tO. TheAR WAAz A SAJ BR AND
I AT TheAR. The End.

The translation is: Once I went to the pool. I had a good time and I played a lot and I swam a lot too. There was a snack bar and I ate there. The End.

FIGURE 16-1

I went to Sandy's house.
I went to the Ice Capades too.

As the teacher wrote the second line, Rebecca admonished, "Oh, oh, you did a goof! Look there! You used those ones before." Rebecca was pointing to the repetition of the words "I went" in both lines. She had evidently formed the hypothesis that the way writing works is to invent a new combination of letters for every word. To understand that the use of the same word *requires* the use of the same letters in the same sequence compelled her to give up a notion that, up to this experience, had seemed to work very well.

Five-year-old Angela has been doing a great deal of her own writing using mostly invented spellings. Angela watched and listened to the conversation her friend Amy was having with the teacher about the label she was putting on her picture of her cat, *"C-A-T."* Angela exclaimed excitedly, "That's the way I write *cat* too!" Judging by her obvious surprise, Angela evidently hasn't yet discovered that when the same word is used, the spelling is always (almost, except for homonyms) identical.

Six-year-old Jim Tyler becomes very agitated when classmate Jim McDonald labels his paintings with the same three letters that are Jim Tyler's name. Jim Tyler evidently assumes ownership of these special letters, not realizing that since Jim McDonald also has the same name, it is predictable that his written name will also be the same.

To summarize, the idea that a unique configuration of letters represents each spoken word (except for the exceptions of a limited number of homonyms) must be discovered and incorporated into learning efforts by each new reader. Once the discovery is made, this principle (the uniqueness of word forms) and the alphabetic principle become the keys which ease the way into literacy.

Once children realize that there are a constant of word forms to be learned about, they observe, discover, inquire and learn independently. When they learned to talk, the question "What's 'at?" dominated their exchanges with adults as they tried to figure out the correspondence between objects and their labels. Similarly, in reading the task becomes learning the conventional way in which words are represented by a configuration of letters. Knowing this, they begin to abandon many of their spelling inventions and notice or ask frequently, "How do you spell . . .?" Their writing gradually includes more and more words which have conventional spelling, although these words are still intermingled with words which are spelled according to guesses of what the conventional spelling might be.

Judith Schickedanz uses the hierarchy shown in Figure 16-2 (on p. 309) to track the progress of children in using word creation strategies. As Schickedanz points out, this schema describes the typical progression of children, but since different environments provide different information, the progression may vary according to children's varying kinds of early literary experiences. Children who have a great deal of encouragement to use invented spellings and limited exposure to conventional spellings through observing others write or in examining and hearing books read which have repetitious text may long continue in what Schickedanz labels "the early phonemic" stage. Children who have experiences which lead them to become aware of the uniqueness of word form principle and little exposure to the alphabetic principle may become voracious readers long before they attempt to produce their own written expression. The advantages or disadvantages of these variations are not well-understood, but it seems likely that a balanced exposure to both meaningful writing and reading opportunities is desirable.

WHOLE-LANGUAGE APPROACH

In countless schools around the country, the *whole-language* approach to teaching has been recently discussed and adopted.* Whole language combines reading, writing, speaking, and listening into a unified set of activities that very gradually introduce children to the joys of literacy. Although the term *whole language* may mean very different things to different people who say that they are using it, one common denominator seems to be the heavy emphasis on reading and enjoying real literature (as opposed to basal readers or workbooks); an emphasis on children's own writing productions; and sharing and discussing what is read and written. The central emphasis of the program is to stimulate and maintain children's involvement in communicating through writing, reading, spelling, talking, and listening without setting up separate instruction for each. For example, children learn skills, including phonic skills, because they want to contribute to the class book or newspaper or to write a letter or to learn about zebras, not because the next page in the workbook or teacher's manual directs them to do so.

Whole-language programs emphasize each child's own construction of knowledge about the writing and reading process and how letters and combinations of letters predictably represent meaningful words. In whole-language approaches, as in all other methods used to teach reading, the more knowledge the teacher has of what the individual child has figured out, to date, about how print works, the better able the teacher will be to provide experiences and comments to help with the next steps. The whole-language approach typically includes an abundant inclusion of the following activities: listening at story time; writing stories and journals; labeling of art work; reading big books; reading the text of familiar poems, song lyrics, and folk tales; creating portfolios of writing samples.

---

*Whole-language approaches incorporate many aspects of a method for initial teaching of reading referred to as *language experience.* The language experience approach, which, like whole language, emphasizes listening, speaking, reading, and writing, is based on the idea that the best text for initial reading instruction is that which the children generate themselves. This approach emphasizes group and individual dictation of ideas and experiences for a teacher to transcribe into print and an emphasis on children's own storywriting, creation of captions for artwork, and so forth. As you will note, these emphases are also part of the whole-language programs. Whole-language approaches put greater emphasis, however, on children's own emergent writing (including scribbling) with "invented" spellings as important stages in the learning-to-read process. Teachers using whole-language approaches are more concerned with how the environment and modeling affect the concepts about print, alphabetic representation, and so forth that children are actively constructing for themselves as they engage in writing and reading activities than they are about how they will *teach* children "how to read."

Physical Relationship

Child tries to relate the number of the appearance of marks to some physical aspect of the object or person represented. The child might use three marks, for example, to write her name if she is three years old.

Visual Design

Child accepts the arbitrary nature of words—that they do not resemble their referents physically. The child tries to recreate some designs. The first design attempted is often the child's name. Placeholders—other letters, circles, solid dots, or vertical lines—often are used in place of those letters that the child cannot form.

Syllabic Hypothesis

Child realizes there is a relationship between the oral and written versions of words and also that spoken words can be segmented into "beats" or syllables. The child codes words syllabically, using one mark for each of a word's syllables.

Letter Strings (Visual Rules)

Children create words by stringing letters together so that they look like words. They use several rules:
1. Don't use too many letters.
2. Don't use too few letters.
3. Use a variety of letters, with not more than two of the same letter in succession.
4. Rearrange the same letters to make different words. Children also ask, "What word is this?"

Authority Based

This strategy often follows on the heels of the letter-string strategy, apparently because children decide that it is more efficient to ask for spellings, since so many of their letter strings yield nonwords. Children ask for spellings of whole words, or they copy known words from environmental print or books.

Early Phonemic

Children begin to generate their own words by coding sounds they hear. This is an idea they might get, when adults provide spellings and make letter-sound associations explicit while giving spellings during the time that children are using an authority-based strategy. Independent spelling may be delayed in children who receive complex answers to their spelling questions during the early part of this stage. No known disadvantage is associated with a delay of this kind.

Transitional Phonemic

Children begin to realize that their sound-based spellings do not look quite like words they see in the environment and that specific spellings they generate are not always identical to ones they see elsewhere. Children often become dissatisfied with their own spellings and begin again to ask for whole-word spellings, or they generate a spelling of their own and ask, "Is that right?" This strategy is not common among preschoolers, although children who read early often use it, presumably because they have more visual information about words than do typical preschoolers.

FIGURE 16-2   Word creation strategies

Story Time

If children are to expend the time and energy necessary to successfully learn to decode other's writing, they need to have a strong conviction that reading is its own reward, that reading is not something done to please others or as a means to another end. One of the most effective ways that teachers and parents can contribute to this motivation is to read to children on a regular basis, choosing books which delight and intrigue. Children who have regular exposure to children's literature have greater success as readers (Chomsky, 1972; Greaney, 1986; Moon & Wells, 1979; Wells, 1986). In listening to stories read, children are exposed in a meaningful way to new vocabulary and complex sentence constructions of the type that they seldom hear in spoken exchanges but which are common fare in written language. When literature provides children with models that basically fit but slightly stretch their existing language abilities, the bene-

SETUPS FOR LITERACY AND LITERATURE

BOOK CORNER

Basic Equipment

- Low open shelving; low tables and chairs; carpeting (not mandatory but very desirable); at least a hundred picture books; thirty to fifty easy-to-read general resource materials; well-illustrated encyclopedias; magazines.

Suggested Location

- Locate apart from heavy traffic areas. Isolate from art and snack areas, which foster "messes" and from noise-producing activities such as blocks and dramatic play.

Accessories

- Small rugs, rug samples, a couch or overstuffed chairs, display rack, bean bag chair.

General Guidelines

- Books crowded together on shelves are less likely to attract children's interest than books standing so that their covers show.
- A fresh supply of books selected to stimulate new interests and to encourage known enthusiasms will increase usage. Try to borrow new books each month to supplement those in the basic collection. Sources for borrowing can include the central school library collection, the public library, other classroom collections, and parents' collections.
- Include on the shelves the books and stories children have produced themselves.
- Sit with individual children as often as possible while they are looking at or reading books. Make it a point to talk informally with each child about books as often as possible. You might wish to keep a record of these contacts to make sure that you do not inadvertently miss certain children. Try to sit even more frequently with those children who resist the group story sessions.
- Children at ages five, six, and seven may enjoy having books classified according to reading level or subject. All the easiest-to-read and easy-to-read books might be kept in particular sections, with others classified topically (such as *animals*) or generically (such as *pretend, real, Mother Goose*). Pieces of colored tape on the binding can be used to indicate the shelf location.
- As you are talking with children about the books they have selected, note their interests and be alert to ways of using these books to facilitate the learning experiences you have designed for them.

Alternatives

- Arrange trips for children to the school or public library to examine and select books.

STORY TIME

Basic Equipment

- Chairs, cushions, or floor space (preferably rug) for seating; low chair for teacher or other story reader.

Preferred Location

- Locate in open area away from activity and toys with light source behind children.
- Keep the group as close together as comfort permits.

Accessories

- Pictures or flannel board cutouts (with flannel board) representing story theme or sequence.
- Objects relating to books to be read; for example, real blueberries to go with Robert McCloskey's *Blueberries for Sal* (New York: Viking, 1948) or a flower to introduce Munro Leaf's *The Story of Ferdinand* (New York: Viking, 1969).

General Guidelines

- Whenever possible, arrange to read or tell stories to a small group of children rather than to a large group. At ages three and four, no more than five or six children at a time is recommended; at age five, ten or so; even at age six or seven, small groups are occasionally desirable because they allow more opportunity for interaction, questions, and discussion.
- It pays to use great care in selecting books to read. Avoid reading a book you have not previously read yourself. In making your selections, consider the interests and attention span of the children and general appeal of the books. Look at picture books from the distance at which children will be sitting to determine whether the illustrations are large enough to be effective. You may find it more effective to read two or more short stories that have greater appeal than to read a longer story that is less interesting.
- Always have alternative books and stories on hand. If once under way, you find that the book you selected has no holding power for the particular group, tell the rest of the story instead of reading it—as you quickly turn the pages, give only the most salient points and sketchy information. Then go on to one of your alternative choices.
- Plan to have group stories at a relaxed time of day—not during cleanup or just before outdoor play! Reading after outdoor play might be preferable, or as the last activity in the day. Reserve enough time, however, for leisurely enjoyment.
- In introducing a book, mention the title and point to the words that give the title. (For children from age five up, you will also wish to give the name of the author and illustrator, making sure that children know the meanings of these terms.) Otherwise, keep the introduction brief. A few sentences or less will probably suffice. "This book is about ___," or "Can you guess what this book is about? I thought you'd like to hear it because ___," and then start reading.

- In reading a book aloud to a group, you may find these guidelines useful:
  a. Maintain eye contact with the listeners as much as possible.
  b. Hold the book open toward the children, turning it as necessary for all to see the illustrations before turning to the next page.
  c. Show your regard for the book by turning the pages very carefully and handling the book gently.
  d. Start the reading in a clear tone and at a lively pace. Once you sense that you have the children's full attention, lower or raise your voice and quicken or slow your pace as appropriate to the text. Lengthen your dramatic pauses to let your listeners savor the words and ideas.
  e. From time to time, point out things in the illustrations to which the text refers.
  f. Periodically, sweep your fingers under the sentences as you read them to reinforce for the children your left-to-right pattern of reading.
  g. When reading rhymes, word repetitions, or predictable outcomes, pause to let the children finish phrases for you. It maintains children's involvement and gives them a feeling of confidence when they can use relevant cues to predict what is coming.
  h. Have the children save their discussion until the story is finished. Some interruption will inevitably occur among young children, but if your request to "Tell us later" is consistent and if you immediately continue with the story, they will accept the delay and a more satisfying story reading experience will be maintained.
  i. Should your story not hold everyone's attention, continue on without interruption if at all possible. Sometimes a hand on a child's shoulder will regain attention, or a rejoinder can be interwoven into the story, such as, "And, Toby, whatever do you suppose will happen now?" Keep the story going, more dramatically than ever. If stopping does become unavoidable, make it as brief as possible and then continue on without additional comment.
  j. As you conclude a book, you may wish to avoid asking, "Did you like that story?" and the inevitable shouts of yes and no. Instead of asking for comment you may find it more effective to simply turn back to the beginning of the book and slowly, without comment, turn through the pages again. Typically, children will be reminded of the things they wished to say or ask and may spontaneously comment, "That's a good book."
  k. After spontaneous discussion, you may wish to pose other questions or suggestions related to what has just been heard, such as, "What other things might ___ have done to solve the problem of ___? Would you be interested in trying ___?

Alternatives

- To use flannel board stories, prepare cutouts of major characters and props for a story and position them on the flannel board in coordination with the reading or telling of the story. To most easily prepare effective cutouts, place fabric lining material (Pellon) over the figures you wish to reproduce from illustrations and trace with a black felt pen. Fill with felt color pens the areas you wish to brighten (such as clothing). These pieces will adhere firmly to the flannel or felt surface of the board.

- Young children can learn to use commercial or teacher-prepared tapes of children's books at listening stations with a minimum of help. In preparing tapes, read the text of a book you have selected into the tape as clearly as possible, pausing at the finish of each two-page spread. Play a signal of some kind at this point so that the listening children will know that it is time to turn the page. It is easy to flick a fork against a glass while you are reading and this sound makes an effective and nondistracting "turn" signal.

WRITING CENTER

Basic Equipment

- Low open shelving; low tables and chairs; bulletin boards; paper of various sizes and types, including an ample supply of unlined white newsprint or other white paper ranging in size from 8 1/2" $\times$ 11" to 24" $\times$ 36"; index cards; blank books; writing folders; felt-tipped marking pens, crayons, pencils; chalkboard and chalk; typewriters; computer with word processing software and printer.

Suggested Location

- Place in close proximity to the Book Corner and apart from heavy traffic areas.

Accessories

- Interesting pictures, photographs, posters and objects labeled to stimulate writing; alphabet models; stamp alphabet printing materials; bookmaking materials such as hole punch, stapler, construction paper for covers; blank books in shapes suggestive of special occasions (apple shape, heart shape); mailboxes, stationary, stamps, envelopes; theme-based or seasonal word charts.

General Guidelines

- Allow children to work individually or in pairs or groups in the writing center. Whether children work alone or together, encourage them to share their writing with you and with other children.

- Expect that some writing "starts" will not be completed and that the most earnest and prolific "writers" will fluctuate in their pursuit of writing involvements. A child may write for long periods daily for a period and then in the next days or weeks lose interest. Although sometimes renewed involvement in writing may be fostered in relation to new interests (e.g., making a sign to post with a block construction), there is no long-term benefit in mandating writing during group free-choice times.

- Show special appreciation for those writing products which children themselves seem to value most by making copies on a copy machine, by providing a bulletin board space, by remembering and talking about them again at a later time.

fits are great. It is important to read children's favorite books again and again, engaging them in conversations about what is being read. Repeated readings encourage children to discuss in depth and to tackle the reading of these books for themselves.

For those children who lack language facility because English is their second language or because they use a nonstandard dialect, stories with simple clear wordings and phrasing are best. The old nursery tales are good choices: *Goldilocks and the Three Bears, The Three Billy Goats Gruff, The Little Red Hen, Chicken Little, The Gingerbread Boy.* The language in many newer traditional tales is almost as clear and simple, such as Beatrix Potter's *The Tale of Peter Rabbit* (New York: William Scott, 1957), H. A. Rey's *Curious George* (New York:Coward-McCann, 1941), and C. W. Anderson's *Billy and Blaze Book Bag* (New York: Collier, 1973). Children who have ample exposure to such engaging stories develop reading abilities earlier and more successfully than children who lack such exposure (Feitelson, Kita & Goldstein, 1986).

By age six or seven, many children can follow stories read from books without illustrations. There are excellent transition books that wean children from total reliance on picture books to enjoying simple stories conveyed primarily in language. The books that teachers read continue throughout the elementary school years to pave the way for children to more complex reading and thinking about reading than they can yet handle independently. Story time continues to be a central feature of programs which result in quality involvement of children in gaining information and enjoyment from reading.

Writing Stories and Journals

Young children believe that they can write. When invited to write they produce some approximation of what they have observed and deducted as the essence of the act of writing. In many traditional classrooms, one of children's early learnings is that what they have previously thought was writing is not correct. They then come to believe (as do their teachers) that they cannot know how to write until they have received a long series of instructional sessions on letter formation. In such classrooms, instruction is given in how to form letters, in how to hear sounds in words, and in how to write names as if the children know nothing about these matters. In whole-language classrooms, to the contrary, children's perceptions of themselves as writers are fully accepted and many opportunities are provided for the exercise of whatever writing abilities have been developed. Then, very gradually the adults in the programs help them make discoveries about how to make their writing more like the conventional forms while maintaining their sense of themselves as authors and their joy in the power of written communications.

Some classrooms have a writing center stocked with unlined paper, pencils, crayons, markers, staplers, tape, small pads of paper, cards for signs, chalkboard, typewriter, computer. Children use this center at various times of day as they have the opportunity to choose between involvements. They produce letters, books, stories, signs and use scribbles, invented spellings, and drawings as they communicate real meanings of various kinds. Children's emergent writing forms are accepted and encouraged. Inquiries about "how to write . . . ?" or "how to spell . . . ?" receive responses, but children's self-reliance is also encouraged, and adultlike products are not the goal. A writing center supports emergent literacy in many early childhood classrooms.

Many whole-language kindergartens set aside a special time for writing, sometimes called *journal time* or *story-writing time.* Teachers initiate such a time by simply providing blank paper and pencils or markers and inviting children to "Write a story." or "Write a letter to your mother." Then children are asked to "Read me (us) what you have written." Hesitant children are encouraged by comments such as "It doesn't have to be like grown-up's writing. Do it your own way." Children share what they have written with the teacher and then with groups of other children. As expressed by Sulzby, Teale, and Kamberelis (1989), "By inviting children to read their own stories, we are inviting them to remember their compositions and to treat written compositions as stable—fixed in time and space by the act of writing" (p. 72). Products are displayed, taken home, preserved in writing folders. The key for teachers is to demonstrate to children that their writing, at whatever stage of emergent development, is valued.

During the kindergarten year, children's writing will include scribbling, drawing, nonphonetic letter strings. Some children will increasingly use invented spellings, and a few will move toward conventional spellings. Some will copy print they see in the classroom environment at times. Some children will use sounds they have learned to get the initial (sometimes final) letter for the words they have in mind. The same child may move back and forth between these various forms of writing at various times. Some children will become thrilled with creating lists of names of friends, telephone numbers, and so forth.

Experts disagree about whether children's awareness of spelling conventions and the resulting interest in spelling everything "the right way" facilitates or discourages their further enthusiastic authoring of letters, journals, stories, and so forth. Maintaining enthusiasm about writing while gradually moving in the direction of greater mastery of concepts and skills is the goal of whole-language teachers. Children are expected to progress through the stages of becoming writers at different rates. With continued involvement, eventual mastery is anticipated even though that mastery may not occur until the primary grade level for some children.

Book Time

At book time all the children and their teacher spend a set period of time in quietly enjoying their own reading materials. These materials often include all kinds of published picture books, magazines, textbooks, comic books, child-made books, etc. Children may browse, read, look at pictures and so forth but must engage quietly in some activity related to their own self-selected reading mate-

Book time affords an opportunity for comfort and concentration. *(Laura Lehmann)*

rial. In some programs, especially for older children, this time period is referred to as USSR or SSR (Uninterrupted Sustained Silent Reading or Sustained Silent Reading).

Children's progression into gaining more and more meaning from books during the book times is greatly facilitated by the availability of books with artfully repetitious and lyrical text about captivating subjects. Such books are sometimes referred to as **predictable books** (Bridge, 1986; Heald-Taylor, 1987, Rhodes, 1981; Tompkins & Webeler, 1983). An exemplary volume is Bill Martin Jr.'s *Brown Bear, Brown Bear, What Do You See?* Brown Bear's answer is "I see a redbird looking at me," and, next, quite predictably, the text continues, "Redbird, Redbird, what do you see?" and so forth. Another favorite is from the series of predictable books edited by Margaret Holland—*It Didn't Frighten Me* (New York: Sterling, 1981) by Janet L. Goss and J. C. Harste. Other longtime favorite story books can quickly help beginners understand what it is like to be able to decode and obtain meaning from print. Perhaps you can recall your own response as a novice reader to Dr. Seuss's *Green Eggs and Ham* (New York: Random House, 1960), P. D. Eastman's *Are You My Mother?* (New York: Random House, 1969), or Elsie Minarik's *Little Bear* (New York: Harper & Row, 1960).

As they branch out from predictable or the so-called easy-to-reads into less easily mastered volumes, some children may only read a couple of lines from a page, sampling many books, while others persist through the entire text of each book they choose and then reread each several times more before moving to another. Unless these reading experiences are influenced by particular teacher expectations, this variation will continue. Some children will read only the easiest materials as rapidly as they can, and others will skip directly to hard materials. Still others will alternate between easy and difficult reading. Most children can find an array of books that suit their reading levels and interests, given reasonable access to the multitude of early reading materials produced over the past decades.

Labeling of Artwork

Children's writing and artwork are closely aligned, but the adult concept of drawing a picture and then writing about it may not make sense to the young child. However, when children express an awareness of difference between what they "write" and what they draw or paint, they are encouraged in many whole-language classrooms to use writing to label their drawings. Often, the labeling process is done by the child using whatever writing knowledge they have and is reread by the child. An alternative approach is for the teacher to ask the child to tell about the drawing and for the teacher to take down as dictation whatever is said, whether simple one-word labels or narrative text. Sometimes children find the task of producing captions for a drawing very puzzling: As children draw they often portray a series of happenings rather than a snapshot of a happening in one point in time. They often talk with their friends about what is happening in the picture they are drawing, using it as just another kind of social play exchange. Friends' ideas may also get incorporated into the drawing. To tell about their picture then after it is completed requires a transposition for which their conceptual and language skills are inadequate. To capture in words this richness of events across the passage of time often proves frustrating. For example, five-year-old Ted talked constantly to his friend, Matt, as he drew elaborately about the adventures of an old dog who went through the woods and went into another dog's dog house and climbed up into a tree and found a bone and climbed down and buried it and then went to play with his owner and then could not remember where the bone was. Asked by his teacher to dictate a story about his picture, Ted looked stymied at first. Then he resorted to simply labeling parts, i.e., "This is the old dog." "This is the bone." "This is the tree." When his teacher urged, "Tell something about what happened in your picture," Ted finally said, "He didn't like it one bit." Ted was referring to the end point of his drawing. The task of recapturing the happenings in a sequence in which they could be reported was quite beyond Ted's capacities. Only gradually can the kind of sequences represented in drawings begin to be transposed into a narrative which has a beginning, a main body of a story, and an ending.

When dictation is taken, the teacher listens carefully to how the child produces the language to facilitate the writing. The child's performance during dictation tells much about the progress made in acquiring literacy concepts. How much the child looks at what is written by the adult taking the dictation and whether the child slows and matches the production of the spoken words with the recording of written words and/or sentences reveals what the child knows about the relationship between spoken and written language.

As children are encouraged to meet the various challenges involved in creating narratives to accompany their drawings, they make the transposition described by Vygotsky (1978, p. 115), "the written language of children develops in this fashion, shifting from drawings of things to drawing of words." Dyson (1991) has described in insightful detail how the young authors she observed during journal-writing periods across kindergarten and primary grades increasingly shared their imaginary worlds through their writing in ways that closely paralleled the how they shared dramatic play and expressive art activities. As Dyson describes it,

> Initially, . . . talk about each other's imaginary worlds occurred primarily during drawing. Talk during writing tended to be focused on spelling, a process that took great effort for most children. In time, though, the children's social talk began to focus more on the content of each other's writing. In fact, the children's very struggle with encoding helped that text world become more accessible to their peers. One child might overhear another reread his or her text; and although the rereading peer was focused on remembering and encoding a message, the listening child might react to the sense of the read message. Thus, the children's imaginary worlds were increasingly embedded within their on going social world (p. 106).

Dyson further describes how the children even put each other as characters into their stories and create ideas together for all kinds of exciting adventures in very complex and rich narratives. Writing becomes a social enterprise, mutually enjoyed; concomitantly, the children grow in their powers to use written language as an expressive tool. The connections between play, drawing, and writing becomes clearer as children are observed developing their abilities in whole-language settings across a number of years.

"Reading" the Text of Familiar Poems, Song Lyrics, and Folk Tales

In addition to reading stories, a resourceful teacher has in memory an assortment of poems, songs, and simple folk tales to share with young children. The advantage of committing these to memory is that they can be repeated and repeated at the drop of a hat, gradually becoming more and more beloved. Language impact is heightened due to better voice inflection and eye contact with memorized rather than read materials. Poetry, particularly, is more effectively presented when it is recited, not read. Unless a teacher has poems on the tip of the tongue, the chances are that they will never be heard. Teachers are well-advised to memorize and practice reciting several poems and then to look for meaningful opportunities to use them. Some of the materials that you will enjoy committing to memory for repeated use will be poems and songs which include motions and which have repeated refrains and choruses.

As children learn to say for themselves the words that you share with them, it becomes useful to post large charts on which you have neatly printed the text.

From that point, you may sometimes wish to sweep along under the lines with your hand as you and the children say them together. You can also model noticing things about the words and about the repetitions of words and of rhyming parts of words. These charts, which for the children become as familiar as the spoken words, become reference documents for a known set of words which they can use for many different purposes. Six-year-old Mary goes searching through the accumulation of charts mounted on a flip chart easel for, as she says, "I want the place where it says, `one misty, moisty morning' cause I want to write `one snowy, blowy morning' and I want to see if I'm right about morning." She has written *morening* and is pleased to see that she is so close to the conventional spelling. Five-year-old Todd just "reads" all the charts through and through, alternately singing and laughing. He, too, sometimes writes some of the words from the charts in his own writing book. He particularly likes to write lines from the chant:

> Who stole the cookies from the cookie jar?
> *(Name)* stole the cookies from the cookie jar.
> Who, me?
> Yes, you
> Couldn't be.
> Then who?
>
> *(Different name)* stole the cookies from the cookie jar.
> Who, me?
> Yes, you
> Couldn't be.
> Then who?

Todd inserts the name of his friends into the rhyme and gleefully shows them what he has written.

Reading "Big Books."

Big books, just as the name implies are books which are much larger than normal. They are large enough to be viewed by a number of children when held by the teacher or placed in a special book rack. There are many appealing commercial versions of big books available such as Bill Martin's *Brown Bear* (Holt, Rinehart, & Winston, 1970), Eric Carle's *The Very Hungry Caterpillar* (Philomel, 1970), and Rodney Peppe's *The House That Jack Built* (Delacorte, 1970). Teachers also often make big books of tagboard which they may *laminate* or cover with contact paper so that the pages survive intact, despite frequent and enthusiastic handling. These teacher-made books are often mounted on rings and hung on a chart stand or easel. The commercial versions, and often the teacher-made books as well, have a repetitive narrative which appeals to children and helps them make some discoveries about how print works as well. As they see the same written refrains reappearing in print and hear them spoken again and again, the words begin to look more familiar and they are able to figure out that there is a predictable relationship between saying a particular word and the appearance of the same set of letters on the big book page. Commercially prepared big books have illustrations which are very appealing. Teacher-made big books may also sometimes be illustrated but may also only include the narrative of a class event, a report of children's activities or preferences, and so forth.

Initially teachers share the narrative from the pages of the big book in individual, small-group, or large-group settings (depending on the age and sophistication of the group), discussing the pictures and the events to the extent children find them involving. The teacher typically will, without comment, move a finger along under the lines and words as they are being read. The book is then left in a special location in the classroom where children can look at it themselves if they choose to do so. As the story becomes more familiar, and depending upon the print interest of the children, the teacher may comment or encourage children to comment on the duplicate words on a page or on subsequent pages of the same story. Some of the words of particular interest and/or of most frequent appearance in a story may be prepared and made available for children to use for matching activities with the big book text.

Many teachers find that children's learning with big books is even further extended if there are a number of regular-size versions of the same stories available for children to use during book times (individually or with others) or to take home to share with family members.

Creating Portfolios

In whole-language programs children's progress toward literacy is documented, not by tests, but by the creation of portfolios for the accumulation of evidence about performance. One type of evidence consists of anecdotal notes written by the adults (teachers or parents) to record each child's perceptions of how print works and his or her preferences for particular kinds of activities. Children's writings (or copies of their writings) are placed in a portfolio on a regular basis (e.g., monthly or weekly). Although the specific path toward literacy and rate of progression vary by individual child, the ways in which each progresses in skill and understanding is thus available for examination.

As children progress to the point of decoding text in some of the commercial books or other teacher- and child-produced materials, they are sometimes asked to read aloud for the teacher, who uses special indication marks on a photocopy of the text to record the miscallings and the strategies displayed in decoding unfamiliar words. This kind of record constitutes an ongoing record of progress.

TEACHING RESOURCEFULNESS FOR LITERACY AND LITERATURE

As discussed above teachers need to be aware of each child's interest in and use of print and be able to illustrate to parents the progress of their own children toward the goal of literacy. Teachers also need to understand that they will be

Book illustrations provide the stimulus for teachers and children to talk together. *(Permission of Bernice Wright Cooperative Nursery School)*

helping children at all stages of working toward literacy. The older the children, the broader the range of development to be found in the group. The resourceful teacher will move easily from the child whose writing is scribbles to the child who writes long and involved paragraphs and will value what each is doing. In addition to understanding and appreciating the stages young learners achieve along their way to literacy, teachers who work with children in early stages of literacy development need some specific skills and knowledge if they are to foster and maintain children's absorption with print. Teachers need to abundantly incorporate meaningful print and writing encounters into the classroom environment. They consciously create a print-rich environment, using signs, letters, notes, lists, daily news, reminders, schedules, notices of special events, theme-related products, and so forth. The print incorporated into the classroom is most effective when it conveys some information of real interest to children.

In creating print for the classroom environment, teachers need to be able to print legibly and to form letters very consistently. The spacing between lines and between words must be ample so that novice readers can more easily follow the word sequences. Reading is laborious for many beginners, and teachers need to be very careful not to further complicate the task with careless penmanship. Those who work with young children do well to practice until they can easily and effortlessly produce text which approximates that shown in the photograph on page 426.

KNOWLEDGE OF CHILDREN'S LITERATURE

In addition to creating classrooms in which there is a great deal of meaningful print for children to experience, teachers of young children need to develop depth and breadth of familiarity with children's books. They also need to become aware of the many contributions literature makes to children. A resourceful teacher finds benefits for many aspects of development, e.g., fostering motor development, strengthening affective and social development, and nurturing cognitive development. The following paragraphs give a sampling of the possibilities within each of these domains.

Motor Development

Since movement is such a dominant aspect of the being of young children, it is not surprising that, quite spontaneously, children often imitate the movements and activities they hear in stories. Given teacher suggestions, their motor participation will become even more extensive and varied:

- The children are listening to Esphyr Slobodkina's *Caps for Sale* (New York: William R. Scott, 1957). As they listen, they cannot resist duplicating the monkey's imitation of the peddler whose wares (caps) the monkeys have stolen. With delight, they shake their right hands, their left hands, both hands; stamp their left feet, both feet; and finally toss an imaginary cap as the story concludes with the peddler collecting the caps and continuing to shout, "Caps for sale!"
- Many four- and five-year-olds, inspired by George Zaffo's *The Giant Nursery Book of Things That Go* (Garden City, NY: Doubleday, 1959), have spent their activity period chasing fires, pulling on coats and boots, winding hoses, and climbing imaginary ladders.
- A few three- and four-year-olds have just heard the book by Wanda Gag, *Millions of Cats* (New York: Coward-McCann, 1938). In this rhythmic tale, a little old man and a little old woman who wanted just one cat find themselves with "millions and billions and trillions" of cats. As their teacher puts some lively music on the record player, they act out their impressions of the playfully mewing, pawing, pouncing, and fighting kittens. Their activity is so appealing that many other children join in. Crawling "kittens" appear to be everywhere, just as in *Millions of Cats*.
- The seven-year-olds have thoroughly enjoyed rehearing Theodore Geisel's (Dr. Seuss) Christmas classic, *How the Grinch Stole Christmas* (New York: Random House, 1957). They ask their teacher to read it again, so that they can act out the parts of the Whoville citizens who almost lost their holiday. At the conclusion, with their teacher's help, they consider the many different ways particular parts of the story could be portrayed. All the children quite spontaneously try out each action suggested, which involves a wide range of posturings and gestures.

- Even three-year-olds adore the suspense and dramatic action of Michael Rosen's retelling and Helen Oxenbury's illustrating of the long-time favorite chant *We're Going on a Bear Hunt* (Margaret McElderry Books, Macmillan, 1989).

Verses can be even more effective in leading children into a variety of motor activities. If you have memorized a series of rhythmic verses that you can recite at any point, you will find it easy to involve children in the actions suggested by the cadence, whether they are in the classroom, on the playground, on a field trip, or simply waiting for the bus to arrive.

Affective Development

Books provide children with models of what is acceptable and admirable, undesirable or deplorable. Children exposed to a variety of character roles with contrasting experiences and feelings can begin selecting and clarifying their own roles and feelings. Through books you as a teacher can offer children a rich set of perspectives for thinking about their own feelings and behaviors.

The scope of children's books has broadened appreciably during the last decades, but you will still find some books to be stereotyped in their portrayal of the world. Use books depicting a variety of male and female roles and behaviors. Among these volumes you will find books such as Joe Lasker's *Mothers Can Do Anything* (Chicago: Albert Whitman, 1972), in which mothers are portrayed as fixing pipes, making films, fixing teeth, flying, and climbing.

The current world of children's books is far from being a fairy-tale world of good and evil, beauty and ugliness, wisdom and stupidity. The characters in many children's books are now quite believable, exhibiting real problems and human frailties that children can easily identify with. Things sometimes go quite badly for these new heroes of children's literature, just as they do for us. In Judith Viorst's *Alexander and the Terrible, Horrible, No Good, Very Bad Day* (New York: Atheneum, 1972), Alexander woke up with the gum he had been chewing the previous evening stuck in his hair. From that point right through bedtime, when his cat deserts him to sleep with his brother, everything goes wrong. Knowing about Alexander should make any young child a bit more tolerant of his or her own bad days and the negative feelings that accompany them.

In Mary Hoffman's *Amazing Grace* (Dial, 1991), the heroine, Grace, an inveterate "pretender," wants to play the lead in the school play production of *Peter Pan*. Her schoolmates insist that she can't play Peter Pan because she is a girl and she is black. Supported by her mother and inspired by her grandmother, she persists and wins the part. The story line is warmly portrayed by Caroline Binch's illustrations of Grace in her various moods and roles.

Through books children can learn that their own occasional "bad" feelings are felt by others as well. Storybook children often are not any happier with their siblings, for example, than are real children. In Charlotte Zolotow's *If It Weren't for You* (New York: Harper & Row, 1966), the main character tells another child about all the things, "I would do if I were the only child" but concludes "except I'd have to be alone with the grown-ups." Aliki's book, *Feelings* (New York: Greenwillow, 1984) shows small figures in dialogue in a wide range of emotions triggered by such events as a birthday party, the death of a pet, and spring weather. Opposites in feelings are illustrated as well, for example, selfishness and generosity.

Storybook children have very realistic problems as when Mary Jo, in Janice May Udry's *Mary Jo's Grandmother* (Chicago: Albert Whitman, 1970), has her first independent visit to her grandmother's home in the country during one Christmas vacation. Everything goes as expected until in the middle of a big snowstorm, Grandmother falls, hurts her ankle, and cannot move at all. Mary Jo faces a problem situation that could happen to any child, and children relish thinking about such dilemmas. In Joe Lasker's *He's My Brother* (Chicago: Albert Whitman, 1974), the problem is an ongoing one involving a slow-learning younger brother whose odd behaviors are sometimes difficult to understand and accept. In Gloria Skurzynski's *Martin by Himself* (Boston: Houghton Mifflin, 1979), Martin's mother is not at home when he arrives from school, a realistic happening, particularly in one-parent homes. And in *Granpa* (New York: Crown, 1985), by John Burningham, a little girl's loss of her grandfather is poignantly portrayed. The book shows their close relationship in doing all sorts of things—planting seeds in the spring, sledding in the winter, and more. At the end of the book, Granpa's chair, where the two had often been together, is empty. Young children readily identify with the sense of caring and loss.

As children vicariously encounter and live through these experiences by identifying with book characters, they gain emotionally. Especially important are those books that deal with situations similar to ones confronted by the young reader or by persons close to him or her. Through books we can all compare and extend our experiences and emerge as stronger people because of it. As a teacher, you can consciously choose books that will facilitate such emotional growth for children.

Social Development

Books can contribute much to children's appreciation and understanding of their own feelings in social relationships. Even the best of friendships have their ups and downs, and this range of feelings is reflected in children's literature. Charlotte Zolotow's *My Friend John* (New York: Harper & Row, 1972) celebrates all that is good about having a friend. "I know everything about John," reads the text, "and he knows everything about me." What each knows about the other is lovingly recounted, "John's the only one besides my family who knows I sleep with my light on at night . . . and [we know] how to get into each other's house if the door is locked." Young listeners respond warmly to this message, one that they are just learning—that it is very good to have a close friend.

That friendships, however good, have their rough moments, is delightfully conveyed in Janice M. Udry's *Let's Be Enemies* (New York: Harper & Row,

1961). Two good friends have a falling out. "James used to be my friend," reads the text, "but not today." Three- and four-year-olds echo agreement as they hear the problem, "James always wants to be the boss." Evidently, they often see their friends in the same light and recognize the uncomfortable mixed feelings in being mad at your friend. The tension begins to break as the angry one declares, "I'm going over and poke James," and then, "I think I'll put his crayons in the soup." What comic relief from the preschoolers' perspective!

Books can also play a crucial role in helping children consider alternative responses to social situations. Recall the discussion in Chapter 6 of the work of Spivack and Shure (1974) in developing children's awareness of alternatives for social problem solving; books can help you develop these abilities in children. By pausing at critical decision points within a story and asking the children what they would do in that particular situation, they will become more aware of the diverse decision-making possibilities in most situations. Such discussions should probably not interrupt the initial reading of a story, however, as they might detract from the story's impact; they can be reserved until the end of the initial reading or until subsequent readings.

Certain stories provide built-in opportunities for children to respond. One such book is Norma Simon's *What Did I Do?* (Chicago: Albert Whitman, 1969). In this book, Consuela faces many small issues in her Puerto Rican neighborhood, such as "I want to play but I can't find my doll. What do I do?" and "Joe wants my wagon. What do I do?" Consuela only tells the reader of the one option she took, that is, she looked for her doll, she suggested to Joe that they take turns. It is only through a teacher-led discussion that listeners can learn that Consuela had many other possible choices.

Book characters often demonstrate their cleverness in solving social problems. In Crosby Bonsall's *I Mean It, Stanley* (New York: Macmillan, 1969), some older bullies are foiled in their efforts to take motorcycle goggles away from Archie, Peter, and their dog Willie. Cleverness prevails over size. However, in the Udry book, *What Mary Jo Shared* (Chicago: Albert Whitman, 1966), the heroine cleverly solves another kind of problem—the very common problem of what to show during sharing period at school. In each of these books, a single solution is offered to some common childhood dilemma. In such cases, teachers can extend a book's usefulness by leading a group discussion of alternative solutions.

Cognitive Development

On the following pages, we offer examples of books that are appropriate to the various types of learning discussed in Part 2: classification, number, seriation, causality, space and time concepts, and spoken and written language. It should be noted, however, that books defy pigeonholing. Clever teachers can adapt most books to a variety of teaching responsibilities.

Classification   Many books demonstrate classifications to children. In books such as Anne Rockwell's (New York: Dutton) *Cars* (1984) and *Boats* (1982), Atushi Komori's *Animal Mothers* (New York: Philomel, 1983), Donald Crew's

Harbor (New York: Greenwillow, 1982), Richard Scarry's (New York: Random House) *Great Big School House* (1969) and *Great Big Air Book* (1971), or George Zaffo's (New York: Doubleday) *The Giant Nursery Book of Things That Work* (1967) and *The Giant Nursery Book of Things That Go* (1959), animals or objects are grouped according to form or function. Children can discover by themselves, or teachers can show why particular things are grouped in the same book or on the same pages.

In other books, such as Bernice Kohn's *Everything Has a Shape* (Englewood Cliffs, NJ: Prentice-Hall, 1964), and Millicent Selsam's *All Kinds of Babies and How They Grow* (New York: William R. Scott, 1953), the classification criteria are explicitly discussed in the text. In the latter volume, baby animals that resemble their parents are contrasted with other animals that go through a series of radical developmental changes during their life spans (frogs, moths, eels, crabs, and swans).

Color is highlighted in Tana Hoban's *Is It Red? Is It Yellow? Is It Blue? An Adventure in Color* (New York: Greenwillow, 1978). Beautiful color photographs throughout the book are accompanied by circles of the colors that predominate in each.

Number   All sorts of number books are available that encourage children to count pictured objects and to recognize written numerals. For the youngest children, Tana Hoban's *1, 2, 3* (New York: Greenwillow, 1985) presents bold colorful photographs illustrating a set of objects and the corresponding material. At the bottom of each page are the corresponding number of dots and the numeral written out. For preschoolers, Sandra Joanne Russell's *A Farmer's Dozen* (New York: Harper & Row, 1982) combines rhyme, colorful illustrations, and numerical borders in an aesthetically pleasing number experience.

Benjamin Elkin presents the tale of *The Six Foolish Fisherman* (Chicago: Children's Press, 1959) who never get beyond *five* when counting themselves. That each has forgotten to count himself is obvious only to the most observant young child. Other particularly appealing counting books are Helen Oxenbury's *Numbers of Things* (New York: Franklin Watts, 1968), James Kruss's *Three by Three* (New York: Macmillan, 1965), Arthur Gregor's *1 2 3 4 5* (Philadelphia: Lippincott, 1964), Dahlov Ipcar's *Brown Cow Farm* (Garden City, NY: Doubleday, 1959), Maurice Sendak's *One Was Johnny* (New York, Harper & Row, 1962), and Mitsumasa Anno's *Anno's Counting Book* (New York: Crowell, 1977) and *Anno's Counting House* (New York: Philomel, 1982). Mary Ree's illustrations in *Ten in a Bed* (New York: Joy Street, 1988) shows sleepover scenes to accompany the rollicking rhyme beloved by children.

There were ten in a bed
And the little one said,
"Roll over! Roll over!"
So they all rolled over
And one rolled out. . . .

"What do you suppose happened next?" (*Permission of Bernice Wright Cooperative Nursery School*)

Seriation   Alignment according to size or other dimensions is best learned by children's active manipulation rather than through books. However, a number of books can help a child formalize or crystallize his or her developing concepts of how objects can be compared with each other. Books that help children with size comparisons are Bernice Kohn's *Everything Has a Size* (Englewood Cliffs, NJ: Prentice-Hall, 1964), Miriam Schlein's *Heavy Is a Hippopotamus* (New York: Dodd, Mead, 1956), Alexi Tolstoi's *The Great Big Enormous Turnip* (New York: Mifflin, 1984). Relative speed is the focus of Miriam Schlein's *Fast Is Not a Ladybug* (New York: William R. Scott, 1953).

Causality   Many fine books covering virtually all subjects are available to help explain various real phenomena to young children. By spending time in the nonfiction section of any children's library, you not only will learn what is available to children but also will inevitably sharpen your own perspective on many topics. Study carefully the presentations that are made in these books, especially those in the natural and physical science areas, and you will gain many valuable ideas for demonstrating cause and effect. Exemplary are Ann and Harlow Rockwell's (New York: Macmillan, 1982) books *How My Garden Grew* and *Sick in Bed* and Peter Spier's *Rain* (Garden City, N.Y.: Doubleday, 1982).

Some illustrators do a masterful job of pictorially explaining to children how things are made, how they grow, how they change. One of the finest examples of this genre of books is Byron Barton's *Building a House* (New York: Greenwillow, 1981). All the important stages of the construction of the house are realistically portrayed. A bulldozer digs a hole; a cement mixer pours cement; the bricklayers lay large white bricks; the carpenters make the floors, the walls, and the roof; the bricklayers make the fireplace chimney. We also see a plumber, an electrician, and painters at work. Finally, the workers leave, and the family moves in. Having encountered a book of this kind, children are wiser about how houses, including their own, came to be.

Some books suggest a number of possibilities for children's investigation of the common things that surround them. In Harvey Milgram's *Egg-Ventures* (New York: E. P. Dutton, 1974), for example, suggestions are given for measuring the length, width, and volume of eggs; for examining their buoyancy in fresh and salt water; for rolling them and comparing their rolling patterns with those of balls and other objects; for examining the effects of heating and beating them. Seymour Simon's *A Tree on Your Street* (New York: Holiday House, 1973) gives more complex suggestions for various activities in measuring, examining, and analyzing changes in a tree.

Space Concepts   Although the preschooler most effectively builds space concepts through active manipulation of objects and self in relation to objects, five- to seven-year-olds can benefit from simple book presentations on measurement and directionality. Among the books that may be useful at this point are Ethel Berkeley's *Big and Little, Up and Down* (New York: William R. Scott, 1960), and Rolf Myller's *How Big Is a Foot?* (New York: Atheneum, 1962). There are also books that help a child consider him- or herself in relation to larger spatial contexts. Herman and Nina Schneider's *You Among the Stars* (New York: William R. Scott, 1951) is one such volume; another is James Hengesbough's *I Live in So Many Places* (Chicago: Children's Press, 1956), which attempts to help the child understand that he lives simultaneously in a house, in a town, in a state, in a country, and in a world.

Time Concepts   Young children's sense of time and history remains quite sketchy from ages three through seven, but their awareness may be heightened by attention to the time concepts presented in many children's books. For example, Virginia Lee Burton's *The Little House* (Boston: Houghton Mifflin, 1942), the story of a country house that is increasingly surrounded by city structures, contains beautiful illustrations of the passage of time. The little house is portrayed through days and nights, through passages of seasons, through the passing of years and generations. The same kind of direct or indirect reference to time is included in many other children's books and can contribute to a child's awareness of these dimensions. Among these are Franklyn Branley's *Snow Is Falling* (New York: Thomas Y. Crowell, 1963) and Maurice Sendak's *Chicken Soup with Rice: A Book of Months* (New York: Harper & Row, 1952).

SUMMARY

Children develop literacy across their early years from myriad experiences with print and books. They are helped in this process when adults create print-rich environments in which they support children's efforts to try out their discoveries about how to read and write. Whole-language approaches which integrate exposure to reading, writing, speaking, and listening facilitate those discoveries. Activities such as story time; book time; writing journals and stories; labeling art work; reading the lyrics of poems, songs, folk tales; and reading "big books" characterize whole-language approaches. Resourceful teachers atune their own input to children's individual progress, produce legible text of high interest to children, and creatively integrate discerning selections from the vast storehouse of children's literature into classroom experience. The remaining chapters in Part 4 provide further perspectives on how literacy is developed within the context of manipulatives, art, pretend, music, literature, and sharing. Each chapter offers recommendations and examples of how to meaningfully involve young children with written language.

SUGGESTED ACTIVITIES

1 Visit several early childhood classrooms and analyze the setups for book areas, noting the following:
   a Where is the area placed in relation to other areas?
   b What kind of floor coverings and other furnishings are used?
   c How are books and other reading materials displayed and stored?
2 Observe in a classroom book or reading area when children are present. Note the following:
   a How do different children react to the same materials? What differences in action and language repertoire are evidenced?
   b How long do children remain engaged with the materials?
   c What kinds of interactions do the materials engender among children?
   d What do teachers say and do when they are in the area? Do they initiate activities or respond to children's initiations?
3 Observe in a classroom or library when an adult is reading or telling stories to groups of children. Note the following:
   a How do adults position themselves in relation to the children? How do they position themselves in relation to the book or other props?
   b What communication and management techniques are used by the adults?
   c What are the qualities of the stories used in terms of level of language sophistication, action versus description, and amount of repetition?
   d How long do such sessions last?
4 Become familiar with children's books by browsing through libraries, book stores, book corners in classrooms. Ask yourself the following kinds of questions about each book you examine:
   a Does it tell a story?
   b Does it teach a concept?
   c Does it provide an aesthetic visual experience?
   d Does it provide an aesthetic language or an internal imagery experience?
   e Is the intent of the book fulfilled primarily by the illustrations? By the text? By both?

5 Collect writing samples of children of various ages across a span of several months, comparing performance both across and within individuals. From observing the writing process and/or examining the products, try to infer the children's knowledge about print and letter-sound relationships.

ADDITIONAL READINGS

Atkins, C. (1984). Writing: Doing something constructive. *Young Children, 39,* 3–7.

Clay, M. M. (1975). *What did I write?* Portsmouth, NH: Heinemann.

DuCharme, C. C. (1991). "Pictures make me know more ideas": Lessons from three young writers. *Day Care and Early Education, 19*(1), 4–10.

Goodman, K. S. (1986). *What's whole in whole language?* Portsmouth, NH: Heinemann.

Goodman, K. S., Goodman, Y. M., & Hood, W. J. (Eds.). (1989). *The whole language evaluation book.* Portsmouth, NH: Heinemann.

Harsh, A. (1987). Teach mathematics with children's literature. *Young Children, 42*(6), 24–29.

Kamii, C., & Randazzo, M. (1985). Social interaction and invented spelling. *Language Arts, 52,* 124–133.

Raines, S. C., & Canady, R. J. (1990). *The whole language kindergarten.* New York: Teachers College, Columbia University.

Schickedanz, J. A. (1981). Hey! This book's not working right. *Young Children, 37*(1), 18–27.

Schickedanz, J. A. (1986). *More than the ABC's, the early stages of reading and writing.* Washington, DC: National Association for the Education of Young Children.

Strickland, D. S., & Morrow, L. M. (1989). *Emerging literacy: Young children learn to read and write.* Newark, DL: International Reading Association.

Tierney, R. J., Carter, M. A., & Desai, L. E. (1991). *Portfolio assessment in the reading-writing classroom.* Norwood, MA: Christopher Gordon.

Warner, L. (1990, Fall). Big books: How to make them and how to use them. *Day Care and Early Education, 18*(1), 16–19.

Willert, M. K., & Kamii, C. (1985). Reading in the kindergarten: Direct vs. indirect teaching. *Young Children, 40,* 3–9.

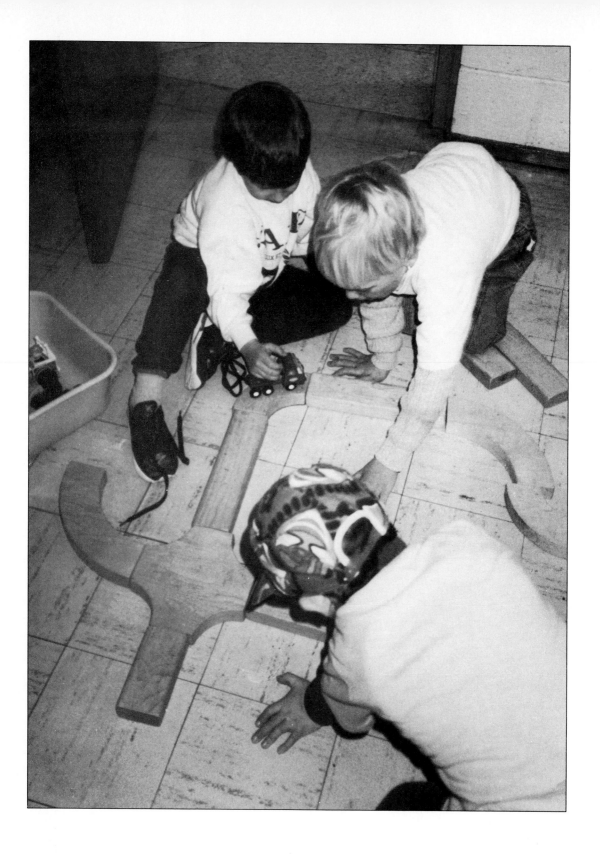

CHAPTER 17

MANIPULATIVE MATERIALS

OVERVIEW

Materials such as sand, water, clay, and blocks offer rich learning possibilities for children. These materials take on whatever meaning and form a child imposes on them, in contrast to many games and toys that replicate something very specific in the real world. The child adapts these materials to his or her own purposes and, consequently, they are used in different ways at different points in development. A three-year-old, a five-year-old, and a seven-year-old will each use the same materials in quite different ways.

Although miniature toys, with their intricate replication of reality, immediately attract children, they tend to be quickly discarded or ignored. On the other hand, unstructured materials, which allow children the opportunity to explore and replicate reality according to their own perceptions, serve month after month and year after year. Dorothy Cohen (1972) points out the need to provide these kinds of materials for children who lack natural access to them:

> In the past parents bought their children the structured play materials, and the children found the unstructured ones in the natural world around them. Dirt, mud, sticks, stones, sand, clay, plant debris, and whatever else nature offers are all fair game for children's use. In industrialized, urban society such natural riches are harder for children to come by. Blocks, paint, manufactured clays, crayons, and various manipulative construction materials are the replacements both at home and at school for nature's gifts. (p. 91)

The appeal of unstructured materials to children is undeniable, whether they are used at early ages or for very complex constructions as their abilities grow. Activity becomes increasingly elaborate and detailed as the children mature and become more experienced with the possibilities inherent in the material. When children construct a highway with a sand tunnel or create a rain storm at the beach or water table, they symbolize these objects and events in their thinking. Sometimes their activity leads them to new discoveries. For example, as the sand caves in on the cars in the highway tunnel, they may begin to wonder what keeps the ground from falling on cars in real tunnels. As the incompleteness of their knowledge becomes apparent, their curiosity will lead them into more precise observations and further experimentation.

As you read this chapter, try to attune yourself to the many possibilities unstructured materials afford. Try to think back to your own childhood experiences and recall the situations in which you played with sand, water, clay, blocks, or other construction or manipulative materials. Think about your feelings, problems, frustrations, and successes. Consider how adults interfered with or assisted your efforts, and how environmental factors encouraged or discouraged you. This kind of recollection should be helpful in recapturing the importance of manipulative materials to young children.*

---

*Specific guidelines for observing how teachers and children use various areas of the classroom for specific activities are provided in Part 4 of Appendix 1.

Sand play is fully engrossing for many young children. *(John James)*

SETUPS FOR MANIPULATIVE MATERIALS

SAND

Basic Equipment

- Container—commercially sold sand table; wooden box lined with heavy plastic; child's small plastic swimming pool; plastic baby's bath; plastic dish pan; flat cardboard box (12″ × 8″ × 3″).
- Sand—beach quality, clean.
- Boxes for storing accessories.

Preferred Location

- Locate where floor covering will be least likely to be damaged by sand, such as a cement area or outside; or use large plastic, canvas, or cloth sheeting with weighted corners under sand play area.

Accessories

- Shovels (miniature); scoops; funnels; containers (varying sizes with some duplications); pans; measuring spoons, cups; plastic see-through containers; spoons; tin cans; gelatin molds; muffin tins; chunks of wood; beach rocks; large marbles; shells; string; miniature boats, trucks, cars, animals; rigid plastic tubing; magnifying glass; bottle caps; tongue depressors; rollers; balance scale; plastic letter forms; netting; cardboard tubing.

General Guidelines

- Sometimes use dry sand, sometimes wet sand for contrasting experiences. Dry sand pours easily through tubing, sieves, sifters, funnels. Wet sand molds more easily and facilitates use of various-sized containers to create molds of different sizes; use miniature toys, plastic letter forms, tongue depressors in making impressions.
- Keep accessories in boxes rather than in sand container. Take out only a few accessories each day. Vary them to create fresh experiences.
- Set firm limits initially for keeping sand in box, sand table, or whatever container is in use.
- Have broom and dustpan on hand and teach children how to use them to clean up spills.

Alternatives

- Rice or cracked corn or wheat, beans of various sizes, wood shavings, pebbles, sawdust, salt (large-grain variety if you can keep it dry and covered between uses). For salt, a plastic cake pan (with cover) serves well for one child's use.
- Where climate permits, sand play may be predominantly an outside activity. Providing a variety of accessories is equally important, and there might be an additional need for larger containers such as pails and pans and for tools such as hoes, shovels, and trowels.

WATER

Basic Equipment

- Container—commercially sold water table; child's small plastic swimming pool; plastic baby's bath; dishpans; water pails; galvanized small tub. (Place smaller containers on top of a table to facilitate use by a standing child.)
- Boxes for storing accessories.
- Plastic or rubberized cover-ups for children to wear to keep their clothing dry.

Preferred Location

- Locate where dampness or spills will not damage surroundings, close to sink or other water supply for ease of filling and emptying.

Accessories

- Floating soap or soap flakes; measuring cups; funnels; plastic baster, or other syringes; rotary eggbeater; pieces of hose; plastic squeeze bottles; blocks of wood; toy boats, animals, people; small watering can (spray attachment); plastic straws; floating and sinking objects—corks, sponges; wooden ball, hollow rubber ball, eraser, buttons, shells; food coloring; medicine droppers, clear rigid plastic tubing (6″ to 24″ long with varying diameters); marbles (giant size); tin cans (varying sizes); materials for boat making—aluminum foil, waxed paper, sticks, tongue depressors, manila paper, masking tape.

General Guidelines

- Establish expectations with children that cover-ups will be worn for water play; be prepared to provide dry changes of clothing even with use of cover-ups.
- Drain water after each day's use.
- Keep a small plastic pail and sponges on hand and teach children how to sponge up spilled water.

Alternatives

- If a water table is routinely available, occasionally place small plastic dishpans in it so that children have individual spaces.
- On warm days outdoors provide a bucket of water and brushes. Children will create designs and intriguing effects as they "paint" with water on walls, sidewalks, play equipment, and bikes.
- Fill water table with ice or snow for variation in experiences.

CLAY

Basic Equipment

- Clay-type material—ceramic potter's clay, salt clay or playdough, plasticene, sawdust mixed with wheat paste. (Potter's clay can be purchased ready for use in a sturdy plastic bag, or it can be obtained in powdered form and mixed with water.)

- Storage container with tightly fitting cover, such as crock, plastic garbage pail, or large covered bowl.
- Masonite boards (about 15″ square).
- Cover-ups (aprons or smocks).

Preferred Location

- Locate relatively close to water supply or sink for ease of cleanup, and away from games and other nonwashable materials.

Accessories

- Tongue depressors; rollers (round wooden cylinders); cookie cutters; yarn; buttons; leather thongs (pieces); sturdy plastic knives and forks; scissors; table knives; wooden mallets; spools; blocks; bits of aluminum foil, waxed paper, plastic; cracked eggshells; toothpicks.

General Guidelines

- When providing clay for children, test to see whether it is in malleable condition before giving it to them. Clay is used and reused by most young children without interest in creating a product to preserve. If potter's clay becomes dry, it can be reconditioned for further use. If it is at all malleable, mold it into small balls (tennis ball size), make an indentation in each ball with your thumb, and place in storage well before giving it to children. If the clay becomes too wet, leave cover off for a period of time and then rework. If it dries into hard, unmalleable lumps, place in a cloth bag and pound with hammer or other instrument until it is reduced to powder form and then remoisten.
- When children reach the stage of wishing to preserve their products, potter's clay can be left to harden and can be fired, with or without glaze, if a kiln is available. Pieces that are not fired tend to be very fragile, although they can be kept if children wish to care for them.
- Plasticene must be relatively warm to be usable by children. Store in a warm place, if possible, or warm through your own hand manipulations.
- Salt clay or playdough may be mixed from one cup salt, one cup flour, one tablespoon alum, and water sufficient to bring it to the consistency of putty. Food colorings can also be added. The products will eventually dry, but if the mass is very large the drying time is usually prohibitive.
- Place newspapers under the work areas to ease cleanup tasks, even when the clay is used on masonite boards.
- Distribute or set out clay in balls intended for individual use, but be prepared to "serve" more if a child has a project under way for which the allotment is insufficient.
- You may wish to encourage children to use clay by sitting with them and manipulating clay while they are working. Beware, however, of making representational objects that they might then try to imitate rather than attempting to develop their own ideas. In clay and other art media, children benefit most by representing their own perceptions and experiences.

BLOCKS

Basic Equipment

- Large wooden hollow blocks and auxiliary pieces; large cardboard hollow blocks; small-unit blocks.
- Open shelving for unit block storage.

Preferred Location

- Locate in an out-of-the-way area so that those passing by will create minimal interference with construction activities.
- Carpeting can be used for noise reduction.

Accessories

- For use with larger constructions in which the children are themselves the users (in contrast to miniature play scenes)—large steering wheel affixed to sturdy base; large foam rubber balls; short pieces of rope; rug remnants; linoleum squares; pieces of sturdy cardboard; pieces of plexiglass; cardboard boxes (various sizes); boards; barrels.
- For use in smaller constructions in which the children create miniature worlds and imaginatively manipulate the actions—colored cubes; pail of smooth beach stones; empty thread spools, empty tin cans; string; Easter grass; miniature objects replicating those familiar to children, such as humans, animals, transportation, furniture. (Children will be more likely to attempt representations of their own experience in block play if the accessories include toy replicas that are familiar to them. Buses, taxis, cranes, and traffic officers may be most appropriate for urban children. Cows, sheep, horses, and pickup trucks might facilitate richer play in rural areas. Try to include regional and subcultural representational toys to the extent possible.)

General Guidelines

- Arrange blocks in storage by size and shape. Place unit blocks in open shelving. Indicate the correct placement of the respective blocks by taped-on block outline.
- Expect that block structures will be regularly knocked down, both by accident and intentionally.
- Always give advance notice of the termination of an activity period in which there is block play under way. This will avert the disappointment of children who spend long periods of time preparing a construction in anticipation of a particular kind of play, only to have the actual play abruptly canceled.
- Block cleanup can be made fun and interesting through the use of one of the following techniques. Say to the children, "You bring them to me, and I'll put them away," or vice versa. Assign particular children to bring all blocks of a given size. Sing or play a lively record to accompany cleanup.

Alternatives

- Use cardboard cartons, taped tightly closed, as a substitute for large blocks
- Use cardboard milk cartons, washed and trimmed to angular shape, as substitutes for cardboard hollow blocks. Cover with adhesive shelf covering.

Balance and symmetry are integral to satisfying block construction. *(Cumberland Hill Associates, Inc.)*

MOTOR DEVELOPMENT AND MANIPULATIVES

Large-muscle activities are predominant in block play and in outdoor sand play. Given the opportunity, children will constantly transport sand and large blocks and, in the process, will develop strength, balance, endurance, and broadened action repertoires. Children gradually increase their ability to perform these actions with ease and agility. The tasks of lifting, pulling, and pushing are practiced initially as separate endeavors and are then gradually interwoven into more complex play actions.

To further encourage large-muscle involvement, you may wish to use the following arrangements and activities with manipulative materials:

- Arrange storage of blocks so that some are as high as children can reach and others are low, to mandate reaching and bending.
- Use blocks to build bins for target shooting with bean bags or foam rubber balls. Mark a starting line on the floor (with masking tape) and let the children "shoot." Lengthen the distance between bin and starting line to increase the difficulty of the task.
- When you are filling or emptying the water table or washing the clay or painting tables, a few helping children can be encouraged to engage in water-carry-

ing activities. If suitable containers are provided in outside water areas, children will spontaneously become involved in carrying and balancing tasks. Expect spills, of course!

- Erect a pulley system that children can use for transporting blocks placed in a sling or blanket, or pails of sand (outside).
- Blocks can periodically be used along with other materials (such as large cardboard boxes, hoops, chairs, and tables) to create obstacle courses. Masking tape or string can be used to mark the trail to be followed through the series of obstacles. To follow the trail, children might need to crawl over objects or through, under, around, and between them. Large wooden hollow blocks can be used with the longest-unit blocks to create tunnels, arches, and steps.
- Children can be encouraged to construct and use a series of blocks in the form of walking rails. The blocks can be placed end to end to provide narrow or wide ridges, or a combination if you are uncertain about the difficulty level. Children can be encouraged to try to walk forward, backward, sideways, halfway, and all the way. This provides excellent practice in balance and motor control.

As children use sand, water, clay, and blocks, they also quite spontaneously engage in activities that foster small-muscle development. Especially when an abundance of varied accessories is available, children gradually extend their repertoire and skill. The following arrangements can prove particularly useful in encouraging children to engage in actions that improve eye-hand coordination and small-muscle control:

- For sand play, be sure to provide sifters, sieves, scoops, containers of different sizes, funnels, and miniature toys, cars, trucks, people.
- For water play, provide cups, spoons, various-sized containers, basters, funnels, tongs, rigid plastic tubing, and rotary beaters. As children use these tools, they become more precise and skilled in their movements. Encourage precision and experimentation with suggestions such as: "Can you pour like that into the bowl from way up high?" "Can you fill this bottle with the watering can without spilling any water?"
- With clay activities, provide tongue depressors, wooden meat skewers (with points blunted), or other marking tools. Comment on the marks children make with these tools, such as, "I see you are making curvy lines," or "Those criss-cross lines look interesting." Or if a tool is used for cutting, you might say, "I see that you have two pieces now that you cut in half," or "Oh, look, you made a square when you cut off those curved edges."
- When children are playing with dry sand, encourage experimentation with different actions by asking "How many different ways could you get sand in that bowl (or whatever container is in use)?" Suggest ways the child has not thought of, such as scooping with hands, scooping with another container, through a funnel, through a tube, and so forth.

Many kinds of skill learning may result from water play. *(John James)*

These ideas are not intended to include all the things that might be done to promote motor development in the context of children's use of manipulative materials; these ideas simply illustrate some of the possibilities. Once you become aware of how children quite spontaneously become involved in motor activities with sand, water, clay, and blocks, you will undoubtedly think of many additional ways to extend these activities.

AFFECTIVE AND SOCIAL DEVELOPMENT AND MANIPULATIVES

Manipulative materials are useful in helping anxious children to relax or angry children to settle down. Concentration on the responsive material and their own manipulation of it can help children regain their composure. To calm an angry child or relax a tense one, suggest water play, or ask for help washing tables with warm, sudsy water. Show the child how to use a sponge in both soaking up and letting out water. Demonstrate procedures such as wetting the sponge, large-muscle scrubbing, bringing in water, and rewetting the sponge, and notice whether the child's tensions dissipate as he or she becomes involved in these actions.

Sometimes the amorphous manipulative materials serve as targets of feelings generated in other situations. For example, you may note that children spontaneously use clay as the object of their aggressive feelings. You may also encourage a child who appears to be having a series of pugnacious encounters to use clay for this purpose, perhaps by saying, "This clay would do better if it was worked around a bit." You might punch it vigorously yourself a few times and then ask, "Would you like to pound this until it is mixed up very well?" Praise vigorous slapping and pounding, saying, "Good, that should be better mixed now."

At other times, children may use the materials to enact a situation that has created conflict. A child who is feeling angry about his or her treatment from others may retaliate in vigorous representational play—with blocks, clay, or sand—in which something or someone really "gets it."

The unstructured quality of these manipulative materials makes them especially useful for the indirect expression of affective states. Teachers may wish at some point to help a child broaden his or her repertoire for dealing with problem situations that have generated tensions and anger, but the immediate value of manipulative materials for indirect emotional release should not be overlooked.

Since there is no right or wrong way to use manipulative materials, especially water and sand, these materials—more than structured toys such as tricycles, dominoes, puzzles, or dolls—allow a child who lacks confidence to experience satisfaction. The following techniques may be appropriate to use with children whose abilities to initiate activities and to be independently involved are not well developed.

- Go with the child to the water or sand area and begin to play there yourself. Smile and praise the child if he or she begins to use the materials. Continue frequent visual contact, smiling and offering periodic comment as long as the child remains occupied. Make your attention contingent on continued activity. With an initial positive experience built on adult support and attention, the child is likely to find that this type of involvement is within his or her repertoire, and he or she will therefore be likely to independently initiate involvement on subsequent occasions.
- For a child who has only used water or sand play, suggest other manipulative materials (such as blocks, clay, or painting) rather than an activity that would require more specific skills, especially those involving interactions.
- After children, especially those who lack confidence, have created a block structure or other similar product, ask if they would like to see themselves with the work. Hold a mirror (preferably the large, stand-up metal variety) so they can see themselves standing beside it. Or take a Polaroid picture.

Contact with manipulative materials can facilitate more comprehensive participation for a hesitant child. The teacher must get the child to handle the materials initially and then follow up with warm attention and quiet praise. Since all levels of performance are well integrated in manipulative play, children are very likely to see their efforts as quite adequate when viewed positively by others.

Social interactions between children when they are using manipulative materials range from early parallel and associative play to the most advanced cooperative play activity. The myriad possibilities for working together, particularly with sand, clay, and blocks, can incorporate very advanced social functioning. Children who have not been involved with peers often have first contacts at the water table or sand area. As they work side by side, one child's action frequently leads to imitation or comment by others and subsequently to increased interaction and joint activity.

Play activities with manipulative materials can also lead to interpersonal conflicts and other social problems, thereby providing opportunities for helping children develop their social sensitivity and problem-solving abilities. The following types of teaching strategies are among those that may prove useful in this regard:

- Demonstrate to children alternative behaviors for obtaining a material that someone else is using, instead of grabbing, crying, or other relatively ineffective behaviors. These possibilities might include asking the other child if they can use it; trading something else for it; looking for something like it; waiting; getting the other child more interested in another activity; or finding a good substitute. If they fail to understand the basic idea of having different options for their actions, concentrate first on developing such concepts as *and, or, same,* and *different* with the concrete manipulative materials. Suggest: "There is a shovel *and* a hoe." "We have blocks this size *and* blocks this size. Which do you want?" "Do you want to shovel sand *or* do you want to swing?" "You have a big pail. Do you want the *same* kind or do you want a *different* kind next?" "You usually play in sand first when you come to school. Today you are doing something different." When you have evidence that children understand the meanings of these terms in regard to their materials and their actions with materials, you may also be successful in helping them apply those terms in their thinking about alternative social behaviors. To make children more aware of their actions, ask, "Do you want to ask Jimmy for it *or* do you want to wait?" or "That didn't work, did it? Is there a *different* way you could do it?"
- If children become bothersome by knocking down others' block structures, suggest alternative activities, such as building their own structures for the express purpose of knocking them down; trying to build structures that are very easy to knock down and some that are so strong that it is almost impossible to knock them down (show them how the base is essential to a building's stability); standing blocks up on end like bowling pins and trying to knock them down with balls or bean bags.
- After children engage in an alternative behavior, explain why it is better than their previous actions, and praise this current activity.
- Watch for the positive alternatives employed by children in solving social conflicts. Make sure that the other children understand the nature of the conflict and are aware of the original, inappropriate behavior as well as the substitute behavior you are praising.

COGNITIVE DEVELOPMENT AND MANIPULATIVES

The opportunities for helping children develop cognitively and intellectually are particularly abundant when they are using manipulative materials. Children will benefit if their teachers have a broad and varied repertoire for furthering development in each of the following areas.

Classification, Seriation, and Number

Manipulative materials and the accessories used with them offer many diverse opportunities for classifying, ordering, counting, grouping, regrouping, and various numerical operations. The following are among the possibilities:

- Help children classify blocks by size as they put them away. "All large cylinders on this block shelf, smaller cylinders here, the longest blocks on another shelf."
- Commercial unit blocks are carefully graduated in size, which facilitates learning. They can be sorted according to size or ordered in sequence to form stairsteps. Smaller units can be combined to replace larger ones, while the teacher says, "This is half as big as that. I'll need two of the smallest ones to match it."
- If you provide a variety of containers for use with wet sand, children will be able to make forms of various sizes and shapes, such as round, square, flat, tall, big and round, little and round. These provide opportunity for labeling and classification.
- With tweezers or kitchen tongs and objects in sand or water, a child can become involved in classification activities such as those involved in picking up everything that is red or everything that floats. Through conversational interchange, descriptors and classifications can be modeled very effectively, such as, "There, you got that large blue boat. Now can you pick up the little red one?"
- In using water, children will soon learn that items such as a cloth, sponge, or paper towel will soak up water, whereas others will not. The classification of a group of things according to which are absorbent and which are not might be insightful to older children.
- As more mature children construct block buildings, ask about the kinds they are making. Talk with them about other kinds of buildings, such as those for living in, for storage, for selling, for making things, for conducting schools, and for caring for sick people.
- If children are pretending that materials such as water and clay are other things, help them extend their thinking even further. For example, if they are serving Coca-Cola in pretend play with water, ask for something else to drink besides Coca-Cola. See what they can think of and then mention others as well, such as orange juice, milk, or root beer. Or if you are served a pretend apple made of clay, ask whether they have additional fruits to go with the apple. Start with their pretend item, and try to extend their awareness of other items within the same category.

- Provide smooth, weathered sticks or beach stones of differing sizes, and encourage children to place them in order according to length, size, and weight.
- As a child is manipulating clay, note what he or she is making, and draw comparisons. Say, "You have such a big round shape. That's the shape of a cookie. It's the shape of a plate too. And let's see, what else?" If the child does not contribute, continue, "The clock face is sort of like that, isn't it? So is the dial on the telephone. So is the top of that can."
- Children will quite spontaneously make piles and rows of blocks, mounds of sand, series of clay balls, all of which can be noted, counted, and described: "You have two blocks here and three blocks there," and as the child places another with the two: "Now you have the same number in each group." As he or she places another: "Now they have different numbers. There are more in that pile." By reacting to children's manipulations you can reinforce those concepts they have not yet mastered, such as *more, same, less,* and *different.*
- Hiding and then sifting objects out of sand is particularly intriguing to the younger child who still has only a meager sense of the constancy of objects. For the older child, counting how many objects are thus retrieved on each sifting is also fun: "That time you got two feathers, three shells, and a piece of string. Let's see how many things that is altogether."
- Supplying real candles or small sticks along with wet sand or clay on a child's birthday will almost inevitably lead to cake making. This allows all kinds of discussion about topics such as how many candles various cakes have, how many years older six is than four, and how many more candles you need for a "four-year-old" cake if you already have two. If a teacher then makes a numeral to match the number of candles on each cake, children can begin to make associations between numerals and counting.
- When children are using blocks, look for opportunities to initiate counting as the blocks are distributed, stacked, and replaced. And use chances to divide blocks, saying, "One for Jim. One for Jack. . . ." Point out the equality of the groups formed in this way.
- With blocks, also look for opportunities to ask children questions, such as "How many more do you want?" or "Do you want me to hand you big blocks first or do you want little ones first and big ones last?"
- Children involved in playing with clay will often arrange rows of objects in one-to-one correspondence. Point out to younger or less mature children what others have placed in one-to-one correspondence.
- If children become engaged in activities such as shooting bean bags or foam rubber balls into bins constructed with blocks (as suggested earlier), they might enjoy keeping score.
- Children create wares which they pretend to sell; blocks are sometimes used as hot dogs, clay as cookies, water as lemonade. This simple dramatic play provides a good opportunity to increase number awareness by asking about cost and then very elaborately counting out money (made from other blocks, bits of paper, and so on). Comments can accompany the interchanges, such

as: "I owe you three cents for the other one, right?" "Let's see, that's one, two, three, four, five, six. Is that right?" "I have only two cents left. What can I buy for that?"

Mass and Liquid Quantity

Children need many experiences in observing through their own manipulations the reversibility of liquids and other substances. Until they have accrued sufficient experience and maturity to remember how the thing was before being transferred to another container (in the case of liquid and sand) or manipulated into another shape (in the case of clay), they will deny or doubt the sameness of its quantity. They will declare it to be either more or less, depending on how it appears. Although most children will not fully develop these conservation insights until age six or seven or later, prerequisite understandings are being accrued in the child's play with unstructured materials throughout the early years. Conservation is not imparted by direct teaching; it is gradually acquired through the child's own activities and observations. Through the following arrangements, however, the likelihood of involvements leading to conservation are enhanced:

- For sand and water play, arrange to have some containers that have a definite relationship to others; for example, one might hold exactly twice as much as another. Also try to have two or more different shapes that hold the same amount. Observe and question children to help them discover these relationships and use the terms for describing what they discover, such as *twice as much* and *half as much.*
- Encourage children to count the number of times they use a small container to fill a large one. They could be helped to make a chart that shows what they have discovered.
- Encourage children to figure out which container in a set holds the most water or sand. Help them label each according to the number of cups it holds.
- A child who has shown considerable interest in learning how many small containers are required to fill a larger one might be led to first guess (estimate) how many, before figuring out the actual number.
- If you supply a large and sturdy homemade balance scale, those children who already have some awareness of conservation of mass and liquid quantity can experiment with containers of different weights and sizes. They can, thus, further confirm their hypotheses of weight invariance of a given amount of sand, blocks, clay, or water despite variations in appearance when placed in different containers.

Causality

By acquiring through experience many specific associations during their early years, children build up a knowledge base that proves helpful to them in mastering the notions of predictability and causality. To provide this kind of experience, the following activities may prove useful:

- Let children help make playdough. Make sure they note the appearance, feel, and smell of the ingredients prior to and throughout the process of mixing. Before adding the water to the salt and flour, ask, "What do you think will happen when we add the water?" Note with them the change from dry to lumpy to sticky. Later ask, "Can you remember what we did to make the clay?"
- Let the children help you smash up the pieces of hardened potter's clay (in a cloth bag) with wooden mallet or sturdy wooden block, to prepare it for reuse. Let them also assist you in adding water, stirring, kneading, and inspecting to see if the clay has reached a desired consistency.
- Encourage children to make holes of various sizes in paper cups for use as sieves with sand and water. Note with them the sizes of the streams of water or sand that escape through the holes. Lead them to predict and then experiment to find out which varieties of small objects will wash through different-sized holes and which will be caught and retained in the cup through repeated washings.
- For water play, prepare a set of tin cans of identical size that have "leaks" of various sizes in various positions. Make one with a large hole, one with a small hole, one with several fine holes, and one with two holes of different sizes. Other cans might have different numbers of small holes punched in the side. (Stuff can with paper or cloth to prevent collapse while hammering holes.)
- Both sand and water play lead children into experiences with gravity and centrifugal force, and teachers can sometimes help extend this interest. For example, if some of the tin cans with holes positioned in different locations are suspended from strings, the differences in their rotation as water is poured into them may encourage experimentation. If a small windmill, pinwheel, or water-wheel is provided, children will delight in using falling water and sand to make it go around. Observing water running downhill often leads to experimentation with dams, waterfalls, and channels.
- In water play, as children are manipulating containers underwater, point out the bubbles of escaping air. Ask, "I wonder if you could hold your bottle in a way so you could make big bubbles?" or "Can you make little bubbles?"
- If children are supplied with a magnifying glass while playing with sand, they might enjoy examining sand crystals. The source of the sand may be of interest to children, especially if different types of sand from different sources are available for close examination.
- Provide the children with sandstone for examination. If mallets are available, they can pound the sandstone into a sand that could be added to the sand table after thorough washing.
- Blocks or block structures (and objects such as sticks or dowels), when stuck into sand or clay, cast shadows in different directions and of different lengths

according to their distance from the light source. Experimentation in creating shadows of different lengths and shapes can follow. Outside shadows can then become the subject of careful observation during different points of the day as well, as in Beatrice Schenk de Regnier's *The Shadow Book* (New York: Harcourt Brace Jovanovich, 1960).

- For more mature six- and seven-year-olds, combine water and clay play with the challenge, "Can you make a clay boat that will float?" If children can successfully do this, let each test his or her boat to see how many paper clips (or similar light objects) the boat can take aboard, and in what position, without sinking.

- Children will experiment with sounds of water splashing or being poured, blocks bumping together and against other objects, and clay as it is pounded against various surfaces and with varying intensity. Encourage this experimentation by suggesting significant variations, such as filling containers to different levels and then striking with other objects (such as a digging spoon, wooden stick, or block), or arranging blocks according to length to produce a xylophone effect.

In each of these instances, children are gaining a greater awareness of specific causal relationships. As they acquire a rich base of these kinds of associations, they will be better prepared to appreciate the more general principles at some later point in development. Without specific associations from personal experience to use as a basis for drawing conclusions, magical and intuitive thinking patterns will tend to persist.

Space Concepts

Some of the most useful experiences children can have in developing spatial orientations come through manipulations of concrete materials. As children build low block barricades around themselves and then add even more blocks to make enclosures with walls as high as they can reach, they gain valuable insights. They learn how large a space must be in order for them to go through it or take other objects through it. They learn that when the largest blocks have been used, several smaller ones can be combined and substituted. And as children build roads, lakes, and towns for their toy cars and people, using sand, water, and clay, they quite literally become cartographers. As a teacher, you can extend these experiences in the following ways:

- Space concepts such as *inside, outside, around,* or *between* are natural learnings in sand and block play. As children engage in activities such as constructing barriers to contain the turtle they have found, you can help them learn the vocabulary that describes their actions through your commentary, such as "Do you think he will be able to go *between* those two blocks?" "Who ever would have thought he could climb *over* that block? Why it's as high as he is." "I see you are making a tunnel for the turtle to crawl *through.*"

- If a child is stretched out on the floor in the block area, place a block on each side to mark how big he or she is, and invite him or her to look. Or involve children in placing blocks at distances they think will allow them to lie down between them. Ask, "How far do you think it is from your head to your feet?" When the blocks are placed you might wish to more permanently mark the child's size by replacing each block with masking tape on which you write the child's name. You might also give the children string, which you and they can measure out to just their height.

- As a child manipulates a miniature horse or other toy along a sand trail, you can describe the actions using space vocabulary. For example, "I wonder how *far* that rider is going? There she goes *around* the bend and *over* the hill. Here she comes to the crossroads. She's making a turn to the *right*. And another turn to the *right*. And another, and here she is back where she started. You know, she went in a *square*."
- If children have constructed what amounts to a three-dimensional map using sand or blocks, examine it admiringly and ask where various things are in relation to each other. You might wish to photograph or sketch it as the children watch. You might also involve them in trying to determine distances and perspectives, saying, "Suppose the driver of that jeep ran out of gas right where he is, what would he do? Would he go back into town or go this way to the airport?" "Why do you think it would be better for him to do that?"

Time Concepts

Children's involvement with manipulative materials provides a meaningful context for helping them become more aware of time sequences and ways to describe the passage of time. For example, simply reiterating to them what they did first, next, and last while creating a clay form or a block scene is helpful. The following suggestions exemplify other possibilities:

- Look for opportunities to relate children's current activities with what they have done previously. Use terms such as *yesterday, last week, this morning, last year, in the fall.* You might say, "Remember when you made strawberry shortcakes from clay *last week?* You made a big one, a little one, and a middle-size one. And *yesterday* you made big, little, and middle-size bowls like the three bears. *Today* I see you are making something in three sizes again!"
- Help children keep track of time as they wait for potter's clay or salt clay products to harden. "Let's see, you made this on *Monday*. Then *yesterday* was *Tuesday* and *today* is *Wednesday*. Let's check it *today*. You might have to wait until *tomorrow*, but it should be dry before *Friday*. I'm sure of that. It usually takes three or four *days*."

Spoken Language

A resourceful teacher can make an exciting language-learning experience out of the most insignificant event—a lost mitten, too much milk money, a dripping faucet. Almost any situation contains stimuli capable of provoking learning in children. You can improve your ability to enhance children's language development by noting the rich possibilities contained in the dialogue accompanying manipulative activities.

- With block play, look for opportunities to use words such as *more, fewer, same, tall, taller, short, shorter, high, higher, wide, many, several, long, even, uneven, same, different, and, or, first, next, last.*
- With water play, look for opportunities to use words such as *dry, wet, soaked, damp, how much, full, empty, thin, wide, deep, shallow, fast, slow, float, sink, evaporate.*
- With sand play, look for opportunities to use words such as *damp, dry, sprinkle, pack, rough, smooth, wide, narrow, thin, thick, short, tall, round, curved, straight, flat, full, empty, half full, half empty, heavy, light, how much, fine, coarse, deep, shallow.*
- In using balance scales with water, blocks, clay, or sand, use words such as *heavy, heavier, light, lighter, balanced, more, less, same, fewer, how many, how much.*
- Ask questions such as: "Is your clay too hard, too soft, or just right?" "How much water should we add to this salt clay—just a little, a cupful, or a half cupful?" "What size trucks do you want for your highway?"
- Children like to hide things in sand for others to find. Encourage them to verbally describe something about the object they have hidden to allow guesses as to its identity before you or another child begin to look for it.
- Particular kinds of vocabulary can be encouraged by the kinds of props provided for sand and water play. Funnels, tubing, and containers encourage terms such as *into, out of, through,* and *half full.* Containers of three different sizes enable discussion of *smallest, middle size, largest, more,* and *less.*

Many children who have retarded speech development or who lack confidence in their talking abilities can be more effectively helped while they are happily involved with play materials than in a special instructional session. For instance, it might be useful to place at the water and sand areas accessories and toy objects whose names or descriptions require sounds that are difficult for a particular child. It is often easier to model the correct pronunciation and to engage the child in producing these sounds in informal, nonpressured situations. While children are involved in play with sand, water, or clay it is often possible to provide elaborations of sentences and phrases and to ask them questions that encourage a more precise language expression than they normally attempt. Ask open-ended questions such as, "What are you going to do now?"

Written Language

Many opportunities for recording ideas in writing are related to play with sand, water, clay, or blocks. Whether children remember the words or not, the more meaningful print they see, the more they will understand that the written word represents the spoken word, that the spaces and the unique sequence of letters comprising words are significant, and that words are written and read in a left-to-right direction. Consider the following possibilities for involving children in written language:

- Invite children to dictate stories to you about their block structures or other products of their manipulative materials. Print clearly in lowercase and upper-case letters. If children, despite requests to "slow down please," seem unable to match their talking speed with your writing speed as they dictate, take down rough notes, and then carefully print out what is said and read it back, "to be sure you have it right." A Polaroid photograph to go with the dictated story would add to its continued appeal.
- Look for opportunities to make signs to embellish block structures. The builder of a hot dog stand, for example, would probably appreciate having the name of the business and a list of produce and prices printed on signs or perhaps having messages to customers placed on signs.
- While with children during sand play, you might write their names or other personal messages, such as "I like Becky," in the sand. If they are interested, read, discuss, and point out words and similar letters and cross out and change parts ("I like Sally") for as long as their interest is maintained.

Whenever you are doing this kind of writing for children, try to print their exact words. Be sure to read it back to the child when you finish writing or invite the child to read it to (or with) you. Some children will enjoy looking for and talking about identical words and similarities between words. Help the children locate their own names and any other high-interest word that appears in the writing. Try to make sure that others note and appreciate the messages the words represent.

You should also encourage children's efforts to engage in writing activities themselves. The following are some possible ways for doing so:

- Involve children in putting their names on papers and beneath their clay products (or other expressive products) to the extent that they are able. This may involve writing a child's entire name, making all but a few less difficult letters, or making one part of one letter. If necessary, make a model (showing only one letter at a time) for them to copy, or write (again one letter or stroke at a time) very faintly on the paper so that the child can mark over it. The important thing is to give the child a feeling of being a writer, a successful writer. As you write the letters for beginners, sometimes discuss their features. You can say, "The *l*'s in your name are just tall straight lines, aren't they, Bill?" or "That is an interesting letter, isn't it, Meg? Look how it goes straight down and then curves up under itself."
- Comment appreciatively on forms, letters, numerals, and symbols that children form on sand or clay. Note especially the aspects that are correctly formed. You might comment, "That's almost a perfect *s*, Sally," or "I can tell that's an

H, Hank." Only if the child is proficient and secure in his or her writing abilities will you find it helpful to note letter reversals or other errors.

FURTHER EXTENSIONS

This chapter has provided numerous suggestions of how children's development can be facilitated through the active manipulation of sand, water, clay, and blocks. We hope that these presentations have attuned you to the educational possibilities of these and similar materials.

The same kinds of activities suggested here can also be very appropriate for the host of manipulative and construction materials that are sometimes referred to as "table toys." These include items such as Tinker Toys, Lincoln logs, counting blocks, parquetry blocks, dominoes, design cubes, marbles, checkers, Cuisenaire rods, attribute blocks, Lego blocks, mosaic shapes, peg boards, and nuts and bolts (assorted sizes). Each of these can serve many of the same functions and be used in the same ways as blocks.

Many other materials can serve similar functions. Some are natural materials readily available in many outdoor situations, such as mud, leaves, rocks, plant debris, and snow. Other manipulative objects can be obtained in industrial and commercial settings, such as barrels, packing cases, ladders, bricks, cement blocks, tires, planks, cardboard cartons, styrofoam packing materials, cardboard tubes, pipes and pipe fittings, pails, hoses, and baskets.

Whether manipulative materials are natural or manufactured, free or costly, they offer wide opportunities for children's learning; any teacher should continue to extend his or her repertoire for using these materials to stimulate particular learnings and skill development in children.

SUMMARY

Children's use of unstructured manipulative materials changes with their development. The nature of these materials allows the imposition of increasingly elaborate use as children move to higher levels of conceptual and physical development. Without adult assistance and intervention, there are benefits to children from access to sand, water, blocks, clay, and similar materials; with skillful arrangements of materials and appropriate commentary from adults, the benefits increase.

Large-block play and outdoor sand play can especially contribute to gross-motor development. Challenges for small-muscle manipulation can be heightened by the skillful introduction of tools and other props and through verbal recognition and encouragement of their varied uses.

Tensions are lessened through concentration on the manipulation of materials such as water and sand. Concerns can be actively explored through projective activity, and the children's repertoires for resolving conflicts can be extended in the context of activities with these materials.

The use of manipulative materials provides especially abundant possibilities for experiencing classification, seriation, and number groupings; for assessing quantity, causality, and space and time concepts; and for oral and written communication. Whatever children's functioning level in these categories of cognitive and intellectual development, there are varied opportunities for enhancing and extending their understanding.

The involvements and learnings provided by sand, water, clay, and blocks are also available through the small manipulative materials referred to as table toys, through many natural materials available in the outdoor environment, and through industrial and commercial castoffs.

SUGGESTED ACTIVITIES

1 Visit several different early childhood classrooms and analyze the setups for manipulative materials, noting the following:
   a Where is the area placed in relation to other areas?
   b What kind of floor coverings are used?
   c How are materials and accessories stored?
2 Observe in a classroom in a particular area where manipulative materials are being used by children. Note the following:
   a How do different children react to the same material? What differences in action and language repertoire are evidenced?
   b How long do children remain engaged with the materials?
   c What kinds of interactions do the materials engender between children?
   d What do teachers say and do when they are in the area? To what extent do they initiate activities or respond to children's initiations?
3 Take photographs of a child's block structures across a period of days or weeks and analyze the patterns of construction. Compare this child's structures with those of his or her peers.
4 Introduce different types of accessories into sand or water play setups, and note whether children's activity is thus influenced.

ADDITIONAL READINGS

Anker, D., Foster, J., McLane, J., Sobel, J., & Weissbourd, B. (1974). Teaching children as they play. *Young Children, 29,* 203–213.

Cartwight, S. (1974). Blocks and learning. *Young Children, 29,* 41–146.

Eggleston, P. J. (1975). Water play for preschoolers. *Young Children, 31,* 5–11.

Folkes, M. A. (1985). Funnels and tunnels. *Science and Children, 22,* 93–97.

Forman, G. E., & Hill, F. (1980). *Constructive play: Applying Piaget in the preschool.* Monterey, CA: Brooks/Cole.

Hill, D. M. (1977). *Mud, sand and water.* Washington, DC: National Association for the Education of Young Children.

Hirsch, E. S. (Ed.). (1984). *The block book* (rev. ed.). Washington, DC: National Association for the Education of Young Children.

Lorton, M. B. (1972). *Workjobs: Activity-centered learning for early childhood education.* Reading, MA: Addison-Wesley.

Provenzo, E. F., & Brett, A. (1983). *The complete block book.* Syracuse, NY: Syracuse University Press.

Stone, J. I. (1987). Early childhood math: Make it manipulative! *Young Children, 42*(6), 16–23.

Whiren, A. (1975). Table toys. The underdeveloped resource. *Young Children, 30,* 413–419.

CHAPTER 18

ART

OVERVIEW

Children are not learning to be artists. They *are* artists. And, as we will point out in this chapter, their art contributes to their learning. They use media quite spontaneously—exploring, expressing, creating. It is a very unusual child who does not like to use paints, paste, colorful papers, crayons, and other art materials. Children's art activity may look to an adult like "messing about," but as the young artists work, they are dealing with the same elements of composition, balance, and representation as adult artists. With ample opportunity to use art media, all children are creative and expressive. They will also become able to use art quite spontaneously in expressing their experiences. Many children at four, five, and six years of age will proudly describe their drawings with words such as the following:

> This is my Mommy and this is my aunt. That's my house and that's me inside. I'm upstairs, and I'm glad Mommy is coming home. She is talking to Aunt Betty in the kitchen. Now she is coming up the stairs. And I'm hugging her.

The drawing may actually show several representations of the child's mother as various phases of the child's experience are related.

Children need only learn some simple techniques to care for and use art materials in order to have very satisfying art experiences. The adult's role is to provide ample access to materials and to respond in interested and attentive fashion to the child's activity as the materials are used. Unfortunately, however, adults can prevent children from finding art expression satisfying in a variety of ways. One of these is to insist that children become concerned about the appearance of final products. Young children often enjoy art for the series of experiences that occur while they are using the media. The product may be valued (if in fact it is valued at all) only because it is the final trace of what has been a sequence of pleasurable effects. A child may not care at all that the end result of the art experiences looks like "mud." The satisfying experience may have been in seeing how the clear yellow paint mingled in such magnificent ways with red and green, creating an array of hues and designs *before* all were blended into the final dull effect. Insistence on lovely final products or suggestion that there is a *right* way of drawing or painting or visualizing an object may well discourage the child. Natural inclinations for spontaneous and satisfying art experiences need to be encouraged at this age.

SETUPS FOR ART

COLORING, DRAWING, AND CUTTING

Basic Equipment

- Open storage cupboard or table with bins and trays.
- Paper—Manila, newsprint, or equivalent (9″ × 12″ or smaller is most satisfactory); construction paper in assorted colors.
- Crayons (fat and flat without wrappers are recommended).
- Scissors of good quality without sharp points, some left-handed ones.
- Pencils—regular and oversized.
- Small paste pots with covers.

Preferred Location

- Any location out of heavy traffic areas is satisfactory. Little supervision is necessary.

Accessories

- Felt pens, stencil forms, tracing paper, multicolor crayons, metallic and other "special" papers.

General Guidelines

- These materials require little maintenance and can be used with minimal supervision. Locate them in a place where they are consistently accessible.
- Teachers may label products with children's names or narratives on drawings and other creations. Such labeling leads to interest in reading and writing and to considerable learning about how the spoken words relate to the written words.
- Avoid telling children what to draw or make or how to draw or make particular things. Respond to children's queries such as, "How do you draw a dog?" with responses such as, "There are all kinds of dogs. Tell me about the dog you want to draw. Is it big or little? Does it like to be patted? Does it like its ears rubbed? Does it lick your face? You know much more about that dog than I do. You can make it however you want it to be. Make it and then tell me about it, okay?"

Alternatives

- Provide stacks of blank books for children to use to draw a series of pictures or produce a sequence of designs. To make the books, simply fold five or six sheets of 9″ × 12″ Manila or other blank paper and staple along the fold.

PAINTING

Basic Equipment

- Children's painting easels (commercially available); long low tables.
- Newsprint sheets (18″ × 24″); Manila sheets (18″ × 24″); rolls of kraft paper (brown wrapping) about 36″ wide.
- Tempera paints (powder or liquid)—basic selection includes white, black, orange, yellow, blue, green, and red. You may find that you need twice as much black, yellow, and white as the others. Magenta, purple, and turquoise may be added on occasion.
- Sink or firm stand for containers of water.
- Drying equipment such as clothes rack (foldable), or stackable units made for the purpose from screening attached to 20″ × 30″ frames, or clotheslines on pulleys that start at 3 feet and reach to the ceiling. Brushes preferably will be flat, made of hog bristle, $^3/_4$ ″ to 1″ wide, with comparatively short handles. (For kindergarten and primary children also provide narrower brushes useful for creation of details in paintings.)
- Aprons or cover-ups (some tempera paints stain clothing.)

Preferred Location

- Near water source.
- On hard-surface scrubbable flooring; on plastic sheeting; on linoleum or acrylic floor protectors; on ample thicknesses of newspapers.
- Away from nonwashable furnishings and supplies.

Accessories

- Additional things to which paint can be applied—cardboard boxes; styrofoam pieces; cardboard tubes; pieces of wood; foam rubber; balloons (inflated); paper plates; shapes of circles, ovals, triangles, and squares cut from newsprint; wallpaper pieces; newspaper; paper doilies; large pieces of cardboard; corrugated paper; colored tissue paper; heavy plastic (add soap flakes to the paint to make it adhere); large brown roller paper (mural size lengths); cloth (burlap, cotton); old window blinds; textured paper.

General Guidelines

- Paints need to be examined on a daily basis, and those that are too thick or thin can be made a better consistency by adding more water or more paint. Thick cream consistency is best. "Muddy" paints are disposed of and replaced with clear, distinct colors. Paper is replenished on the easels or within access of children. A brush is placed in each container of paint. Brushes are washed at the end of each day's use, and paint jars are covered to prevent drying.

- Children are shown how to choose the color with which they wish to paint, how to use the brush available in the jar, and how to return the brush to the same container. They may also be shown how to place a fresh paper on the easel, although for some children, especially the youngest, teachers may have to assist with this process.
- When a child has a turn to paint, allow him or her to keep using additional sheets of paper as needed, as long as serious effort or experimentation continues. One or two lazy brush strokes per sheet may be an indication that a child is ready to stop, but fewer turns during the week are more desirable than limiting the children to the number of pieces of paper or the number of minutes they can paint per turn. If easels are available on a daily basis, children can usually paint for long periods without denying access to others.
- Consistently write children's names (the first letter in uppercase with the remainder of the letters in lowercase in an upper corner of 2-D paintings and prepare press-on labels for 3-D works if it is not easy to write the child's name on the surfaces.
- As children describe paintings, you may wish to print a portion of what they say to attach to their product. Do not expect to do this with all art productions, however. Some of the children's efforts are for experimentation, and only occasionally will they care to have their words of description incorporated onto their work.

Alternatives

- In place of brushes, provide tongue depressors, cotton swabs, weeds, feathers, toothbrushes, brayer rollers (on large sheets of paper), sponges.
- Vary the paint consistency. Create a creamier effect by adding liquid starch; create an oily effect by adding bentonite, a volcanic ash-based clay (available from art suppliers); vary texture by adding such items as coffee grounds or sawdust.
- Paint on windows or mirrors. Add soap flakes to make the paint adhere to glass and to make it easier to remove.

PRINTING

Basic Equipment

- Low tables.
- Trays or bins for objects.
- Stamp pad or shallow dish containing slight amount of paint or other thick liquid, porous sponge soaked in tempera paint, or heavy absorbent cotton flannel or terry cloth with tempera paint worked into it.
- Drying racks.
- Aprons or cover-ups.

Preferred Location

- Near water source and away from books or other materials that might be damaged by spills and splashes.

Accessories

- Gadgets—cork pieces, paper cups, sponge pieces, fork, large bolts, jar lids, wood blocks, dowels, checkers, spools.

General Guidelines

- Place only a little liquid in a dish or on a stamp pad for clear prints.
- Place several layers of newspapers on the tables where children will be doing printing for protection of the table and for easy cleanup.
- Since children can create a great many arrangements and special effects with little effort on their part, printing is a popular activity. Be prepared for heavy production with concomitant need for storage of products for drying.
- Some children may "brush" paint on paper with printing gadgets. Let them experiment in this way if they wish.
- Final product is of less concern than experimentation with effects.

Alternatives (for older children)

- **String design prints** Children brush acrylic glue (Elmer's glue) on small wood block or other firm surface that is small enough to be grasped by the child and used as a stamp. Place lengths of string on the acrylic glue in any design pattern. When dry, use as a stamp for printing. For best results a roller (ink brayer roller) can be dipped in paint or ink and rolled in a pan or aluminum foil to spread the paint over the roller surface uniformly. If the roller is then rolled across the string design attached to the block, it will produce a more even coating on the string than if the block were directly pressed into the liquid.
- **Texture prints** Children use acrylic glue to attach a number of small flat objects such as paper clips, wire, washers, coins to a block of wood or piece of cardboard. When dry, they print as described above.
- **Hands or feet printing**
- **Fold printing** Children use tongue depressors to place dabs of fingerpaint on paper. They then fold and press the paper. On reopening the sheets of paper, they see "mirror" designs and overlapping colors. (Be prepared to store a vast number of these quickly produced works. Once into this activity, children enjoy seeing the many different symmetrical effects they can produce so easily.)
- **Loose-string printing** Children dip string of varying lengths into tempera paint and then guide it as it falls on the surface of a foil sheet (or other washable surface such as a cookie sheet, acrylic sheet). Printing paper is pressed on top of the string and then lifted. A few identical prints can be made of the configuration before it is rearranged to produce another design.
- **Rubbings** Primary-aged children can make relief designs by taping paper over objects that have raised features and by firmly pressing as they rub the broad side of a crayon across the paper surface. Using this method, children can make impressions of cardboard shapes, wood grain, coins, leaves, designs and raised lettering, designs on toys and household objects.

COLLAGE

Basic Equipment

- Sturdy shallow boxes or bins to hold scrap materials.
- Scissors
- Glues and tapes: acrylic medium (Elmer's glue), masking tape, scotch tape.
- Staplers.
- Hand paper punches.

Preferred Location

- Near other art expression areas (painting, coloring, cutting, pasting).

Accessories

- Sturdy 2-D base materials—pieces of cardboard, paper bags, paper plates, corrugated paper.
- 3-D base materials—cardboard cartons, styrofoam forms, wooden pieces, cardboard tubes.
- Cloth and fabric scraps—felt, ric-rac, thread, velvet, net, ribbons.
- Natural objects—seeds, weathered stones, wood, pebbles, beach glass, shells, twigs, barks, feathers, seed pods.
- Scrap and junk—drinking straws, string, yarn, wood shavings, magazines, boxes or cartons, wallpapers, egg cartons, cellophane, wire, popsicle sticks, corks, styrofoam packing materials, wrapping papers, fabric scraps.

General Guidelines

- Scrap materials can be a regular classroom option located on a shelf or table where children can use them independently during free activity times.
- "Special" materials such as old holiday greeting cards and wrapping papers may be arranged as a special art activity initially and then placed with other collage materials for subsequent use.
- Final products are of little importance in contrast to children's explorations of properties of materials.
- Children and their families may help to keep the scrap boxes supplied with raw materials. In most homes, offices, and factories a great abundance of useful raw materials is routinely discarded. Collecting and saving them for use by children is often welcomed by a variety of adults.
- Name labels (press-on labels are easy) can be attached to those creations that children want to preserve. There is no reason to assume, however, that children will or should care about all the things they produce.

MOTOR DEVELOPMENT AND ART

Kellogg (1970) describes the relationship between art and movement as follows:

Child art integrates movement and vision, the perception of overall shapes and the perception of details, familiar line formations and new ones, stimulation and reaction,

Children's interest in each other is often surpassed by their interest in their own art expression.
(Ursula Moeller)

aesthetic pleasure and muscular satisfaction. This integration is not supplied by the mere contemplation of art. To be effective, it must be experienced through one's own muscles, those of the hand as well as those that control the eye. Child art integrates not through communication from artist to viewer, but through self-stabilization of the aesthetic activity itself (p. 265).

The fascination children have with art media draws them toward practicing muscle control as early as age one or two. As soon as they can maneuver a crayon across a page, children will do so with interest. At the very beginning, the marks on the paper appear random, their placement somewhat accidental. There may be some repetition of lines, as the arm is swung back and forth, but initially, there is little effort to direct the markings. In fact, the child's eyes may be directed elsewhere while he or she is making scribbles, looking afterward to see what resulted. The child may grasp the crayon in the fist or clench it in the fingers only. The scribbling is at first a result of a movement of the entire arm or body. Although the markings appear small to the adult, they require a big motion for the toddler making them.

Scribbling is a very important activity for the young child. If paper and pencil or crayon are not available, the child will find other means for engaging in these same processes. Media may include sticks in dirt; mud on walls; fingers in food, feces, sand, snow, steam on windows; and so forth. Wise adults will provide ample opportunity for children to scribble. It is a universal natural step in development that seems to serve as a foundation for more differentiated behavior in a number of areas.

At some point in time as the child scribbles, the relationship between the kinds of motions made and the appearance of marks on the paper is discovered. The consequence is increased practice in placement of markings to create effects. This is a very important achievement that serves as a prerequisite to many complex eye-hand coordination tasks. Conceptions of space, directionality, and form are derived. Lines are systematically repeated or drawn at varying angles in concentrated efforts at achieving a gestalt that pleases. The small muscles of the hand are increasingly used in practicing different kinds of marks. The earliest scribblings are usually done in continuous lines. These are not likely to be small repeated patterns or dots. The scribbling is increasingly under the child's control, however, and is very engrossing. Although eye-hand coordination comes as a side benefit from the child's explorations through scribbling, it is a significant benefit.

Many three-year-olds hold a crayon, pencil, or easel brush much as adults do, but may continue to have difficulty in guiding these tools in precise markings. Their continued enjoyment of drawing, painting, and related motor skills of art expression can be easily discouraged at this stage by the reactions of those about them. If the adults' responses are appreciative and encouraging, further efforts will probably follow. If, on the other hand, the adults show displeasure by trying to show the child how to *really* draw, the child may be far less likely to continue this activity and will miss out on the aesthetic satisfactions from the art activities and the practice of fine-motor coordination they require. Setting expectations for preschoolers' performance is inappropriate. What is important is to maintain productive and spontaneous involvement. Maintaining the child's involvement not only ensures the continuation of ample small-muscle practice but also contributes to affective, social, and cognitive development. These benefits are elaborated in the sections that follow.

AFFECTIVE AND SOCIAL DEVELOPMENT AND ART

If natural interest in scribbling is not "turned off" by thoughtless or uninformed adults, children will usually progress through a series of drawing stages. Children master the control of lines on paper in the following order: discontinuity versus continuity, straightness versus crookedness, changes in direction, orientation, intersection (Smith, 1972). Producing controlled shapes follows from the ability to produce controlled lines. For example, at ages three and four, children create rectangular shapes by drawing two parallel vertical lines and then drawing the top and bottom lines to complete the rectangular shape. At a later point, they learn that they can draw the same shape with a continuous line. Once they have developed a proficiency with the creation of lines and shapes, they begin to create organized designs. A great deal of experimentation is necessary, however, before a child is capable of intentionally creating designs. For many children, this does not occur until age three or four. From that point, the same kind of universal symbols that are found in all children's art begin to appear. Rhoda Kellogg (1970) has made a lifelong study of approximately 1 million drawings. Among the symbols she describes as commonly found in young children's art are *mandalas* (Sanskrit word for *circles*), suns, radials (one or more lines radiating from a point or a small area), and human figures. These forms appear to satisfy an innate preference for symmetry, balance, and design and, once discovered, are repeated and embellished and consistently used in art expression. The human figure may initially be less an expression of a child's experience of self or the viewing of others than a logical extension of the prior use of the mandala, sun, and radial techniques by adding the facial features. Kellogg notes the frequency with which the oval that serves as the human figure in early drawings is embellished with lines projected out from all sides. These seem less to be used as limbs or hair representations than as means for creating a balance in the drawing. The placement of features, lines, and embellishments on the human figure may be more an effort to create symmetry than to describe pictorially an event or a visual image.

By age three and a half or so, children typically begin to give their drawings names. A scribble that looks no different from previous ones may be described as "This is my daddy," or "I'm eating." This is seen by some art educators (Lowenfeld & Brittain, 1975) as an important landmark in a child's use of art in self-expression. Often the child's drawing at this point is still begun without a preconceived idea of what is being represented. What is drawn may remind the child of something experienced, and so he or she calls it by that name and then may add details to further represent that event or object. Lines drawn quickly or slowly, smoothly or jerkily are as much a part of the intended representation as the look of the marks that result.

Once children begin to name and intentionally embellish their representations, they increasingly may use drawing and painting and other art activities as a means for recording images of things experienced. Some children develop quite elaborate scenes and actions on paper in which they are able to experiment with situations they have created and over which they have total control. When children achieve this kind of imagery on paper, it appears to be a very satisfying resource and a very positive force in their affective development. Other children continue to concentrate most of their energies, while using art materials, on harmoniously balancing color and form in abstract works, which they also appear to find highly satisfying. Each child's art is uniquely his or her own, and individual styles of expression become very evident to observant adults.

When children are using art to reflect their imagery of persons and events, their drawings are likely to vary according to the central features of the experiences. What is included in the drawing is indicative of what is active in the child's imagery at the time of the drawing. For example, a picture of throwing snowballs will often have figures with at least one arm because of the predominance of throwing actions. A picture of eating will probably include a big mouth, even tongue and teeth, but perhaps no legs or feet or ears. A picture of telling secrets, on the other hand, will be more likely to have oversize ears, and climbing stairs may stimulate the inclusion of legs. These are natural and healthy variations and should not concern the responsible adults. If a child consistently omits a part of the body, he or she should be encouraged to envision an action before beginning to draw. Such an observation is preferable to a comment like, "You didn't make any arms on your man" after the drawing is done.

What may appear to adults to be distortions in children's drawings are actually truer representations of the experiences of children than the real-life portrayals the children will later want to learn to make. Young children use art for expression of feelings and experiences. Since they are little concerned with how things *should* look, they are free to make them in any way they may have experienced them. The complexity of mother's refrigerator, for instance, can be reduced by a hungry four-year-old to a simple drawing with one important forbidden object—chocolate pudding (being saved for supper) overshadowing all else drawn.

Whether the lines are produced by crayon or brush stroke, the spontaneous drawings of the young child have the same unspoiled spontaneous quality as the work of artists who are identified as creative geniuses. Children are able to let impulse guide their art forms without regard to how what they produce matches the more typical portrayal of the subject matter. The story is told of Picasso's interchange with a woman who had just viewed an exhibit that included a range

Crayon drawing entitled "Four cows inside a fence."

of works from his productive career. "Why is it," she queried, "that your early works appear so mature and polished while your later works are so immature and uncontrolled?" Picasso hugged, kissed, and hugged her again saying, "Ah, yes, it takes a long time to become young."

In art as in other matters, children are eager to adopt whatever gives the appearance of being the grown-up way. When children become aware of how others represent objects in more visually realistic fashion, they begin to modify their own expression accordingly. Visually realistic may not, however, be experientially realistic. For example, objects that were scattered about a page by the four-year-old will almost certainly be placed by the six-year-old on a plane, a line, or a strip that has been carefully drawn across the lower portion of the paper. Even before the relative sizes of objects are differentiated—say, the size of houses versus toys versus people—the use of the base line becomes standard for all drawings.

The movement by a child to draw in the style of older peers, siblings, and adults is to be expected and, in fact, could be a sign of developmental difficulty if it were not to occur by age six or seven. When a child foregoes his or her own self-expression, however, and thinks instead of how things *should* be drawn, a very different function is being served. Many art educators feel that a child's emotional and aesthetic development is best served by delaying movement into this stage or, to the extent possible, by not attempting to hasten the child's interest in drawing like others (Kellogg, 1970). Art educators, concerned about helping preschool children maintain their own self-expression, suggest the following:

- Do not provide coloring books or worksheets on which young children fill in the colors for objects drawn for them by an adult artist.
- Do not draw objects for children. When asked to do so, say something like, "You're the only one who can make it the way you want it to be. Tell me something about what a _____ is like." Despite all insistences by the child to "Please draw me a _____," steadfastly refuse.
- Do not tell children that trees should be green or that faces should not be green, or other things of this nature.
- Do not pick out children's most realistic drawings (from your perspective) to comment on, praise, or display.
- Do comment on and display a child's drawing or painting if the child has shown keen involvement while working on it.
- Do not set up expectations for what children will produce with art materials. For example, do not provide orange circles and small black or yellow triangles at Halloween for jack-o'-lantern representations. Instead, provide children with direct experiences in making a jack-o'-lantern. If you provide black, orange, yellow, and green paint, crayons and paper, children may produce jack-o'-lantern drawings that are related to their own experiences. If not, they will produce other more meaningful products. The seasonal colors will in any case prove festive for holiday bulletin boards.

Preserving a child's artistic and self-expressive instincts is often difficult. There are so many counter expectations from others. Parents may expect to see children bringing home "standard" drawings or constructions of Easter bunnies, autumn trees, and other seasonal or holiday items. Some teachers may show their children how to make "clever" things such as a Thanksgiving turkey by drawing around their hands, using the fingers for tail feathers and the thumb for a head. Uncles and aunts may buy coloring books and how-to-draw books that show the child how to transform, step-by-step, circles into cats, bunnies, or teapots. A teacher must have very firm beliefs and considerable self-assurance not to follow suit and engage in teaching practices that further diminish the child's likelihood of using art materials to benefit development. The greatest pressure comes from the children themselves, who quite naturally want to do things the grown-up way and are eager to be taught how to draw and make things "correctly."

Even within a climate that respects and encourages a child's own aesthetic inclinations and representational style, the child, at age six or seven, will settle into a pattern of making trees in a certain way, people in a certain way, and so forth. Although each child's schema for a person will be different from his or her peers, by age seven, most children will adopt an overall standard kind of representation for common objects. These schemata are then varied to meet new drawing demands. At this stage, children benefit from encountering various cre-

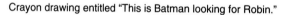

Crayon drawing entitled "This is Batman looking for Robin."

THE LITTLE BOY by Helen E. Buckley

Once a little boy went to school.
He was quite a little boy.
And it was quite a big school.
But when the little boy
Found that he could go to his room
By walking right in from the door
  outside,
He was happy. And the school did not
  seem
Quite so *big* any more.

One morning,
When the little boy had been in school
  awhile,
The teacher said:
"Today we are going to make a
  picture."
"Good!" thought the little boy.
He *liked* to make pictures.
He could make all kinds:
Lions and tigers,
Chickens and cows,
Trains and boats—
And he took out his box of crayons
And began to draw.

But the teacher said: "Wait!
It is not time to begin!"
And she waited until everyone looked
  ready.

"Now," said the teacher,
"We are going to make flowers."
"Good!" thought the little boy,
He *liked* to make flowers,
And he began to make beautiful ones
With his pink and orange and blue
  crayons.

But the teacher said, "Wait!
And I will show you how."
And she drew a flower on the black-
  board.
It was red, with a green stem.
"There," said the teacher,
"Now you may begin."

The little boy looked at the teacher's
  flower.
Then he looked at his own flower.
He liked *his* flower better than the
  teacher's.
But he did not say this,
He just turned his paper over
And made a flower like the teacher's.
It was red, with a green stem.

On another day,
When the little boy had opened
The door from the outside all by him-
  self,
The teacher said:
"Today we are going to make some-
  thing with clay."
"Good!" thought the little boy,
He *liked* clay.
He could make all kinds of things with
  clay:
Snakes and snowmen,
Elephants and mice,
Cars and trucks—
And he began to pull and pinch
His ball of clay.

But the teacher said:
"Wait! It is not time to begin!"
And she waited until everyone looked
  ready.

"Now," said the teacher,
"We are going to make a dish."
"Good!" thought the little boy,
He *liked* to make dishes,
And he began to make some
That were all shapes and sizes.

But the teacher said, "Wait!"
And I will show you how."
And she showed everyone how to
  make
One deep dish.
"There," said the teacher,
"Now you may begin."

The little boy looked at the teacher's
  dish.
Then he looked at his own.
He *liked his* dishes better than the
  teacher's.
But he did not say this.
He just rolled his clay into a big ball
  again,
And made a dish like the teacher's.
It was a deep dish.

And pretty soon
The little boy learned to wait,
And to watch,
And to make things just like the
  teacher.
And pretty soon
He didn't make things of his own any-
  more.

Then it happened
That the little boy and his family
Moved to another house,
In another city,
And the little boy
Had to go to another school.

This school was even Bigger
Than this other one,
And there was no door from the outside
Into his room.
He had to go up some big steps,
And walk down a long hall
To get to his room.

And the very first day
He was there,
The teacher said:
"Today we are going to make a pic-
  ture."
"Good!" thought the little boy,
And he waited for the teacher
To tell him what to do.
But the teacher didn't say anything
She just walked around the room.

When she came to the little boy
She said, "Don't you want to make a
  picture?"
"Yes," said the little boy,
"What are we going to make?"
"I don't know until you make it," said the
  teacher.
"*How* shall I make it?" asked the boy.
"Why, any way you like," said the
  teacher.
"And any color?" asked the little boy.
"Any color," said the teacher,
"If everyone made the same picture
And used the same colors,
How would I know who made what
And which was which?"
"I don't know," said the little boy.
And he began to make pink and orange
  and blue flowers.

He liked his new school . . .
Even if it didn't have a door
Right in from the outside!

Source: "The Little Boy" by Helen E. Buckley. First appeared in *School Arts Magazine,* October 1961. Used by permission.

ative tasks (for example, creating illustrations for a story they have written), that stimulates them to adapt their schemata to new drawing demands and, to the extent possible, to continue to put something of their own experience in their drawing and painting efforts. It is easy at this age for the self-expressive aspect of drawing to fade, and, thus, to cease to be a support for affective development.

These early years are important for the development of aptitudes and attitudes toward artistic expression. Concomitantly, the expression of feelings and experiences through art media is important to emotional development throughout the early years. Sometimes adults can learn a great deal about children's feelings by observing their art expression. Free-flowing variation in representation and subject matter is likely to be indicative of healthy feelings about self and others. The opposite is also possible; that is, rigid repetition of patterns over a period of time may be indicative of emotional problems. A young child's plaintive "I can't draw," along with refusal to try, however, is not necessarily an indication of emotional insecurity. Such a creation is more likely to reflect experiences in which the child's scribbling, drawing, or painting has not been accepted by persons important to him or her. Although unfortunate, the child's reluctance represents a lack of confidence in this specific area and is not a reflection of more generalized feelings. Every effort to reinvolve such a child in art expression is therefore in order. A child who will not attempt representational drawing may be drawn into experimentation with color and lines and occasionally may then gingerly initiate some art expression independently. Often, however, the child's confidence in her or his ability to represent experience through art is difficult to retrieve, once lost.

Teachers or parents should not attempt to draw psychological interpretations from children's drawings with any degree of certainty under any conditions, especially on the basis of single drawings. The particular use of symbols as an unconscious expression of feelings can be guessed at only through the careful study of a child's work collected over a period of time. Objects or placements or choices of color by one child may have particular meanings, but one should not expect the next child to use these configurations for the same reasons. Whereas one child may choose somber dark colors as an expression of feelings of sadness, another child may choose a dark crayon simply because it makes such clear, bold lines. A monster may represent an underlying fear when it appears in one child's drawings, but for another child a monster may be introduced only in secure but boring circumstances when a challenge is being sought. For one child, the drawing of a house with all windows and door beyond the reach of a human figure drawn small and without arms may be indicative of feelings of helplessness and insecurity. Having observed the recurrence of this symbolic representation by the child, the adult may watch for these configurations as signals that it may be important to provide assurance and to express confidence in the child's ability to cope with tasks and situations successfully. For another child, the same general configuration may not have a similar meaning. Although adults may want to study children's drawings for clues to feelings, they should realize that there is no reason to expect a simple correspondence between feelings and drawings for any one child, and certainly not among children.

COGNITIVE DEVELOPMENT AND ART

Piaget (Piaget & Inhelder, 1967) observed that children's earliest drawings (beyond scribbling) show the beginnings of awareness of topological representation. Things near each other in physical space may be placed close to each other in the drawing, and there is likely to be separation in space between the elements being drawn; for example, the eye will be separate from the mouth. Only later do children begin to place the elements in relation to each other in any ordered pattern. Even then, a hat may be drawn some distance above a head, a roof may project down into a house instead of above it, an animal's tail may come from the same side of the body as the head. These universally observed drawing modes of the young were described by Piaget as less a result of motor ineptitude or improper or incomplete perception than a reflection of the child's lack of spatial concepts. As Piaget pointed out, spatial concepts are internalized actions, not mental images of external things or events. Not until the children, through their own actions and experiences, have constructed concepts that illustrate how objects in space can be placed, replaced, and manipulated in relation to each other will their drawings reflect this kind of ordering. Drawings are thus seen as indicators of the concepts children have developed for thinking about spatial relations. It also seems likely that drawing provides children with useful direct experiences that contribute to the development of more adequate spatial concepts.

The possibility of further linkages between art expression and mental development is believed by some to have great significance for educators to consider. There are those who see a direct causal relationship between a child's mental growth and the opportunity he or she has for expressive activities. The following are said to be among the learnings children derive as they paint and use other art media:

- Children learn that they can create images with materials.
- Children learn that the images they create can function as symbols—as something intended to stand for something else.
- Children learn that symbolic images can be used in playful manipulation, creating a fantasy world in which they can take on new roles and learn from them.
- Children learn that they can rely on their own sensibilities and perceptions in making judgments about imagery.
- Children learn that images can be related to other images in more visually complex configurations that require attention to both parts and whole.
- Children learn that paintings, drawings, and sculptures provide visual feedback on their own ideas; furthermore, the process of forming ideas for the creation of images is in itself clarifying. (Eisner, 1978)

Learning how to control the placement of color is serious work. *(Lee C. Lee)*

Through drawing and painting and similar activities, children engage in a dual differentiation process. Ideas or impressions are separated from the totality of experience and are represented via media. The effect created then exists apart from the child and serves as feedback for both the idea and the execution. Few other activities in which children engage provide such direct data on their own thinking and doing. The increased differentiation in representational ability is well chronicled through art products for the child and all interested adults.

Some researchers and practitioners who stress the benefits of art in intellectual as well as in aesthetic development are interested in how the two hemispheres of the brain appear to be involved with different kinds of functioning. The left hemisphere has been found to be more actively involved with sequential and analytic thinking abilities and language ability. The right appears to be superior in pattern recognition, spatial abilities, and imagery. When a child is involved with art activities, the right, or the visual, side of the brain seems to be dominant. If full development of the varied mental capacities of both hemispheres is to be achieved, involvement with activities like art, which fully engage the right hemisphere, are as important as verbal activities, which engage the left hemisphere and are more predominant in schools. To quote Dr. Jean Houston (Williams, 1977), a researcher concerned with brain function, a child without access to a stimulating art program "is being systematically cut off from most of the ways in which he can perceive the world. His brain is being systematically damaged."

As a child creates and uses symbols in art expression, the entire mind-body system benefits. It is considered important that the younger child exercise all of his or her sensory functions through art activities, thus providing an integration and balance of experience. Although educators and psychologists continue to assume that intelligence or brain functioning is concerned with analytic and traditional academic subjects, there is increasing recognition that many persons who contribute significantly to our lives are not only proficient in the traditional academic subjects but are also able to make rich connections with their prior experiences. They are more in touch with imagery of things previously experienced and, thus, are able to make interconnections between ideas and sensory modalities in approaching learning or problem-solving situations. Art experiences are thought to provide an imagery base for this kind of functioning. Proponents of the arts for overall mind development point out that in several experimental settings gains in math and reading achievement have been thought attributable not to a scholastic program but to an arts-centered program in which visual, auditory, and kinesthetic experiences as well as verbal experiences are included (Williams, 1977).

FURTHER EXTENSIONS

Teachers often wonder about the extent to which they should arrange to have adult art products available for children to see and talk about. Children seem to benefit from exposure to adult art if there is considerable variety in what is shown and if appreciation for that variety is expressed by the adult who makes it available. The combination of aesthetic experiences in selected art pieces and in books can do much to support children's developing aesthetic standards and tastes.

Reproductions of paintings, drawings, prints, and sculptures representing many art styles might be rotated in and out of a "beauty spot" in the classroom. Klee, Cezanne, Picasso, Monet, Manet, Degas, Seurat, Calder, Miro, and Wyeth are among the artists whose works appeal to young children. Sculpture can be interchanged with or displayed in conjunction with pleasing natural objects such as plants, rocks, flowers, tree branches, and pine cones. Wall hangings, photographs, stained glass creations, pottery, and other works of art can be featured in turn in classrooms to provide aesthetic enjoyment for children and to extend their awareness of the many different ways in which adults create and use visual symbols. A prolonged experience with a limited number of adult art products might channel children's expression in the direction of those artists' conceptualizations, but exposure to a wide array of art forms would allow children to intuitively sense that adult artists strive for the same sort of balance and composition that is so often evidenced in the scribblings, drawings, and paintings of child artists.

The illustrations in children's books are another way a child has exposure to the great variety of forms of adult imagery. Many of these illustrations are of such high quality that they are truly outstanding art pieces, and today's young are tremendously fortunate in having them so easily available. With very little effort, adults can find books containing a great variety of styles and media to share with children. Among the best of the illustrators whose work you, as a teacher, may wish to share with young children are Robert McCloskey, Garth Williams, Roger Duvoisin, Bruno Minari, Brian Wildsmith, Feodor Rojankovsky, Leo Politi, Evaline Ness, Ezra Jack Keats, Beni Montresor, and Maurice Sendak. Each of these artists has a distinctive style and achieves memorable visual effects.

SUMMARY

Young children cannot be taught how to represent their experiences or how to be creative with art media. They learn this on their own as they experience using art materials. Therefore, they must have ample opportunity to draw, paint, cut, collage, print, and construct. Sometimes they need to be taught basic procedures for obtaining, using, and storing art materials. They also need quality materials to use—crayons that make bold markings, scissors that cut easily, clear tempera paint that is of thick, creamy consistency, sufficient paper supply to allow for "easy" experimentation.

Providing the raw materials for children's growth in art expression requires time and commitment from adults. The effort is rewarded, however, by the obvious pleasure derived by the child artist. Further, there are obvious benefits to motor coordination, self-understanding, and perhaps surprisingly, cognitive development. Art, particularly for young children, is not a "frill" or a special activity for the talented few; it is basic to every child's full development, and it needs to be an integral part of every preschoolers' experience.

SUGGESTED ACTIVITIES

1 Visit several early childhood classrooms and analyze the setups for art, noting the following:
  a Where is the area placed in relation to other areas?
  b What kind of floor coverings are used?
  c How are materials and accessories stored?
2 Observe in a classroom within a particular area where art materials are being used by children. Note the following:
  a How do different children react to the same material? What differences in action and language repertoire are evidenced?
  b How long do children remain engaged with the materials?
  c What kinds of interactions do the materials engender between children?
  d What do teachers say and do when they are in the area? Do they initiate activities or respond to children's initiations?
  e What happens to art products? How are they labeled and stored?

3 Collect art products from one or more children over a period of time and note the continuity or discontinuity in what the child produces. Describe the changes and the factors that might have been an influence on the child's art expression. Note how the child's products are similar to or different from other children's.

4 For individual children, assess the level of maturity in art expression. List the behaviors (evidence) that lead you to judge a particular child as more or less advanced than others in abilities to use art as a medium for expression.

5 For teachers you observe, assess repertoire for constructively interacting with children who are engaged in art activities. List the different types of behaviors you observe these teachers exhibiting in response to children's involvement while drawing, painting, or using clay.

ADDITIONAL READINGS

Bos, B. J. (1987). *Don't move the muffin tins: A hands-off guide to art for the young child.* Roseville, CA: Turn the Pages Press.

Brittain, W. L. (1979). *Creativity, art and the young child.* New York: Macmillan.

Clemens, S. G. (1991). Art in the classroom: Making every day special. *Young Children, 46*(20), 4–11.

Eisner, E. (1978). What do young children do as they paint?: Creating visual images teaches many things. *Art Education, 31,* 6–10.

Feeney, S., & Moravcik, E. (1987). A thing of beauty: Aesthetic development in young children. *Young Children, 42*(6), 7–15.

Franks, O. R. (1979) Scribbles? Yes, they are art! *Young Children, 34,* 15–22.

Fucigna, C., Ives, K. C., & Ives, W. (1982). Art for toddlers: A developmental approach. *Young Children, 37*(3), 45–51.

Gardner, H. (1980). Artful scribbles: The significance of children's drawings. New York: Basic Books.

Golomb, C. (1974). *Young children's sculpture and drawing: A study in representational development.* Cambridge, MA: Harvard University Press.

Goodnow, J. (1977). *Children drawing.* Cambridge, MA: Harvard University Press.

Kellogg, R. (1969). *The psychology of children's art.* New York: CRM/Random House.

Kellogg, R. (1970). *Analyzing children's art.* Palo Alto, CA: Mayfield.

Lasky, L., & Mukiji, R. (1980). *Art: Basic for young children.* Washington, DC: National Association for the Education of Young Children.

Schirrmacher, R. (1986). Talking with young children about their art. *Young Children, 41*(5), 3–7.

Silver, R. A. (1982). Developing cognitive skills through art. In L. Katz (Ed.), *Current topics in early childhood education* (pp. 143–171) (Vol. 4). Norwood, NJ: Ablex.

Sparling, J. J., & Sparling, M. C. (1973). How to talk to a scribbler. *Young Children, 28,* 333–341.

CHAPTER 19

PRETEND

OVERVIEW

Given time, props, and opportunity, most children will act out in fantasy the relationships and events they know about that are important to them. Pretending is serious business for children. They will create their fantasy worlds with whatever objects are at hand and will act out their roles in pretend. "Pretend you are ___ " and "Let's play that I'm ___ " are such common phrases to children that there seems little doubt that pretending play fulfills some central role in development. Only in those few cultures where children are thrust into adult responsibilities from an early age is the kind of role-playing so familiar to us in Western culture not often observed (Ebbeck, 1971). Although the amount of fantasy play differs from one culture to another, there appears to be a relationship between it and the richness of the adult culture (Whiting & Child, 1953). Within the more complex cultures, fantasy activities abound among the young and are assumed to be helpful to children as they attempt to understand the world about them. In pretend play, or **dramatic play,** children take on an identity not their own (Let's pretend I'm ___), convert common objects into imaginary uses (Let's say this is a ___), and set up imaginary conditions (Let's pretend we're downtown and ___). A child can engage in a dramatic play alone, with a single friend, or in a group. In your observations of children, you have probably noted the extent to which they engage in **sociodramatic play,** that is, play involving others. When engaged in sociodramatic play, children act out complex social situations that involve the reconciling of players with differing needs and background experiences and contradictory views.

According to Smilansky (1968), sociodramatic play contributes to children's development by providing practice in adapting their scattered experiences to the demands of a particular role; they must discern the central features of the role behavior and simultaneously take into account the physical context and the ideas and actions of others. Such complex involvement is believed to develop powers of observation and abstract thought.

Despite the observations of Smilansky and others regarding the value of sociodramatic play, adults and children alike commonly refer to it as "just playing." Parents may wonder about the value of this kind of school activity. Since children play at home and in the neighborhood, why should they do the same thing in school? This is a legitimate question, and as a teacher of young children you must be prepared to answer it often. Each of the following sections presents a rationale for including pretend play in the program setting as well as ideas for making these activities more beneficial than when they occur spontaneously

Pretend play with others enhances language skills. *(Cumberland Hill Associates, Inc.)*

outside the school. Part of your contribution in establishing beneficial pretend play will be in providing settings that encourage particular and varied kinds of dramatic activity. Only the most basic "staging" arrangements are included here.

SETUPS FOR PRETENDING

Basic Equipment

- Child-size furnishings are commercially available to stock housekeeping areas for children's dramatic play. These include refrigerators, kitchen ranges, sinks, rockers, ironing boards, chests of drawers, beds, and doll carriages that all beautifully replicate real-home furnishings. Children certainly enjoy these ready-made replicas, and young children especially can benefit from them, since their imaginations may be inadequate to the task of "making do" with common objects, as older children can. The following materials are very desirable for children ages three through seven: low tables, child-size chairs, shelving, full-length mirrors (metal), sturdy crates, boxes (perhaps reinforced beverage boxes or other sturdy containers), small barrels, smooth and sturdy boards, dress-up clothes (older boys' and girls' sizes are more appropriate than adult men's and women's such as simple gathered skirts, vests, and so forth, of washable material), a rack for hanging dress-ups, floor cushions, small bean bag chairs, rug samples, toy telephones (at least two), durable dolls (both sexes, varied features and skin coloring), doll clothing and accessories, small metal or sturdy plastic dishes, silverware, pots, pans, bowls.

Preferred Location

- Within "walls," either a miniature house or within screens, room dividers.
- Within a space sufficiently large to allow easy movement of several children both inside and outside the "wall" boundaries.
- Near the block area, since blocks often are used as props for various pretend activities.

Accessories

- Old sheet, blanket, bedspread, tarp.
- Cloth remnants of different textures (cotton, satin, velveteen, terry cloth, silk, nylon netting).
- Other remnants (fur, fish net, heavy plastic).
- Ties (pieces of lace, ribbons, sashes, scarves).
- Carrying cases (suitcase, briefcase, satchel, shoulder bag, lunch box, shopping bag, mailboxes).
- Dress-up extras (eyeglass frames without glass, purses, billfolds, jewelry, neckties, bow ties, gloves).

- Odds and ends (note pads, calendar, clock, pillows, grocery bags, small boxes, cans of food, food boxes, cash register).
- Dramatic play kits—the following collections of materials might be stored in boxes and made available to support or stimulate particular types of dramatic play activities:

  Office   Discarded portable typewriter, pads, paper, envelopes, pencils, pens, rubber stamp and ink pad, pictures of office settings.
  Restaurant   Tray, pads, tablecloths, napkins, paper dishes, real food, pictures of restaurant scenes.
  Store   Paper bags and boxes, play money, note pads, cash register, cartons, cans, pictures of store scenes.
  Fire station   Firefighters' hats (plastic), hose lengths, ladder lengths, tall boots (older children's sizes), pictures of firefighters in station and in action.

  Kits might also be prepared for a hair salon, a library, camping, fishing, a train, a bakery, a picnic, a clinic or hospital, a post office, a gas station.

General Guidelines

- An ample period is necessary for children to have satisfying experiences in dramatic play. A half-hour is probably minimal, and a longer time is preferable. A warning that a time period is almost over should be given somewhat prior to terminating children's activity in dramatic play.
- At the start of each activity session make sure that the dramatic play area is clean and orderly, with dress-ups, dishes, and other props neatly arranged.
- Frequently launder all dress-ups and cloth remnants and remove, repair, or discard all articles that are broken or torn.
- Establish a clear policy on whether water, clay, and other messy materials may be used in the area established for pretend play. In some situations, it is easy to accommodate and clear away spills. In other situations, the carpeting, flooring, or the nature of the "props" preclude the use of these materials with dramatic play.
- Establish a clear policy on whether toy guns or other kinds of props children will inevitably bring from home may be used in pretend play. Keep in mind that the nature of the play will be significantly influenced by the kinds of props available.

Alternatives

- Puppets of all varieties often serve to engage children in dramatic representation. An impromptu stage can be created by simply turning a table on edge and allowing the performers to be behind the table (between the table legs) while the audience sits on the other side. Durable and attractive hand puppets are commercially available from many sources, and others can be easily constructed for or by children. These can include hand puppets made of fabrics, socks, mittens; finger puppets; paper bag puppets; and papier-mâché puppets. Almost anything can be turned into a puppet, given a bit of imagination.

MOTOR DEVELOPMENT AND PRETENDING

While children are "just playing" being firefighters, pioneers, monsters, wild dogs, horses, Batman and Robin, or other such roles, they often appear to be in constant motion. They may pause for plans and consultation ("Let's say I find a note one of the robbers left"), but when the action resumes, so does the incessant running, diving, rolling, dodging, sneaking, crawling, jumping, and climbing. The healthy child in pretend play quite naturally practices and perfects motor skills and, especially, muscle coordination.

Pretend play can also be used to encourage motor activities that are not performed spontaneously. Children's repertoires of movements can be expanded as they follow your suggestions, and they can pretend to be jack-in-the-boxes, rubber bands, firecrackers, balloons, popcorn, alligators, snails, fish, skaters, Raggedy Ann or Andy dolls, soldiers, giants, clowns, racing cars, puppets, tightrope walkers, propellers, jumping beans, rocking boats, jeeps, bouncing balls, jets, helicopters, tops, trees, or daisies. The possibilities for things to imitate and the related actions are nearly limitless. Almost any child will enthusiastically respond to suggestions that he or she pretend to be something else. The following role suggestions may encourage children to practice particular motor skill:

- **Body alignment for strength**   Strong man at the circus pushing and lifting "heavy" objects; football lineman pushing against opponent; farmer lifting hay bales or bags of feed; horse pulling heavy load; sanitation workers moving heavy garbage cans; movers pushing pianos, sofas, refrigerators; bulldozers pushing heavy rocks
- **Body alignment for balance**   High-wire performer at the circus; animals or people crossing stream on log or series of rocks; firefighter walking narrow ledge to save stranded kitten; ballet dancer on toes; construction worker on steel girder
- **Rhythmic movements** (can have musical or clapping accompaniment) Bouncing balls; swimmers, dancers; marionettes; sea gulls; grass blowing in the wind; rowing or paddling; shoveling or chopping
- **Body alignment for speed**   Superman; power boat; jet plane; baseball player; racing cars; racehorse

Children's physical endurance is more likely to be encouraged through participation in dramatic activity than by any other means. In normal play, they may take quick runs, gallop across the room, or turn a somersault, but they are not likely to sustain these activities for as long as they will when playing a role. As wild horses, they may gallop about for long periods of time, neighing enthusiastically through it. As a lame dog trying to get back to its master against all kinds of obstacles, a child will struggle long distances on two hands and one foot. While scooting along on their backs with knees up and feet on the floor, pretending to be submarines, children will traverse great distances, turning and changing directions but continuing to sustain these rather tiring actions.

Although you seldom wish to interrupt children's spontaneous sociodramatic activity to suggest beneficial motor movements, you will find ample opportunity to make such suggestions when children are not involved, and some of these suggestions will later become incorporated into their impromptu dramatic actions, often in more complex and creative ways than you imagined.

Hyperactive and impulsive children may especially benefit from your direct suggestions for engaging in dramatic actions. Activities that involve conscious tensing followed by relaxation can be particularly effective for these children. Suggest, for example, that children become racers. Begin with preparatory actions that are fun (such as shaking hands and giving autographs to the fans). Next, encourage them to become tight set, muscles hard, waiting for the starting signal. Then get them to run a hard, quick race followed by total relaxation— collapsed, stretched out, exhausted, "like the bones are all out of the muscles." Again, let them pretend that they are fierce lions, all tense and waiting for a chance to pounce. Then let them quickly capture the prey and devour it before taking a carefree lope over the grasslands. Finally, let them find a place in the sunshine for a nap, stretched out in total relaxation like a big, tame pussycat. Practice on yourself, when you are tense. What kinds of dramatic imagery help you alternatively tense and relax your muscles? Perhaps you can translate your own imagery into suitable relaxing activities for the hyperactive, tense child.

The impulsive child might especially benefit from dramatic activities that require conscious control of movements, alternately moving slowly and quickly. To this kind of child, you may suggest series of actions: a cat stealthily approaching and pouncing on a mouse; a little dog trying to steal a big dog's bone; a mechanical man performing a variety of activities; or someone fishing, slowly reeling in a line to change the bait and then rapidly reeling when there is a catch. Any of these roles must of course be embellished with suggestions not related to the desired movements; for example, the dog might stop to scratch a flea, or the person fishing might wave away the mosquitoes and wipe his or her forehead. Within a fun context, it is possible to insert many suggestions that require the conscious control of movement rates.

It is also possible to find ways of promoting eye-hand coordination and use of unfamiliar small-muscle skills in the dramatic play activities. Supply raw materials that encourage small-muscle activity, such as apples and celery that can be cut up and served in a play restaurant, dress-ups and doll clothes requiring buttoning, scissors and pads of paper for children to make play money or grocery lists. Real resourcefulness and sensitivity, however, are required to offer these at the appropriate moment, so that the main thread of play is not interrupted.

AFFECTIVE DEVELOPMENT AND PRETENDING

The therapeutic value of fantasy play is frequently cited in books about early education, to the exclusion of motor, social, and cognitive development. It is easy to understand this emphasis; pretend activities do offer children possibilities for (1) exerting control over a situation rather than being controlled; (2) safely expressing negative feelings and unacceptable impulses; (3) working out feelings about disturbing situations and coming to better understand them; and (4) reliving or anticipating pleasurable experiences. In pretend play, children are free to deal with their particular concerns and to pursue their interests at their own pace.

Teachers have only limited possibilities for assisting with the therapeutic aspects of dramatic play. Perhaps the most important ways of helping are simply by providing play time and recognizing when not to interfere. For example, when a child in the role of mother or teacher is scolding or beating a doll-child, this is probably not the time to interject alternative views on how a teacher or mother might treat a misbehaving child. When a child, playing a big-sister role, is ruthlessly teasing a little sister, there is no need for moralization. Nor should you infer that such actions necessarily reflect the true reality of the child's experience. A teacher need not understand precisely why a child acts a role out in a certain way; it is often sufficient to recognize and respect the intensity of the child's involvement.

It is sometimes possible to provide specific experiences and props that stimulate children's role experimentation in critical areas. Having the props (a chair, a stethoscope, a syringe, Band-Aids, carrying cases, white jackets) to act out the traumatic experience of blood tests for lead poisoning was helpful to children in one day-care center. In another situation, when several kindergarteners expressed resentment about their treatment from "that school patrol boy," their teacher set out the school patrol insignia along with other paraphernalia needed for a street scene. Their experimentation with the roles of patrol boys and girls, bus drivers, and school children were intense and pointed.

After seeing an older group acting out a rather frightening Snow White drama, a group of first-graders, gingerly at first but with increasing confidence, tried on the witch costume and mask their teacher had borrowed. They gradually began to enjoy feigning the fierceness of the witch and the fright of Snow White. Of course, children should never be forced or even encouraged to play out frightening or puzzling experiences. Some children will refuse even if given the props and the opportunity. However, many will benefit from such play, as evidenced by their increased confidence in similar, real-life situations thereafter.

SOCIAL DEVELOPMENT AND PRETENDING

In dramatic play, children often have more opportunities to work cooperatively with a greater variety of children than they do in the home and neighborhood. Sociodramatic play typically represents the first effective social education in a child's life. As mentioned earlier, the regulation of personal fantasies so that they mesh with those of others in a way that is mutually satisfying to all is a challenging task. This kind of sustained and mutually satisfying sociodramatic activity, when it occurs, reflects a milestone in social development.

Most children need only the opportunity, time, and props to stimulate cooperative pretend play. For a few, however, direct teacher intervention may be nec-

In sociodramatic play, children often act out complex social situations. *(Ursula Moeller)*

essary to get them under way with this very specialized social interaction. When children appear unable to successfully engage in sociodramatic activities, you may wish to invite them to play a specific role, saying, "Why don't you pretend that you are the customer at the bakery, and I'll be the clerk?" Demonstrate to them how specific objects can be used to represent other objects, for example, "We can pretend these long blocks are bread and the round ones are cakes," and set the fantasy stage verbally, saying, "Pretend that you are coming into the bakery and that you are *very* hungry."

Smilansky (1968), in investigating the lack of sociodramatic play activities in Israeli children from socioeconomically deprived families, induced teachers to participate with those children who had previously engaged in very little or no dramatic play. She found that these children's involvement in dramatic interactions with each other increased markedly both in total amount and in complexity. By demonstrating how to translate specific experiences into dramatic activity, the teachers were able to significantly increase the children's repertoire for this kind of interaction. Thereafter, the children's ability to learn from and to enjoy group fantasy play greatly increased. When the children you teach appear to be incompetent or uninterested in dramatic play and appear to have poor social interactions, you may wish to take the lead by playing with them, in order to ensure their familiarity with the processes involved in cooperative sociodramatic play.

The line between helpful and nonhelpful intervention in children's dramatic play is often difficult to determine. However, when children already skilled in group pretend play are having conflicts over who will take which role, your intervention to solve their problems would probably be inappropriate. For instance, in playing house, children like to have someone play the role of baby, but they may not be willing to take the role themselves. And many children will vie with each other for the lead role in whatever drama is under way at the moment. You will frequently be asked by children to intercede to make sure that they are fairly treated: "He always wants to be Peter Pan and won't let anyone else." A helpful rejoinder might be, "I can see why you wouldn't like that. How might you get him to take turns with you?" This may be ineffective in solving the immediate problem but could set the stage for more effective problem solving later. It is seldom helpful for a teacher to assign roles in a voluntary dramatic activity; the playing usually disintegrates, everyone is dissatisfied, and nothing is learned about problem solving.

The noting and commending of children's social problem solving is especially effective in regard to cooperative play. For example, "That was really a good idea you had about Jimmy playing your dog, wasn't it? He wanted to play dogs and Janie wanted to play house, and by suggesting that he be the family dog, everyone was happy. That was certainly a smart idea!" Or, "When you and Tanya both wanted a purse to carry to play secretaries, you had a good idea. You pretended the hat was your purse. It worked out well, didn't it?" As a reinforcement for children who have done particularly well in merging their separate fantasies in a coordinated play theme, you can invite them to act out their "play" before the class at sharing time. Six- and seven-year-olds, and even some five-year-olds, especially enjoy "doing a play," and this is the natural progression into more formalized cooperative endeavors. The tasks of jointly creating individual scenes and then sequencing these in a coherent presentation leads to the satisfactions inherent in all cooperative drama.

COGNITIVE DEVELOPMENT AND PRETENDING

While children are engaged in pretend play, they often attempt to better integrate new and puzzling encounters and situations into their understanding. As they structure their activities, they invent ways to make the actions they have seen in adults, peers, or the media fit within their own conceptions of the world. Things that have been encountered but not fully incorporated are re-created in fantasy, reworked, and gradually assimilated. The greatest values from pretend play are derived from these self-initiated processes. Adults can make additional interjections that stimulate further explorations and learning in play situations. It is these special arrangements and situations that are primarily discussed in this section. Keep in mind that although many of the following ideas for intervention can prove useful, they may have far less significance for children's cognitive and intellectual development than the processes in which children spontaneously engage.

"Let's pretend that I'm the baby sitter." *(Robert Burdick)*

Classification, Number, and Seriation

Without detracting from children's ongoing play, there are many indirect strategies you can use for involving them in thought about classification, numbering, and ordering. The most effective way is to stock their dramatic play areas with materials that invite these processes. The following are examples of props that will serve this function:

- Silverware, dishes, pots and pans, napkins, and other kitchen items selected so that they represent differing kinds, shapes, sizes, and colors
- Fabric samples (differing fabrics—satin, cotton, corduroy; differing sizes—4″ × 8″, 8″ × 8″, and 16″ × 16″; differing colors)
- Cans and cartons of differing sizes and colors
- Dowels that vary in diameter and length
- Play coins (varying in size and composition)
- Doll clothes (differing in size, fabric, and design)

If these materials have been carefully selected to provide several instances of each variation, children will spontaneously use and reuse them to classify, order, and count. Frequently, these processes will be interwoven with dramatic play sequences after a child or group of children has been given direct practice with them. For example, in an instructional situation a group could be presented with fabric samples to sort according to color, type of fabric, and size and given help in differentiating concepts (size, color, and texture). When the materials are then returned to the dramatic play area, you can observe whether the children have incorporated any of the words or concepts into their spontaneous play.

There are many opportunities to unobtrusively work numbers into the exchanges that children initiate with you while playing. Playing store offers constant opportunities to ask eager sellers, "How much will that cost?" For example, when the baker says, "Ten dollars," or "Three pennies," you can count out something (bits of paper, play money, twigs, or simply hand-pats) to match the number cited. Also, when children are assembling props for a particular set and ask you for something, a sensible reply would be, "How many do you need?" Or, after counting out two or three, "Is this enough or do you need more? How many more do you need?"

Mass and Liquid Quantity

In pretend activities in which products are produced and sold, children sometimes express interest in quantity. At a lemonade stand, for example, with only a limited supply on hand, it behooves both the buyer and seller to note how much various containers hold. By age six or seven, some children are ready to begin making comparisons on a more accurate basis than appearance. By providing them with measuring utensils, weighing instruments, and a varied array of containers, you can increase the likelihood of their investigating and learning about conservation of quantity.

Causality

As children are acting out various pretend experiences, questions about phenomena they only partially understand are likely to surface. Most children will stop only long enough to ask a quick question and get a quick answer. They usually do not want to become involved in doing an experiment, looking in a book, or listening to a long answer; they just want quick information in terms they can understand, based on what they already know. In fact, rather than asking questions, some children will simply create their own answers, announce them, and wait to see whether they are countered. What kind of response would you make to the following children's comments?

- Jimmy is playing car wash outside on a sunny day, washing bikes for two cents (stones) each. He suddenly notes that the pavement, which had been wet, is now dry. "Where did that wet go," he asks, "into the ground?"
- Janey has spread her doll clothes out on the grass on a hot day and has gone to get the dolls. When she comes back she notices that the dark cloth feels much hotter than the white. "This one was in the oven," she says looking at you for confirmation.
- The light suddenly goes out during an electrical storm. Several children playing house say, "Who did that?" One says, "Probably Mrs. Dubrey (the principal) didn't pay the bill."
- Randy and Elmer are playing policemen. They are trying to tell some children who are engaged in another kind of playing that they must stop and be

searched. The other children declare that they do not have to. Randy asks, "You have to do what police say 'cause they got guns." Elmer adds, "And they can shoot anyone they don't like!" They look to you to support their contentions.

In each of these situations, you must make two decisions. First, how to explain the immediate question, and, second, how to provide for future elaboration. By carefully listening to and observing children while they are involved in dramatic play, you can often identify potentially productive areas for later instruction.

Time and Space Concepts

The essence of pretending is the manipulation of space and time. Most pretend play involves superimposing a different time and setting on the real "here and now." A single dramatic play episode can even include several locations and several points in time. Consider the following excerpts, taken from the planning segments of children's play:

"Now let's say that's over and now it is much later, and we've gone out to the park."

"Hey, let's pretend I go to the movie. Okay, I'm at the movie show now. Pretend you are the person who sells tickets. Wait, let's make the chairs and stuff for the movie first, okay?"

"Let's say we feed the baby and then she cries a lot so we have to spank her and then she goes to sleep. When she wakes up, it's the next day. And let's say she's sick, so I will be the doctor in my office, and you can call me up. Okay?"

Perhaps such mental excursions are the precursors of an appreciation of literature and history: Each situation requires keeping in mind a time and place and then considering a series of events within that context.

Between the ages of three and seven, spatial understanding is derived from the creation of settings for children's role-playing or the manipulation of miniature toys in pretend activities. To successfully convert the same props and the same space into such diverse settings as a movie theatre, museum, motel, office, or hospital, as many five- through seven-year-olds will do, requires considerable spatial expertise. Of course, those children who have already become adept at playing house are more likely to tackle more imaginative staging enterprises. Less experienced children will remain content with domestic or other familiar scenes.

The beginnings of a sense of geography can be spawned through children's efforts to create play worlds for their dolls, toy soldiers, and miniature animals. In one elementary school, a bear fad—involving tiny three-inch Steiff bears—developed and spread throughout the entire student body. Nearly every child kept a bear close at hand and many children even created and furnished tiny bear homes. Some of the older children created a factory in which their bears produced bear furniture that was sold to other bears—at a good profit, of course.

At the height of the bear mania, the first- and second-graders, with the help of their teacher, created a miniature bear world on a six-by-eight-foot wooden platform. Using a mix of sawdust and wheat paste, they formed a continent with mountains, hills, valleys, and a couple of small islands. Surrounding these land forms was an ocean, and within the continent were an inland lake and two rivers. For weeks, little bears sailed the oceans, built houses on the land, fished in the rivers, climbed the mountain, and skated on the lake. The children "lived" geography through their little bears' adventures. The creating of miniature worlds for their small objects is an excellent way for children to develop their spatial understandings.

Spoken Language

Children's participation in sociodramatic play puts intensive demands on their language abilities, and at the same time motivates them to become more precise in their use of language. They must verbally influence their fellow players if their own ideas are to be included in the play activity, so most children work at learning how to express themselves effectively.

Teachers can also enhance language development through the medium of pretend play. This can be done by arranging play settings that encourage the reenactment of new experiences and their associated new words. When children have been to a fire station, on a picnic, or to a library, it is likely that the

"I'm the biggest monster." *(John James)*

trip will be reenacted via dramatic play if visited objects (or replicas) are available in the play setting during activity periods. Also, if photographs or illustrations of the places visited or similar settings are posted nearby, children will continue to talk and play through those experiences and, in the process, will add some of the new words to their vocabulary.

Language development can also be stimulated by introducing new objects into the dramatic play area. For example, you might bring in **realia** from your excursion to the seashore, if you think this would represent a new experience for some children. You might show them your shells, sunglasses, beach towels, beach chairs, and a collection of representative postcards or photographs. If you then leave these objects in a box near the dramatic play areas, some children will incorporate them into their play, and will ask, "What did you call this? What do you do with that?" In short, by thoughtfully introducing new objects into the play area, you can ensure children's exposure to new vocabulary and, depending on the degree to which they incorporate these objects into their play, you may succeed in expanding their permanent vocabulary.

You might consider the following kinds of objects for this purpose: scuba diving equipment, bathroom scales, real flowers, a vacuum cleaner, a flashlight, a backpack, a life vest, a plastic thermos jug, crutches, rubber boots, a coil of heavy rope, a parachute, a picnic basket, a rowboat. Many other such objects can be used to enrich children's play and vocabulary.

Written Language

The making of signs, labels, and other written materials can become an integral part of many dramatic play activities. Because written language abounds in the real world, the re-creation of this writing adds authenticity to children's play. If children are making a restaurant, for example, they may want any of the following: a large sign bearing their restaurant name, duplicated menus, a wall price list, order pads, advertising posters, table signs, and name tags. As children create play settings from what they perceive as the essence of the situation they are depicting, you can be alert to opportunities to ask, "Do you want a sign?" or "Do you want me to write that out for you?" Children will usually be delighted to add this extra dimension of reality.

Once children of age six or seven have begun producing plays for others to see, you can often involve them in preparing their "playbills," which tell the audience the name of the play, the scenes, the actors, and offer short character sketches. Whether these are duplicated to be passed out or are read by a child announcer, such writing enhances both the dramatic endeavors and the children's competency in reading and writing.

Even the very young can sharpen their visual discrimination skills within the context of dramatic play. By interjecting into their play props such items as rubber stamps (library, post office), stick-on forms (post office, stores), playing cards (homes, camping), picture collections (stores, homes), play money (stores, homes, restaurants), and price tags (stores), children will examine, sort, and use them.

FURTHER EXTENSIONS

Our consideration of pretend play has been within the context of the activity periods in the typical early education setting. It may also be used to consider how a child's pretending experiences can be extended through other expressive modes or in other settings. For instance, a vivid representation of the world as seen and imagined can be created in dance. Bruce (1965) suggests that movement accompanied by music may be a prime means of expression for children.

> The child expresses through dramatic movement ideas which are of his imagination and arise from his experience. Pictures, stories, the world around, television and cinemas provide the stimuli. He can be like an animal, a bird, a space man, or father digging the garden. He can also be like a train or a river, the wind or the snow, a rock or a star. In children, music will often excite movement which is spontaneous and unselfconscious. A child responds especially to the rhythm with gesture, which is unplanned and on the whole unremembered (pp. 7–8).

For this kind of movement activity, large open space may be preferable to the regular classroom. A gymnasium, hallway, or other large space without furnishings provides opportunities to freely create in movement without psychological or physical impediments.

Children are normally enthralled with pretending through the production of sound effects. They delight in making sounds with their voices and by manipulation of objects—striking, scraping, tapping, and so forth. The sounds children produce are frequently disturbing to adults, and there are often sanctions against shrieks, whistles, and motor imitations. Although such noise prohibitions may be necessary to preserve the well-being of most adults and certain children, there should be some recognition of the fact that the producing of sounds is an important avenue of pretending for many children. In each child's daily experience, there should be some time and place where the creation of sounds in all variations—loud, raucous, soft, rhythmic, staccato, and shrill—is allowed and encouraged.

Because children prior to age seven or eight, as Piaget (1969) points out, do not have the capacity for internally representing movement and change but instead think in terms of static imagery, it is small wonder that creating and recreating scenes in pretend play are so important to development. Through pretending, children can reexperience changes and sequences of events so as to better understand them. Sound and motion can contribute to this understanding.

SUMMARY

The benefits of pretend play for young children are many and varied. They engage in pretend activities without instigation but under adult guidance can derive even greater benefits.

Through pretending, children can be encouraged to engage in a wide variety of gross-muscle actions and will often sustain them, without urging, for long periods. Positive outcomes can be derived by some children from movement imitations in tensing and relaxing, slowing and speeding, and other contrasting actions. The provision of appropriate props encourages involvement with small-muscle actions.

Given the opportunity, children will typically engage in spontaneous dramatizations of episodes that concern them. A teacher may be able to further encourage this therapeutic use of pretending by furnishing props related to situations that appear to be stressful.

Participation in sociodramatic play is particularly valuable and demanding. Teachers may need to initially help some children translate specific experiences into dramatic activity. In general, however, direct involvement of teachers in sociodramatic play is counterproductive.

Particular kinds of props may encourage classification, consideration of number and seriation, awareness of quantity, spatial awareness, and language usage. The situations that arise during play may present further opportunities for considering causality, time sequences, and written communication.

Given the developmental status of children ages three to seven, it is not difficult to understand why pretending has positive consequences, nor is it difficult to understand that movement and the production of sound effects might contribute significantly to children's pretending.

SUGGESTED ACTIVITIES

1 Visit several early childhood classrooms and analyze the setups for pretending, noting the following:
   a Where are dramatic play areas placed in relation to other areas?
   b What kind of furnishings or floor coverings are provided?
   c How are materials and accessories displayed?
2 Observe in a classroom when children are engaged in pretending. Note the following:
   a How do different children react to the same props? What differences in action and language repertoire are evidenced?
   b How long do children remain engaged in pretend play activities?
   c What kinds of interactions do the materials engender among children? How is pretending initiated, sustained, terminated? How are roles and actions determined?
   d What do teachers say and do when they are in the area? Do they initiate activities or respond to children's initiations?
3 Observe and record a dramatic play situation that involves a group of children engaged in cooperative play. Analyze the dynamics of the situation and the kind of communication behaviors that were used to initiate and sustain the interaction. Identify the frustrations experienced by (or within) the group, if any, and how these were resolved.
4 For individual children, assess the level of maturity in pretending activities. List the

behaviors that lead you to judge a particular child as more or less advanced than others in abilities to engage in cooperative pretending.

5 For teachers you observe, assess repertoires for constructively interacting with children who are engaged in pretend play. List the different types of behaviors you observe these teachers exhibiting in response to children's pretending activities.

ADDITIONAL READINGS

Almy, M. (1967). Spontaneous play: An avenue for intellectual development. *Young Children, 22,* 265–280.

Bender, J. (1971). Have you thought of a prop box? *Young Children, 24,* 164–169.

Garvey, C. (1977). *Play: The developing child series.* Cambridge, MA: Harvard University Press.

Paley, V. G. (1984). *Boys and girls: Superheroes in the doll corner.* Chicago: University of Chicago Press.

Paley, V. G. (1988). *Bad guys don't have birthdays: Fantasy play at four.* Chicago: University of Chicago Press.

Singer, D. G., & Singer, J. L. (1985). *Make believe: Games and activities to foster imaginative play in young children.* Glenview, IL: Scott-Foresman.

Smilansky, S. (1968). *The effects of sociodramatic play on disadvantaged preschool children.* New York: Wiley.

Smilansky, S., & Shefatya, L. (1990). *Facilitating play: A medium for promoting cognitive, socio-emotional and academic development in young children.* Gaithersville, MD: Psychosocial and Educational Publications.

CHAPTER 20

MUSIC

OVERVIEW

There is no scarcity of music in the lives of most children. They hear background music at the grocery store, in shopping malls, in restaurants, in the dentist's office, in airport terminals. Music is frequently heard on home and car radios. Some children have their own radios and phonographs. Music is ever-present during television viewing, keying the listener's emotions to what is visually and verbally presented. Preschool children spend two to four hours watching television daily (Houston, Wright, Rice, Kerkman & St. Peters, 1990). During much of that time, they are exposed to musical background sounds.

Despite the constant exposure to music, children may not have the opportunity to see musical performances in which attention is focused directly on the music and the musician. Although it is a rare child who has not heard the sound of a harp, banjo, bassoon, and a wide array of other instruments, few of those same children have ever had the experiences of seeing these sounds being produced or hearing what each of the blended sounds is like if heard apart from the others.

The task of the early educator may well be to bring aspects of music generally available to children into greater personal awareness. Because children are so used to hearing music without really listening to it, experiences that will prove most meaningful to them initially may involve the production of music. If they can be encouraged to experiment with variations in rhythm, pitch, and volume in producing sounds, they will develop a more intensive awareness. Through their own creations, children can be sensitized to listening to music and to hearing what previously had been primarily pleasant noise.

Enjoyment is the prime benefit of music. For children particularly, there are a number of other positive effects. As you read this chapter, you will learn about the importance of pleasurably involving children with music and about how that involvement contributes to several aspects of their development.

MOTOR DEVELOPMENT AND MUSIC

Many children first relate to music through movement. Some children easily match their own movements to the music they hear; others, especially the youngest, enjoy having adults match music to rhythmic movements that they initiate. For example, the child who is stalking with long steps and heavy treading may be pleased that the teacher intones "VOOM, VOOM, VOOMM . . ." in time to the steps or beats out the matching rhythm on a table top or on a resonant toy or instrument. The tiny fingers of the three-year-old tapping insistently on the teacher's arm for attention can be repeated on the xylophone or song bells to the delight of the child. Teachers who are accomplished pianists, guitarists, or the like have much to offer children in amplifying their actions to more elaborate music. Less involved translation of movement to sound is something, however, that even the least musically talented teacher can accomplish via voice or percussion.

"I like this song. Look at me go!" (*Cumberland Hill Associates*)

SETUPS FOR MUSIC

GROUP SINGING

Suggested Location

- Any location away from distractions such as toys, dress-ups. It is desirable to have comfortable seating where children can easily see the song leader and sit close enough together to hear each other's voices.

Accessories

- Chording instruments—autoharp, guitar, ukelele.
- Melody instruments—tone bars, step bells, xylophone, piano.
- Other—pitchpipe, song list, music books.

General Guidelines

- Prepare a list of songs that the children in the group know and keep it in a handy location as a reminder to yourself. Or if you are to sing with a new group, prepare a list of songs children commonly know or can very easily learn.
- Make sure that you know all the words to the songs you want to sing and that you know the tunes well enough so that you can stop and start anew in the middle if you should need to do so.
- Don't ask children if they want to sing a particular song. Just announce it and begin to sing. Or just begin to sing. Judge by children's reactions whether it was a good choice and, if not, quickly switch to another.
- Intersperse action songs with nonaction songs so that there is some motor participation—clapping or feet tapping. Also use some chants or fingerplays for variation.
- Sing a few songs happily. Don't prolong the singing to the point where children are tired and bored.
- Generally choose songs that are strongly rhythmic, have repetition of lines and verses, and are in the low range children can manage. Five or six adjacent notes upward from middle C are usually most appropriate but some variation from this is often okay, depending on the children's enthusiasm for the song's tune, rhythm, or subject.
- Expect requests for well-liked seasonal songs at all times of the year. Don't be surprised if "Rudolph the Red-nosed Reindeer" appears to be preschoolers' favorite springtime song.
- Beware of cumulative verse songs. Six- and seven-year-olds may appreciate *all* the verses in songs such as "The Fox," "Tree in the Woods," or "The Twelve Days of Christmas" but children who are three, four, and five years old may do better with several shorter selections.
- When teaching a new song, it may be helpful to provide the children with something to see while they listen to the words the first time through, such as, a related picture, a puppet moving to the song's rhythm, a sequence of movements. Merely listening to an unfamiliar song may not be sufficiently

interesting for many young listeners. Sing it all the way through once or twice on the first day you introduce it, and then go on to other songs. Do the same thing the next day, inviting children to sing with you if they can remember it. Soon the new song will become familiar. Saying the words of a song and having children say or sing them line by line is not particularly helpful. Try not to distort the song as you introduce it.

- Use instruments (piano, song bells, guitar) to accompany singing only if you can do it with sufficient ease to allow your attention to remain with the children singing, not with the accompaniment.

Alternatives

- Put lively songs on the phonograph during cleanup time and, by example, encourage children to sing along.
- Play calming lullabies on the phonograph during rest periods and encourage children to sing to a pretend baby, to a doll, or to a stuffed animal. Try "Kumbaya" and "Hush Little Baby."
- Rhythm instruments can be distributed to one or two children at a time for accompanying group singing. Beware of the extensive use of instruments with singing, since the voices will be so easily overshadowed by the produced sounds.

MOVEMENT

Suggested Location

- Any large space will do; a gymnasium is not necessary. A large classroom space or a hallway can be used, or the activity can be held outdoors.

Equipment

- Record player or tape recorder of good quality.
- Piano or other instruments such as tom-tom or tambourine.

Accessories

- Scarves, hoops, ribbons, rhythm instruments.

General Guidelines

- Establish a means for signaling to children that they are to come to a set location. You may wish to use a drum signal, a piano chord, or a mellow bell sound. Practice this initially before attempting other activities. Once children begin moving about in a large space, gaining their attention without a preset signal is difficult.
- If children are to take their shoes off, have them do so first and leave the shoes in a location away from the space to be used for the movement activities. The alternative is to place all shoes in a box that is out of reach. If shoes are left willy-nilly about the perimeters of the space you are using, young children will

attend to them at periodic intervals, detracting from their involvement in the movement activities. If you won't have time or assistance for getting shoes on and off, it is better to have children leave them on.

EXPERIMENTING WITH SOUNDS

Suggested Location

- Experiments for creating musical sounds are best conducted as individual activities or in small groups. A music center can be created in any area of a classroom where experimentation can be carried out by a small group during activity periods. Some separation from other areas is desirable so that idle toying with instruments does not occur during other time periods and sounds produced will be less disturbing to others.

Equipment

- Shelf or table.
- Screen to separate music center from other activity areas.
- Rhythm instruments—triangles, maracas, finger cymbals, clappers, wooden sticks, sand blocks, wrist bells, ankle bells, tambourines, drums (various sizes and shapes). (Introduce only a few at a time.)

Accessories

- Raw materials for creating instruments—tumblers or bottles (glass), water pitcher, wood or metal rods; sturdy box without a top; rubber bands; cardboard; boiled shank bones; cord; juice cans; nails; pebbles; shells or beans; coconut shell cut into halves.

Guidelines

- Expect noisy experiments before the music making becomes a serious endeavor.
- Children need to have opportunities to make choices. They can choose an instrument to play (or to create). They can choose to work alone, with a partner, or with a group. They can choose to create music for only their own ears or to share with an audience.
- Point out to children how different sounds are produced if they hold instruments in one way compared to another, or if they use forceful movements rather than gentle ones.
- Produce a tape recording of the children's musical efforts and replay it for them to hear. You might want to reserve this for special "compositions" that have been planned and rehearsed.
- The instruments can also be brought into action as accompaniments for other musical activities—to accompany the beat of a song or recording, or to add sound effects for a story, poem, rhythmic movement, or creative dramatics.

Children's ability to differentiate their movements in response to music increases with age and experience. At three, most children can join others in clapping simple rhythms and in performing movements such as pounding, hitting hands to knees, moving hands vertically or horizontally in time and to music. The youngest preschoolers are more likely to move parts of the body than the whole body, for instance, swinging hands, moving head, shaking fingers. At four and above, they become increasingly differentiated in matching their movements to music and are able to alternate between tiptoeing, swaying, hopping, and running. They also become interested in taking on particular roles or imagery as they move to music. As mice scurrying, seagulls soaring, leaves falling, and so forth, children engage in actions that promote rhythm, agility, and balance and, at the same time, become more appreciative of the variations in music. As children play a particular role in which they follow music (or create patterns of movement from which musical patterns can be derived), they engage in an array of movements. Adults can increase the children's awareness of their movements by noting and emphasizing variations in the following areas:

- Direction (forward, backward, sideways, and around)
- Level (high or low or in between)
- Range (using small or large space)
- Focus of movements (toward specific spots in space)
- Floor patterns (paths followed in moving about the floor)

Notice that in these recommended areas emphasis is placed on increasing the child's awareness of the range of possibilities for movement rather than on directing the children how to move. If, however, some children are observed not to engage in certain kinds of movement, they may be invited to pretend to be in a role that promotes the kinds of movement desired. For example, children who never move out of standing positions may be invited to become kites (or gliders or seagulls or bees), which begin high and dip and rise, sometimes settling to a low level before swooping up again. Of course, the children must be very familiar with the designated objects to be able to portray them in movement.

Children who seem always to run in circles in relatively undifferentiated movement responses to music might be drawn into a dramatic improvisation in which they become squirrels running out from a nest to gather nuts, returning, gathering, returning; or sailboats moving back and forth across a lake. Or they might portray a sequence of animal actions—sleeping, waking, playing, eating, drinking, chasing, becoming tired, and again, sleeping.

It is the adults, not the children, who should keep the dimensions of direction, level, range, focus, and floor patterns consciously in mind in guiding movements to music. Because of this awareness, the adult can suggest characters and scenes that stimulate children to develop a more varied movement repertoire. Through suggestions for improvisations, children can be encouraged to engage in movement of the whole body or certain body parts (head, arms, fingers). Movements can be from sitting, kneeling, and reclining as well as from standing positions. In addition to developing children's repertoire for movement, adults can simultaneously provide music leading to awareness of the following variations in music:

- Tempo (fast or slow)
- Accent (loud or different beat or sound)
- Rhythmic patterns (steady beat or recurring accents)
- Intensity (loudness or softness)

Providing too complex a musical stimulus is a common error adults make when helping children relate music to movement. As discussed in Chapter 6, young children cannot sort objects according to double classifications; neither can they easily attend to aspects of tempo and variations in volume or other dimensions at the same time. They will spontaneously note and respond to volume shifts at some points and to other variations at other points. Most, however, cannot shift their attention from one to the other at the request of an adult. They may react to a loud, slow song as though it were loud and fast, attending only to loudness but not to tempo. Beware of expecting a child who can differentiate between high and low tones to be able to do the same thing when the tones are embedded in a composition that includes variations in tempo as well as in tone level.

In addition to the relationship between movement of the body in response to music (or the creation of music in response to the movements of the body), motor development and music have an additional kind of linkage. To produce music, one must have command of small muscles. Only a small part of the task of creating music on a musical instrument has to do with auditory or cognitive abilities; the rest is motor. Children improvising music on instruments gain the practice with motor control essential for receiving music instruction. Although children's "messing about" in creating sounds is sometimes painful to adult ears, the resulting physical control provides a base for more aesthetic efforts. With this motor practice, the initial effort to pattern movements and sounds to another's modeling is greatly facilitated. Further, if children at ages five, six, and seven can be shown how their musical inventions can be represented by symbols so that they can be preserved and "read" by others, essential steps are taken that lead toward interest in musical notation and music reading.

AFFECTIVE DEVELOPMENT AND MUSIC

When the role of the arts in education is considered with any degree of seriousness, there appears to be agreement that the arts need to be central to individual learning experiences, in and out of school and at every stage of life (Arts, Education, & Americans Panel, 1977). The early childhood experience sets the stage for this lifelong involvement.

In music as in the other arts, the experiences of the early years may greatly influence the extent to which emotional and aesthetic satisfaction are derived from the medium at later ages. Children can learn to close out and avoid music, or they can learn that it is enhancing and enjoyable. To some extent, of course, the responses of children to sound are a function of inborn physiological sensi-bilities, albeit modified according to early experience. Feelings about music, though, are the result of experiences with music. Adults can share their enjoy-ment of music with children at an appropriate level; adults can also turn chil-dren's experiences with music into disciplinary fiascos through inappropriate expectations and unappealing musical selections. All too often four- and five-year-olds, whose prime interest while in groups is in their peers, are put into a group situation and then are expected to ignore one another and attend only to uninspiring singing or listening activities. This is not the way to enhance affec-tive or social development, nor is it the way to encourage involvement with music. Voluntary participation in musical activities by individual children or small groups of children is far more likely to result in further interest in these activities than required, whole-group musical activities. Greenberg (1979) sug-gests how this is done:

> The preschool teacher notices the four-year-old playing "soldier" and beats the drum to accompany the child's marching footsteps. As children rhythmically pound the clay or Play Doh or build castles in the sandbox, the teacher picks up the beat or the move-ments on a drum or rhythm sticks and chants about what the children are doing. As a child moves on the seesaw or bounces a ball, the teacher rhythmically chants "up and down" or "high—low" to correspond with the child's movements. As a child plays with a doll, the teacher encourages him to make up a lullaby to put the doll to sleep. As the child becomes fascinated with the sound he hears when he knocks against the metal water pipe, the teacher encourages him to hit other objects and discover their sounds. And as a child watches the butterfly flit from flower to flower, the adult encourages him to move like a butterfly and sings as the child moves. The adult who capitalizes on these everyday situations will promote musical growth in the child in the most natural way possible.
>
> Your day-to-day, ongoing role in music instruction with the preschool child is pri-marily one of supporting, encouraging, and interacting with him. You can capitalize on the child's songful jabbering in the playground by joining in with him or by adding a drumbeat to the child's rhythm. You can encourage the child as he role plays the part of his older brother or a television star strumming the guitar. You can hear the child's chant or rhyme and repeat it for him and for other children. You can encourage the child to find different ways of playing the tambourine. Once a feeling of warmth and support permeates the relationship between you and the child, then the child will readily seek you and other adults to share his experiences.*

Only if the group music period can be kept from becoming an unpleasant dis-ciplinary situation should it happen at all. But let us assume the best and look at the practices that lead to a satisfying group music experience. Plenty of move-ment and action as well as brevity are recommended. Ten or fifteen minutes is quite long enough. Better for preschoolers to enjoy a very brief march to a seg-ment of "In the Hall of the Mountain King" and a lusty singing of one or two

---

*M. Greenberg (1979). *Your children need music.* Englewood Cliffs, NJ: Prentice-Hall, pp. 110–111.

Let's sing "If you're happy and you know it, touch your nose." *(Permission of Bernice Wright Cooperative Nursery School)*

songs than a stressful and dispirited session in which the teacher tries to cover content that a curriculum guide suggests is appropriate for the age. Some of the following scenes may suggest principles to follow in helping children grow in their appreciation of music and their abilities as musicians:

- Jimmy appeared at first not to become positively involved in any of the music activities presented in his Head Start program. He proved a real problem whenever there was group singing, whenever rhythm instruments were used, or movement activities encouraged. After his teacher visited Jimmy's home and saw blue grass and country records in evidence, she added to the classroom song repertoire more folk music, such as "Gray Goose," "Boll Weevil," "Clementine." Sometimes she played record selections featuring musicians like Mike Auldridge, Brother Oswald, Bob Brozman, and Tut Taylor. Jimmy began to participate in music when these artists were offered, and he gradually became involved in other musical activities as well. *Principle:* Include in the musical period music that is most familiar to children as well as additional new types of music for them to experience and become familiar with over a period of time.
- Although the children in the first grade participated with great joy in creating and performing their own musical compositions with rhythm instruments, the teacher found that any comment he made about the instruments heard on

records seemed to go over the heads of the children. There was no interest at all. It was only when an artists-in-residence program brought a series of artists (violinist, clarinetist, harpist) into the center to play for the children that the children responded with any degree of understanding to discussion such as, "That's the violin's voice. Now you will hear the cello saying the same thing. Here's the answer from the flutes." *Principle:* Provide live experiences of seeing as well as hearing music performed by accomplished musicians rather than relying totally on recorded works.

- Whenever the day-care teacher led her children in circle games such as "London Bridge," "The Mulberry Bush," "Looby Loo," troubles erupted. There were problems in forming the circle by joining hands and then, once in the circle, pulling seemed to be more interesting than moving around the circle to the music. The confusion was resolved by making a circle of approximately the right size with masking tape on the floor. Children were first asked to come to the circle. Only then were they asked to join hands. The game began immediately, without the period of inactivity while waiting for everyone to join a circle. Also, to draw the children back into singing instead of pulling on the circle, the teacher began to intersperse a singsong action chant between the regular verses:

Put your hands up high *(hands reach up)*
    Put your hands down low *(hands at sides)*
Now clap, clap, clap *(clap three times)*
    And here we go! *(rejoin hands in circle)*

Principle: Think of ways to gain and to keep the children's involvement; avoid making the children feel that they are "bad" for engaging in behaviors that are as legitimate for their age and stage as the ones you are trying to encourage.

- In the musical period, the nursery school teacher found that many children became restless. She found that their enthusiastic participation could be maintained for a longer period of time by singing songs that included use of their names or included some personal reference. She was able to regain the involvement of children who were beginning to become bored by singing the following sorts of songs: "Hey, Betty Martin" (sing child's name instead of Betty Martin); "Mary Has a Red Dress" (substitute names and descriptions—for example, Jose has a striped shirt); "Are You Sleeping" (substitute names and actions).

Are you singing? Are you singing?
    Freddy Jones? Freddy Jones?
Here we sing together. Here we sing together.
    Hear us sing. Hear us sing.

Principle: Adapt music to the interests and needs for personal recognition of your participants.

Provide the opportunity, and children will improvise with gusto. *(Ursula Moeller)*

Exposure to real musicians rather than to records is certainly an important way to involve children in more actively responding to the music they hear, but having children, especially in groups, attend adult concerts may prove difficult. Most concerts, even those intended for children, are beyond the level of most children aged three through five. Only the most good-natured and pliant of children will not repeatedly ask, "When will it be over?" or, worse yet, become disruptive. Dr. Eleanor Robinson, one of our valued colleagues, took a young friend, age five, to such a children's concert. In one of the less dramatic stretches of music, the child appeared to be tiring, and Dr. Robinson whispered, "The music will be livelier again soon." The child looked puzzled and whispered back, "How do you know? Have you been here before?" Without perspective on how musicians rather predictably use time and contrast to create their special effects, a child may fear that the segments they find less interesting will continue interminably. No wonder they sometimes find concerts tiring and abrasive.

Certainly adults can help to work the strangeness or unfamiliarity out of musical works through their explanations and carefully selected experiences. "If you listen now, you may hear something like the wind blowing very hard." "I've always liked the part where the instruments are all quiet except the bassoon. Doesn't it make an interesting sound?" "Listen to how the different instruments join in with that bmm . . . bmmm . . . bbbbmmmmmm." Out of such experiences comes an enjoyment of music that, once gained, is an enrichment in the child's life.

SOCIAL DEVELOPMENT AND MUSIC

To create music with others is a very social activity and one in which young children can often engage very successfully. Even small children can produce sounds in music with others that provide for a sense of sharing. Toddlers beating out a simple rhythm together on a table top are able to experience social cooperation in this activity, even though their lack of verbal skills and egocentrism prevent them from doing so in many other activities.

The songs children learn in preschools are common bonds that can be used for making social initiations. Starting to sing ". . . farmer had a dog, and Bingo was his name . . . B-I-N-G-O . . . " in many preschool groups is a sure-fire way to get others to join in. Knowing some of the standard childhood songs also gives children at ages three, four, and five a means for relating to older siblings and adults. "Let's sing `Jingle Bells' is a social initiation that will work in many situations. A child's discovery that older brothers and sisters, and even Mommy and Daddy, know a song he or she has just learned is very rewarding. There is good reason to include in your repertoire of children's songs some that will be familiar to the families of the children you teach.

As small groups of five-, six-, and seven-year-olds work together to create and then perform musical compositions, advanced social skills are developed. Musical performance requires cooperation and communication; the invention of new forms and their subsequent repetition require abilities to both lead and follow. Working together, without adult leadership for music or dramatic planning, facilitates the development of social skills. This kind of activity is valuable both for musical and social development.

Some adults who work with children are very conscious of the social implications in the lyrics of some of the songs that children sing. Others argue that children are not at all interested in the content of the words and are thus not adversely affected by any of the values that are conveyed. Examples of some of the kinds of songs that cause concern follow:

"One Little, Two Little, Three Little Indians"   The concern is that Native Americans are not objects to be counted as is implied in this song. Would we, for example, sing: "One little, two little, three little Englishmen"?

"The Rabbit in the Wood"   Although this song about a hunter "bopping" the bunny is greatly appealing to young children, some adults wonder if they want to encourage children to so relish this comic violence.

"Old Grey Mare"   Does this old favorite suggest that old is inferior?

As a teacher you will want to select songs to sing that are rhythmic and have an appealing melody. You may sometimes find that you will want to change lyrics for songs that seem to you to belittle particular groups of people or appear to support questionable values. Look for appealing tunes requiring tones around middle C (the range that is easiest for most young children) and then, if necessary, design your own lyrics for these selections.

COGNITIVE DEVELOPMENT AND MUSIC

The connections between music experience and cognitive or intellectual development are far from clear. There are those who believe that children involved in arts programs progress at a more rapid rate with reading and other academic skills than comparison groups without this kind of involvement. These proponents suggest that a multimodal approach, using sight, sound, and touch together, is more successful in reaching all learners than programs that use primarily verbal approaches to learning. According to the hemispheric (brain) theory, such a multimodal approach involves the brain hemispheres and thus increases the likelihood of retention and recall of that which is encountered in the learning situation. By increased usage of music or art expression within learning contexts, the speculation is that the learning will be both more complete for all learners and more effective for a greater number of learners than would verbal approaches used alone. It is expected that if all of the senses are involved in the learning activities, that which is learned will be more accessible for recall and more available for use in problem-solving situations.

Tunes children learn easily

"If You're Happy and You Know It"
"Kumbayah"
"Here We Go Round the Mulberry Bush"
    ("The Wheels on the Bus")
"Go Tell Aunt Rhodie"
"Are You Sleeping?" ("Frere Jacques"; "Where is
    Thumbkin?")
"Old MacDonald's Farm"
"Goodnight Irene"
"B-I-N-G-O"
"Did You Ever See a Lassie?"
"Go Round and Round the Village"
"London Bridge"
"The Hokey Pokey"

"Here We Go Looby-Loo"
"The Muffin Man"
"Michael Row the Boat Ashore"
"Shoo, Fly, Don't Bother Me"
"Bear Went Over the Mountain"
"Da-ye-nu"
"Hey, Betty Martin"
"She'll Be Comin' Round the Mountain"
"Skip to My Lou"
"This Old Man"
"Zum-Gali-Gali"
"Hush Little Baby"
"We Wish You a Merry Christmas"
"The More We Get Together"

Classical selections that appeal to children

"Peter and the Wolf" Prokofieff
"Sorcerer's Apprentice" Dukas
"Carnival of the Animals" Saint-Saens
"Danse Macabre" Saint-Saens

"The Sleeping Beauty" Tchaikovsky
"Til Eulenspiegel" Strauss
"The Firebird" Stravinsky

Beyond the possible general relationships between music and intellectual development or learning, there are other connections. Some have to do with the discriminations and classifications that are made in regard to music. As the child becomes familiar with and appreciative of musical compositions, discriminations are made between high and low (pitch); fast and slow (tempo); loud and soft (dynamics); long and short (duration); and source of tones (voices and types of instruments). The labeling and classification of sound stimuli occur through cognitive processes, as in other learning areas, and proceed from vague awareness of gross differences to more refined perceptions. For each type of musical experience offered, a more detailed awareness of the possibilities in that experience results. Some of the discoveries children may make about melody bells are suggested by Francis Webber Aronoff:

The Melody Bells

Each bell has a different sound
  low
  high
  somewhere in between

You can use more than one to go up and down
  making melody shapes
  in steps
  with wider spaces
                               but no sliding
The sounds are soft
              and they gently   fade   away

They ring
      they can't be jumpy

When you hit the metal with the mallet
  it starts to sound

You can stop the sound by touching the metal
                    but you don't want to

You can play two bells at the same time
  one mallet in each hand

Two or more people can play
  at the same time
  one after the other to make a melody*

There is yet another way in which resourceful teachers use children's involvement with music to lead toward accomplishment in other areas of learning. As discussed in Chapter 16 lyrics for children's favorite songs are often recorded on charts. Since lines and rhyming words are frequently repeated, there is good

---

*From Francis Webber Aronoff, *Music and Young Children,* expanded ed. (New York: Turning Wheel Press, 1979), p. 47. Reprinted by permission.

opportunity for learning about the manner in which print and speech are related. The young child learns something of the left-to-right progression of writing and reading as the teacher swings his or her hands under the lines while they are being sung. Children also have the opportunity to note how words look the same, how rhyming words start differently but have similar endings, and so forth. For some children, this can be a major learning-to-read experience, especially if the words are available in a picture book and sung on a record or tape with sound signals for when to turn the pages. Since they can be used independently, these materials will be used again and again by children with increasing awareness of how the words on the page are matching the words sung on the record. For a number of children, hearing and singing the words they see in print can provide a pleasant and successful introduction to initial reading.

A brief commentary about the origins of the music is appropriate when you introduce children to songs and other musical compositions, particularly lullabies, sea chanteys, work songs, cowboy songs, ethnic and folk music. They can learn that music and lyrics are someone's invention—that people like us have contributed all the songs and music we hear about us. Children can also learn that some of our songs were made up so long ago that everyone has forgotten who actually did them first. And, of particular importance, they can learn that the people who have sung the songs have often changed them also. The message you will want to communicate is that they, too, can make up tunes and lyrics or make changes in old songs to make them more to their liking. Even awkward wordings requested by children can be put into a favorite song. It makes no difference if you have to sing very fast to fit in "Shoo, big fat elephant, don't bother me. . . ." Children's ideas, not the songs' traditional word patterns, have the priority.

Children like their involvement in music to be active, and as they experiment with the production of sound, they gain the experiences that lead to cause-and-effect inferences. Children's strumming, drumming, blowing, and bowing with a variety of sizes and arrangements of materials result in awareness of how to systematically produce different effects. These insights will serve them well in turning their noise into music.

FURTHER EXTENSIONS

Eclectic practice in music education is prevalent, but as an early childhood educator you will want to become familiar with several of the distinctive approaches currently used with young children. One approach was developed by Hungarian educator Zoltan Kodaly. The Kodaly method has as primary goals the reading and writing of musical notation. The sequenced progression begins with two-syllable "teasing" chants and builds to the use of simple folk songs. The tone direction is emphasized, and children are taught to match the progression they hear with body and then with hand movements. The progressions are then represented visually. The Hungarian folk songs used by Kodaly have been replaced by American folk songs in an American adaptation of the program.

A second method, the Orff method, was designed by German music educator Carl Orff. It combines movement and speech with the use of special instruments (xylophones, metallaphones, and glockenspiels with removable tone bars). Only five steps of the diatonic range are used; the fourth step *(fa)* and seventh step *(ti)* are deleted. The tones produced are those obtained by playing only black keys on a piano. Creative improvisation is particularly emphasized in the Orff approach.

Schinick Suzuki of Japan developed the Suzuki method, in which parents as well as children are involved in the music education process. Parents first receive several months of instruction. The parent learns to model for the child the playing of simple compositions on the violin or piano. The child is encouraged, primarily by the parent, to imitate what is heard on a piano or miniature violin. The process is basically one of rote learning and imitation. Festivals in which children have the opportunity to perform for an audience are an important aspect of the method.

Each of these three methods is quite distinctive, but all have in common the active participation of the child. Further references to these and other music curricula are included in the Additional Readings at the end of the chapter. Although nonspecialists in music education need not be concerned with a careful analysis of these methods, it may be useful to note that in each approach children are given a means of engaging themselves pleasurably and successfully in musical activity. As a teacher of young children, you will do well to provide such experiences by building your own repertoire of activities that will have such an effect.

SUMMARY

Most children have ample experiences in hearing music sounds. What they need, however, are activities to help them become more consciously aware of salient dimensions in music—rhythm, tone, pitch, and intensity. Teachers of young children can develop this awareness through singing activities, listening activities, movement activities, and opportunities they provide for children to create music.

With experience and maturation, children become increasingly able to coordinate their movements with music and to respond to a greater range of musical variation. If they find early experiences pleasant and satisfying, they will develop a taste for music that will last beyond childhood. The experience of seeing adult artists producing music will be beneficial if the exposures are brief and informal. Cooperating with others in producing dances, singing, or instrumental music can be aesthetically pleasing, and can have positive affective and social benefits as well. The coordination of music and other arts with verbal learning tasks is thought to be beneficial in reaching some learners who fail to learn through verbal presentations, with the result that more lasting learning is achieved in all areas.

SUGGESTED ACTIVITIES

1 Visit several early childhood classrooms and analyze the setups for music activities, noting the following:

    a What types of music activities are initiated by the teachers? By the children?

    b In what situations are music activities initiated? During which time periods?

    c How are materials and accessories for music involvement stored?

    d How do different children react to opportunities for involvement with music activities?

    e What differences in children's repertoires for music involvement are evidenced?

    f How long do children remain involved with music activities of various types—singing, playing instruments, listening to records?

    g What kinds of interactions do different types of music involvement engender between children?

2 Compile a list of simple and appealing songs that you can sing with children, making sure you know all the words, and of the recordings of rhythmic music you can provide for listening, movement, and other musical experiences.

3 Compile a list of the various music activities, other than singing, that you can provide for children that make use of simple and inexpensive materials.

4 Experiment with musical or rhythm instruments in ways in which a child might do so, to understand the various discoveries a child might make.

5 Create new words to familiar tunes that fit particular occasions you have observed in classrooms. Consider the value of this ability for a teacher.

ADDITIONAL READINGS

Andress, B. (1980). *Music experiences in early childhood.* New York: Holt, Rinehart & Winston.

Andress, B. (1991). From research to practice: Preschool children and their movement responses to music. *Young Children, 47*(1), 22–27.

Bayless, K. M., & Ramsey, M. E. (1978). *Music: A way of life for the young child.* St. Louis, MO: Mosby.

Benzwie, T. (1987). *A moving experience: Dance for lovers of children and the child within.* Tucson, AZ: Zephyr Press.

Bradford, L. L. (1978). *Sing it yourself: 220 pentatonic folk songs.* Sherman Oaks, CA: Alfred.

Choksy, L. (1974). *The Kodaly method.* Englewood Cliffs, NJ: Prentice-Hall.

Glazer, T. (1973). *Eye winker, tom tinker, chin chopper: Fifty musical fingerplays.* New York: Doubleday.

Glazer, T. (1980). *Do your ears hang low? Fifty more musical fingerplays.* New York: Doubleday.

McDonald, D. T. (1979). *Music in our lives.* Washington, DC: National Association for the Education of Young Children.

CHAPTER 21

SHARING

OVERVIEW

There are both informal and formal ways of promoting children's sharing. **Informal sharing** is talking that occurs in an unstructured situation. For younger children, informal sharing in which they initiate talk about themselves or show off their possessions and creations should predominate. To promote this kind of sharing, there must be many opportunities for spontaneous exchanges among children and between children and adults.

Whereas the greatest benefits for young children are typically derived from informal sharing, from the ages of four through seven children also become increasingly capable of engaging in **formal sharing,** which refers to those situations especially structured by the teacher for interchanges within a group.

The most common type of formal sharing is sometimes referred to as *show and tell.* Children take turns talking about anything they wish, whether or not it is related to what others have said. These sessions are usually a potpourri of topics, objects, and experiences. They are also referred to in some situations as sharing time, news time, talking time, or circle time.

A second type of formal sharing revolves around the accomplishments of the school day. Between ages five and seven, many children begin to appreciate the end products of their creative efforts, rather than the mere physical manipulation of materials, and at this stage they are encouraged in further efforts if they have frequent opportunities to share what they have produced. At the end of a work session or a program day, they may be given the opportunity to hold up or talk about things such as paintings, constructions, inventions, written stories, books they have read, or problems they have resolved.

A third type of formal sharing involves group planning or group problem solving. Individuals are invited to share the ideas they have about a particular topic. In group planning, children are told of an upcoming situation, such as a trip to an apple orchard to pick apples, and are then invited to contribute their ideas about what could be seen, investigated, and learned there, and about what preparations should be made. This kind of discussion is initiated and led by the teacher but can be quite open-ended in allowing children's expressions of concerns, questions, and thoughts about the subject in focus.

Group consideration of a problem, in which individuals are invited to share their ideas for resolution, can be initiated and conducted by either the teacher or a concerned child. A child who is personally confronted by a problem situation may request that others join in and give their views of the situation. The child, rather than the teacher, can then recognize speakers and manage others' participation. Initiative of this sort, of course, usually requires prior experience in sharing situations in which adults or older children have demonstrated these procedures. Examples of the problems that young children may wish to discuss with their peers are disruptive incidents on the playground or during work periods, damage to possessions, unfairness, and invasions of privacy. These sessions do not usually resolve the immediate concern of the child, but if such sessions occur consistently over a period of time, a greater sensitivity to the needs and feelings of others evolves and fewer such incidents arise. The discussion process itself usually seems to satisfy the offended or concerned child.

As a teacher, you should know how to provide the settings within which children can develop an ability to both informally and formally share their ideas,

---

SETUPS FOR SHARING

INFORMAL SHARING

Basic Arrangements

- As children arrive from home, be available to them at or near the entrance to the classroom or center. You can simultaneously assist with wraps and listen to them as they make the transition from home and neighborhood to school. This, of course, requires that all advance preparations for the school day be completed before the children's arrival.
- Intermingle with the children during indoor activities and outdoor play so that you can be the recipient of their sharing. Circulate in much the same manner as a host or hostess at a social function.
- Try to be available to children as they complete their activities and share with them their final enjoyment of the process or the product. Be ready to label objects they have made with their names and a caption or a full description.
- Arrange display spaces within the classroom—a bulletin board, open table space, or open shelf space. These will accommodate a random assortment of

items rather than a coordinated or thematic display. For younger children, display items can simply be labeled with their names. As children mature in their awareness of written communication, the amount of labeling will increase. Displays will change frequently, even daily, as a reflection of children's shifting interests.

- To facilitate the transformation from oral to written sharing, have on hand felt pens, crayons, newsprint sheets, file cards, strips of paper, and stand-up display cards (fold 5″ × 8″ file cards in half). You may wish to prepare a special container with these raw materials so that they can be kept close at hand. Some teachers keep these supplies and others (such as scissors, tape, safety pins, paper clips, stapler, and Band-Aids) in a "teacher basket" that can be carried from place to place in the program setting (even outdoors).

General Guidelines

- You can encourage children to share by staying at their eye level at least part of the time, kneeling or sitting rather than standing above them. Establish eye contact and signal with a smile your willingness to listen.
- Learn to decipher children's nonverbal body language (their bearing, expressions, and gestures). For example, note the way a child bounces newly styled hair or carefully wipes off new shoes. Note looks of dejection or pride. Verbal expression is only one of many ways young children communicate about themselves.
- Note any objects children are carrying. Anything valuable enough to children to be transported from home to school or from one location to another within the classroom is likely to have some personal significance.
- Avoid being monopolized by children who want to share constantly. Make sure that you give roughly equal attention to all children during the course of a week, if not daily.

Alternatives

- When you cannot be personally available to children, arrange for another adult or for more mature children to assume your role. Their effectiveness will depend in large measure on your ability to communicate what is expected of them.

FORMAL SHARING

Basic Arrangement

- Some teachers prefer to have children sit on chairs during group discussions. They feel there is less confusion once the chairs are placed. It is more difficult to move about in a chair, they point out, and thereby to divert attention away from the speaker. Other teachers prefer having children sit on the floor, which eliminates the need for transporting and arranging chairs as well as the temptation to tilt them precariously on two legs. Still others prefer to use seating mats that identify each child's spot, which also eliminates the problem of transporting and arranging chairs.

- Most teachers find that a circular arrangement promotes attentive listening better than either rows or random groupings. Masking tape is often used to indicate the circle size and to help children arrange themselves for group discussions.

Preferred Location

- It is important that the discussion circle not crowd the children. Any large open space, such as the block or reading area, can be converted into a discussion area. Ideally, the space should be separated from the room entrance and from other activity areas that might be used simultaneously.
- A chalkboard or an easel stocked with chart paper and felt pens can be used to record the sharing experiences. The extent of this recording will vary with the maturity of the children.

General Guidelines

- Transitions from informal to formal sharing are best made very gradually, beginning with very short periods and limited expectations for order and formality. These transitions are most easily accomplished when younger children can simply join or observe older peers who have already learned to share their ideas in an orderly manner. Taking turns, listening to others, and questioning or commenting on others' ideas are more easily learned through observation and imitation than through verbal instructions.
- If older children are not available to model formal group discussion, then it becomes your job to make the transitions as painless and productive as possible. Initially, you might ask for volunteers to join you in a "talking time" (or whatever label you want to use). You will need to repeatedly model the appropriate behaviors and procedures. Try to do this with your most dramatic flair! Demonstrate how to sit or stand while listening or talking, how to talk in bold tones to make sure everyone hears, how to listen to, and later to question the speakers, and how to signal readiness to talk. Make your points clearly, dramatically, and definitively.
- Your guidelines for group discussion should emphasize what to do rather than what not to do. There must be fun, ceremony, pride, and recognition. If the sharing becomes a time of prohibition, of child-misconduct and teacher scolding, it will take a great deal of effort to rebuild a positive atmosphere. Careful attention to keeping the sharing periods brief, lively, and pleasurable will do much toward making it a time for real communication.
- Emphasize all positive behaviors and good efforts while ignoring less desirable behaviors. In the long run, you will find that the praising of specific desirable behaviors is more effective than general instructions or the correcting of inappropriate behavior. Praise the child who is attending to the speaker; ignore the child who is clowning while another speaks. Comment on the child who speaks in audible, well-modulated tones; pass over your concerns for the child who speaks too loudly. In other words, praise and reward all those who model the

kind of communication you desire in the group-sharing situation, and avoid attending to those who do not. When you find that you must attend to a disruptive or inappropriate behavior, do it swiftly and briefly, and then continue on without further delay.

- Clarification of the following procedural concerns may be especially helpful to children just learning to participate in group discussions. Although the adoption of one procedure over another is strictly arbitrary, having an initial set of procedures provides security for the novice. Modifications can easily be made as children mature. Rigid adherence to a set of procedures is of course inadvisable and might discourage communication rather than enhance it. For young children, though, the ceremony of sharing is half the fun and will typically encourage participation rather than discourage it.

experiences, and concerns. You will also need to learn how these sharing activities can be used to satisfy a variety of developmental needs.

MOTOR DEVELOPMENT AND SHARING

Topics such as becoming half as tall as Mother, losing a tooth, learning to swim, learning to ride a two-wheeler, jumping off a fence "as tall as me," and outgrowing last year's snowsuit are typical sharing fare. These topics reflect children's keen awareness of their physical and motor development.

The resourceful teacher can use children's reports of physical feats as a springboard for involvement with motor activities. Given a bit of encouragement and direction, the child who is showing or telling about something can also act out what he or she did, saw, or created. Young listeners are also able to relate better to what they have heard if it is accompanied by motoric expression. The following are examples of how teachers encourage motor participation in regard to sharing activities:

- When Julie reported that she had gone to a local amusement park, she was encouraged to enact as well as describe the things she saw there: the "dodgem" cars that twirled and careened as they narrowly missed or bumped into each other, the undulating animals on the merry-go-round, and so on.
- Stevie told about his birthday party and about the games and presents there. He was invited to demonstrate as well as tell about how the biggest balloon expanded and expanded and then *popped!* All the listeners enjoyed joining him in the Hokey-Pokey when he mentioned it as one of the activities.
- As Jimmy arrived at school he described to the teacher the TV show he watched the previous day. He was asked to demonstrate how the cowboys stopped the oncoming train to save it from derailment and then how they captured the "bad guys" without firing a shot. As others gathered around to see, he pretended to climb a pole holding a jacket in his teeth and then waved it vigorously. As he described the capturing of the bandits, everyone

became involved in crawling, hiding, rolling, dodging, feigning, hitting, and being hit.

AFFECTIVE DEVELOPMENT AND SHARING

Many teachers feel that by sharing important thoughts and experiences children develop positive feelings about themselves that significantly influence other aspects of their physical, social, and cognitive development. When you observe children who seem to be lacking in independence, initiative, and persistence, note whether they also appear to lack awareness of themselves as individuals who have distinct characteristics. Considerable self-awareness is usually necessary to support a healthy sense of autonomy. For those children who do not seem to have developed such self-awareness, you might wish to use both informal and formal sharing situations to increase their acceptance of themselves. Most children in the preschool and early school years are already developing a healthy self-awareness, but some may benefit from your assistance in these areas. If so, the following types of activities may prove useful.

- Help children develop book, picture, or object collections that contain items of personal significance. Label these with their names and help them share the collections with others. A book might include such items as photographs of themselves, their families, and pets or pictures selected from magazines. It is

"Bet you didn't see a snake. What did it do? Show us if you can." *(Ursula Moeller)*

important that they have something concrete to share (easier than verbal sharing) that they identify as very personally theirs.

- Note the new skills children develop, which they may not have considered sharing with others, and suggest that they do so. You might say, "Susan, I was wondering if you might want to show everyone how you have learned to skip." Emphasize that what is important is the newness of the experience for that particular child, whether or not it has been mastered by others.
- Point out to others things about a child of which he or she may have only a dim awareness. For example, "Have you noticed what a good friend Tim is? He ___," or "Have you noticed how carefully Susan holds the bunny?"
- Have smiling, sad, and mad faces prepared and attached magnetically to a metal chalkboard (or with Velcro to a felt board) and ask a child undergoing an obvious emotion whether any one of these faces shows how he or she feels. Encourage children to tell how they feel, that is, to "own" their own feelings.
- When you note that a child has distinctive clothes, looks particularly well groomed, or has a special possession, creation, or a newly acquired skill, encourage self-observation in front of a full-length mirror. Such visual awareness can lead to heightened self-awareness.

Children with developmental retardation or physical disabilities may need the encouragement of teachers in order to share their feelings and experiences. Children who feel themselves to be different from others may equate their differences with inadequacy and consequently may avoid attention. When this appears to be the case, intercede very directly to make sure that each child does have a successful sharing experience. Sometimes this requires close cooperation between home and school. Parents might be asked about important events that a child could be led to talk about with you or the classroom group. Personal day-to-day observation of a child's behavior is another way of identifying special characteristics that might be shared with others.

Keep in mind that each of us has unique traits and abilities and that sharing these with others usually enhances our own appreciation of them. Children who lack the confidence to talk about themselves or who fail to recognize what about themselves is worthy of sharing will benefit from your tactful acknowledgment and publicizing of their special characteristics. By first soliciting and accepting the feelings, concerns, and experiences of insecure children in one-to-one discussions, you can gradually lead them to further self-disclosure and eventually to group sharing.

SOCIAL DEVELOPMENT AND SHARING

Until children have reached the stage of voluntarily entering into sustained cooperative play with other children, it is unlikely that they will participate with any competence in formal group discussions. Prior to this point, informal sharing strategies are generally preferable, although some children may feel comfortable in group discussions if their roles involve listening but no active participation.

Conversely, some young children who find cooperative play very enjoyable may be quite uncomfortable with the restrictions imposed by formal group discussion. As suggested previously, unpleasant group experiences will contribute nothing of value to children's development and can even delay the willing acceptance of group discussion activities.

However, once children have successfully participated in group sharing situations of the show-and-tell variety, they are also usually ready to participate in group planning or problem-solving discussions. The following examples illustrate likely themes for such discussions:

- After recess, Lynn and Janey ask for a group discussion to talk about a problem. Lynn announces to all those who come to listen that she and Janey do not like the way some big kids are teasing little kids. The teacher interjects, "Do you want us to help you think what you could do when you see something like that happening?" The girls indicate that that is what they want, and Lynn calls on children who have suggestions. The ideas offered include:

On returning to the classroom, this small group will be invited to tell other children and adults about the road construction they observed. *(Cumberland Hill Associates, Inc.)*

You could go over to the mean kids and say, "Pick on someone your own size!"

You could tell the mean kids' mothers.

You could be especially nice to the little kids yourself.

You could tell the mean kids' teacher.

You could tell the little kids that if they don't pay any attention, the mean kids will probably get bored and stop.

- Mr. Whitney calls the children to the circle and says, "Some of the sixth-graders have discovered a nest of baby garter snakes on the playground. They want to show them to you, but they want to be sure that you know how to catch and hold snakes without hurting them. What do you think we should do?" Answers include the following:

I don't want to catch no snakes anyway.

Maybe they could show us.

I know how. You cup your hands like this and don't squeeze.

Only people who knows how should catch them.

- Miss Jones uses her special piano chord signal to call the children to the circle for discussion. Some continue to work quietly at their previous activities, an option that has been established in this classroom. She addresses those who gather around her. "I wanted to talk with you because we have a problem. Miss Peters just told me that some of her children had to stop their work when we went out to the playground today because we were so noisy. What do you think we could do to help us remember to go out more quietly?" The children's ideas flow freely as she calls on the many who indicate they want to talk. They have the following ideas:

We could put a sign outside our door that says *Be Quiet.*

You could always remind us just before we go out the door.

We could have someone whose job it is to stand by the door and say *shh* to everyone.

These kinds of sharing sessions, focusing around topics of genuine concern, contribute substantially to children's social development. The rapidity with which children become sophisticated in these kinds of group discussions sometimes surprises their teachers. For example, by age seven or so, children can often carry on a coordinated discourse without adult intervention. Their commentary reflects their understanding of each others' comments; for example, they might say, "The problem with Tod's idea about ___is that ___might ___"; or "I agree with you, Jay, but I think a better way might be to ___"; or "I disagree with what Chris said because I'm afraid that what would happen is ___"; or "Would you tell me your idea again, Rob? I didn't understand what you meant when you said ___." Children's abilities to interact usually depend on their having had ample opportunity to hear their teachers or older children engage in such discussions. In terms of developmental benefits, these discussions not only increase awareness of alternatives for social problem solving but build discussion skills as well.

COGNITIVE DEVELOPMENT AND SHARING

There are many opportunities to use the content of children's show-and-tell sessions to develop skills, concepts, and knowledge. A resourceful teacher can see abundant learning possibilities in almost any object or event. The trick is to select from among the many possibilities those that are particularly appropriate for a given child or group. This is sometimes called incidental teaching, since the teacher does not know in advance precisely what will be emphasized. There is nothing incidental, however, about the teacher's constant watching for situations or incidents that can be used to introduce or reinforce appropriate learnings.

Classification, Seriation, and Number

Very often the collections of things that children bring to school for sharing lend themselves quite naturally to classification, seriation, and counting activities. Among these are such items as shells, buttons, leaves, nuts, cones, pebbles, flowers, picture collections, baseball cards, playing cards, marbles, bottle caps, feathers, seeds, and seed pods.

Children also can be led to classify the object they show with other similar objects already present. For young children, such classification might be limited to aspects of color, size, and shape. For older children, more advanced classification criteria, such as the function or derivation of objects, might be used. The following are examples of ways an alert teacher might use a shared object to trigger involvement in classification.

- **Felt pen** What else in our room can we use to write with?
- **Clay bowl** What else do you see that might be used to hold water like this bowl?
- **Plastic raincoat** Do you see some other people who are wearing something made of plastic today?
- **Transparent sheet of acetate** Do you see anything else in this room that is transparent, that we can see right through?
- **Miniature horse** Did you know that the word *miniature* means something that is made smaller than it would naturally be? What else is there around here that is miniature?

The opportunities to focus on numbers are particularly plentiful during sharing sessions. The following are only some of the many possibilities.

- **Clothing** How many buttons? How many of each kind of button? How many pockets? How many pockets in both shirt and pants? How many of each kind of decorative item (flowers, birds, loops, and so on)?

- **Birthdays**   How old were you last year? How old next year? How many candles are on the cake? How much older are you than your brothers and sisters? How much younger? How many years until you are eight?
- **Trips**   How many went? How many were in the seat where you sat? In other seats? How many stops did the bus make?

A teacher should be resourceful enough to see that there may be other more interesting and productive possibilities, or children may be too often asked, "How many?" in regard to the things they share.

Causality

Sometimes sharing sessions can be used to encourage children to make careful observations and to speculate about causality in a rudimentary way. If you wonder aloud about phenomena, as in the following examples, children may take the cue and become wonderers also:

- **Icicle**   Where did it come from? What causes it? What happens to it in the classroom?
- **Pussy willows**   What will happen if we just put them in a vase without water? With water?
- **Toy cars**   Why will some cars roll such a long way while others stop so soon?
- **Rock**   That rock looks very heavy. I wonder which weighs more, the rock or one of our large blocks?

Space Concepts

When children talk about places they have been, you may be able to improve their typically fuzzy grasp of distance and location. They may speak easily of going to California, visiting Grandmother in the adjacent city, going across the ocean, or getting a present from Africa without any idea of the relative distances or the directions involved. They may know that Japan is far away, but have no idea whether it is a country, an ocean, a state, or a city. All these things are, of course, learned very gradually, those that have the greatest personal significance serving as a reference point for later learning.

For this reason, children's sharing activities provide an excellent basis for developing such understandings. The state and city where the child's grandmother lives will likely be learned first and will serve as a good example for further comparisons. Similarly, a TV show that children report on is a better reference point for understanding geographical relationships than something they do not identify with. The following types of comments and questions may help children clarify terms and concepts:

- Do you know what street your new friend lives on? What is your street? There are lots of streets in our city. Does your friend live on your street or on a different one?

- Were you farther from home when you went to Cleveland to visit your aunt or when you went to Florida at vacation time? Let's look at our big globe and see if we can find Cleveland, Ohio, and Orlando, Florida.
- How many days will it take you to drive to Texas? Texas is a big state. Do you know what city or town in Texas you are going to? What city do we live in? What state is our city in?

Time Concepts

As children talk about their experiences, teachers can help them clarify the time frame within which the events took place. Children's talk is full of *and then's*. A teacher can gently inquire whether events happened this morning, yesterday, the day before yesterday, last week, last year, or a long time ago; and whether anticipated events will be in a few minutes, today, tomorrow, the day after tomorrow, next week, next month, or next year. Even when children do not know the answer, they can become aware that there is terminology related to time that can be learned and used to good advantage.

Recording shared events on a calendar can also be helpful in developing a time sense. Upcoming birthdays and holidays can be anticipated as the number of days to the event are marked off. The dates of plantings and record of growth can be recorded for children who share their experiments with gardening. Children's reports of seasonal events can be recorded on a calendar until it is obvious that the season has fully arrived. For example, as spring approaches, the flowers, returning birds, people in summer clothing, kites, bees, and swimming can all be recorded as "firsts" of the new season.

Spoken Language

Many children still in the egocentric stage are unable to share experiences in a way that their listeners can understand. Trying to tell a group of peers about incidents such as "flying a kite with Daddy yesterday" so that they appreciate the event is a language task of the highest magnitude. Without teacher assistance, trying to share such experiences may be too frustrating for many children. Consequently, a resourceful teacher will try to capture the child's imagery and, through questions such as the following, will supply some of the words and concepts the child is struggling for:

Was the wind blowing very much?
How big was the kite? As tall as you? Could you reach across it?
Did it have a tail?
Was it shaped like this (drawing on chalkboard), or was it different?
How did your daddy get it started?
Was it difficult to hang on to the string? What would have happened if you let go?
Did it go as high as the door? As high as this room? As high as this building? As high as birds fly? As high as airplanes go?

Did it hold still, or did it move about?
What else was happening at the park while you were there?

Teachers are in a far better position to assist children in sharing out-of-school happenings if they are familiar with the child's family, home, and neighborhood. The more a child's socioeconomic, cultural, or ethnic background differs from that of the teacher, the more important it is that the teacher make a special effort to become familiar with what the child is likely to talk about. Knowing such things as what the family members are called, the ages of siblings, who the prominent neighborhood adults are, and what holidays are celebrated, all aid in understanding a child who is struggling to relate some personal experience.

This kind of knowledge helps a teacher become engaged in productive listening-questioning patterns. In describing a study conducted in the British infant schools, R. M. Brandt points out the predominance of these patterns of behavior in the exemplary teaching he observed and elaborates as follows:

> Often this took the form of a child's showing his teacher something he was working on; asking for assistance, information, or permission; or telling about an experience he had. Although the teacher occasionally provided information, reaction, or direction, more often her response consisted of raising questions designed to draw the child out further with respect to his feelings, plans, or experiences. Hughes (1959) maintains that such eliciting of additional thinking in response to students' bringing up potential instructional content represents the essence of good teaching. In the classrooms she studied, however, she found it occurred infrequently and accounted for less than 20 percent of most teachers' behavior.
>
> Because of the greater evidence for this type of behavior in the British infant school, it seemed important to study the specific types of questions teachers raised. I made a tape recording, therefore, of a "show-and-tell" class discussion that teacher A conducted one Monday morning. Although weekend experiences constituted a major portion of the discussion, children were permitted to bring up anything that seemed important to them. Opening questions such as "Who has something he wants to tell us?" encouraged them to talk. The teacher would ask the child responding a number of questions about the experience until a rather full elaboration of its details was forthcoming. Typically, this listening and questioning on the teacher's part took the form of an open dialogue between child and teacher; other children were permitted to ask questions, furnish additional details (if they had been involved also), and make related comments only after the responding child seemed to have completed his story. The teacher would often hush another child momentarily with such remarks as "We are listening to John now; your turn will come." At other times she would purposefully bring other children into the discussion by asking such questions as "Who else has been to see the Cutty Sark?" (i.e., the item being described). This particular morning the show-and-tell period was kept going for over an hour, until almost all forty children had shared one or more experiences and until obvious restlessness appeared.*

While a show-and-tell session of this length is very unusual with young children, even for this British teacher, the interest of children in listening to

---

*From R. M. Brandt, "Observational Portrait of a British Infant School," in B. Spodek & H. J. Walberg (Eds.), *Studies in Open Education* (New York: Agathon Press, 1975), pp. 111–112.

others can often be extended by skillful adult interjections and enthusiastic responses.

When a child is attempting to share an experience with you or with peers, this is obviously not the time for training in pronunciation or grammar. As a teacher, you may wish to echo back the child's message in clearer speech or better language, but you should not break the sharing mood by pointing out incorrect usage.

Written Language

There are many ways to encourage children's interest in writing down what they have told about. As you greet children upon their arrival at school, you will find opportunities for recording what they say to you. For example, a chart can be used to record whatever news children informally share as they arrive at school.

Later, the chart can be read to the entire class, or it might be posted in a prominent spot where visitors could read and enjoy its messages throughout the

"What we talk about, we also can write about." *(Cumberland Hill Associates)*

day. At the end of the day, such a chart can be cut into individual strips so that interested children can take their news home to show their families.

During group sharing times, you may occasionally wish to prepare such a news chart while the children are talking and then conclude the session by reading the things you have heard them say or by letting them read their own messages, if they can. For variation, the news can be written on a master sheet and duplicated so that each child has a copy. Or, instead of making a compilation of news items on a chart or master sheet, you may wish to make individual stand-up signs to be placed on the display table.

Teachers can also write down children's descriptions of paintings, drawings and constructions. Children often enjoy talking about their creations, and these descriptions can either be written as they are dictated or, at a later stage, written by the children with whatever adult help is necessary. This writing can take the form of brief labels, longer captions, stories, or even a book text (to accompany a series of paintings, illustrations, or other products).

What children write (by themselves or via dictation to an adult) can be available for later sharing periods at school or to take home. Such writings often culminate children's productive effort and for some may even serve as the major vehicle for learning the mechanics of writing and reading.

In addition to recording what children say as they arrive at school, a resourceful teacher will look for interesting labels and directions on the objects that are brought to share. Depending on the maturity of a particular child or group of children, they may become interested in titles of books, prominent phrases (*Made in USA; Caution; Open Here*), or directional signs (*On; Off; Stay Off the Grass*). Children will become increasingly print conscious as they see written language attached to their personal possessions.

FURTHER EXTENSIONS

Sharing will increase your familiarity with children. Only when you know what children have previously experienced are you in a position to help them associate that experience with new concepts.

For example, while reading a story about a woodcutter who lived deep in the forest, a child might ask you, "What's a forest?" You can, of course, answer very generally, "It's a place where there are lots of trees growing. A forest is also called a *woods*." If, however, the child is unable to grasp your meaning, you can try to supply concrete examples derived from sharing, as follows: "Remember where your family went for a picnic last week? All around the fields where the picnic tables are there are lots of trees and trails you can follow through the trees. The place where the trees are is called a *forest*." For another child, you might refer to the place where he and his aunt went to get a Christmas tree, and, for another, her experience of being in the woods while on a snowmobile ride. Different children have different associations. Being able to establish personal associations as a result of listening to children share their experiences can greatly improve your teaching effectiveness.

You will also find that you can better predict which pictures, games, and activities will be of interest to particular children through knowledge gained during their sharing activities. One teacher, for example, when selecting books from the public library to supplement a meager classroom collection, tries to make many special selections to fit children's recent significant experiences. She might choose Robert McCloskey's *Make Way for Ducklings* (New York: Viking, 1941) for a child who went to the park to feed the ducks, or Taro Yashima's *Umbrella* (New York: Viking, 1958) for a child with a new umbrella.

SUMMARY

There are both informal and formal means for promoting children's sharing. Informal sharing is more appropriate and beneficial for young children. From ages four through seven, however, many children become increasingly able to engage in formal group sharing activities.

If you are resourceful, you can find many ways to use children's sharing as a stimulus for activities to enhance learning and development. Physical growth and accomplishments are common sharing fare, and just as children enjoy telling of their feats and activities, they also enjoy conveying their own and others' news items in movements.

Through sharing, children can be helped to develop a healthy sense of identity; a few may need assistance from teachers in determining what about themselves is worthy of sharing. The sharing of ideas about group problems can contribute to an increased awareness of others' perspectives and of alternative ways of behaving in social situations.

The varieties of objects children bring to share and the experiences they describe can be used very effectively to develop skills, concepts, and knowledge. The teacher must have the ability to elicit additional thinking in response to the child's sharing. Language experience approaches to reading and writing are based, to a considerable extent, on what children share, both formally and informally.

From sharing comes much information about children that you as a teacher can use to good advantage in providing matches to promote their learning.

SUGGESTED ACTIVITIES

1 Visit several classrooms and note any evidence in each environment that individual children's unique expression or experiences are valued. Compile a list of the various ways in which teachers facilitate children's sharing through classroom displays or arrangements.
2 Visit several different classrooms with children of various age levels while formal sharing sessions are occurring, noting the following:
   a Where does formal sharing occur in relation to classroom activity areas?
   b What kind of floor coverings or seating arrangements are used?
   c How is sharing elicited?
   d How do teachers position themselves in relation to the children?

e What do teachers say and do in response to children's sharing?

f What communication and management techniques are used by teachers?

g How are objects and possessions displayed and stored prior to, during, and after a child's use of them during sharing?

h How do different children react to the same sharing milieu? What differences in action and language repertoire are evidenced?

i What kinds of interactions do the sharing events engender among children?

j How long do formal sharing sessions last?

ADDITIONAL READINGS

Adams, A. (1984). Talking and learning in the classroom. *Language Arts, 61,* 119–124.

Berry, K. S. (1985). Talking to learn subject matter/Learning subject matter talk. *Language Arts, 62,* 34–42.

Bohning, G. (1981). Show-and-tell: Assessing oral language abilities. *Reading Horizons, 22,* 43–48.

Cazden, C. B. (1985). Research currents: What is sharing time for? *Language Arts 62,* 182–187.

Hubbard, R. (1985). Write-and-tell. *Language Arts, 62*(6), 624–630.

Moffett, J., & Wagner, B. J. (1976). *Student-centered language arts and reading: A handbook for teachers* (2nd ed.). Boston: Houghton Mifflin.

Oken-Wright, P. (1988). Show-and-tell grows up. *Young Children, 43*(20), 52–57,

Plourde, L. (1989). Teaching with collections. *Young Children, 44*(3), 78–80.

PART FIVE

ISSUES AND PERSPECTIVES

As we pointed out in Chapters 2 and 10, the field of early childhood education has been strongly influenced by conflicting ideas and movements, many of which offer very different perspectives on basic issues concerning human growth and learning. It is therefore not at all surprising that as part of our heritage, we still have contrasting and conflicting views on such issues as the following: What is the responsibilty of society for the health and welfare of families with young children? What is the responsibility of the family, and what is the responsibility of programs and teachers in caring for and teaching children? Who is accountable and for what? What is a good school? How do we know whether a school is good for a child? Who should decide and on what basis?

This final part of the textbook is intended to extend your consideration of a few selected issues that are currently controversial. Many devastating conditions affecting children are not discussed in this chapter. Among these are the problems of racism, malnutrition, neglect, and abuse. We encourage you to independently pursue some of these societal issues.

You will want to do more than just read about early education issues; you will gain more if you discuss them with others. Be warned, however, that discussion of early education issues often results in conflict. You may find to your surprise that friends who usually agree with you on other issues have counter views on the care and education of the young. You will find that in your discussions of early education issues you will have ample opportunity to analyze your own values and to explore the thinking and values of others.

ISSUES AND PERSPECTIVES

OVERVIEW

The first section of this chapter discusses the pressing issue of the problems of poverty in childhood. The plight of poor children is one of the issues that must be quickly addressed in our country and around the world. Abundant documentation establishes the prevalence of poverty and the dangers of allowing children to continue in economically deprived situations. Early childhood educators are needed as advocates for change for young children who cannot crusade on their own behalf; advocacy requires awareness, knowledge, skill, and commitment.

In addition, Chapter 22 focuses on the changing U.S. family and the kinds of arrangements for child care made by today's parents. As a teacher, you will certainly work with children who are receiving their primary care outside the home, either because both parents are in the work force or because the household is headed by a single working parent. It is important that you understand the problems and satisfactions of such families, including those of the parents as well as the children.

The remaining sections of the chapter present controversial educational practices. They cover controversies regarding early learning; entry, grouping, and appropriate programs for kindergarten children; and testing throughout the prekindergarten, kindergarten, and primary grades. These are issues that currently demand attention. Analysis of these issues will prepare you for considering related issues as they occur.

THE PROBLEMS OF POVERTY IN CHILDHOOD

Mary Burkett's car was damaged in a freak accident as she drove from her rural home to the nursing home twenty miles away where she works as a nurse's aide. This is more than an annoyance for Mary. The loss of transportation is a major dilemma. Her minimum wage provides the only steady income for the family. Mary's husband, Bob, works on construction jobs when they are available, and he is a dependable, cheerful, strong worker, but opportunities for construction work are few and far between. No other jobs are available either. Businesses are cutting employees, and many other family members and friends are also without income. Mary and Bob have three young children, aged fourteen months, three, and five years of age. Mary's minimum wage job has provided the only steady income for the family throughout their marriage.

Bob and Mary and their children live in a partially completed house. Bob has plenty of time to work on their own house since he is largely unemployed, but the Burketts have no money for materials. He is able to care for the children while Mary is at work.

There is no money to have the car repaired or replaced, and there is no other means of transportation. The Burketts cannot afford to move closer to Mary's work and pay rent. Thus far, because they live in a rural area on a piece of family property donated to them by Bob's father and they can depend on garden produce and wild game for food and their own wood supply for heating, Bob and Mary have been able to remain self-sufficient, despite recurring problems of the sort they are facing now. They are now at the brink of becoming totally destitute and dependent on public support.

Mary and Bob's plight is not unlike that of many other struggling young families across the country. Only a small portion of the United States' poor fit the stereotyped image of poverty as part of the inner city ghettos. For example, "only one in 50 poor children is a black child born to a single, teenage mother on welfare in a central city. A minuscule one in 1,000 poor children lives in such a family with a mother who has never held a job (Children's Defense Fund, 1991). In the Burkett family one of the immediate effects of not having a functioning car is that the five-year-old will have to drop out of kindergarten. Only half-day programs are available in the local school district. Special mid-day kindergarten buses are not provided, and parents must drive their own kindergarten children to or from school at noon. Mary has done this daily, but now she will no longer be able to. This, of course, is just one of the consequences of being poor. Although Mary has been working full-time, except for very brief maternity leaves, since her marriage at age 18, and Bob has worked at intervals, they have never been out of poverty.

The federal government has an official definition of poverty based on family size and income. A family was considered poor, according to the 1990 definition, if the earnings were less than $8,420 for a family of two, $10,560 for a family of three, and less than $12,700 for a family of four, and so on. Based on this definition, more children live in poverty than any other segment of our population.

Poverty affects children very directly and a great many, 22.5 percent, of our nation's young children are born into families that are poor. Child poverty worsened during the decade of the 1980s; for example, an average of 22.5 percent of children younger than six were in families below the poverty line throughout the 1980s as compared to 17 percent during the 1970s (Children's Defense Fund, 1991). The parents of these poor children are not necessarily among the unemployed. A minimum-wage full-time year-round job in 1991, bringing $4.25 an hour, provides earnings of $8,840, less than 80 percent of what is needed to bring a three-person household out of poverty. When children are born to families who are working at minimum-wage level, they are in poverty. It is among the working poor of this country that we find a great many of our youngest children.

As children grow older, poverty is still very much a problem: Poor teens are much more likely to become parents than nonpoor teens, and in 1989 almost one in six young people ages twelve to seventeen were poor. By dropping out of school to become parents, teens and their offspring become stuck in a cycle of poverty. In addition, when teenage pregnancies occur in poor families, medical care is rarely available. Neither the pregnant teens nor their parents, being unemployed or marginally employed, are covered by health insurance. Neonatal intensive care units are filled with babies who were born too soon or too small or damaged because their mothers had no or little access to decent prenatal care. For children of teenage mothers in poverty, medical care, dental care, and nutrition are often so marginal that both physical development and cognitive development are affected.

Nationally 10.7 million U.S. children younger than eighteen (one in six) lacked any form of health insurance in 1988. These are often the children of low-income working families, many of whom are single mothers, who are not eligible for Medicaid, have no employer-sponsored insurance, and cannot afford to pay for insurance privately. The National Health Interview Survey conducted in 1988 found that children under five living in families with incomes under $10,000 were much more likely to have physical or mental disabilities and other chronic health conditions which impaired daily activity (Children's Defense Fund, 1991).

Many children are at risk from the beginning of their lives and, without intervention, the cycles of poverty continue. Many of the most critical—and potentially cost-effective programs—have been woefully underfunded. The WIC (Food for Women, Infants, and Children) nutrition program for pregnant women and children supported by the federal government reduces infant mortality and increases birthweight. For example, the House Select Committee on Children, Youth and Families reported that each $1 invested in WIC saves $3 in short-term hospital costs for low-birthweight babies. Schorr and Schorr (1988) report on eight South Dakota babies whose mothers did not receive prenatal care and whose neonatal nursery costs were nearly half a million dollars. Good prenatal and infant nutrition can do much to prevent mental retardation with its huge costs. Nevertheless, the House Select Committee reported that WIC reached only slightly over half of those eligible because of lack of funds.

FIGURE 22-1   Moments in America

Every 35 seconds an infant is born into poverty.

Every 2 minutes an infant is born to a mother who received late or no prenatal care.

Every 2 minutes an infant is born at low birthweight (less than 5 pounds, 8 ounces).

Every 11 minutes an infant is born at very low birthweight (less than 3 pounds, 8 ounces).

Every 14 minutes an infant dies in the first year of life.

Every 31 seconds an infant is born to an unmarried mother.

Every 55 seconds an infant is born to a mother who is not a high school graduate.

Every 21 seconds a 15- to 19-year-old woman becomes sexually active for the first time.

Every 32 seconds a 15- to 19-year-old woman becomes pregnant.

Every 64 seconds an infant is born to a teenage mother.

Every 5 minutes an infant is born to a teenage mother who already had a child.

Every 74 seconds a 15- to 19-year-old woman has an abortion.

Every 14 hours a child younger than 5 is murdered.

Every 5 hours a 15- to 19-year-old is murdered.

Every 2 hours a 20- to 24-year-old is murdered.

Every 2 seconds of the school day a public school student is suspended.

Every 4 seconds of the school day a public school student is corporally punished.

Every 10 seconds of the school day a student drops out of school.

Source: Children's Defense Fund (1991). *The state of America's children 1991*, Washington, DC: Author.

Many of the poorest families in our nation are minorities, particularly blacks. Over 40 percent of U.S. black children, as contrasted with approximately 15 percent of white children, were living below the poverty line in 1989. Latino children now fare only a little better than black children—a whopping 36.2 percent are in poverty families (Children's Defense Fund, 1991). The long-term consequences of such inequities are difficult to contemplate.

We have many precedents across the history of our country for government action to undo the effects of poverty. Often there has been support from both sides of the political spectrum for government intervention to better the lives of poor and/or neglected children. A recent example of such federal legislation is the Family Support Act passed in 1990 intended to benefit children of poverty families by building family self-sufficiency. Major components of the 1990 law are Job Opportunities and Basic Skills (JOBS) program, guarantees of child care for AFDC parents who work or are in education or training, child support enforcement mandates, and a requirement that all states provide Aid to Families of Dependent Children (AFDC) benefits to two-parent families where there is at least one unemployed parent. Local and state economic woes have limited the extent to which funds have been forthcoming to match the federal dollars and support implementation.

The most controversial issues regarding child poverty involve questions about how the needs of children balance out against the needs for national defense, for military retirements, for veterans' benefits, for agriculture and farming, for space exploration, for bail-outs of financial institutions, and so forth. These are the issues that legislators wrestle with as they consider expenditures for children.

In this country, whether we provide for children's health, well-being, learning and development depends on how we establish our national priorities. In some less industrialized nations, children exist in even more hopeless situations, living pitiful and brief lives. In our increasingly interdependent world, the problems of one part of the world directly impact on the political, economic, and, hence, daily lives of fellow humans in the rest of the world. Many early childhood educators point out that we cannot avoid becoming concerned about how the children of our planet fare. An egocentric or ethnocentric view is no longer viable. As you consider the plight of U.S. children as portrayed in Figure 22.1 and children in need in other parts of the world, what are your thoughts?

THE PROBLEMS OF CHILD CARE

Janie Eldred and Dawn Cummings are best friends. Both are three years old. Both have baby brothers. They live in side-by-side identical houses in a subdivision development in the suburbs of a large city. In many ways they are alike, but one part of their life experience has been very different. Janie's mother and father both work. Janie's mother drops her and the baby off at Happy House, the child care center near her law office. Except for a brief maternity leave, Carol Jones-Eldred has maintained her law practice. Even during the maternity leave she was busy with case preparation. Tom Eldred travels during the week and returns on weekends. Carol follows a very regular routine during the week and usually finds it very satisfying. Sometimes she glances next door and thinks of how delightful it must be to have a more leisurely opportunity to enjoy the children and to observe and assist with their development. But, sighing, she knows that she enjoys the challenge of her work and would not have it any other way.

Leslie Cummings, Dawn's mother, stays at home and describes herself as a "full-time homemaker." She was in advertising with a promising career start prior to her first pregnancy but made the decision that her career could wait until her children were all in school. She finds that being a full-time wife and mother is satisfying, and she never lacks for things to do at home. She arranged for a Tuesday play group of four area preschoolers so that Dawn will have some social experiences. Dawn likes best to play with Janie, but Janie is usually at the day care center and not available. Sometimes Leslie glances next door and thinks of how delightful it must be to go off to an adult world each morning, as her neighbor does, and to leave the diapers, the Play Doh, and the peanut butter sandwiches to a day care center. But as she looks at her children, she sighs, knowing that she wouldn't have it any other way.

Janie and Dawn are both bright and happy youngsters. Janie has nine hours of each weekday spent in the company of fifteen other children. She relates to many different adults in her center. She is very sophisticated about how to

"What is a kangaroo doing with all the farm animals?" *(Cumberland Hill Associates, Inc.)*

behave in a group setting and loves the stories, the songs, the blocks, the field trips. She knows that she is just one of many children and that she must often wait her turn for opportunities to talk with adults and to play with the favorite toys. She has had many colds, viruses, and other infections through contact with her peers. Sometimes when she isn't feeling well, Janie wishes that she could just stay home and play in her room. Nevertheless, she must always go to the day-care center or the emergency baby sitter.

Dawn is very sophisticated in her knowledge of cooking, of marketing, of sewing, of care of babies. All the things her mother does she observes very thoroughly. She has almost unlimited opportunities to converse with her mother and, except for the weekly play group, unlimited access to her favorite toys. She, however, has never even seen many of the toys that are Janie's favorites, and she has little interaction with adults outside of her family. Sometimes Dawn asks her mother when she will be able to go to the day-care center like Janie.

There is much that we have yet to learn about the consequences and long-term effects of differing child-rearing styles on the health, well-being, development, and learning of young children. The choices are never clear-cut; trade-offs dominate the decision making of many families as they contemplate child-care options. Approximately half of children younger than age six have mothers in the work force. The 10.2 million mothers of children younger than age six who work outside their own home constitute a sizable portion of the labor force.

The entry of women into the work force has significantly altered traditional family child-rearing patterns, and there are reasons to be pleased with the changes. The new life-styles appear to offer all family members more options and enriching experiences. Some, however, argue that young children need the guidance and love of a mother and father and that this is best provided when fathers support the family through gainful employment and mothers remain at home. The economics of this situation evidently do not appear viable to many of today's parents. Indeed, mothers often work to support their families rather than for personal fulfillment. For good or ill, child rearing and homemaking are not considered the primary work of many of today's women.

There are, of course, many kinds of arrangements that working parents make for their children's care. Group day care is one arrangement. Approximately one-quarter of all children whose mothers work are placed in center care. Another quarter are placed in family day-care homes, where caregivers provide for a small group of children in their own homes. Sometimes the caregiver's own children are included in the group. Over half of the children are cared for by relatives or by a sitter in their own home (Children's Defense Fund, 1991). Each situation, in the best of circumstances can be very desirable; in the worst of circumstances, each can be disastrous. The issue is not so much the kind of care arrangements that are used but the quality of those arrangements.

Finding quality child care frequently presents a dilemma for many parents. They feel themselves wonderfully blessed if they find caregivers they feel are loving, aware, and responsible. Many working parents lack the assurance that their children are as well-cared for as they would wish. It is a constant concern. Sometimes there are reasons for parents to worry, since some caregivers are not well-qualified for the important work that they do. The low pay does little to attract and retain qualified personnel. This is a critical problem, one that children's advocates cannot ignore.

Not surprisingly, given the low salaries, there are high turnover rates in the child-care profession. This is especially alarming since there is some evidence (Howes & Rubenstein, 1985) that there are ill effects for children resulting from changes in providers. People who understand the importance of the early years for children's continued health, well-being, and development must increasingly advocate for children in improving the conditions of child care and the status of well-qualified child-care providers. Although there are instances of parents who share child rearing, who arrange their work lives with flexible hours so that they themselves may provide care for their offspring, these arrangements are rare. Increasingly, parents are looking toward group care arrangements for their children while they work. Consequently, most parents accept what is available regardless of quality. A critical issue for our society, therefore, is to identify the dimensions of day care that have an impact on health, well-being, development, and learning and to ensure that those dimensions are available in programs for as many children as possible. Some of the dimensions of quality that have been tentatively identified are listed here:

- **Adult-child ratios**   Ratios of adults to children are very important indicators of quality. The number of children with whom each caregiver can interact in sensitive and resourceful fashion is limited. If there are too many children for whom a caregiver is responsible, the amount and quality of interaction suffers.
- **Caregiver training and education**   Caregivers with child-related training provide more developmentally appropriate experiences for children, which results in higher social and cognitive competence. Caregivers' total years of schooling are less certain to have an influence on their behavior as caregivers, and hence on children's behavior, than specialized training.
- **Caregiver-child verbal interactions**   When caregivers engage in conversations with children in their care on a frequent basis, there are positive consequences for cognitive and language growth.

Findings are inconclusive or mixed on a number of other dimensions that might be hypothesized to have effects on children. It will be important in the years ahead to determine more precisely what circumstances of child care contribute to the welfare of each new generation.

On behalf of children who are unable to lobby for their own interests, many early childhood educators feel that it is important to support governmental and other organizational efforts to ensure that children have adequate care arrangements. Through the current publications of professional organizations such as the National Association for the Education of Young Children and the Association for Childhood Education International, you can learn how to be an active advocate for child-care improvements.

MISEDUCATION OF YOUNG CHILDREN*

The events of the last thirty years regarding early childhood education have left a great web of confusion about appropriate practices. Some people are tremendously eager to have young children develop as rapidly as possible and want to provide all the advantages for early development from prenatal stages onward. Others assume that hugs and acceptance of childish ways are sufficient for optimal development and are aghast at the special arrangements (lessons, learning devices, computers, trips, vacations) many parents think it is important to provide.

As pointed out in Chapter 2, a great deal of writing and research conducted during the 1960s and 1970s emphasized the importance of the early years for children's learning. Many early childhood professionals, however, point out that beliefs about the critical nature of early learning have lead some practitioners to inappropriately "push down" the conventional academic curriculum of the elementary school, virtually unchanged in format, to earlier age levels. The following statements from commercial advertisements are examples of that trend:

*The term *miseducation* has been used by Elkind (1987) to describe the developmentally inappropriate experiences and possessions parents are providing for their children "to give them an edge that will make them brighter and abler than the competition" (p. xiii).

- "For beginning readers, early success is a critical step toward making the grade. The younger a child learns to read effectively, the sooner he begins the exciting, lifelong adventures reading affords." (Paid advertisement, *Instructor,* Nov./Dec. 1988, p. 7.)
- "*Early Reader Library* 20-volume series even a preschooler can read. Charming stories with a vocabulary ranging from 11 to 170 words per book." (*Educational Teaching Aids 1987–1988 Catalog,* p. 90.)

Increasingly, there is concern about the plight of today's children who are expected to respond to the same kinds of instruction and the same kinds of learning that their parents encountered at much later ages. The widespread nature of the pushdown curriculum has lead to the recent adoption of guidelines by the National Association for the Education of Young Children (Bredekamp, 1987) and other professional organizations that clarify practices appropriate and inappropriate for children at various age levels. The central problem seems to have come from inappropriately equating the importance of early learning with early direct instruction. It is true that young children are ready to learn a great many things. They are eager learners. But, even though they may appear to

"Four black buttons and two white buttons. I guess I'll get one more and make it seven."
(Cumberland Hill Associates, Inc.)

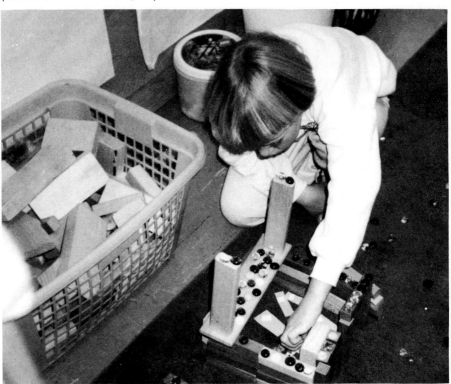

adapt and to respond adequately to direct instruction, it may be done at a price. To follow adult instruction, they give up their own efforts to construct knowledge and increasingly wait patiently (or impatiently) for teachers to tell them what to do. This leads to less real learning and to a motivational numbing that may interfere with health, well-being, and development, as well as later educational achievement. Loss of enthusiasm for learning, loss of curiosity, burnout, or dropout at later levels may be some of the consequences.

Elkind (1987) points out that miseducation is seen in young children's extracurricular as well as school experiences. Parents who feel obligated to provide series of lessons for their preschoolers may be engaging in practices more harmful than helpful to their children. Dancing, foreign language, swimming, learning to play a musical instrument, and yoga are among the classes offered to young children. Although children are certainly capable of learning a great deal in these areas and may indeed benefit greatly from their early learning, they will not benefit if the instruction is geared either above or below their capabilities, if they must remain passive while instruction is given, or if affection from parents or other important adults is contingent on successful participation.

At school, miseducation most often takes the form of formal programs that require children to listen quietly while their teacher presents lessons. Young children are also being miseducated if they are expected to spend their time completing prepared worksheets—coloring an already prepared picture, pasting shapes drawn or cut out by an adult, drawing lines and making marks to indicate correct answers.

KINDERGARTEN: CONTROVERSIES ON PLACEMENT, SCHEDULING, AND GOALS

In the opinion of many early childhood educators, miseducation of U.S. children has reached a crisis state in our kindergartens. With the advent of increased availability of prekindergarten programs (Head Start, nursery schools, day care) and the overall increased push for academic emphases, the nature of kindergartens has been altered significantly. What was formerly done in first and second grade is now routine in many kindergartens. Five-year-old children in many school districts spend their kindergarten days in sedentary, teacher-directed tasks. They receive direct instruction in reading, mathematics, and handwriting in the formal methods many believe are inappropriate for their level of development. Many school systems have developed very specific objectives for kindergarten children, such as "Children will recognize numerals 1 to 10." In at least one state that has mandated kindergarten for all children, approximately 200 objectives are mandated to be met during the course of the year. This is in contrast to a kindergarten program that emphasizes the development of "the whole child" in which "everything should be done to ensure that children go on developing their love of learning, expanding their general knowledge base, their ability to get along, and their interest in reaching out to the world all through the kindergarten year" (Peck, McCaig, & Sapp, 1988, p. 35). Developmentally appropriate programs are tailored to the individual children who enter them in recognition that there is always a range of skills in any group and that children learn best in a heterogeneous group because they learn so much from each other.

As kindergartens have increased academic preparation and have taken on tasks formerly handled in first grade, child failures have increased, necessitating a number of changes in policies associated with kindergarten entrance and promotion to first grade. These changes include (1) modification of birth date requirements, for admission into kindergarten, (2) testing requirements to determine readiness for admission to kindergarten, (3) increased incidence of kindergarten retention, and (4) the development of special programs, which have the effect of adding an extra year ("a gift of time") to an "unready" child's schooling. These changes, now common in many schools, stem from the fact that many kindergarten children do not function well in a program that sets expectations which in prior generations were seen as more appropriate for older children. Let's examine each of these practices in greater depth.

Modification of Birth Date Requirements for Kindergarten Entry

Some educational decision makers have attempted to avoid inappropriate experiences for young children by moving up the cutoff date for entry so that children are older on admission to kindergarten. Thus, many states or local districts have moved the date for qualifying for kindergarten entrance. Whereas, being five by December 31 was traditionally the age criterion for kindergarten admission in many states, this date has been moved back to ensure that entrants are older—to October, to September, and so forth. Given our system of starting the school year in September for the entire kindergarten cohort (as contrasted with having each individual child enter on his or her birthday as practiced in some other countries), however, there are always children who are younger and who may be less mature than classmates who are nearly a year older. Changing the cutoff date for entry in order to exclude younger children seems to simply result in further push downs of grade-level expectations. The real problem is less what cutoff date is used and more the expectation for uniform performance.

Testing for Admission to Kindergarten

Legislation in sixteen states and more than half of the districts in another seven states mandates that schools conduct kindergarten entrance screening (Ellwein, Walsh, Eads, II & Miller, 1991). Children are tested to determine their degree of readiness and the likelihood of their successful participation in the kindergarten program. If judged "unready" in some locales, children are excluded from entry until greater readiness has been achieved. In certain cases, children are not directly excluded but parents are advised that if they enroll their child, he or she will probably experience frustration and failure and that another year at home (or in a prekindergarten or junior kindergarten program) is advisable. Many parents comply. One problem associated with this practice is that test results from children at this age are not always accurate, and thus erroneous judgments can be made. Researchers (Graue & Shepard, 1989; Shepard & Smith, 1985) have concluded that the popular admission test, the *Gesell School Readiness Test* (1980), can result in misidentification of 50 to 60 percent of the children tested and placed in extra-year programs. Four other tests (Brigance, Daberon, DIALR, KIDS) commonly used for admission testing were reported by Ellwein, Walsh, Eads, II, and Miller (1991) to misidentify nearly as many. The authors of this latter study condemned admission screening and stated flatly that the tests were "no more accurate [in predicting kindergarten performance] than the toss of a fair coin" (Ellwein, Walsh, Eads, II & Miller, 1991, p. 171).

Even if the tests were perfectly accurate, another important problem with this practice exists. Children who are denied entry to kindergarten programs even though they are of legal kindergarten age may need the benefits of a school program more than children who are admitted. Often it is children who have not had home experiences with drawing, painting, enjoying books, building with blocks, doing puzzles who score less well on the screening tests used to weed out the unready. The idea of giving a "gift of time," as the practice of denying admission is often called, is based on the maturationist perspective discussed in Chapter 10, which assumes that the important forces influencing the current state of the child are primarily internal to the growth rate of that child. As you will recall, others feel that the child's experience is a very important determinant of readiness and, therefore, a decision to simply wait for readiness to develop with the passage of time is not wise. As the policy statement of the National Association of Early Childhood Specialists in State Departments of Education (NAECS/SDE) (1987) described it, "the very children being counseled out of school are the ones who, if provided a flexible, appropriate kindergarten curriculum, could benefit the most" (p. 5).

Kindergarten Retentions

In some school districts, kindergarten children who do not successfully complete the objectives set for that level are required to repeat the kindergarten year. They simply do the program over. It has been estimated that between 10 and 20 percent of kindergarten children are recommended for retention or for transition classes (Elkind, 1988). Many early childhood educators challenge this practice. Admittedly, a few children make gains and do well during their second year in kindergarten; others do not fare any better than they did their first year and, in addition, may suffer loss of self-esteem if parents, teachers, siblings, and playmates react in a negative fashion. The harmful consequences of grade repetition have been well documented (Norton, 1983; Shepard & Smith, 1986, 1989; Plummer, Liniberger & Graziano, 1987; Smith & Shepard, 1987, 1988). However, there are those who believe that the earlier in school a child repeats a grade the greater the chances of long-range success. Others point out that taking a year of a persons' adulthood to give a gift of time, or an extra year at the kindergarten level, assumes greater assurance of the "gift's" benefits than actually can be claimed.

Transitional Programs

One way in which schools have attempted to deal with the concerns for children's lack of readiness for the formal kindergarten program without excluding the child is to set up separate classes, or transitional classes, for those determined by test or observation to be too immature to enter the regular kindergarten. These classes are sometimes set up to parallel the kindergarten year and are known as prekindergarten and junior kindergarten (for five-year-olds), transitional kindergarten, developmental kindergarten. Or they may be set up to follow a regular kindergarten experience but are required for children deemed unready to enter first grade. These are referred to as developmental first grade or transitional first grade. Whatever the name or the timing of the transitional program, it is well understood that these classes are for children who are "slow." Children assigned to such programs almost always spend an additional year in the school system beyond that of their agemates. The segment of the school population most often assigned to these groups are males, minorities, children for whom English is a second language, and those from low-income families. Because they are judged unready by indicators, which may or may not be accurate, at the start of their schooling, they are tracked into a different kind of experience than their peers. The liabilities of such placement include the stigma of being labeled "unready" as well as the later loss of a year of adult earning power.

None of these practices addresses the issue of the nature of the kindergarten curriculum. As Peck, McCaig, and Sapp (1988) say:

> In any or all of these patchwork, quick-fix approaches to the problem, the most important factor is overlooked: the curriculum itself. Children are being blamed for their inability to keep pace with the curriculum. Instead of looking at entry criteria, we should be re-examining the curriculum to see whether it is appropriate for the children, because all children succeed when the curriculum is appropriate (p. 10).

Concern about kindergarten programs has led to the development of position papers by a number of professional organizations, which are listed here:

Association for Childhood Education International. (1987). *The child-centered kindergarten.* Wheaton, MD: Author.

Bredekamp, S. (Ed.). (1987). *Developmentally appropriate practice in early childhood programs serving children from birth through age 8.* Washington, DC: National Association for the Education of Young Children.

Early Childhood and Literacy Development Committee of the International Reading Association. (1985). *Literacy development and pre-first grade: A joint statement of concerns about present practices in pre-first grade reading instruction and recommendations for improvement.* Newark, DE: International Reading Association.

National Association of Early Childhood Specialists in State Departments of Education. (1987). *Unacceptable trends in kindergarten entry and placement.* Lincoln, NE: Author.

Southern Association on Children Under Six. (1984). *Position statement on developmentally appropriate experiences for kindergarten.* Little Rock: Author.

Consulting these documents and the Additional Readings is strongly suggested. The type of kindergarten program recommended in these position statements is exemplified by the following:

> In a traditional, developmentally appropriate kindergarten children learn mostly through play and through freely choosing and using a variety of learning centers all around the classroom, figuring out how things work, interacting with each other, trying out new roles, experimenting with their own ideas, building on their experiences, and solving real problems. Teachers prepare many projects in what we think of as "subjects" (science, language arts, math, social studies, early literacy, and so on). . . . Projects integrate "subjects" as much as possible (Peck, McCaig & Sapp, 1988, p. 36).

THE INFLUENCES OF TESTING

Testing primary-age children with annual standard achievement tests to determine progress relative to a normed sample has been routine practice for a number of years. Formal testing of younger children, however, is a relatively new phenomena greatly encouraged by two efforts designed to alleviate societal inequities. The first of these was the effort during the 1960s and 1970s to evaluate the effects of the Head Start experience on program participants. Government planners felt the need to determine the extent of advantage of intervention programs to justify continued governmental support. New testing instruments were therefore developed and used extensively to determine whether children gained through participation in Head Start and other comparable intervention efforts. The other major effort was due to the Education for All Handicapped Children Act. To ensure that all disabled children were receiving appropriate services, it was deemed necessary to test and then to use the results of these tests to guide planners in the selection of appropriate services and in the formation of individual educational plans (IEPs). Both of these are admirable efforts, but unfortunately one of the consequences has been the increased popularity of testing young children.

When young children are tested, the objective is usually one or more of the following three purposes:

1 **Screening**   Used to determine (a) whether children may need early intervention or special services for any condition that could prove disabling or (b) whether children might profit from a modified or individualized educational program due to disabilities or giftedness

2 **Readiness testing**   Used to determine (a) the child's readiness to benefit from a specific academic program (for example, a given level of a reading program) or (b) the level or type of instruction to be used with the child at his or her current level

3 **Accountability testing**   Used to determine (a) whether a child has benefited

from participation in a particular program or (b) whether a teacher has been effective in instructing pupils

Nearly half the states in the United States require developmental screening for children between the ages of three and six to identify children who may be in need of special services or intervention. Screening tests are used in an effort to disclose the child's potential for learning as well as any disabling conditions that would prevent learning. Even though the purposes for screening are quite different from those concerned with readiness or accountability, it is not unusual to find that the same types of tests are inappropriately applied to all three purposes. There are many misconceptions about the role of testing and, therefore, it is important for early childhood educators to become aware of the issues and the problems.

There are two major aspects of tests that are essential to understand—reliability and validity. **Reliability** refers to whether a test gives dependable or consistent scores. The issue is whether test scores can be attributed to the performance of the test taker or to errors of measurement. **Validity** concerns whether a test accurately measures whatever it claims to measure. For example, does a screening test actually measure potential for learning and disclose disabilities or does it measure what has been achieved thus far in the child's life, which may simply reflect lack of environmental opportunity, not disability. Tests that are not reliable or do not have validity can lead to inappropriate conclusions. To date, only a few tests for young children have adequate evidence of validity and reliability. Moreover, there is good reason to treat test results obtained from preschool, kindergarten, and primary grade children with considerable skepticism. The younger the child, the less likely that test scores can be viewed as valid and reliable.

Ideally, the kindergarten screening process includes data from parents and teachers who have observed children in a variety of settings over a long period. In many locales, however, the screening process requires the child to appear on a special screening date and to respond to questions and commands from a team consisting of a psychologist, a physical education teacher, a speech and language specialist, a nurse, a principal, and a kindergarten teacher. The following describes such a screening process:

> Many of the children . . . may be puzzled, others frightened by the questions posed during required kindergarten screening. The child may wonder, "Why did he ask me what my name was? He already knew it, 'cause he said, 'Hello, Mark!' " "Why did she want to know what color that circle was? She's big. Can't she tell it was a kind of orangish red?" "Why did I have to draw a circle?" "Why?"
>
> Questions such as these, questions which ask a child to name body parts, to identify letters, numbers, shapes, and colors are part of many screening instruments currently in use. Children may be asked to hop, skip, and follow directions such as, "Please open the door, then walk around your chair, and then say, "Hello!" They may be asked to draw a square; to build a bridge from three one-inch wooden cubes; to place a car beside, or on, or under a block; to identify various "common" objects; or to place things in a predetermined sequence. The child who asks why in his or her

relentless search for meaning, may wonder at this world of adults who ask for arbitrary fragments of information which must, indeed, seem meaningless.*

The controversy over developmental testing and the associated practices of exclusion or developmental placements is but one aspect of the issue of testing of young children. There is also a great deal of concern about the influence achievement testing for accountability purposes wields over teacher decision making about what to provide in children's programs. When teachers feel that they or their children will be judged by how well the children perform on tests, the content assumed or known to be on the test is sometimes overemphasized, often by direct instruction. Since testing in all but the rarest and most innovative instances consists of determining whether there is a correct predetermined response to discrete questions with a very narrow focus, teachers are influenced to use direct instruction along with worksheets and workbooks that mirror the appearance of tests to prepare children to do well.

Because of the influence of accountability testing, teachers sometimes engage in practices they otherwise believe to be unwise and developmentally inappropriate. This is a widespread phenomenon every teacher must be prepared to encounter. These pressures are particularly problematic for teachers in the primary grades where it has become common knowledge that, for some learners, focused direct instruction leads to higher scores on academic achievement tests than indirect methods. Chapter 2 discussed evidence supporting this view. However, there is also evidence that introducing basic skills before a child is ready may undermine the child's motivation to use these skills in the long run. Further, there are many who point out that the items in achievement tests are not representative of the important aspects of what a child actually does in the act of reading or in encountering a real mathematical problem in his or her own life. According to Altwerger, Edelsky, and Flores (1987), "Tests fail to test what they claim to be testing" (p. 152). From this perspective, the efforts of teachers to improve their children's test scores may be distracting them from the real tasks of helping children understand and use their abilities in more constructive ways.

The National Association for the Education of Young Children (1988) has adopted a position statement on standardized testing that emphasizes the following "utility" criterion:

> The purpose of testing must be to improve services for children and to ensure that children benefit from their educational experiences. Decisions about testing and assessment instruments must be based on the usefulness of the assessment procedure for improving services to children and improving outcomes for children. The ritual use even of "good tests" (those that are judged to be valid and reliable measures) is to be discouraged in the absence of documented research showing that children benefit from their use (p. 44).

Other decision-making groups have taken similar stands. The National

---

*S. Updike. "Why?" *New York Early Education Reporter,* 25 (1) (1988, Fall), 1,3. Reprinted by permission.

Young children construct understandings of how to read and write by trying alternatives and asking for confirmation. *(Steve Sartori)*

Association of State Boards of Education concurs with the NAEYC stand on the utility criterion, citing the waste that occurs when teachers use valuable time "teaching for the test" rather than focusing on the developmental needs of children. They have recommended a review of educational programs currently provided for four- through eight-year-olds and stated the following regarding testing of children of these ages:

> We recommend that young children be assessed through observation and recording of their developmental progress. Periodic samples of writing and drawings, oral tapes of reading, and videotapes or observations of social interaction and problem solving become examples in a portfolio for each child. This information should then be used to adapt the curriculum, plan activities to meet the needs of the children, and provide feedback to parents. This type of assessment should take place informally on a daily basis for program planning rather than for placement purposes. . . .
>
> We are not suggesting abandoning the effort to assess appropriately the progress of students and the effectiveness of programs. We still need to hold schools, programs and professionals accountable and develop better ways of informing the public about the results of educational programs. Our concern is to find new ways to do this that do not stigmatize children and create a sense of failure at a young age.*

*National Association of State Boards of Education. (1988). *Right from the start.* Washington, DC: p. 14.

Despite the appearance of the statements we have just presented, the common practice in many primary schools, and increasingly in kindergartens and prekindergartens as well, is to depend almost solely on testing to provide information for purposes of screening, readiness, and accountability.

SUMMARY

Early childhood educators have recently made great strides in reaching consensus on a number of well-publicized troublesome issues. Individuals and professional organizations are becoming increasingly active as advocates for legislation action on behalf of children in poverty. There has also been increasing recognition that since most parents are working outside the home, greater attention must be given to the amount and quality of available child care. With growing public support for programs to benefit children, the 1990s may see greater movement toward intervention on their behalf. As an early childhood educator, the resolution of these issues, or lack thereof, will directly affect you and the children you teach.

Professional organizations are taking highly active roles in clarifying appropriate practices in relation to programs for young children; these actions will likely significantly modify some of the current practices regarding curriculum development, testing, grouping, and teacher preparation. As a professional, you will have opportunities to influence the direction of those modifications. Your career as a teacher will certainly be affected by the outcomes.

SUGGESTED ACTIVITIES

1 Scan current professional and popular periodicals to determine whether the issues discussed in this chapter appear and what other issues regarding young children are discussed.
2 Interview experienced teachers about the changes they have observed throughout their years of teaching concerning the life circumstances of children and the expectations of society for school programs.
3 Interview friends and acquaintances about their views on issues such as government programs to intervene in the care, health, nutrition, education, and protection of young children.

ADDITIONAL READINGS

Bredekamp, S. (Ed.) (1987). *Developmentally appropriate practice.* Washington, DC: National Association for the Education of Young Children.

Bredekamp, S., & Shepard, L. (1989). How best to protect children from inappropriate school expectations, practices, and policies. *Young Children, 44*(3), 14–24.

Child Care Employees Project. (1990). *Who cares? Child care teachers and the quality of care in America.* Child Care Employees Project, 6536 Telegraph Ave. #A201, Oakland, CA 94609.

Elkind, D. (1987). *Preschoolers at risk.* New York: Knopf.

Hatch, J. A., & Freeman, E. B. (1988). Kindergarten philosophies and practices: Perspectives of teachers, principals, and supervisors. *Early Childhood Research Quarterly, 3,* 151–166.

Kamii, C. (Ed.). (1990). *Achievement testing in the early grades: The games grown-ups play.* Washington, DC: National Association for the Education of Young Children.

Katz, L. G., Evangelou, D., & Hartman, J. A. (1990). *The case for mixed-age grouping in early education.* Washington, DC: National Association for the Education of Young Children.

National Association for the Education of Young Children. (1988). NAEYC position statement on standardized testing of young children 3 through 8 years of age. *Young Children, 43*(3), 42–47.

National Association for the Education of Young Children. (1990). NAEYC position statement on school readiness. *Young Children, 46*(1), 21–23.

Peck, J. T., McCaig, G., & Sapp, M. E. (1988). *Kindergarten policies: What is best for children?* Washington, DC: National Association for the Education of Young Children.

Phillips, D. A. (Ed.). (1987). *Quality in child care: What does research tell us?* Washington, DC: National Association for the Education of Young Children.

Schorr, L. B., & Schorr, D. (1988). *Within our reach: Breaking the cycle of disadvantage.* New York: Doubleday.

Seefeldt, C. (Ed.) (1990). *Continuing issues in early childhood education.* Columbus, OH: Merrill.

Wingert, P. & Kantrowitz, B. (1989). The day care generation. *Newsweek, 114,* Special Issue on the Family, 86–87, 89, 92.

EPILOGUE

Throughout this book, you have considered the implications of becoming a teacher of young children. In Part 1, you examined background information on the profession and learned about the historical heritage of early childhood education. Part 2 was designed to develop your knowledge of children's development and your observational acuity.

In Part 3, you learned of three contrasting perspectives on child development and of alternatives for the organization of programs as illustrated by five prototypic models. You were told about ways to manage the classroom environment and children's behavior. Teaching strategies for dialogue, activities, and lessons were described. Communication skills were also emphasized, with examples given of how these skills are applied in working with children, parents, and co-workers.

Part 4 contributed to your teaching resourcefulness. You developed a broad repertoire for identifying learning possibilities within a variety of situations and with diverse materials.

Part 5 helped you understand some of the issues that are currently of concern regarding the care and education of young children. It was suggested that advocacy is included among the role responsibilities of the early childhood educator.

If you have thoughtfully studied these sections, you have made an excellent start toward preparation for teaching. And, what may be even more important, you now have an idea of the kinds of activities in which you can continue to engage to prepare yourself more fully prior to actual employment. Regardless of your current level of accomplishment in preparing yourself, you cannot expect to perform as a "veteran" until you have accrued considerable experience. The program you provide in your first years of teaching will not be as comprehensive or as individualized as those you will ultimately be able to provide. The eventual goal—at least from our bias—is to provide programs that contribute to the broadest possible development in the most individualized way, but it is only as you mature in experience, competence, and confidence that this goal can be approached. We therefore emphasize continued development within the broad framework we have proposed. Your continued activity will prove especially beneficial in two areas: (1) modification of your program plans in light of the actual circumstances of your eventual employment and (2) consideration of how you will sustain your own basic intentions in the face of forces and situation factors in the real world. Your survival, effectiveness, and satisfaction in teaching will depend on how you adapt to the situation in which you will actually teach and on whether you find ways to both fulfill your own personal needs and meet your teaching goals.

Although it is impossible to project the circumstances you may face during your professional career, it will be helpful for you to visit and learn about characteristics of different programs whenever you have the opportunity. From this, you can determine the settings within which you personally could or could not find satisfaction in teaching and also learn how teachers operate differently, according to their own convictions, in similar settings. Through this kind of observation, you may learn to what extent particular contextual factors can support a range of different styles and orientations—including those similar to your own. Clearly, there is significant variation among organizational structures, and it may make a tremendous difference to you whether you are in a child-care context, a half-day nursery, or a primary classroom. You can best learn of these and similar situational effects through direct experiences. Make sure, for example, that you know the characteristics of the various program settings in your local community. You can also use your vacations and trips to other locations and regions as opportunities to visit various types of early childhood programs. You will gradually acquire a very realistic view of variations among programs for young children that are influential in supporting or constraining teachers' efforts.

Beyond the immediate context, there are also, of course, broader cultural influences that will affect your practice as a teacher and about which you will wish to be informed. The cultural expectations for schooling and the role of teachers have changed markedly during this century and can be expected to change at an ever-increasing rate as we move toward the twenty-first century.

The issues discussed in Part 5 will be of concern as you begin your career. There will also probably be increased controversy over the use of media technology to contribute to the education of young children. There is continuing concern about how mainstreaming and multicultural education, including bilingual training, can be most effectively achieved. There is increased interest in studying how young children learn. Some of the understandings reached will likely result from research on brain functioning. These and similar trends may assist or complicate what you consider to be your mission in teaching, depending on your goals, objectives, and overall orientation.

By the year 2000, other trends may have emerged. The one trend that does seem quite stable is an ever-accelerating rate of change. A solid perspective on oneself and one's basic values will be essential for maintaining both stability and flexibility in light of new demands, expectations, and opportunities. At this point, you can profitably begin to adapt strategies both for your survival and growth as a beginning teacher and for your continued development in the years ahead. In concluding, therefore, we suggest the following two strategies for this effort:

1 **Be as realistic as you can be in your endeavors.** Strive to make accurate discriminations about the requirements of situations, your own needs, and the extent to which your own abilities are adequate for the responsibilities you are accepting. Keep your goals and priorities within reason, seeking a balance between personal and professional efforts. No one can do everything; sort out your priorities, plan, and work ahead, but also reserve time for relaxation.

2 **Take active responsibility for continuing your own professional development.** Do this systematically. You are now familiar with the areas in which you need further work. Build and strengthen these.

Develop a classification scheme for storing plans, points of view, illustrative materials, activities for self-development, and ideas for things to do with children. Test the usability of your scheme by periodically trying to locate something on short notice.

Start or join a professional work group and find a "buddy" with whom you can test and share ideas, plans, materials, problems, solutions, and who will help you keep on target regarding your goals. Develop other support systems, such as finding people who can help you out on short notice, finding sources of inexpensive and free scrap materials. Practice explaining ideas to children as well as to sympathetic and hostile adults.

Your ultimate goals will include survival, effectiveness with children, and personal satisfaction in teaching. We have suggested that this means the provision of the most comprehensive and individualized program possible, given the constraints of the setting, the resources you are able to muster, and your own teaching repertoire. With these goals in mind, you can perhaps see why the realistic assessment of your professional commitment and the continual enhancement of your repertoire are so essential in becoming a teacher of young children.

FIELDWORK GUIDELINES

In Part 1 of this book we stated that fieldwork or an internship in an early childhood setting will be useful to you as you are studying the material in the textbook. The materials in this appendix are intended to guide your participation in that fieldwork. They have been arranged into four parts to correspond with the first four parts of the book.

PART 1: OBSERVING TEACHERS AT WORK

To maximize your learning from your fieldwork and to help retain what you learn, establish a fieldwork notebook that contains a number of subsections with categories such as the following: *Basic Information, Log, Observations, Ideas, Other.* We advise you to carry file cards or a small notebook with you to your fieldwork and, after your session, transfer notations of particular interest into a more permanent record. Distilling your notes at a later point will help you to reflect on what you have seen and will ensure that your notes are retained in more readable form. If responsibility for participation in your fieldwork setting prevents sustained note taking, you will need to reserve time soon after your participation to recall and to record what you have seen.

During your first fieldwork visits, you will want to obtain as much information as possible about the children and the setting. Try, through observation, to learn the answers to the following questions:

- What is the daily schedule? What names are given to the different time blocks (snack time, outdoor play time)? What are children expected to do during each of these time blocks? What do teachers do?

- How is the indoor program space arranged? Make a floor plan of the space showing furniture placement. What equipment and materials are present, and how are they placed in the room(s) used by the children? What names do the teacher and children use to refer to the different areas in the room (book corner, science center)?
- What are the major activity areas in the outdoor space? Make a bird's-eye-view map of the outdoor space showing major equipment and natural landmarks.
- What is the composition of the class? Make a list of the names of the children, noting interests and characteristics.
- What are the adults' expectations for children's behavior? How do these vary according to time periods throughout the program day and according to different locations in program space?
- When a child's behavior is not in accord with the program expectations, what do the adults do? What do other children do?
- What guidelines are followed to protect the health and safety of children in the program setting in regard to potential health problems or injuries?
- Are there children with special needs such as language differences or disabilities? How are they handled?
- How does the teacher interact with parents and other program or community personnel?

This kind of information would, of course, be placed in your notebook section *Basic Information*. If you have the opportunity to talk with the teacher responsible for the program in which you are observing or participating, try to get his or her responses to these questions as well as to the following:

- Do you feel that your work as a teacher is important? How do you think it compares with other professions in making an important contribution to the lives of others and to the betterment of society?
- In teaching, do you usually feel satisfied that you have done as much as possible for the children you teach? Or do you find yourself worrying about whether you should do more or do things differently?
- Do you feel you have opportunities to be creative as a teacher? Or is what you do quite prescribed and repetitive?
- Do you feel there is general agreement among the teachers you work with about how to teach? Or are there many differences of opinion?
- Do you find that other people—friends, acquaintances, strangers—try to tell you how to teach and how schools should be managed and organized? Do you think this happens to teachers more than to people in other professions?
- Can you generally decide how you will manage and organize the program? Or are you told how to do so?
- How much supervision do you have? What kind of supervision?
- Does someone evaluate your teaching? How is this done?
- How much contact do you have with other teachers in your school on a typical day? with adults other than teachers?
- What is most enjoyable for you in working with children?

- What personal characteristics do you feel are important for success in teaching? What kind of self-development do you think a prospective teacher might attempt?

For each day you participate in the fieldwork setting, you would do well to prepare a summary sheet for your *Log* notebook section, recording items such as the following:

Time of arrival and departure
Time blocks observed
My role
Situations of interest
My reactions

You may also make daily entries in the notebook subsection *Ideas.* Record just enough detail to help you remember at a later time what was done so that you can use the idea in your own subsequent work as a teacher of young children, if you so choose. These entries might take the form of lists under headings such as:

Art activity ideas
Dramatic play ideas
Language/reading/writing activity ideas
Math activity ideas
Movement ideas
Music activity ideas
Poems
Science activity ideas
Songs
Stories and books
Other

The following general guidelines for unobtrusive observation apply to almost any setting:

- Children will be less distracted by your presence if you sit or kneel than if you are a tower within their visual landscape.
- Be as unobtrusive as possible and do not become involved in the children's activity, or you will have little opportunity to be an observer.
- If a child tries to talk with you, asks for your help (in a nonemergency situation), or asks what you are doing, reply that you are doing your work, that you are learning about what children are like (or something of the kind), but do not encourage further conversation. Remove yourself briefly, if necessary, to lose a persistent child.
- Try not to laugh, frown, or in any way react to either the child you are observing or the other children in the setting, or you may find that you are not only recording but are influencing behavior.
- Never talk about a given child to other adults if either that child or the other

children are within hearing. The old saying that "little pitchers have big ears" is sometimes truer than you may realize.

- Avoid casually discussing the behavior or characteristics of any particular children you have observed (especially by name) with anyone other than the responsible person who gave you permission to observe. Consider information you obtain through observation as privileged professional matter that has no place in casual conversation.

Participation guidelines appropriate to most settings include the following:

- Dress comfortably in washable casual clothing.
- Arrive on time and determine how you can assist in the preparation for the daily session.
- If you have an assignment to supervise a particular area or activity, listen carefully to the teacher's plans for it or ask for information about what you are expected to do. Examine the equipment and materials so that you are familiar with them and how they are used. Experiment, if necessary, to gain a sense of how things work. For example, if you are to supervise an art activity, you may wish to experiment a bit with the media yourself before the children's arrival to learn what to expect. Think through the process of how children will acquire materials, what you will do while they are working, how you and they will clean up, how products will be handled. Better to ask questions of the teacher in advance than to wait until you are in the middle of the activity.
- Listen carefully to the directions teachers give to the children so that you know what their expectations are and can avoid giving contradictory help or directions.
- Converse with children in a quiet clear voice and friendly manner. Avoid teasing (physically or verbally) or testing (asking "What color is this?"). Instead, comment on what they are doing, about the materials available, and so forth.
- Ask for advice in how to handle materials or in responding to child behaviors if you feel uncertain. If children ask you to do something for or with them that you have not observed other adults doing, say to the children, "Let's ask (teacher's name) about that."
- Read the Guidance Strategies (pp. 223–226) and Alternative Strategies for Dialogue (pp. 240–244) sections of this textbook. They will prove useful to you now and can be restudied at a later point as well.
- Keep unnecessary conversations with other adults in the program setting to a minimum (whether indoors or out), saving comments and chitchat until the end of the program session.

PART 2: OBSERVING INDIVIDUAL CHILDREN

We suggest the following general procedures in observing and recording children's behavior. At the beginning, obtain basic information such as the child's name, age, sex, and the name and relationship to the child of the person giving you permission to observe. Learn as much as you can through observation before asking for additional information. During your first observation, try to gain a general impression of the setting and of the child's general appearance and demeanor and then prepare several descriptive narratives of approximately five-minute segments of behavior. Try to be as detailed as possible. Be sure to save these observations for later reference.

Descriptive Narrative

In producing a descriptive narrative of a given child's behavior, the observer begins by recording the time and the setting and then proceeds to write down in as much detail as possible what the child does, including responses to the actions of others. The following is an example of a five-minute descriptive narrative:

> Setting: Lucy's (age five) backyard
> Time: 3:30 P.M.
> Lucy is filling a plastic swimming pool with water from a hose. She directs the stream of water to make swirls and waves in the pool. She moves the stream of water as close to the pool's edge as possible and goes twice around in this fashion. George (neighbor, age five) asks Lucy to fill the watering can he is holding: "Gimme some gasoline." She guides the stream of water into the one-and-a-half-inch opening and fills, saying, "That's all you get." Betsy (neighbor, age four) comes over with another can saying, "I want some gasoline." Lucy says, "You can't have any more 'cause you aren't my friend." Sprays hose on edge of pool and onto Betsy's feet. Betsy says, "My mother said not to get wet." Lucy does not reply but looks at her and then swings stream of water across her shorts. Betsy shrieks. Lucy grins, then turns and walks about ten feet from pool pulling hose along at her side. Wets down concrete patio flooring. Turns hose toward each dry area until all are wet.

In recording behavior in descriptive narrative format, the goal is to describe only actual behaviors and to exclude statements of inference or evaluation. Describing actual behaviors is often referred to as reporting. It is important that you learn to clearly differentiate between reporting, inferring, and evaluating. **Reporting** is simply focusing on what is before you in as much detail as possible. **Inferring** is going beyond what you actually see and trying to guess at the underlying feelings, goals, or causes that might explain the behavior. **Evaluating** is making a judgment about the behavior you see, whether it is desirable or undesirable, positive or negative, mature or immature. A teacher, of course, engages in all three types of observation, often simultaneously, and benefits from proficiency in each. It is useful, however, to clearly differentiate between these processes and, especially, to develop the habit of relating each inference and evaluative statement to the actual behavior that was observed. Only if a report of actual behavior is available for consideration can alternative inferences and evaluations be considered. Without a descriptive report there is no possibility for considering whether other kinds of statements have validity.

EXAMPLES OF REPORTING, INFERRING, AND EVALUATING

Report

Sara is drawing on the chalkboard. She makes a circular figure about which she says, "Look at the cookie I made." Tom replies, "I'll eat that cookie," and with his hand reaches over and wipes across the drawing. Sara lunges toward him and pushes him away. In doing so, the piece of chalk breaks, falls to the floor, and shatters into several pieces. Sara goes to the teacher and says, "Tommy broke my chalk."

Inference

Sara is pleased to be able to produce figures and wants Tom's recognition for her ability. Tom, however, is more interested in the social interchange than in Sara's product and demolishes it, bringing forth her anger and physical aggressiveness. However, when the chalk breaks, she is unwilling to accept the responsibility for her own action and so attributes it to Tommy.

Evaluation

Both Sara and Tom are behaving less maturely than might be expected for children of their age. Sara should be given help in learning to verbally express her displeasure rather than physically striking out. She also needs to be encouraged to "own" her own actions—even when they have unfortunate consequences. Tom should be helped to understand that the destruction of another's product is not likely to produce the positive response he evidently wants. He should be shown ways of relating in a situation where someone asks him to look at his or her work.

There are no set limits for the time span covered by such a narrative, but since the writing load is intense, many observers restrict themselves to a brief episode. During this time, observers are involved with rapid note taking, after which they fill in the details. The initial episode can be followed by another stretch of observation, note taking, and note expansion. Psychologists call this practice of making a record for preset time periods at regularly recurring intervals **time sampling.** The observer assumes that by regularly sampling behavior during a period of time, sufficiently representative behaviors will be obtained to make reasonable inferences about the person's typical pattern of behavior. For example, if an observer has a collection of six narrative descriptions of Lucy, each reporting on five minutes of activity during the day, there is sufficient base for discussing Lucy's behavior patterns. Another approach to sampling is called **event sampling.** Again, the observer does not try to record behavior continuously, but instead waits for some particularly relevant event or situation to occur and then records all behaviors that occur during that event. The observer may decide in advance to record only instances of conflicts, or interactions with adults, or the use of toys. This kind of sampling is used when the observer (1) wants to have a controlled set of contexts for making better inferences about behavior, or (2) wants to assess a child's behavioral repertoire in a particular type of situation. As with time sampling, the observer records as rapidly as possible all relevant actions and reactions, and upon termination of the event, makes sure the record is readable and complete.

Especially in the initial observations of a child, detailed descriptive narratives of segments of behavior are useful. The disadvantages of narrative descriptions stem from the fact that they are relatively time-consuming and require total concentration on a particular child to the exclusion of all others. Although such a period of concentration on each child is easily justified by the insights obtained, it is often difficult for a person who has responsibility for a group to find the opportunity to make such observations. It is an excellent way for a student to observe, however, since the novice observer of children needs to learn how to avoid following the action of the group, thus missing the nuances of the individual child's ongoing behavior.

As indicated previously, a series of questions about individual children's behavior were posed in Chapters 5, 7, and 9. Your task is to study these categories, and in your observations of each child for whom you are doing an assessment, to record from your descriptive narrative notes (very briefly) any evidence that bears on the questions. For example, one question posed in Chapter 5 was "What is the child's ability to use his or her body in rhythmic fashion?" During your observation, you might see absolutely no evidence of rhythmic performance, or you might note something such as the following:

- Janey tries to skip across the room as her friend Suzy is doing; manages a skipping pattern about halfway across and then runs the rest of the way.
- Listens to music from record player while writing on chalkboard; continues in activity of writing and moves in dance pattern while doing so.

In each of Chapters 5, 7, and 9, many such questions are asked to guide you in looking for specific behaviors that might otherwise go unnoticed. As you attempt to answer specific questions about the children you observe, you will find that some of the answers will be obvious given a very brief observation; others will require repeated contacts. You may even find that you do not observe any behavior relevant to some of the questions.

You should only record actual descriptions of the child, obtained as you are watching him or her. For instance, in studying the child's hand dominance, you might note, "combs hair with left hand"; "uses both hands in doing puzzle"; "marks with crayon using left, sometimes right." Avoid general statements such as "no hand preference." Only after repeated notations of specific behavior would the inference that the child has not established hand dominance be justified. Beware of jumping to immediate conclusions on the basis of limited evidence. Even if your early impressions do turn out to be correct, you will be on safer ground if you can support your statement with repeated examples of the child's actual behavior.

There are a number of ways to organize your notes. You may wish to put together a notebook for each child for whom you will make a full behavioral assessment, about twelve pages or so, recording category heads and questions for motor and physical development leaving sufficient blank space for writing in descriptions of the behaviors you see.

Or you may prefer to use a three-by-five-inch card file. If so, the questions might be written on dividers, with tabs indicating the numerical codes. Your notes could then be jotted on three-by-five-inch note pad sheets (one sheet for each note you make) and filed under the appropriate heading after each observation. You may also wish to label each card with an identifying number for the child, the place of observation (sand area, story time), and so forth.

Whatever your organization of materials, we encourage you to be a liberal note taker. It is easier to discard extraneous information later than to try to recall half-remembered details. It will probably help you to read through the list of questions just before your observation period. Make notes while you are actually observing if it is feasible to do so. Immediately after the observation period, reread the list of questions and record any additional behaviors that seem to be relevant to your records. Be sure to put a date on each entry so that you will have a means for following a child's behavior pattern across time.

You will probably find that when you first begin to observe a child you will have countless notations, and you will feel frustrated that you are seeing more than you can possibly record. However, you will soon find that what you miss will typically occur again and again and can be recorded later. During observation periods spanning several days or longer, new behaviors will become increasingly rare. The process of learning about a new child is always heavy initially, but stick with it! You will find that persistence pays off and that the task becomes increasingly manageable.

Each individual, whether adult or child, has a limited repertoire of behaviors used in daily interactions. Whereas some individuals have a far greater repertoire than others, particularly in certain areas, there is far greater repetitiveness than at first appears. Your task as an observer is to assess this repertoire, making extensive notes at first contacts and determining new or previously unused facets of the repertoire through continued observations.

Chapters 5, 7, and 9 also contain models for organizing your information into full behavioral assessments. Ultimately, you will have the information necessary to compile a detailed report on the child you observe that includes his or her physical characteristics and motor behavior; affective behavior and social behavior; cognitive behavior and intellectual behavior.

PART 3: OBSERVING CLASSROOM INTERACTION

In Part 2 of the textbook, you learned to observe individual children through the use of narrative descriptions and then to use those narratives to answer questions representing categories of children's behavior. Those observational approaches were open-ended; that is, you were told to record everything that you observed that was relevant to the category. We now suggest that you use narrative descriptions of the event-sampling type to document and study the teacher behavior you are observing in your fieldwork setting. While you are in your fieldwork setting, observe what the teachers do and say during problematic situations. The following are only a few examples of such situations:

- Child crying upon separation from parent
- Conflicts between children
- Spills (paint, milk, and so forth)

- Children using very loud voices indoors
- Fire drills
- Child biting another child
- Name calling
- Sex play
- "Bad" language
- Child refusing to do cleanup

You may find it useful to share the descriptive narratives you prepare of these kinds of events with your classmates and your instructor. Since these are common incidents in early childhood classrooms, you need the opportunity to develop an effective repertoire to respond to such situations in your own teaching.

In addition to the open-ended descriptive narrative, however, you may also wish to learn how closed category systems can be used to analyze behaviors in the classroom setting. These systems are very useful when the observers wish to note only the occurrence of certain selected behaviors in which they may be especially interested.

There are many variations of closed category systems. In one variation in which children's behavior is to be the target (or focus) of the observation, the observer watches an individual child during a set time interval (sometimes for regularly recurring periods) or for a particular event, such as story time. The observer can record the occurrence of each kind of **target behavior** in one of two formats: (1) whether it occurs at all, or (2) the frequency with which it occurs.

Any discrete behavior can be included in a closed category system, and many kinds of behavior can be looked for simultaneously. The observer may, for example, check during a set interval, say thirty seconds, whether Child A is engaging in a social interaction and, if so, whether it is nonverbal or verbal, positive or negative. The observer might then rotate through the group, observing Child B, followed by Child C, and so forth. After observing all of the children and noting on a simple form the nature of the social interaction, the observer then begins again with Child A. The rotation through the class continues for several rounds. The total allows an examination of the group's interactions as well as comparisons between individuals in the group (see Figure A1-1). Data gathered at intervals throughout a year document individual and group changes. Or data gathered for the same group within the same general time frame (that is, the same week) under different conditions may prove insightful. For example, observations might be made during group time versus free-choice time; with regular teachers versus substitute teachers; during cleanup time with music versus cleanup time without music. Your course instructor may help you devise other interesting comparisons to make.

Closed category systems can also be used for gathering data on teacher behavior. We might observe different teachers to determine how they respond to children's behaviors. Suppose we observe Ms. Grath and Ms. Young, both first-

Date _____ Observer _____

Time at start _____ Teachers _____

Activity description _____

	Time 1	Time 2	Time 3	Time 4	Time 5	V	N	+	−
							Total		
Child A	V+	V+	0	V−	N+	3	1	3	1
Child B	0	0	N−	0	0	0	1	0	1
Child C	N−	V+	N+	0	V+	2	2	3	1
Child D	V+	V−	N+	N+	V+	3	2	4	1
Child E	N+	N−	V−	V−	N−	2	3	1	4
Child F	V−	V−	V+	0	0	3	0	1	2
Child G	V+	0	N+	0	N+	1	2	3	0
Child H	V+	V+	V+	V−	V+	5	0	4	1
Child I	0	V−	V−	N−	N+	2	2	1	3
Child J	N+	N+	N+	V+	0	1	3	4	0
					Group Total	22	16	24	14

Code:
V = Verbal
N = Nonverbal
0 = No interaction
+ = Positive
− = Negative

FIGURE A1-1   Example of a closed category system for recording children's behavior.

grade teachers, for three ten-minute periods at different points during their program days. During each of the ten minutes, we attend to those instances in which they speak to individual children, ignoring any talk directed to the whole group. We watch to determine what their physical orientation is to each of these individuals to whom they speak. For example, in observing Ms. Grath each time she turns her attention to a different child, we indicate, by placing a tally in the appropriate box, whether she is standing, sitting at adult chair height, sitting at child chair height, kneeling, or sitting on the floor. The chart in Figure A1-2 reveals that Ms. Grath has many more interactions with individual children than Ms. Young and is more often physically located at the children's eye level.

The two closed category systems described here are only examples. You will find it interesting to design your own systems so you can gather data on topics of particular interest to you.

In addition to descriptive narratives, open category systems, and closed category systems, you may also find it useful to keep additional notes on how various classrooms you see in operation at your fieldwork site organize space and time and how various teaching strategies and techniques are implemented, especially those with which you feel most comfortable. This may prove helpful in incorporating these practices into your own repertoire. Keep in mind that the broader your repertoire, the more likely it is that you will be effective in your teaching efforts.

	Teacher Ms. Grath				Teacher Ms. Young			
	Period*				Period*			
Posture	First	Second	Third	Total	First	Second	Third	Total
Standing	/	//	/	4	//	///	//	7
Sitting (adult chair)				0	///	//	///	8
Sitting (child chair)	////	///	HH	12				0
Kneeling (floor)	//	///	//	7	/		/	2
Sitting (floor)	///	HH	//	10				0

Total individual child interactions   _33_   Total individual child interactions   _17_

Percent child's eye level   _88%_   Percent child's eye level   _12%_

*Ten-minute observation periods

FIGURE A1-2   Example of a closed category system for recording teachers' behavior.

PART 4: OBSERVING CLASSROOM ACTIVITY AREAS

To learn more about classroom activities, focus on specific areas or activity centers. For example, see what happens in a single area (book area, block area) during an entire free-choice period. Record which children go to the area; what they get involved in; the kinds of interactions they have; whether the teachers are present in the area and, if so, what they do; how long each child stays in the area. On another day, focus on a different area.

A second way to learn about classroom activities in a fieldwork setting is to compare the behavior of teacher and children during different time periods. You might compare, for example, the amount of conversation that occurs at different times of day. In the Suggested Activities sections at the end of each of the six chapters in Part 4, you will find specific questions to guide your observations.

If your fieldwork involves participation, you may be able to take dictation from one or more children. Offer to write down a story as the child tells you what to write. The story may be about a drawing or painting the child has produced, about a magazine picture, or just a "made up" story. You will need to write neatly, using whatever writing system is used by the teacher. As you write, place the letters making up a word quite close together; then leave ample space between words and between lines to make the discrimination of words as entities clearer for the children. Try to answer the following questions regarding what the child understands about print:

- Does the child show any interest in looking at the words you are writing?
- Does the child slow down his or her speech to match your rate of writing? Does the child seem aware of the one-to-one correspondence between each word that he or she says and the word that you write?
- Does the child show any evidence of recognizing any of the words you write?
- Does the child point out any interesting features of letters or words? Does he or she point out any of the letters by name? Does he or she notice any similarities between words?
- Does the child show an interest in having you read back the words that have been written? Does the child have an interest in reading the words that have been written? If so, what clues does the child appear to get from the print versus recall of the story told?
- Does the child value the story product, asking to have it for himself or herself or giving it to another person?

As you analyze the answers to these questions, try to determine what opportunities or lack of opportunities and what satisfying or frustrating experiences might have led to the child's current reactions to this kind of experience with print.

OUTLINE FOR A
PORTFOLIO

We recommended in the Introduction and Epilogue that you develop a portfolio of materials related to your professional growth. Whether or not you ever show others the materials in your portfolio, their accessibility will assist both your teacher preparation experiences and your actual teaching.

You will probably acquire materials in diverse forms—loose papers, clippings, xeroxed sheets, pictures, photographs, booklets, books, notebooks, and so forth. You may decide to keep them in file folders, card files, loose-leaf notebooks, envelopes, boxes, or filing cabinets. Keeping track of such a variety of materials requires a fairly detailed system for classifying and labeling. The following is a suggested outline for classification. It is merely illustrative, since any such system is highly arbitrary and depends on one's particular bent. Whatever scheme you use must not only make sense to you, but should be comprehensive enough to encompass quite diverse sets of materials on a range of topics related to early education. Finally, the outline should be constructed to allow for expansion through branching of the original categories.

One advantage of the following classification system is that it follows the general format of this text and should, therefore, be easy for you to learn and remember. The numerical divisions and the logical extensions of this outline permit expansion and are easily applied to collections of materials in various forms through consistent numerical labeling and sequencing. To look for materials on a particular subject, you need only know the category number to identify each type of collection—cards, files, and so forth.

Whatever classification scheme you use initially, you should continue to modify it to make it fit your own teaching priorities. The following sample outline is offered as an example:

1   Foundations
    1.1   History
    1.2   Cultural and socioeconomic influences
    1.3   Current trends
    1.4   Future perspectives
2   Early childhood education as a career
    2.1   General information about the profession
    2.2   Training requirements
    2.3   Job requirements
        2.3.1   General
        2.3.2   Specific to a given state, program
        2.3.3   Personal qualifications for teaching
3   Children's development
    3.1   Physical and motor development
    3.2   Affective and social development
    3.3   Cognitive and intellectual development
    3.4   Observation and assessment of children's development
4   Organization and management
    4.1   Orientations (theories, philosophies)
    4.2   Models (prototypic program configurations)
    4.3   Program descriptions (specific local programs)
    4.4   Management and discipline
        4.4.1   Space arrangement
        4.4.2   Time scheduling
        4.4.3   Facilities (equipment and materials)
        4.4.4   Behavioral management
        4.4.5   Planning and teaching strategies
        4.4.6   Communication skills and strategies
5   Teaching resourcefulness
    5.1   Resourcefulness in activity-specific situations
        5.1.1   Manipulative materials
        5.1.2   Art
        5.1.3   Pretend
        5.1.4   Music
        5.1.5   Literature
        5.1.6   Sharing
        5.1.7   Other
    5.2   Resourcefulness in subject-matter areas
        5.2.1   Language development
        5.2.2   Reading and writing
        5.2.3   Natural and physical sciences
        5.2.4   Mathematics
        5.2.5   Social sciences
        5.2.6   Other

RESOURCE ORGANIZATIONS

American Academy of Pediatrics, 141 Northwest Point Boulevard, P.O. Box 927, Elk Grove Village, IL 60009

American Federation of Teachers, 555 New Jersey Avenue N.W., Washington, DC 20001

American Foundation for the Blind, 15 W. 16th Street, New York, NY 10011

American Montessori Society, 150 Fifth Avenue, New York, NY 10011

American Physical Therapy Association, 1111 N. Fairfax Street, Alexandria, VA 22314

American Speech-Language-Hearing Association, 10801 Rockville Pike, Rockville, MD 20852

Association for Childhood Education International, 11141 Georgia Avenue, Suite 200, Wheaton, MD 20902

Autism Society of America, 8601 Georgia Avenue, Suite 503, Silver Springs, MD 20910

Children's Book Council, 568 Broadway, New York, NY 10012

Children's Defense Fund, 122 C Street N.W., Washington, DC 20001

Child Welfare League of America, Inc., 440 First Street N.W., Washington, DC 20001

Council for Early Childhood Professional Recognition, 1718 Connecticut Avenue N.W., Suite 500, Washington, DC 20009

Council for Exceptional Children, 1920 Association Drive, Reston, VA 22091

Epilepsy Foundation of America, 4351 Garden City Drive, Landover, MD 20785

ERIC Clearinghouse in Elementary and Early Childhood Education, University of Illinois, 805 W. Pennsylvania Avenue, Urbana, IL 61801

International Reading Association, 800 Barksdale Road, P.O. Box 8139, Newark, DE 19714

National Association for the Education of Young Children, 1834 Connecticut Avenue N.W., Washington, DC 20009

National Association for Gifted Children, 4175 Lovell Road, Suite 140, Circle Pines, MN 55014

National Association for Retarded Citizens, P.O. Box 6109, East Arlington, TX 76011

National Black Child Development Institute, Inc., 1463 Rhode Island Avenue N.W., Washington DC 20005

National Council of Teachers of English, 1111 Kenyon Road, Urbana, IL 61801

National Easter Seal Society, 70 E. Lake St., Chicago, IL 60601

National Education Association, 1201 16th Street N.W., Washington, DC 20036

Society for Research in Child Development, University of Chicago Press, 5720 Woodlawn Avenue, Chicago, IL 60637

Southern Association on Children Under Six, Box 5403 Brady Station, Little Rock, AR 72215

United Cerebral Palsy Association, Inc., 7 Penn Plaza, Suite 804, New York, NY 10001

Women's Action Alliance, 370 Lexington Avenue, Suite 603, New York, NY 10017

World Organization for Early Childhood Education, c/o Dr. Jan McCarthy, School of Education, Indiana State University, Terre Haute, IN 47809

PERIODICALS

Arithmetic Teacher National Council of Teachers of Mathematics, 1906 Association Drive, Reston, VA 22091. $40; published nine times a year.

Child Care Information Exchange Exchange Press, Inc., Box 2890, Redmond, WA 98073. $35; published bimonthly.

Child Care Quarterly Human Sciences Press, Inc., 72 Fifth Avenue, New York, NY 10011. $36; published quarterly.

Child Development Society for Research in Child Development, Inc., University of Chicago Press, 5801 S. Ellis Avenue, Chicago, IL 60637. $110; published bimonthly.

Child Development Abstracts and Bibliography Society for Research in Child Development, Inc., University of Chicago Press, 5801 S. Ellis Avenue, Chicago, IL 60637. $40; published three times a year.

Childhood Education Association for Childhood Education International, 11141 Georgia Avenue, Suite 200, Wheaton, MD 20902. $38; published five times a year.

Children's House Children's House, Inc., Box 111, Caldwell, NJ 07006. $9.50; published bimonthly.

Children Today U.S. Health and Human Services, 200 Independence Avenue S.W., Washington, DC 20201. $7.50; published bimonthly.

Classroom Computer Learning Peter Li, Inc., 2451 E. River Road, Dayton, OH 45439. $24; published eight times a year.

Day Care and Early Education Magazine Human Sciences Press, Inc., 72 Fifth Avenue, New York, NY 10011. $19; published quarterly.

Early Childhood Research Quarterly Ablex, 355 Chestnut Street, Norwood, NJ 07648. $32.50; published quarterly.

Early Education and Development Psychology Press, Inc., 39 Pearl Street, Brandon, VT 05733. $175; published quarterly.

Educational Leadership Association for Supervision and Curriculum Development, 125 N. West Street, Alexandria, VA 22314. $32; published eight times a year.

Elementary School Journal   University of Chicago Press, 5720 S. Woodlawn Avenue, Chicago, IL 60637. $28.50; published five times a year.

Exceptional Children   Council for Exceptional Children, 1920 Association Drive, Reston, VA 22091. $35; published bimonthly.

The Instructor   Scholastic, Inc., 730 Broadway, New York, NY 10003. $20; published monthly.

Journal of Research in Childhood Education   Association for Childhood Education International, 11141 Georgia Avenue, Suite 200, Wheaton, MD 20902. $430 to nonmembers; published semiannually.

Language Arts   National Council of Teachers of English, 1111 Kenyon Road, Urbana, IL 61801. $35; published monthly.

Pre-K Today   Scholastic Inc., 730 Broadway, New York, NY 10003. $24.95; published monthly.

The Reading Teacher   International Reading Association, Inc., 800 Barksdale Road, P.O. Box 8139, Newark, DE 19714. Membership; published nine times a year.

Science and Children   National Science Teachers Association, 1742 Connecticut Avenue N.W., Washington, DC 20009. $35; published eight times a year.

Teaching K–8   Early Years, Inc., 40 Richards Avenue, Norwalk, CT 06854. $18; published nine times a year.

Young Children   National Association for the Education of Young Children, 1834 Connecticut Avenue N.W., Washington, DC 20009. $25 to nonmembers.

GLOSSARY

accommodation   The process, according to the Piagetian view, whereby an internal mental organization is altered to incorporate certain aspects of new experiences that previously could not be assimilated (see *assimilation*); or, as more broadly used, the process whereby existing patterns of behavior are modified to cope with new situations.

accountability testing   The administration of tests to determine whether a child has benefited from participation in a particular program or a teacher has been effective in instructing pupils.

active listening   Taking in accurate and comprehensive information about a speaker's message and feelings.

activity plan   A plan, usually written, for a period of children's involvement in a particular activity; may include the materials to be used, the preparation required, the procedures, the possible learnings, and an evaluation plan.

adaptation   The process of change after which an individual is better fitted to cope with his or her environment; involves, according to Piagetian theory, the dual processes of assimilation and accommodation.

advance organizer   The knowledge base possessed by learners to which new information can be linked.

affective behavior   Behavior related to the feeling function or functions; includes motivations, interests, and values.

agility   The ability to move flexibly to stretch, bend, spin, arch, leap, turn, throw, run, jump.

aide   A person, typically with little or no professional training, employed to perform specified tasks under the direct supervision of professional personnel.

assimilation   The process whereby new experiences (objects, events) are incorporated into existing mental structures.

associate degree   The degree conferred at the completion of a two-year junior college, community college, or technical training program.

associative play   Play involving two or more children in which there is some sharing of materials but little other interaction.

attachment   A bond of affection between two or more individuals; implies a relationship that endures through time.

balance   The effective alignment of body parts to maintain the vertical center of gravity to allow movement without falling.

behavioral assessment   A description of an individual's current status in various areas of functioning that fully supports, with reports of observed behavior, any inferences and evaluative statements.

behaviorist   Person who analyzes the conditions or events shown to have an effect on overt behavior; modern behaviorists often use their findings to manipulate conditions and events to control (manage or modify) behavior.

behavior modification   A change in an accustomed mode of behavior resulting from external encounters; in more specific current usage, the application of systematic principles, especially reinforcement technology, to change behavior.

biological maturation   Changes in the characteristics of an individual that result from anatomical, physiological, and neurological development; different from changes due to experience or learning.

catharsis   The release of accumulated feelings and emotions through awareness and expression (verbal, kinesthetic, dramatic, and artistic).

certification   The issuing of a license to teach by an agency legally authorized by a state to grant such a license.

child development associate (CDA)   A person awarded an associate degree as an early childhood specialist; the degree, based on demonstrated competence, is awarded by the Council for Early Childhood Professional Recognition.

classification   The act of systematically grouping objects or events according to identifiable common characteristics.

classroom management   The actions of the teacher in keeping children constructively engaged in developmentally and educationally appropriate activities.

cognitive structures   The coherent and integrated cognitive systems by which an individual organizes experience and relates to the environment.

commitment   The act of pledging or engaging oneself; in this text, refers to personal identification with the occupational role of teaching.

compensatory education   Educational programs, often sponsored by federal or state governments, intended to lessen or eliminate those differences considered to be disadvantageous for members of various subcultural or economically deprived groups.

computer-assisted instruction (CAI)   The systematic presentation of information to a student through computerized storage and retrieval.

concept   The common element or feature of cognition that functions to identify groups of classes; a concept usually has a name, but the word itself is not the concept, only the symbol of the concept.

concept attainment   The derivation of a concept or generalization inductively by a learner recognizing common elements or attributes from a number of otherwise different objects, events, or situations.

concrete operations   Mental activities concerned with actual objects, including ordering, seriation, classification, and mathematical processes, all of which are reversible (see *reversibility*); characterizes the thinking of children from age seven or eight to approximately eleven or twelve; problem solving is limited to events that can be visualized in concrete terms.

conservation   A term used by Piaget referring to the awareness that number or other quantitative attributes (weight, volume) remain the same despite changes in appearance unless there are additions or deletions.

constructive play   Play in which objects and toys are manipulated to create representations of selected aspects of the external world.

constructivist   Person concerned with how children derive the concepts through which they make sense of the world, what means they use in their explorations and thinking, and how their interactions with their environment move them toward more mature thinking.

contingent   The degree to which one thing depends on another; for example, the degree to which reinforcement is aligned with the occurrence of a given behavior.

continuous reinforcement   A schedule in which every instance of a given target behavior is reinforced.

cooperative play   Play in which a group works together toward a common purpose, such as making some material product, dramatizing a situation, or playing formal games.

corpus callosum   A band of transverse fibers connecting the left and right halves of the cerebrum.

culture   A shared organization of ideas that includes the intellectual, moral, and aesthetic standards prevalent in a community and the meaning of communicative actions (Levine, 1984).

decenter   To be aware of the secondary or prior compelling immediate features; incorporation of secondary aspects of stimulus into the total perception.

decode   To obtain meaning from written symbols; reading.

descriptive feedback   A form of teacher-child dialogue in which the teacher comments on what the child is doing to increase the child's self-awareness and to model the use of language and concepts.

developmental crises   As proposed by Erikson, the succession of eight stages universally encountered in psychosocial development, each of which presents polar possibilities that require resolution.

differentiation   The progressive series of changes in an individual's development whereby generalized movements and relatively simple conceptualizations become more precise; results in increased abilities.

direct instruction   An approach to teaching that emphasizes a prescribed sequence of teacher-controlled verbal interactions designed to lead children to emit responses relevant to specific academic objectives.

disadvantaged   Lacking normal or usual advantages, such as safe and healthful living conditions, opportunities to learn facilitating skills and attitudes.

discipline   The actions of the teacher when a child, despite classroom management efforts (see *classroom management*), continues to engage in behavior that is not considered acceptable.

distancing   The linking through thought processes of immediate behaviors or events with similar ones outside the immediate environment.

dominance   The preference for the use of either the right or left hand, foot, or eye.

dramatic play   The acting out or dramatization of a direct, vicarious, or imagined experience through personal identification with the characters involved.

egocentric   Lack of discrimination between what is and is not self; lack of awareness of anything outside one's own immediate experiencing.

encode   To record ideas by means of written symbols; writing.

endurance   The extent to which movement(s) can be continued without need for rest.

environmentalist   Person primarily concerned with determining how environmental forces shape particular kinds of behavior in individuals or characteristics of species (see *behaviorist*).

evaluating   The process of determining the meaning of behavior or other phenomena in terms of a standard.

event sampling   Obtaining a record of observed behavior only during certain preselected types of incidents, such as play time, conflicts, or interaction with peers.

exploration   Investigation of the physical and functional properties of an object.

fine-motor development   The ability to use one's hands to grasp and manipulate objects.

fixed interval schedule   A reinforcement of behavior according to the amount of time elapsed since the last reinforcement of that behavior.

fixed ratio schedule   The reinforcement of behavior according to the number of occurrences of the behavior required for reinforcement.

Follow Through   Evaluation project initiated in 1968 as part of a federal compensatory education effort; variations in types of programming in kindergarten and primary grades were studied with the goal of sustaining the advantages of participation in Head Start programs.

formal operations   Mental activities concerned with abstract thought, such as hypotheses and logical propositions.

formal sharing   An exchange of ideas or information within a group situation structured by a leader (typically, a teacher) for that purpose.

frames   See *play frame*.

fundamental lesson   The initial introduction by a Montessori teacher to a child of the precise use of a particular type of learning material.

gender identification   Those aspects of an individual's imagery of self, relative to maleness or femaleness, that are differentiated as relatively stable.

gender-related behavior   Those behaviors that, according to social consensus, are identified with males or females.

handedness   Preference for use of the right or left hand either in tasks requiring the use of one hand or in the more difficult aspects of tasks in which both hands are used.

Head Start   A federally funded program designed to provide experiences for low-income children that would allow them to enter public school with the attitudes and skills necessary for their successful participation.

Head Start Planned Variation   A study of the implementation and effects of differing program approaches to compensatory education.

hemispheres   The lateral halves of the cerebrum and the cerebellum (anatomical).

heritage language   The language commonly spoken within the family during childhood; also referred to as the "native" or "first" language.

images   Memories of past experiences; centrally aroused internal experience based on perceptions of external experience.

inferring   Drawing a tentative conclusion regarding the likely meaning of facts and observations; going beyond the evidence available through logical extensions of what is known.

informal sharing   A spontaneous exchange of ideas or information without formality or ceremony.

in loco parentis   To serve in the role of parent or guardian.

integration   The state of having fully incorporated an action, skill, or idea into an overall behavior pattern so there is little need for conscious effort.

intellect   The capacity to integrate experience using cognitive processes.

intellectual behavior   Aspects of behavior that involve the cognitive integration of experience.

interactionist   Person primarily concerned with studying how children attempt to make sense of what they encounter; what means they use in their explorations and thinking; and, especially, how their interactions with their environments help them move to more complex stages of development.

intermittent reinforcement   A schedule in which reinforcement is not given at each instance of an identified behavior but instead is given only periodically.

intervention   Providing new experiences, such as educational programs, in order to modify the performance or state of the recipient of these experiences; applied especially to change the status of the economically or culturally disadvantaged (see *disadvantaged*).

invariance   A term used by Piaget to describe the unchanging aspects of phenomena, such as the constancy of number or quantity; learned by a child in performing operations on objects (see *conservation*).

invented spellings   Spelling of words based on individual children's existent knowledge of sound-letter relationships rather than conventional spellings.

language immersion   Participation in a setting in which discourse is almost totally conducted in a nonfamiliar language.

large-muscle development   Development of the muscles used in gross bodily movements, primarily the muscles of the arms and legs.

lateral dominance   Sidedness; preferential use of one hand, foot, or eye rather than the other; a combination of handedness, footedness, and eyedness; assumed dominance of one cerebral hemisphere over the other in respect to motor functions.

lateralization   Brain organization in which each of the hemispheres control different psychological functions; for example, for most right-handed people, there is a lateralization of speech and language in the left hemisphere.

least restrictive environment   Educational setting for children with disabilities which is, to the maximum extent appropriate, with children who are not disabled.

lesson plan   A plan, usually written, for a short period of instruction to be devoted to a specific limited set of objectives; typically includes a statement of objectives, preparation required, materials to be used, procedures, and an evaluation plan.

literacy   The ability to read and write.

literacy acquisition   The process of becoming able to read and write.

mainstreaming   The integration of students with disabilities into the most normal environments possible that can accommodate and provide for their special needs.

manipulative materials   Abstract shapes or pliable forms which are used as play materials, e.g., blocks, clay, Tinker Toys.

maturationist   Person who holds the view that the pervasive and important changes in individuals occur primarily as a result of biological development rather than experience or learning.

mental structure   See *cognitive structure.*

metacommunication   Communication about communication; self-talk or social talk about what is to be said and done.

mixed dominance   A preference for the use of the right hand and the left eye (or vice versa).

model   A distinctive and coherent organizational or procedural pattern that is specific enough to be replicated (program).

modeling   A teaching strategy emphasizing the demonstration by example of new or appropriate behaviors.

motor behavior   Aspects of behavior related to movement and overt action.

motoric competence   The facility with which an individual can accomplish various physical acts involving strength, muscular coordination, speed of reaction.

motor intelligence   Early modes of thinking that, according to Piaget, consist only of an infant's own actions and the direct sensory qualities of objects encountered; internal symbolic representations of reality are lacking (see *sensorimotor*).

multiple classification   The act of systematically and simultaneously grouping objects or events according to two or more identifiable dimensions; for example, sorting simultaneously according to both color and size.

negative reinforcement   A circumstance in which behaviors are reinforced through the reduction or removal of annoying or painful events.

neurolinguistic programming   Management of human interactions including the enhancement of communication through the intentional selection of behaviors based on knowledge of one's own and other's preferred modes of interaction.

norms   The expected; average (mean, median, or mode); usually according to age, grade, or other criteria.

objectives   Purposes to be realized directly through instructional actions; statements of what behaviors are anticipated as the outcome of a planned program or lesson.

object permanency   The constancy of objects; the awareness that a previously viewed object still exists, even though out of sight.

operant behaviors   Any behavior whose frequency of occurrence can be controlled, at least in part, by the consequences that follow its appearance.

parallel play   Play in which one child is near another and both are engaged in the same sorts of activities but with no active cooperation or sharing and no attempt to achieve a common goal.

paraprofessional   See *aide.*

phoneme   Basic unit of sound that signals difference in meaning in a given language.

plasticity   Capacity for functional changes in the central nervous system induced by external influences.

play frame   The result of a decision to ignore present realities and create an imaginary event or situation.

positive reinforcement   Reinforcement after the occurrence of a particular behavior that increases the probability of that behavior's being repeated or strengthened.

preconceptual thinking   A term used by Piaget to describe early thinking processes based on immediate perceptions and imaginative self-projection.

predictable books   Picture books with limited text which can be easily anticipated because of a chained sequence (e.g., questions and answers), rhythmic cadence, and other context and pictorial clues.

Premack principle   The principle, proposed by Donald Premack, whereby an individual's high-probability behavior is used to reinforce and increase his or her low-probability behavior.

preoperational period   The stage of cognitive development that, according to Piaget, precedes the emergence of logical, reversible operations (see *concrete operations, formal operations*); characterized by intuitive and egocentric thinking linked to perception.

print-rich environment   Environment containing a large amount of print to be seen which serves diverse and meaningful communication functions.

projection   The unconscious act of attributing one's own thoughts or feelings to another (or to self in role of other), especially those thoughts and feelings which are seen as socially unacceptable.

psychosexual conflicts   The developmental crises proposed by psychoanalytical theory as inevitable, since socializing events of weaning, toilet training, and sexual control run counter to predominant sources of bodily satisfactions (oral, anal, genital).

punishment   An unpleasant experience that is a consequence of specific acts or behaviors; typically administered with the expectation that it will reduce the probability of the behavior's recurring.

ratio schedule   Schedules whereby reinforcement is given contingent on the number of times a target behavior has occurred since the previous reinforcement (see *fixed ratio schedule; variable ratio schedule*).

readiness testing   The administration of a test to determine a child's readiness to benefit from a specific type of academic program or the level or type of instruction to be used with a child at his or her current level.

realia   Tangible objects (in contrast to representations such as pictures, models).

reflexive behavior   Instinctual patterns and automatic reactions (which may be a combination of both learning and instinct) that occur involuntarily and are not under conscious control.

reinforcement   Anything that increases the likelihood that an act will be repeated at the next opportunity.

reliability   The extent to which a test gives dependable or consistent scores.

repertoire   The skills, talents, or response patterns that an individual (or animal) possesses and can use in given circumstances.

repertoire building   The act of extending an individual's array of alternative actions or behaviors.

reversibility   A term used by Piaget to describe the aspects of logical thinking operations in which one's mind reverses actions and mentally "undoes" the previous action in order to coordinate the present circumstances with what was previously observed.

rhythm   The ability to pattern movements in a predictable, repetitive sequence.

scheduling of reinforcements   The timing and sequencing of reinforcements presented to an individual to increase or strengthen the probability of selected behaviors.

schema   A pattern of behavior (at the sensorimotor stage) or the internal general form of a conceptualization (at later stages); a mental structure for a specific aspect of "knowing" (plural: schemata).

screening   Process of testing and observation to determine whether a child needs special services or a modified or individualized educational program because of disabilities or giftedness.

scripts   The learned network of associations with particular settings or situations which generate culturally prescribed actions and behavior.

self-concept   Those aspects of an individual's imagery about self that have been differentiated as relatively stable and characteristic.

self-correcting   The attribute of a learning device or learning equipment that allows a user to determine independently whether actions or responses are appropriate or inappropriate without the presence of a teacher or other experienced user; often used to describe Montessori equipment, with which inappropriate alignment of the apparatus is apparent to the user.

sensitivity   The state or quality of being sensitive and perceptive; in this text, specifically refers to awareness of variations in individual children's behavior and development.

sensorimotor   An initial means whereby the individual comes to "know" and learn of the world through specific sensory input and motoric actions.

sensorimotor period   The initial stage of development, as proposed by Piaget, encompassing the years from birth to approximately age two.

sensorimotor play   The use of motor behaviors to create effects for one's own enjoyment or for exploratory purposes.

seriation   The process of ordering or aligning objects or events according to variations in identifiable characteristics such as size, weight, color intensity.

shape/shaping   Reinforcement of each successive approximate response toward a desired behavioral goal.

signaling systems   External behaviors whereby the infant consistently communicates inner states; for example, crying indicates discomfort, cooing indicates pleasure.

social behavior   Aspects of behavior that involve interactions with one or more others.

sociodramatic play   Dramatic or pretend play involving cooperative effort with one or more others to enact a contrived situation.

solitary play   Play in which a child plays alone with toys or materials without interaction or regard as to other children's play.

speed   Rapid and efficient movement; in human movement, requires the effective alignment of body parts.

specific learning disabilities   Disorders in one or more of the basic psychological processes resulting in problems with listening, thinking, speaking, writing, spelling, or doing mathematical calculations.

stereotype   A fixed mental pattern precluding awareness of individual variation.

strength   The effective alignment of body parts to push or release power.

symbolic action   To use motor behaviors to represent other situations or configurations and to thus assist one's thinking.

symbolic play   Play that involves the use of an object, action, or gesture to substitute for or represent something else; pretend play.

symbolize   To use one thing, such as an object, gesture, visual configuration, or utterance, to represent something else.

tabula rasa   Clean slate; according to Locke, a mind not yet affected by experiences or impressions.

target behaviors   The behavior or class of behaviors identified for observation, assessment, or modification.

temporal conjunction   A word indicating a time relationship which is used to join other words, phrases, clauses, or sentences, e.g., "I go *after* you come back."

text features   The visual arrangement of written and printed materials customarily used for particular types of communication.

time sampling   Obtaining a record of observed behavior for present time spans at recurring intervals.

validity   The extent to which a test actually measures what it is intended to measure.

variable interval schedule   A schedule whereby reinforcement is given only after certain random time intervals.

variable ratio schedule   A schedule whereby reinforcement is given according to the number of times a behavior has occurred since the last reinforcement; the number of times required is varied at random.

whole language   An approach to children's learning that links children's involvements and talents in communicating to a gradual development of understanding about the finer points of listening, talking, writing, and reading.

REFERENCES

Ainsworth, M. D., & Bell, S. M. (1972). Individual differences in the development of some attachment behaviors. *Merrill-Palmer Quarterly, 18,* 123–143.

Ainsworth, M. D., & Bell, S. M. (1974). Mother-infant interaction and the development of competence. In K. Connolly and J. Bruner (Eds.), *The growth of competence* (97–118). New York: Academic.

Ainsworth, M. D., & Bell, S. M. (1977). Infant crying and maternal responsiveness. A rejoinder to Berwitz and Boyd. *Child Development, 48,* 1208–1216.

Almy, M. (1984). A child's right to play. *Young Children, 30,* 80.

Altwerger, B., Edelsky, C., & Flores, B. M. (1987). Whole language: What's new? *The Reading Teacher, 41*(2), 144–153.

Ames, L. B. (1946). The development of a sense of time in the young child. *Journal of Genetic Psychology, 68,* 97–127.

Ames, L. B., & Learned, J. (1948). The development of verbalized space in the young child. *Journal of Genetic Psychology, 68,* 97–127.

Aronoff, F. W. (1969). *Music and young children.* New York: Holt, Rinehart & Winston.

Arts, Education, & Americans Panel. (1977). *Coming to our senses: The significance of the arts for American education.* New York: McGraw-Hill.

Ausubel, D. P. (1963). *The psychology of meaningful verbal learning.* New York: Grune & Stratton.

Ausubel, D. P. (1968). *Educational psychology: A cognitive view.* New York: Holt, Rinehart & Winston.

Bailey, D. B., & McWilliam, R. A. (1990). Normalizing early intervention. *Topics in Early Childhood Special Education, 10*(2), 33–47.

Baker, J. N. (1991, May). Beating the handicap rap [Special issue]. *Newsweek,* pp. 36–37, 40–41.

Ball, S., & Bogatz, G. A. (1970). Appendix A. A summary of the major findings in the first year of "Sesame Street": An evaluation. In G. A. Bogatz and S. Ball (Eds.), *The second year of "Sesame Street": A continuing evaluation: Vol 1.* Princeton, NJ: Educational Testing Service.

Bandura, A. (1971). *Social learning theory.* New York: General Learning Press.

Bandura, A. (1975). Analysis of modeling processes. *School Psychology Digest, 4,* 4–10.

Bateson, G. (1979). *Mind and nature.* New York: E. P. Dutton.

Becker, W. C., & Gersten, R. (1982). A follow-up of Follow Through: The later effects of the Direct Instruction Model on children in fifth and sixth grades. *American Educational Research Journal, 19,* 75–92.

Bereiter, C., & Engelmann, S. (1966). *Teaching disadvantaged children in the preschool.* Englewood Cliffs, NJ: Prentice-Hall.

Berrueta-Clement, J. R., Schweinhart, L. J., Barnett, W. S., Epstein, A. S., & Weikart, D. P. (1984). *Changed lives: The effects of the Perry preschool program on youths through age 19.* Ypsilanti, MI: High/Scope.

Bloom, B. (1964). *Stability and change in human characteristics.* New York: Wiley, 1964.

Boocock, S. S. (1977). A crosscultural analysis of the child care system. In L. G. Katz (Ed.), *Current topics in early childhood education: Vol. 1.* (pp. 71–103). Norwood, NJ: Ablex.

Bowman, B., & Brady, E. H. (Eds.). (1982). Today's issues: Tomorrow's possibilities. In S. Hill & B. J. Barnes, (Eds.), *Young children and their families: Needs of the nineties* (pp. 207–217). Lexington, MA: Lexington Books.

Brandt, R. M. (1975). An observational portrait of a British infant school. In B. Spodek & H. Walberg (Eds.), *Studies in open education* (pp. 101–126). New York: Agathon Press.

Braun, S. J., & Edwards, E. P. (1972). *History and theory of early childhood education.* Worthington, OH: Jones.

Bredekamp, S. (Ed.). (1987). *Developmentally appropriate practice in early childhood programs serving children from birth through age 8* (expanded ed.). Washington, DC: National Association for the Education of Young Children.

Bretherton, I. (1984). *Symbolic play: The development of social understanding.* New York: Academic Press.

Bridge, C. (1986). Predictable books for beginning readers and writers. In M. Sampson (Ed.), *The pursuit of literacy: Early reading and writing* (pp. 81–96). Dubuque, IA: Kendall-Hunt.

Brigance, A. H. (1982). *Brigance K & 1 Screen for Kindergarten and First Grade.* Billerica, MA: Curriculum Associates.

Bruce, V. (1965). *Dance and dance drama in education.* Oxford, England: Pergamon.

Bruner, J. (1956). *A study of thinking.* New York: Wiley.

Bruner, J. (1983). Play, thought, and language. *Peabody Journal of Education, 60*(3), 60–69.

Caplan, P. J., & Kinsbourne, M. (1976). Baby drops the rattle: A symmetry of duration of grasp by infants. *Child Development, 47,* 532–534.

Cazden, C. B. (1971). Language programs for young children: Notes from England and Wales. In C. S. Lavatelli (Ed.), *Language learning in early childhood education.* Urbana, IL: ERIC Clearinghouse for Early Childhood Education.

Charles, C. M. (1985). *Building classroom discipline: From models to practice.* New York: Longman.

Chen, C. L. (1984). Growing up with an Asian American heritage. *Interracial Books for Children Bulletin, 15*(6), 11–12.

Children's Defense Fund. (1991). *The state of America's children 1991.* Washington, DC: Author.

Chomsky, C. (1972). Stages in language development and reading exposure. *Harvard Education Review, 42,* 1–33.

Chomsky, N. (1965). *Aspects of a theory of syntax.* Cambridge, MA: MIT Press.

Cicirelli, V. (1969). *The impact of Head Start. An evaluation of the effects of Head Start on children's cognitive and affective development.* Washington, DC: U.S. Government Printing Office.

Clay, M. (1975). *What did I write?* Auckland, New Zealand: Heinemann.

Clements, D. H. (1985). *Computers in early and childhood education.* Englewood Cliffs, NJ: Prentice-Hall.

Cohen, D. H. (1968). The effect of literature on vocabulary and reading achievement. *Elementary English, 45,* 209–213.

Cohen, D. H. (1971). Continuity from pre-kindergarten to kindergarten. *Young Children, 26,* 282–286.

Cohen, D. H. (1972). *The learning child.* New York: Pantheon.

Combs, A. W. (1974). *The professional education of teachers: A humanistic approach to teacher education* (2nd ed.). Boston: Allyn & Bacon.

Corballis, M. C., & Beale, I. L. (1976). *The psychology of the right and left.* Hillsdale, NJ: Erlbaum.

Council for Early Childhood Professional Recognition. (1990). *The 1988 CDA National Survey Results.* Washington, DC: Author. (ERIC Document Reproduction Service No. ED 317 288)

Cousins, N. (1983). *Human options.* New York: Berkley.

CSR, Inc. (1985). *The impact of Head Start on children, families, and communities* (DHHS Publication No. OHDS 85-31193). Washington, DC: U.S. Government Printing Office.

Danzer, V. A., Gerber, M. F., & Lyons, T. M. (1982). Daberon: *A screening device for school readiness* [manual]. Portland, OR: Applied Systems Instruction, Evaluation, Publishing Education.

de Mause, L. (Ed.). (1974). *The history of childhood.* New York: Harper & Row.

Derman-Sparks, L., & A.B.C. Task Force. (1989). *Anti-bias curriculum: Tools for EMPOWERING young children.* Washington, DC: National Association for the Education of Young Children.

Dewey, J. (1897; 1929 reprint). *My pedagogic creed.* Washington DC: The Progressive Education Association.

Divoky, D. (1973). Education's hard-nosed rebel: Ziggy Engelmann. *Learning, 1*(3), 29–31, 68.

Durkin, D. (1966). *Children who read early: Two longitudinal studies.* New York: Teachers College Press.

Dyson, A. H. (1991). The roots of literacy development: Play, pictures, and peers. In B. Scales, M. Almy, A. Nicolopoulou, & S. Ervin-Tripp (Eds.), *Play and the social context of development in early care and education* (pp. 98–116). New York: Teachers College, Columbia University.

Ebbeck, F. N. (1971). Learning from play in other cultures. *Childhood Education, 48,* 2–3.

Education for All Handicapped Children Act of 1975, § 1401, 20 U.S.C.

Education Products Information Exchange Institute. (1972). *Early childhood education: How to select and evaluate materials* (Education Product Report No. 42). New York: Author.

Eisner, E. (1978). *Reading, the arts and the creation of meaning.* Weston, VA: National Art Education Association.

Elkind, D. (1987). *Miseducation: Preschoolers at Risk.* New York: Alfred Knopf.

Elkind, D. (1988). *The hurried child: Growing up too fast too soon* (rev. ed.). Reading, MA: Addison-Wesley.

Elkind, D. (1988, September 11). Overwhelmed at an early age. *The Boston Globe Magazine,* pp. 18, 40–46, 54–58.

Ellis, S. S., & Whalen, S. F. (1990). *Cooperative learning: Getting started.* New York: Scholastic Inc., Instructor Books.

Ellwein, M. C., Walsh, D. J., Eads II, G. M., & Miller, A. (1991). Using readiness tests to route kindergarten students: The snarled intersection of psychometrics, policy, and practice. *Educational Evaluation and Policy Analysis, 13*(2), 159–175.

Emmer, E. T., Evertson, C. M., & Anderson, L. M. (1980). Effective classroom management at the beginning of the school year. *Elementary School Journal, 80,* 219–231.

Engelmann, S., & Bruner, E. (1969). *Distar Reading 1.* Chicago: Science Research Associates.

Erikson, E. (1950). *Childhood and society.* New York: Norton.

Ervin-Tripp, S. (1991). Play in language development (pp. 84–97). In B. Scales, M. Almy, A. Nicholopoulou, & S. Ervin-Tripp (Eds.), *Play and the social context of development in early care and education.* New York: Teachers College, Columbia University.

Fagan, J. F. (1976). Infants' recognition of invariant features of faces. *Child Development, 47,* 627–638.

Fein, G. G., & Apfel, N. (1979). Some preliminary observations on knowing and pretending. In M. Smith & M. B. Franklin (Eds.), *Symbolic functioning in childhood.* Hillsdale, NJ: Erlbaum.

Feitelson, D., Kita, B., & Goldstein, Z. (1986). Effects of listening to stories on first graders' comprehension and use of language. *Research in the Teaching of English, 20,* 339–356.

Ferreiro, E. & Teberosky, A. (1982). *Literacy before schooling.* Portsmouth, NH: Heinemann.

Fiske, E. B. (1985, May 19). A few words of caution on schooling the very young. *New York Times,* p. 22E.

Flavell, J. H. (1963). *The developmental psychology of Jean Piaget.* New York: Van Nostrand.

Forys, S. K. S., & McCune-Nicolich, L. (1984). Shared pretend: Sociodramatic play at 3 years of age. In I. Bretherton (Ed.), *Symbolic play: The development of understanding* (pp. 159–191). Orlando, FL: Academic Press.

Fuson, K. C., Pergament, G. G., Lyons, B. G., & Hall, J. W. (1985). Children's conformity to the cardinal rule as a function of set size and counting accuracy. *Child Development,* 56, 1429–1436.

Gardner, H. (1983). *Frames of mind: The theory of multiple intelligences.* New York: Basic Books.

Garvey, C. *Play.* (1977). Cambridge, MA: Harvard University Press.

Garvey, C. (1979). Communicational controls in social play. In B. Sutton-Smith (Ed.), *Play and learning* (pp. 109–125). New York: Gardner Press.

Garvey, C. & Berndt, R. (1976, April). *The organization of pretend play.* Paper presented at the annual meeting of the American Psychological Association, San Francisco.

Gazzaniga, M. S. (1983). Right hemisphere language following brain bisection. *American Psychologist, 38,* 525–537.

Gesell Institute for Human Development. (1980). *Gesell School Readiness Test.* Rosemont, NJ: Programs for Education.

Gibson, E. J., & Levin, H. (1975). *The psychology of reading.* Cambridge, MA: MIT Press.

Gilkeson, E., & Bowman, G. (1976). *The focus is on children: The Bank Street approach to early childhood education as enacted in Follow Through.* New York: Bank Street College of Education.

Goodall, M. M. (1980). Left-handedness as an educational handicap. In R. S. Laura (Ed.), *Problems of handicap* (pp. 55–66). Melbourne: Macmillan.

Graue, M. E., & Shepard, L. A. (1989). Predictive validity of the Gesell School Readiness Tests. *Early Childhood Research Quarterly, 4,* 303–315.

Greaney, V. (1986). Parental influences on reading. *The Reading Teacher, 39,* 813–818.

Greenberg, M. (1979). *Your children need music: A guide for parents and teachers of young children.* Englewood Cliffs, NJ: Prentice-Hall.

Guralnick, M. J. (1990). Major accomplishments and future directions in early childhood mainstreaming. *Topics in Early Childhood Special Education, 10*(2), 1–17.

Guralnick, M. J., & Bennett, F. C. (Eds.). (1987). *The effectiveness of early intervention for at-risk and handicapped children.* New York: Academic Press.

Hadley, N. (1987). Reaching migrant preschoolers. *Children's Advocate, 14,* 19–20.

Hale-Benson, J. (1982). *Black children: Their roots, culture and learning styles* (rev. ed.). Baltimore MD: Johns Hopkins University Press.

Hall, E. T. (1959). *Silent language.* Garden City, NY: Anchor Books.

Harste, J. C., Woodward, V. A., & Burke, C. L. (1984). *Language stories & literacy lessons.* Portsmouth, NH: Heinemann.

Heald-Taylor, G. (1987). Predictable literature selections and activities for language arts instruction. *The Reading Teacher, 41,* 6–12.

Hiebert, E. H. (1981). Developmental patterns and interrelationships of preschool children's print awareness. *Reading Research Quarterly, 16,* 236–259.

Hobbs, N. A. (1975). *The futures of children.* San Francisco: Jossey-Bass.

Hohmann, M. M., Banet, B., & Weikart, D. P. (1979). *Young children in action: A manual for preschool educators.* Ypsilanti, MI: High/Scope.

Houston, A. C., Wright, J. C., Rice, M. L., Kerkman, D., & St. Peters, M. (1990). Development of television viewing patterns in early childhood: A longitudinal investigation. *Developmental Psychology, 26*(30), 409–420.

Howes, C. (1985). Sharing fantasy: Social pretend play in toddlers. *Child Development, 56,* 1253–1258.

Howes, C., & Rubenstein, J. L. (1985). Determinants of toddlers' experience in day care: Age of entry and quality of setting. *Child Care Quarterly, 14,* 140–151.

Hughes, M. M., (1959). *The assessment of the quality of teaching: A research report* (Office of Education Research Project No. 353). Salt Lake City: University of Utah.

Hunt, J. McV. (1961). *Intelligence and experience.* New York: Ronald.

Hymes, J. L., Jr. (1955). *A child development point of view.* Englewood Cliffs, NJ: Prentice-Hall.

Hymes, J. L., Jr. (1991). *Early childhood education: Twenty years in review. A look at 1971–1990.* Washington, DC: National Association for the Education of Young Children.

Ilg, F. L. & Ames, L. B. (1964). *School readiness.* New York: Harper & Row.

Johnson, D. W. & Johnson, R. T. (1989) *Cooperation and competition: Theory and research.* Edina, MN: Interaction Book Company.

Kamii, C. (1985a). Leading primary education toward excellence. *Young Children, 40*(6), 3–9.

Kamii, C. (1985b). *Young children reinvent arithmetic.* New York: Teachers College Press.

Katz, P. A. (1982). Development of children's racial awareness and intergroup attitudes. In L. G. Katz (Ed.), *Current topics in early childhood education: Vol. 4* (pp. 17–54). Norwood, NJ: Ablex.

Kellogg, R. (1970). *Analyzing children's art.* Palo Alto, CA: Mayfield.

Kohlberg, L. & Lickona, T. (1987). Moral discussion and the class meeting. In R. DeVries with L. Kohlberg (Eds.), *Constructivist early education: Overview and comparison with other programs* (pp. 143–181). Washington, DC: National Association for the Education of Young Children.

Kounin, J. (1970). *Discipline and group management in classrooms.* New York: Holt, Rinehart & Winston.

Lawton, J. T., & Reddy, P. (1983). *Effects of advance organizer and guided self-discovery instruction on preschool children's understanding of conservation.* Paper presented at annual meeting of American Educational Research Association, Montreal. (ERIC Document Reproduction Service No. ED 230 279)

Lazar, I., Darlington, R., Murray, H., Royce, J., & Snipper, A. (1982). Lasting effects of early childhood education. *Monographs of the Society for Research in Child Development, 47* (1–2, Serial No. 194).

Lein, L., & Brenneis, D. (1978). Children's disputes in three speech communities. *Language in Society, 7,* 299–324.

Lenneberg, E. H. (1967). *Biological foundation of language.* New York: Wiley.

Lavine, L. O. (1977). Differentiation of letter-like forms in prereading children. *Developmental Psychology, 13,* 89–94.

Levine, R. A. (1984). Properties of culture: An ethnographic view. In R. Schweder & R. Levine (Eds.), *Culture theory: Essays in mind, theory and emotion* (pp. 67–87). Cambridge, England: Cambridge University Press.

Levine, S. C. (1983). Hemispheric specialization and functional plasticity during development. *Journal of Children in Contemporary Society, 16,* 77–98.

Lewis, M. (1977). Early socioemotional development and its relevance for curriculum. *Merrill-Palmer Quarterly, 23*(4), 279–286.

Lichtenberg, P., & Norton, D. G. (1972). Cognitive and mental development in the first five years: A review of recent research. (DHEW Publication No. HMS 72-9102). Washington, DC: U.S. Government Printing Office.

Lowenfeld, V., & Brittain, W. L. (1975). *Creative and mental growth* (6th ed.). New York: Macmillan.

Lozzoff, B., Brittenham, G. M., Trause, M. A., Kennell, J. H., & Klaus, M. H. (1977, July). The mother-newborn relationship: Limits of adaptability. *Journal of Pediatrics, 91,* 1–12.

Mardell-Czudonowski, C. D., & Goldenberg, G. S. (1983). *Developmental indicators for the assessment of learning, revised* [manual]. Edison, NJ: Childcraft Education.

Marion, N. (1981). *Guidance of young children.* St. Louis: Mosby.

McLean, M., & Hanline, M. F. (1990). Providing early intervention services in integrated environments: Challenges and opportunities for the future. *Topics in Early Childhood Special Education, 10*(2), 62–77.

McNeill, D. (1970). *The acquisition of language: The study of developmental psycholinguistics.* New York: Harper & Row.

Merton, T. (1955). *No man is an island.* New York: Doubleday.

Miller, P. & Garvey, C. (1984). Mother-baby role play: Its origins in social support. In I. Bretherton (Ed.), *Symbolic play: The development of social understanding* (pp. 101–130). Orlando, FL: Academic Press.

Missouri Department of Elementary and Secondary Education. (1981). *Missouri kindergarten Inventory of Developmental Skills—Alternate Form Guidebook.* Jefferson City, MO: Author.

Molfese, D. L., Freeman, R. B., & Palermo, D. S. (1975). The ontogency of brain lateralization for speech and non-speech sounds. *Brain and Language, 2,* 356–368.

Montessori, M. (1964). *Reconstruction in education.* Wheaton, IL: Theosophical Press.

Moon, C., & Wells, G. (1979). The influence of the home on learning to read. *Journal of Research in Reading, 2,* 53–62.

Moore, R. S., & Moore, D. R. (1973). How early should they go to school? *Childhood Education, 50,* 14–20.

Moore, R. S., & Moore, D. R. (1979). *School can wait.* Provo, UT: Brigham Young University Press.

Morrow, R. D. (1989). What's in a name? In particular, a Southeast Asia name? *Young Children, 44*(6), 20–23.

National Association for the Education of Young Children. (1988, March). NAEYC position statement on standardized testing of young children 3 through 8 years of age. *Young Children, 43*(3), 42–47.

National Association of Early Childhood Specialists in State Departments of Education. (1987). *Unacceptable trends in kindergarten entry and placement.* Lincoln, NE: Author.

National Association of Elementary School Principals. (1987). *The Education Almanac 1987–1988.* Alexandria, VA: Author.

National Association of State Boards of Education. *Right from the start: The report of the NASBE task force on early childhood education.* Alexandria, VA: Author.

National Center for Education Statistics. (1990). *Digest of education statistics.* Washington, DC: U.S. Government Printing Office.

Needels, M., & Stallings, J. (1975). *Classroom processes related to absence rate.* Menlo Park, CA: Stanford Research Institute. (ERIC Document Reproduction Service No. ED 110 199)

Norton, S. M. (1983). It's time to get tough on student promotion—or is it? *Contemporary Education, 54,* 283–286.

Odom, S. L. & Karnes, M. B. (Eds.). (1988). *Early intervention for infants and children with handicaps: An empirical base.* Baltimore: Brookes.

Padilla, A. M., Lindholm, K. J., Chen, A., Duran, R., Hakuta, K., Lambert, W., & Tucker, G. R. (1991, February). The English-only movement. *American Psychologist, 46*(2), 120–130.

Parten, M. B. (1932). Social participation among pre-school children. *Journal of Abnormal Psychology, 27,* 243–269.

Peck, J. T., McCaig, G., & Sapp, M. E. (1988). *Kindergarten policies: What is best for children?* Washington, DC: National Association for the Education of Young Children.

Pellegrini, A. D. (1984). The social cognitive ecology of preschool classrooms: contextual relations revisited. *International Journal of Behavioral Development, 7,* 321–332.

Pflaum, S. W. (1974). *The development of language and reading in the young child.* Columbus, OH: Merrill.

Piaget, J. (1952). *The origins of intelligence.* New York: Norton.

Piaget, J. (1962). *Play, dreams and imitation in childhood.* New York: Norton.

Piaget, J. (1969). *The psychology of the child.* New York: Basic Books.

Piaget, J., & Inhelder, B. (1967). *The child's conception of space.* New York: Norton.

Piaget, J., & Inhelder, B. (1969). *The psychology of the child.* New York: Basic Books.

Plummer, D. L., Liniberger, M. H., & Graziano, W. G. (1987). The academic and social consequences of grade retention: A convergent analysis. In L. G. Katz, (Ed.), *Current topics in early childhood education: Vol. 6* (pp. 224–252). Norwood, NJ: Ablex.

Porterfield, J. K., Herbert-Jackson, E., & Risley, T. R. (1976). Contingent observation: An effective and acceptable procedure for reducing disruptive behaviors of young children in group settings. *Journal of Applied Behavior Analysis, 9,* 55–64.

Postman, N. (1982). *The disappearance of childhood.* New York: Delacorte.

Postman, N. (1985). The disappearance of childhood. *Childhood Education, 61*(4), 286–293.

Premack, D. (1959). Toward empirical behavior laws: I. Positive reinforcement. *Psychological Review,* 66, 219–233.

Premack, D. (1965). Reinforcement theory. In D. Levine (Ed.), *Nebraska Symposium on Motivation* (pp. 123–180). Lincoln, NB: University of Nebraska Press.

Prescott, E. (1972). *Who thrives in group day care?* Pasadena, CA: Pacific Oaks College.

Rhodes, L. K. (1981). I can read! Predictable books as resources of reading and writing instruction. *The Reading Teacher, 34,* 511–518.

Rosenshine, B. V. (1978). Academic engaged time, content covered, and direct instruction. *Journal of Education, 160,* 38–66.

Samuelson, R. J. (1988, August 8) Child care revisited. *Newsweek,* p. 53.

Schaffer, H. R., & Emerson, P. E. (1964). The development of social attachments in infancy. *Monographs of the Society for Research in Child Development, 29*(94).

Scherer, M. (1991). How many ways is a child intelligent? An interview with Howard Gardner. In N. Lauter-Klatell (Ed.), *Readings in child development* (pp. 21–25). Mountain View, CA: Mayfield Publishing Company.

Schickedanz, J. A. (1981). Hey! This book's not working right. *Young Children, 37*(1), 18–27.

Schorr, L. B., & Schorr, D. (1988). *Within our reach: Breaking the cycle of disadvantage.* New York: Doubleday.

Schwartzman, H. B. (1978). *Transformations: The anthropology of children's play.* New York: Plenum.

Seaver, J. W., Cartwright, C. S., Ward, C. B., & Heasley, C. A. (1979). *Careers with young children: Making your decision.* Washington, DC: National Association for the Education of Young Children.

Shepard, L. A., & Smith, M. L. (1985). *The Boulder Valley kindergarten study: Retention practices and retention effects.* Boulder, CO: Boulder Valley Public Schools.

Shepard, L. A., & Smith, M. L. (1986, November). Synthesis of research on school readiness and kindergarten retention. *Educational Leadership, 44*(3), 78–86.

Shepard, L. A., & Smith, M. L. (1989). *Flunking grades: Research and policies on retention.* London: The Falmer Press.

Shure, M. (1980). Real-life problem-solving for parents and children: An approach to social competence. In D. P. Rathjen & J. P. Foreyt (Eds.), *Social Competence.* Elmsford, NY: Pergamon.

Siegel, I. E., & Saunders, R. (1979). An inquiry into inquiry: Question asking as an instructional model. In L. G. Katz (Ed.), *Current Topics in Early Childhood Education: Vol. 2* (pp. 169–194). Norwood, NJ: Ablex.

Skinner, B. F. (1957). *Verbal behavior.* New York: Appleton-Century-Crofts.

Smilansky, S. (1968). *The effects of sociodramatic play on disadvantaged preschool children.* New York: Wiley.

Smith, F. (1977). Making sense out of reading—and of reading instruction. *Harvard Education Review, 47,* 386–395.

Smith, M. L., & Shepard, L. A. (1987, October) What doesn't work: Explaining policies of retention in the early grades. *Phi Delta Kappan, 69,* 129–134.

Smith, M. L., & Shepard, L. A. (1988). Kindergarten readiness and retention: A qualitative study of teachers' beliefs and practices. *American Educational Research Journal, 25,* 307–333.

Smith, M. S. (1975). Evaluation findings in Head Start Planned variation. In A. M. Rivlin & T. M. Timpane (Eds.), *Planned variation in education.* Washington, DC: Brookings Institute.

Smith, N. R. (1972). *Developmental origins of graphic symbolization in the paintings of children three to five.* Unpublished doctoral dissertation, Harvard University. (University Microfilms No. 179-9892)

Soar, R. (1973). *Follow Through classroom process measurement and pupil growth.* Gainesville, FL: Institute for Development of Human Resources. (ERIC Document Reproduction Service No. ED 106 297)

Spier, P. (1980). *People.* New York: Doubleday.

Spivack, G., Platt, J. J., & Shure, M. B. (1976). *The problem-solving approach to adjustment: A guide to research and intervention.* San Francisco: Jossey-Bass.

Spivack, G., & Shure, M. B. (1974). *Social adjustment of young children: A cognitive approach to solving problems.* San Francisco: Jossey-Bass.

Stallings, J. (1975). *Relationships between classroom instructional practices and child development.* Menlo Park, CA: Stanford Research Institute. (ERIC Document Reproduction Service No. ED 106 297)

Sternberg, R. J. (1985). *Beyond IQ: A triarchic theory of human intelligence.* Cambridge, MA: Cambridge University Press.

Sulzby, E., Teale, W. H., & Kamberelis, G. (1989). Emergent writing in the classroom: Home and school connections. In D. S. Strickland & L. M. Morrow (Eds.), *Emerging literacy: Young children learn to read and write* (pp. 63–79). Newark, DL: International Reading Association.

Switzky, H. N., Ludwig, L., & Haywood, H. C. (1979). Exploration and play in retarded and nonretarded preschool children: Effects of object complexity and age. *American Journal of Mental Deficiency, 83,* 637–644.

Tan, L. E. (1985). Laterality and motor skills in four-year-olds. *Child Development, 56,* 119–124.

Tompkins, G. E., & Webeler, M. (1983). What will happen next? Using predictable books with young children. *The Reading Teacher, 36,* 498–502.

U.S. Department of Commerce, Bureau of the Census. (1988). *Statistical Abstract of the United States.* Washington: U.S. Government Printing Office.

University of the State of New York. (1984). *Public school professional personnel report: New York State: 1983–84.* Albany, NY: Information Center on Education, The University of the State of New York.

Updike, S. (1988, Fall). Why? *New York Early Education Reporter, 25*(1), 1,3.

Voss, H. (1987). Possible distinctions between exploration and play. In D. Gorlitz & J. F. Wohlwill (Eds.), *Curiosity, imagination, and play: On the development of spontaneous cognitive and motivational processes* (pp. 44–58). Hillsdale, NJ: Lawrence Erlbaum Associates.

Vygotsky, L. S. (1976). Play and its role in the mental development of the child. In J. Bruner, A. Jolly, & K. Sylva (Eds.), *Play: Its role in development and evolution.* Middlesex, England: Penguin Books.

Vygotsky, L. S. (1978). *Mind in society: The development of higher psychological processes.* Cambridge, MA: Harvard University Press.

Washington, E. D. (1989, Winter). A componential theory of culture and its implications for African-American identity. *Equity and Excellence, 24*(2), 24–30.

Wasserman, S. (1990). *Serious players in the primary classroom.* New York: Teachers College, Columbia University.

Webster, N. K. (1984, May/June). The 5s and 6s go to school, revisited. *Childhood Education, 60* (5), 107–111.

Wells, G. (1986). *The meaning makers: Children learning language and using language to learn.* Portsmouth, NH: Heinemann.

Whitehurst, K. (1971). Motor activities for early childhood. In American Association for Health, Physical Education and Recreation, *Report of NAEYC and AAHPER conference on the young child: the significance of motor development.* (ERIC Document Reproduction Service No. ED 069 331)

Whiting, J. W. & Child, I. L. (1953). *Child training and personality.* New Haven: Yale University Press.

Willert, M. K., & Kamii, C. (1985, May). Reading in the kindergarten: Direct vs. indirect teaching. *Young Children, 40,* 3–9.

Williams, R. M. (1977, September 3). Why children should draw: The surprising link between art and learning. *Saturday Review,* 10–16.

Wohlwill, J. F. (1984). Relationships between exploration and play. In T. D. Yawkey & A. D. Pellegrini (Eds.), *Child's play: Developmental and applied* (pp. 143–170). Hillsdale, NJ: Lawrence Erlbaum.

Wolf, D. P., Rygh, J., & Altshuler, J. (1984). Agency and experience: Actions and states in play narratives. In Bretherton, I. (Ed.), *Symbolic play: The development of social understanding* (pp. 195–217). Orlando, FL: Academic Press.

INDEX